D0903438

: t

Lasting Legacy to the Carolinas

LASTING

LEGACY

TO THE

CAROLINAS

The Duke Endowment, 1924–1994

ROBERT F. DURDEN

Duke University Press   Durham & London   1998

Robert F. Durden is Professor Emeritus of History at Duke University, and the author of numerous works on southern history.

© 1998 Duke University Press

All rights reserved

Printed in the United States of America on acid-free paper ∞

Typeset in Sabon by Keystone Typesetting, Inc.

Library of Congress Cataloging-in-Publication Data
Durden, Robert F.
 Lasting legacy to the Carolinas : the Duke Endowment, 1924–
1994 / Robert F. Durden.
  p. cm.
 Continues: The Dukes of Durham, 1865–1929.
 Includes index.
 ISBN 0-8223-2151-3 (cloth : alk. paper)
 1. Duke Endowment — History. 2. Endowments — North
Carolina — History. 3. Endowments — South Carolina —
History. I. Title.
HV98.N82D853 1998
361.7'632'09756 — DC21   97-31427

This book is lovingly dedicated to

two Tar Heels turned Wahoo,

G. O. R. and I. B. R.

Godspeed to them.

CONTENTS

PREFACE

THE DUKE ENDOWMENT was for a number of years the third largest charitable foundation in the nation. Although the appearance in recent years of several new and quite large foundations has pushed the Endowment farther down the ever-changing list in terms of size, it is still one of the top dozen or so foundations in the United States.

It is different from many foundations, however, for several reasons. For one thing, James B. Duke, as is more elaborately explained in the chapters that follow, had quite definite ideas as to how the annual income from his charitable trust was to be distributed. He even included in the indenture, the legal instrument establishing the trust, the exact percentages of the annual income that he wished his trustees to allocate to the various beneficiaries.

Many of the creators of large foundations have approached the matter differently, giving only broad or somewhat vague directions about the uses to which the annual income should be put and leaving to the trustees of the foundation the task of defining its program or mission. John D. Rockefeller Sr., for example, in establishing the Rockefeller Foundation in 1909 stated its purposes in this fashion: "To promote the well-being and to advance the civilization of the peoples of the United States and its territories and possessions and of foreign lands in the acquisition and dissemination of knowledge, in the prevention and relief of suffering, and in the promotion of any and all of the elements of human progress."[1] Not only, then, were the trustees of the Rockefeller Foundation given a global sphere of action, but they were also left to decide just how they would proceed to promote well-being and advance civilization through the acquisition of knowledge, the prevention of suffering, and the promotion of human progress.

Since many other creators of large foundations matched John D. Rockefeller Sr. in the broadness, even vagueness, of their purposes, the Duke Endowment is actually not a typical foundation but a charitable trust with quite specific, legally mandated purposes. Moreover, the trustees of the Duke Endowment are legally liable for their actions in carrying out the provisions of the indenture in a manner that is probably not the case with the trustees of many other foundations.

Because beneficiaries are specifically designated in the indenture, some by institutional name and others (hospitals and orphanages) by category, the Endowment also differs from many other foundations in that it has entered into a more or less permanent relationship with many of its beneficiaries. This continuity has protected the Endowment from the sort of hit-and-run philanthropy practiced by some foundations. Moreover, the trustees of the Endowment are not free to pick and choose among a dazzling array of opportunities for "doing good" and of people and groups eager to do it. A witty person once defined a foundation as a large body of money surrounded by people who want some of it. The Endowment, because of J. B. Duke's careful design, is not thus surrounded; rather, it is linked with its beneficiaries in an ongoing relationship.

The Duke Endowment is also distinctive geographically in that its charitable purposes are limited to North and South Carolina. J. B. Duke candidly faced this matter in his indenture when he explained that he "might have extended this aid to other charitable objects and to other sections, but my opinion is that so doing would be productive of less good by reason of attempting too much."[2]

J. B. Duke had three primary reasons for confining his philanthropy to the Carolinas, but only one of these reasons was explicitly explained in the indenture: the bulk of his assets that he gave to establish the Endowment consisted of a large part of his stock in the Duke Power Company. J. B. Duke had been the major builder of that pioneering electric utility, and it operated exclusively in the Piedmont region of the two Carolinas. Moreover, J. B. Duke envisioned an ongoing, extremely close relationship between the Endowment and the

Duke Power Company. He carefully planned for the Endowment to own the great majority of the Duke Power stock and also requested in the indenture that the trustees "see to it that at all times these [Duke Power] companies be managed and operated by the men best qualified for such a service." His hope, as he explained in the indenture, was that the revenues from the hydroelectric developments of the power company "shall administer to the social welfare, as the operation of such developments is administering to the economic welfare, of the communities which they serve."

In addition to this symmetrical and symbiotic relationship between the Endowment and the Duke Power Company, there were two unstated reasons for the geographical focus of the Endowment. One was that J. B. Duke in creating the Endowment was, to a large extent, simply replicating and elaborating, on a princely scale, a pattern of giving that his father, Washington Duke, had begun in the late nineteenth century and that his older brother, Benjamin N. Duke, had supervised for the family during nearly a quarter-century before the Endowment was established. It is true that J. B. Duke's inclusion in the Endowment of assistance toward the medical care of indigents and the building of community hospitals, as will be explained, was largely his own addition to the family's long-established, general pattern of giving. But the basic point remains that J. B. Duke did not just select the beneficiaries of the Endowment out of the blue but rather was strongly influenced by an inherited family tradition and pattern that had focused on North Carolina.

The other unstated reason for the Endowment's geographical focus was that J. B. Duke fully realized and deeply deplored the fact that the South in the 1920s was still, as it had been since the Civil War, the poorest, most backward section of the nation. In terms of per capita income and various other measurements, the two Carolinas were among the most poverty-stricken of all the states. While J. B. Duke hoped that the industrialization that the Duke Power Company was facilitating would gradually help change that situation, he also meant for the Endowment to do what it could to ameliorate certain conditions in the two Carolinas.

J. B. Duke audaciously planned for his philanthropy to be perpetual, to last forever. There has always been debate about the wisdom, at least from the standpoint of public policy, of allowing tax-free foundations to be established on a perpetual basis. When the first of the truly large foundations began to appear in the United States early in the twentieth century, various critics assailed them not only because of the power that such vast sums of money gave to private, tax-free entities but also because most of them were established in perpetuity. Proposals for setting time limits on the operation of foundations have cropped up intermittently throughout this century.

One important philanthropist in the early decades of the twentieth century, Julius Rosenwald, felt strongly about what he perceived as the folly of a perpetual foundation, no matter how well intentioned. He believed that the passage of time and unforeseen changes made any attempt to establish a perpetual philanthropy unwise. Accordingly, Rosenwald, who strove to provide better educational opportunities for African Americans in the South, among other things, carefully designed his foundation so that it would expire after a certain number of years.

J. B. Duke, however, did not share Rosenwald's misgivings about thinking in terms of forever. Like the majority of the donors who have created the larger foundations, he bet that the Duke Endowment could usefully continue its charitable activity perpetually.

The thesis of this study is that, seventy years after the establishment of the Duke Endowment, one can see that J. B. Duke has both won and lost his bet. In so far as the charitable objects he selected—higher education, hospitals and health care, orphans and child care, and certain Methodist causes in North Carolina—he has won. Not only have the four areas of activity remained at the forefront of society's needs and concerns, but the trustees and staff of the Endowment have been flexible and creative in interpreting the indenture so that various policies have been changed in response to changing circumstances. In that respect, then, Duke has clearly won his bet, at least so far.

J. B. Duke has also lost his bet, however. A vital part of what might be termed his Grand Design for philanthropy in the Carolinas was the careful, elaborate interlocking relationship between the Duke Endowment and the Duke Power Company. After World War II, for many reasons that are discussed later, this arrangement began to pose problems. While the propriety of linking together a tax-free foundation and an investor-owned, profit-making business was not questioned in the 1920s, the situation had changed by the 1950s, and the Federal government increasingly looked askance at the practice. Even before the climax of this federal concern arrived in the Tax Reform Act of 1969, representatives for the Endowment had gone into the courts in the early 1960s and sought relief from certain restrictions that J. B. Duke's indenture placed on the Endowment's investment policy. That effort failed, but in the early 1970s, after the passage of the Tax Reform Act and in response to other developments, representatives returned to the courts and this time gained the relief they sought; that is, the courts allowed the Endowment, at long last, to invest its funds in something besides stock in the Duke Power Company and certain types of government bonds.

Thanks to J. B. Duke's Grand Design, however, the Duke Endowment still owned a massive amount of the Duke Power stock. Moreover, the indenture required the unanimous agreement of all the trustees of the Endowment before any Duke Power stock could be sold — and then only in an "extraordinary emergency." One important trustee, Doris Duke, J. B. Duke's only child, became alienated from the Endowment during the later years of her life. She continued as a trustee, however, and absolutely refused to agree to any sale of Duke Power stock, despite repeated efforts by various other trustees and the Endowment's lawyers to persuade her of the expediency and wisdom of such a sale.

Doris Duke died in October 1993. At the end of that year, the Endowment owned over 26 million shares of Duke Power stock, valued at more than $1.1 billion. In March 1994 the trustees unanimously voted to sell 16 million shares of the stock. While the Endowment continued to be the largest single holder of Duke Power stock, with approximately 10 million shares or about 5 percent of the outstanding stock, the great sell-off of 1994 meant that an important part of J. B. Duke's Grand Design no longer existed. That part of his bet he lost. In other words, as far as the Endowment's philanthropic purposes are concerned, J. B. Duke has, as of 1995, won; but as far as the financial structure or underpinning of the Endowment goes, he has finally lost his bet.

This study has been neither authorized nor subsidized by the Duke Endowment. Rather, it is intended as a work of independent scholarship and as another sequel, in a sense, to an earlier book of mine, *The Dukes of Durham* (Duke University Press, 1975). The last two chapters of that book about Washington Duke and his family deal, respectively, with J. B. Duke's establishment of the Endowment in December 1924 and the beginning of Duke University later in the same month. Accordingly, *The Launching of Duke University, 1924–1949* (Duke University Press, 1993) may be viewed as a sequel to *The Dukes of Durham,* with the focus shifting from the Duke family in the latter volume to the new research university's first quarter-century in the former one. The present volume also continues a story that was barely begun in *The Dukes of Durham.* In a way, therefore, the three volumes constitute a trilogy, though each may be read independently and each has a different focus and purpose.

While this volume was not authorized, the trustees and officers of the Endowment share my interest in authentic history. Accordingly, a significant number of them have generously supplied information and checked the manuscript for accuracy. The interpretations remain my own, but I am most grateful for help from Eugene Cochrane, John Day, Albert Fisher, Myrna Fourcher, Juanita Kreps, Elizabeth Locke, W. B. McGuire, Joseph Mann, Robert Mayer, John Mebane, Mary and Jim Semans, and Jere Witherspoon. Russell Robinson and John Spuches made valuable suggestions concerning those portions of the introduction and last chapter that I combined and published separately as an article.

Douglas Knight and Terry Sanford kindly assisted me in certain matters touching on the Endowment's relationship with Duke University. I am grateful also to the Arts and Sciences Research Council of Duke University for assisting me in making research trips to Charlotte and New York City.

My colleague Margaret Humphreys not only read critically the entire manuscript but also gave me invaluable help about key histories of the American hospital and medical care. I deeply appreciate her generosity.

The indispensable typist in the preparation of this book was Jane Twigg, and I thank her for faithful and always good-natured help. While she bore by far the largest share of the word-processing labor, others who also pitched in at various points were Jenna Golnik and Keith Knight.

In Duke's Perkins Library, I have always found, for forty-five years now, many invariably helpful people. For this volume Linda McCurdy and her coworkers in the Special Collections Department were particularly obliging and efficient. And in one of my long-time stomping grounds, the Duke University Archives, William King and Thomas Harkins stood always ready to help.

Portions of this volume, in somewhat different forms, have appeared earlier in the *North Carolina Historical Review,* and I am grateful to its publishers for permission to reprint them.

Not only did Anne Oller Durden, my wife, again lend a patient, sympathetic ear over a period of several years, but she also at one point typed a chapter for me. Moreover, she promises again to help me compile the index — the author's final, tedious task in bookmaking. I sincerely and deeply thank her.

Robert F. Durden
Duke University
March 1997

I ·

THE

ORIGINS

OF THE

DUKE

ENDOWMENT

WHILE JAMES BUCHANAN DUKE'S father, Washington Duke, and his older brother, Benjamin Newton Duke, were certainly not slouches in the business world, they were also not possessed of the business genius and drive that characterized the youngest member of the family. Known only to his family and a few intimate friends as "Buck" during his life time, J. B. Duke played a key role in persuading his father and other business partners to gamble on machine-made cigarettes in the 1880s. After that gamble paid off handsomely and W. Duke Sons and Company became the leading cigarette manufacturer in the nation, J. B. Duke took the lead in persuading the nation's four other largest cigarette manufacturers to join with the Duke company in forming the American Tobacco Company in 1890. Young J. B. Duke, at age thirty-three, was then named president of the company, and he proceeded to build one of the first giant holding companies in the nation.

Long before the Supreme Court of the United States ordered the dissolution of the vast "tobacco trust" in 1911, however, J. B. Duke helped to organize in 1902 the world-girdling British-American Tobacco Company, headquartered in London. While he totally separated himself from the domestic American tobacco industry after 1911, he continued to play a major role in the British-American Tobacco Company until his death in 1925 and served as its chairman for more than a decade.

Textile manufacturing in Durham and elsewhere in the two Carolinas also attracted Ben and J. B. Duke from the early 1890s onward, and they became major players in that booming economic sector. Moreover, as an outgrowth of their involvement in textile manufacturing and their interest in water-power sites for their mills, early in the twentieth century they became involved in a burgeoning new industry: the production of hydroelectric power. The last major economic activity of J. B. Duke became, therefore, the building of a vast network of electric-power plants in the Piedmont region of the two Carolinas. In the mid-1920s it would become the Duke Power Company. While this company, which soon became state-regulated but investor-owned, never brought the Dukes as much personal profit as had the tobacco industry, it grew to have a special place in J. B. Duke's mind and heart. Not only did he particularly enjoy the kind of construction and problem-solving that was involved in the electric-power business, but he also held a passionate belief, which turned out to be absolutely correct, that the power company was destined to play a key role in the industrial development of the Piedmont region of the two Carolinas.[1]

In light of J. B. Duke's business career, even a casual observer could discern that he both liked and had the ability and persistence to plan and build on a large scale. When he turned to the idea of permanent philanthropy, therefore, it was altogether in character for him to think big. While Washington Duke had carefully raised his children to share his interest in charitable giving, especially to Methodist causes, as will be discussed, J. B. Duke was the only member of the family to institutionalize philanthropy on a princely scale.

Precisely when J. B. Duke first conceived of using the electric-power system as a basis for philanthropy for the Carolinas is not known. When a Virginia-born lawyer named William R. Perkins became Duke's chief legal counselor in 1914, however, he placed in one of his desk drawers an early, rough draft, prepared for Duke, of what eventually became a decade later the indenture creating the Duke Endowment.[2]

J. B. Duke's movement toward his own, large-scale philanthropy was thoroughly entangled with the family's long-standing involvement with Trinity College. Because it was the Methodist church's college for men in North Carolina, Washington Duke and his family began to take an active interest in the small, struggling institution in the late 1880s. At a time when the college was almost bankrupt, Ben Duke gave it $1,000 in 1887 and soon became a trustee. The leaders of Trinity decided in 1890 that it needed to move from its isolated, rural location in the North Carolina Piedmont—five miles from the nearest railroad, telegraph, or telephone—to a growing city. Several North Carolina cities made bids accordingly, but Washington Duke, after conferring with his son Ben and other members of the family, contributed the money that brought the college to Durham, where it commenced operations in the fall of 1892.

Since the full story of Trinity College's gradual development into one of the South's leading liberal arts institutions by the time of World War I has been well told elsewhere, it need not be repeated here.[3] Washington Duke and his family, by providing the regular financial support that Trinity had long sought but never before found, played a major part in that development, with Washington Duke giving the bulk of what endowment the college had prior to his death in 1905 and with Ben Duke contributing largely to the annual budget and serving as the chief link between the family and the college. At Ben Duke's urging, J. B. Duke, who had moved from Durham to New York in the mid-1880s, also made important gifts to the college. In short, Trinity College and its needs, as transmitted to J. B. Duke by his older brother, Ben, and the presidents of the college, first John C. Kilgo and then William P. Few, were what might be called the "starter dough" which, when some other ingredients were added, rose finally into the great loaf that became the Duke Endowment.

Methodist higher education was not, however, the only charitable concern of Washington Duke and his family. The Orphan Asylum at Oxford, North Carolina, some twenty-five miles north of Durham, was owned and operated by the Grand Lodge of North Carolina Masons, to which Washington Duke belonged. From the 1890s onward, he and Ben Duke took a close, personal interest in the institution, often taking the train up to spend the day, or a part of it, seeing what the most urgent needs and problems were, and then doing what they could to help.

The Oxford Orphan Asylum was then maintained for white children only, and the walls of the Jim Crow system of racial segregation, the South's second "peculiar institution" (antebellum slavery having been the first), were rapidly rising higher around the turn of the century. Washington Duke and his family, however, rather than helping to segregate the races, befriended African Americans and their institutions, both in and beyond Durham. The African American school north of Raleigh that became Kitrell College was one early example, and there were numerous others.

Having acquired money and therefore power and social status by the 1890s, the Dukes therefore displayed the paternalistic and benevolent attitudes toward African Americans on which many upper-class white southerners traditionally, and often hypocritically, prided themselves. In the case of the Dukes, however, there was an unusual aspect of the relationship that transcended paternalism, and it was rooted in politics. The overwhelming majority of African American adult males became Republicans in the stormy years after the Civil War, and so did Washington Duke first and then later his sons. If the blacks knew all too painfully what it meant to be an oppressed minority, so too, in an admittedly different way, did those southern whites, like Washington Duke, who became Republicans. They were despised and ridiculed as "scalawags" by the Democratic majority. For Washington Duke, therefore, African Americans became political allies as well as, in many cases, friends, and the relationship influenced not only his sons and the family's philanthropy but also had a certain liberating influence on Trinity College after 1890.

The Dukes' business partner, George W. Watts, gave a general hospital, one of the early ones in the state, to the white people of Durham in 1895. While the Dukes also contributed to Watts Hospital, they were sensitive to the fact that Durham's African Americans sorely lacked such a facility. Accordingly, in response to an appeal from a prominent leader in the black community, Ben and J. B. Duke gave the money to establish Lincoln Hospital for Durham's African Americans in 1901 and continued to help support it in later years.

Lincoln Hospital was, in fact, the first and only major venture of the Dukes in the field of medical care, for Trinity College and other Methodist causes headed the list of Duke philanthropies. In addition to significant support to Methodist colleges for women in Louisburg, North Carolina, and in Greensboro, North Carolina, the Dukes also generously befriended Quaker-sponsored Guilford College, near Greensboro, which had grown out of New Garden School. Since the younger Dukes had briefly attended New Garden back in the early 1870s, it had a special claim on them. Moreover, Trinity College itself had evolved from a one-room school jointly sponsored by Methodist and Quaker farmers back in 1838, so in helping Guilford, the Dukes were also honoring an old collaborative effort.

Having been converted to Methodism as a young adolescent in the early 1830s, Washington Duke honored the tradition of the dedicated itinerant ministers, the circuit riders, who built the church into a major Protestant denomination. He had known first hand the hard work and poverty that filled the lives of both ministers and church members, and he always responded to appeals for help that came from both preachers and congregations, especially in such rural, agricultural communities as his had been.

Countless examples of this could be cited, but perhaps a letter that Ben Duke in Durham wrote to his brother J. B. Duke in New York right after Christmas in 1893 is the best, briefest way to suggest the pattern of fam-

ily philanthropy that was clearly emerging in the 1890s. "Dear Buck," Ben
Duke wrote:

> I am much disappointed at not seeing you here [in Durham] this Xmas,
> but I suppose your business would not allow you to leave N.Y. I want to
> talk to you about money matters. During the past year I have paid out
> money as follows
>
>   Trinity College
>   (on account of our offer to the conference last year) $7,500
>   All other church & charity $4,016
> $11,516.00
>
> I believe it was understood that Mary, you and myself were to share in this
> Trinity College expenditure. The other item of $4,016.00 was expended
> about as follows: contributions to the poor fund of the town during the
> severe weather last winter, amounts given to the pastor of our church for
> the poor during the year which he used in doctoring the sick, burying the
> dead &c, &c (all of which he rendered itemized statement of), Oxford
> Orphans Asylum, current expenses of our church of every kind. Colored
> School at Kittrell N.C. $500. Worn out Preachers of the N.C. Conference
> $500. To poor churches over the state &c &c. What I mention is in
> addition to what Pa gave or rather it is two-thirds (2/3rds) of the total of
> such payments, the total being $6,024.00. I expect you have given away
> money individually during the year — if so & you are disposed to assist me
> as usual with these expenses you should have credit for such amounts as
> you have expended. The total amount I've paid ($11,516.00) looks large
> but $7,500 of it went in one place & I do not see how I could have made
> the other items less, as the pressure from the poor &c has been urgent, &
> as for myself I feel better for having given it than if I had not done so. Of
> course this does not include money I've given to favor kin people.[4]

J. B. Duke promptly paid his share, of course, as his older brother had
requested. While J. B. Duke did make charitable contributions on his own,
especially to certain Methodist churches in New York City and in New Jersey,
among other causes, he generally had no time to spare for the correspondence
involved in philanthropic work, much less for the tedious hours of conferring
with educators, Methodist preachers, and various other petitioners. That was
left to Ben Duke, who took the trouble to answer, even if negatively sometimes, the hundreds of requests that poured in to him and his father, requests

that became especially voluminous after the announcement of each of the family's larger gifts to Trinity. Gifts from the Dukes along the lines suggested in Ben Duke's letter of 1893 grew larger as the years passed, with Trinity College always the prime beneficiary. The pattern was also recapitulated in Washington Duke's will in 1905.

One may well ask why the Dukes began to engage in systematic, annual philanthropic giving from the late 1880s onward, that is from the time that they began to enjoy true wealth. Their motives were no doubt mixed, as in the case in most human affairs. One quick explanation, however, that many in a later era would certainly rush to offer, must be ruled out: since there were no income taxes in the United States in the late nineteenth century, and would not be until after the Sixteenth Amendment was added to the Constitution in 1913, the Dukes obviously were not seeking tax deductions.

Most people most of the time enjoy the approval of those among whom they live, and the Dukes were no exception. Although they generally acted quietly when possible and never hungered for publicity, they sought, certainly in some measure, the approval of their fellow North Carolinians. After the storm of angry opposition to the "tobacco trust" arose in the 1890s, some critics charged that the Dukes were simply attempting to "buy off" public opinion. The simplest rebuttal to that suggestion, however, lay in the large amount of time, thought, and worry, even more than money alone, that Washington Duke and especially Ben Duke gave to charitable causes, and they began doing so even before the American Tobacco Company became the target for widespread attack.

Pride in Durham and a desire to help enhance its respectability and progressive modernity played a part in some of the family's early giving, as in the case of the Dukes' wanting Durham to become the home of Trinity College. They were not alone, of course, in possessing a strong sense of community, of southern love of place, but in their case, money began early to give tangible expression to the sentiment.

When all cautionary qualifications are made, however, the simplest answer seems to be the principal one: the Dukes gave because the Methodist church emphasized the desirability, even the necessity for salvation, of giving on the part of those who were able. Washington Duke came to philanthropy via the Methodist church and raised his children accordingly. In a time when the southern churches still kept the new social gospel at arm's length and focused on the actions and responsibilities of individuals, the old biblical doctrine of the stewardship of wealth remained very much alive: those who possessed wealth had the dual responsibility, according to the church's teaching, of both using and giving it wisely.

While J. B. Duke had traditionally deferred first to his father and then to his brother Ben in the matter of the family's philanthropy, beginning around 1915 things began somewhat to change. For one thing, Ben Duke began to experience serious health problems around that time, and while there would be periods of improvement, he gradually slipped into semi-invalidism. This forced a certain modification of the old division of responsibility between the two brothers, who were unusually devoted to each other as they had been to their father. At any rate, J. B. Duke began, tentatively and warily at first, to establish his own lines of communication with Trinity College. Most members of its faculty had probably never actually met J. B. Duke, but in 1914 President Few went to New York to confer with him and his brother and then wrote one of his first letters directed solely to J. B. Duke. "We want you to understand what we are doing [at Trinity] and to approve of it," Few explained. "But I do want you to feel that we will live within our means; that we will incur no added financial responsibilities without the approval beforehand of your Brother and yourself; and that any further contributions are to be free will offerings made because you feel like making them and not because they are expected of you." In closing, Few struck a note that reappeared many times in his letters and public addresses: "And speaking for myself I am particularly anxious that you shall get enduring personal satisfaction and happiness out of what you have done for Trinity College, because you are able to feel that through it you have done some permanent good upon the earth."[5]

Just precisely how J. B. Duke felt about doing "permanent good upon the earth" is not known, for, prior to 1924, he rarely went on record about his private beliefs and aspirations. In addition to Ben Duke and President Few, however, there was another person who carefully lobbied J. B. Duke on behalf of Trinity College, and that was its former president, John C. Kilgo. Although he became a Methodist bishop upon giving up the presidency in 1910, he remained close to the college, serving as both a trustee and member of the executive committee. Kilgo had rekindled Washington Duke's interest in Trinity back in the 1890s and was greatly admired by Ben and J. B. Duke.

After visiting the Duke brothers in New York and at J. B. Duke's estate near Somerville, New Jersey, in the summer of 1915, Kilgo reported enthusiastically to Few: "I feel that I used the opportunity for its full value, and if there had been nothing except the companionship I should have written down the trip as one of life's highest points. But as things turned out, it became a mountain peak event in my life." Kilgo added, in unhappy words for the historian, that it was all too lengthy for him to try to relate in a letter.[6]

The various nudges and suggestions obviously worked on J. B. Duke, for he soon put his own landscape architects to work preparing plans for the Trinity campus, and he gave a special fund of $10,000 for the grounds, always a matter of great interest to the Dukes. Also starting in 1915 he commenced making an annual contribution to supplement the funds of the two Methodist conferences in North Carolina for their "worn-out preachers" and the widows and orphans of deceased preachers. He requested Trinity College to make the annual disbursements, a chore that President Few performed happily and gracefully just before Christmas each year. In addition, J. B. Duke began giving $25,000 annually to the Board of Church Extension of the Methodist Episcopal Church, South; $15,000 of that gift was earmarked for assistance in the building of rural churches and $10,000 for help with the operating expenses of such churches. In 1920 Duke requested Trinity College to administer these funds also, explaining to the Board of Church Extension that he made the change not through any dissatisfaction but simply because "I have always been very closely identified with Trinity College, and not only would like for them to handle it for me, but think it would help the college by its so doing."[7]

At Ben Duke's suggestion, J. B. Duke agreed to become a trustee of Trinity in 1918 but, intensely disliking what he called "town meetings," he chose not to attend the trustees' sessions. A happy "workaholic," J. B. Duke was, in fact, not by any means an easy person to see or pin down for a conference, and Few had to exercise considerable effort and ingenuity to communicate with or convey information to him. In early 1919, however, after a particularly forceful and graceful letter to J. B. Duke, Few managed to secure an interview. Duke had earlier, once in 1916 and on one or two other occasions, referred vaguely to his long-range philanthropic plans in conversation with Few, but in 1919 matters became more specific. In a frustratingly short letter after the conference, Few wrote: "As I have thought of your plan, it grows in my mind. I think it is really a sounder idea than that around which any other large benevolence in this country with which I am familiar has been built. I have done a good deal of thinking concerning your suggestions, and I should be glad of an early opportunity to talk with your again."[8]

A few weeks later Few followed up with more specific suggestions for implementing the ideas that J. B. Duke had advanced. "If you and your lawyer find that the property cannot be administered under the charter of Trinity College," Few noted, "I would suggest that you create a separate corporation, perhaps to be called the James B. Duke Foundation or Fund, as you might prefer." The trustees of the foundation could be self-perpetuating and be seven in number, the seven members, in fact, of the executive committee of the Trinity trustees. Since there was a vacancy coming up on the executive committee, Few hoped J. B. Duke might be willing to fill it. "To carry out your ideas as I understand them," Few continued, "I think the charter of the Foundation ought to provide that the income is to go to Trinity College, Durham, N.C., and to the building of rural Methodist churches and the supplementing of rural Methodist preachers."[9]

J. B. Duke had finally revealed to Few something of his plan for basing a philanthropic foundation on a substantial portion of Duke's equity in the electric-power company. At that point, the scope of the projected foundation was apparently limited to Trinity College and to certain Methodist causes. Nothing had thus far been said, in other words, about Trinity College's fulfilling a dream that went back to the 1890s of becoming a university; about grants to other educational institutions; or about aid in the areas of health care and child care (orphanages). As Few was about to discover, however, J. B. Duke was simply not ready to act in the matter, for one reason because the stock of the power companies was not paying what he regarded as adequate dividends and could not do so until the rates could be adjusted upward. Another reason for the delay was Duke's continued absorption in the affairs of his fast-growing electric-power companies in the Carolinas and in a vast hydroelectric project he had undertaken in a hitherto underdeveloped region in the northern part of Canada's province of Quebec.[10]

As J. B. Duke and his lawyer successfully battled to gain rate increases from the North Carolina Corporation Commission in the early 1920s, Few, whose hopes for Trinity had soared in 1919, struggled with acute budgetary problems that were rooted in the sharp inflationary spiral that afflicted the county around 1919 and 1920. While both Duke brothers increased their annual support for the college because of the emergency, Few desperately wanted a long-term solution in the way of endowment. Overworked and badly stressed by college problems, Few had to be hospitalized in the summer of 1920, continued to be unwell on and off through the winter of 1920–21, and finally developed pneumonia. Convalescing from that in the spring of 1921, he had much time for thinking, and a number of ideas, many foreshadowed by past efforts or proposals, finally fell into place in his mind. Few had come up with his initial blueprint for a new institution, one he suggested be called "Duke University," that could be organized around Trinity College. It was no hastily conceived scheme designed to lure a large benefaction; rather, it was the carefully considered synthesis of a number of ideas that had long been evolving and of developments in Trinity College that were already underway.[11]

One should particularly note that the idea for naming the new, enlarged institution "Duke University" came from Few. His principal reason was that there was already in the United States alone a Trinity University in San Antonio, Texas, and several other Trinity Colleges. In Great Britain and elsewhere in the English-speaking world there were numerous other educational institutions named "Trinity." Not wishing to share a name with so many others, Few turned to the name that various people first began to suggest in the 1890s, but there is not a shred of evidence that any member of the Duke family had ever shown any interest in changing the institution's name.

At any rate, as a result of his brainstorm in the spring of 1921, Few drew up the following statement that he hoped J. B. Duke would sign:

> I wish to see Trinity College, the law school & other schools expanded into a fully developed university organization. It has been suggested to me that this expanded institution be named Duke University as a memorial to my father whose gifts made possible the building of Trinity College in Durham, and I approve this suggestion. I desire this university to include Trinity College, a coordinate College for Women, a Law School, a School of Business Administration, a School of Engineering (emphasizing chemical & electrical engineering), a Graduate School of Arts & Sciences, and, when adequate funds are available, a Medical School. I desire this enlarged institution to be operated under the present charter with only such changes, if any changes at all, as this enlargement may require. To this university that is to be thus organized I will give   millions of dollars. I agree to pay in within   years   millions in cash or good securities.[12]

Having gained Ben Duke's enthusiastic approval of the proposal, Few traveled to New York to confer with J. B. Duke. While he was still not ready to commit himself so definitely and refused to fill in the monetary blanks that Few had left or to sign the document, J. B. Duke apparently gave some sort of general approval to the scheme. When Trinity's trustees met in June, 1921, at any rate, Few alluded briefly to a possible reorganization looking toward university status. And to one or two close friends he referred to "great plans which I think in due course will be completely realized" and to "our reorganization for the future." Conferences about the matter between J. B. Duke and Few followed, one later in 1921, but there is no record of what was said or agreed upon.[13]

Few's plan for the university included a medical school, "when adequate funds are available." The qualifying phrase was important, for Few had been learning about medical education and its extremely high costs from the most authoritative teacher on the subject in the country, Dr. Abraham Flexner. Author of a report for the Carnegie Foundation that helped revolutionize medical education in the United States after 1910, Flexner began advising Few as early as 1916, when Trinity's president resumed thinking about something that had interested his predecessors, on and off, since the 1890s. With no four-year medical school in North Carolina, there was a growing awareness in the state of the critical need. Nor was there, in fact, a first-class medical school anywhere in the South at that time.

After the distraction caused by the nation's involvement in World War I had passed, Few again picked up the idea of the medical school but hoped to avoid the financial burden that Trinity would have to bear if it alone tried to build a four-year school. He therefore came up with a bold, highly imaginative scheme whereby a new medical school in Durham could be linked with Watts Hospital, an idea which George W. Watts supported, and with the existing two-year, preclinical medical school at the nearby University of North Carolina. The Rockefeller-backed General Education Board was also eager to help a soundly conceived and well-financed medical school in the southeastern region of the nation and indicated that it would consider supplying half of the $6 million needed if Few could obtain the other half.[14]

In 1922 Few's bold plans were frustrated by objections from those who hoped that the University of North Carolina might build its own medical school (which it would not be able to do until after World War II) and by some who claimed to see, in the linking together of a church-related institution and a state-supported one, a possible violation of the principle of the separation of church and state. In short, Few failed in his early effort to secure a medical school, but the episode was quite important in educating J. B. Duke not only about the great cost of medical education but also about the larger situation concerning health care in the Carolinas.

One of Few's strongest supporters in the effort to secure a four-year medical school for North Carolina was Dr. Watson S. Rankin, the secretary of the State Board of Health. One of the most highly respected public health officers in the nation, Rankin keenly recognized the acute need for a full-fledged, high-quality medical school, but he also warned that such a school would not by itself alleviate the widespread shortage of doctors in much of North Carolina. Still one of the most rural states in the nation, as well as one of the poorest, North Carolina consequently faced daunting deficiencies in the area of health care. Rankin had come to believe that the main remedy for the shortage of doctors in rural areas and small towns would be the establishment of a system of local, community-supported hospitals. He had closely studied a system of government-supported community hospitals in the sprawling, agricultural province of Saskatchewan in western Canada; as a result, he had become a veritable apostle on behalf of not-for-profit, local hospitals as an essential step toward better health care for Carolinians.[15]

Rankin's ideas, relatively novel and advanced in the United States at that time, clearly had a great influence on J. B. Duke. Among his other talents, one of the essential keys to Duke's long train of successes in the business world was a pronounced knack for spotting uniquely talented and dedicated persons, treating them fairly and generously, and thereby winning their lifelong loyalty. An early example of this had come almost at the beginning of J. B. Duke's rise when in the mid-1880s, he found a mechanical genius in William T. O'Brien, who was able to make the hitherto undependable Bonsack cigarette machine actually perform smoothly. O'Brien subsequently became an important contributor to the success of W. Duke Sons and Company. A few years later the Duke brothers together picked a remarkably gifted textile manufacturer, William A. Erwin, to run their extensive and highly successful operation in that sector, and Erwin remained on the job for his lifetime. In the electric-power business, William States Lee proved to be an incomparably talented engineer, as much of a genius in his line of work as J. B. Duke was in his, and the two men together must share a great deal of the credit for the successful building of the Duke Power Company. The examples could be multiplied endlessly; but the evidence is clear that J. B. Duke not only had an eye for unusual talent but also possessed those qualities of character and judgment that enabled him to make lifelong associates out of most those with whom he chose to work.

Unlike Ben Duke, J. B. Duke actually had for most of his life rather little direct, hands-on experience with higher education in general or Trinity College in particular. Yet in deciding to work with William P. Few to build a great university, J. B. Duke showed the same shrewd judgment that he had in the case of O'Brien, Erwin, Lee, and others. So it was also in the case of Watson Rankin, for J. B. Duke had had even less contact with the field of health care than with higher education. True, the Duke brothers had given Lincoln Hospital to Durham's African American community in 1901, and they subsequently made additional, substantial gifts to it. They were not, however, in any sense closely involved in the hospital's operation.

As the outline of what would become the Duke Endowment gradually took shape in J. B. Duke's mind over a period of a decade or so, it is clear that, in one sense, he was institutionalizing for posterity, on a princely scale a pattern of family giving — to higher education (Trinity College), to orphanages, and to the rural Methodist church — that Washington Duke had initially inspired in the latter quarter of the nineteenth century and for which Ben Duke had taken the major responsibility between around 1890 and 1915.

One of the most creative and original aspects of the Duke Endowment, however, would be its provision in the area of health care. As will be more fully discussed in a subsequent chapter, in assisting communities in the Carolinas to provide hospital care for indigent Carolinians, both white and black, and to build not-for-profit community hospitals, the Duke Endowment performed one of the classic and most valuable functions of America's private foundations: finding a great social need and trying to show how it might be at least partially met. A good generation or more before the state or federal government would acknowledge any responsibility in the matter of local hospitals, the Duke Endowment's Hospital Section began in the mid-1920s to point the way. When the federal government enacted the Hill-Burton legislation after World War II to spur the building of community hospitals, the Duke Endowment's pioneering effort in the Carolinas served as both inspiration and model.

Since that important part of the Endowment was actually not derived, except in a quite limited way, from the family's traditional pattern of giving, J. B. Duke himself must be credited with including the health-care area in the Endowment's work. He, in turn, owed a large debt to Watson Rankin, whom Duke would subsequently select to design and direct the work of the Hospital Section.[16]

President Few's abortive effort in 1921–22 to build an unconventionally supported medical school was not, therefore, a total loss, for it had brought J. B. Duke into contact with Rankin. Moreover, the pace toward the creation of J. B. Duke's foundation quickened in 1923. Early in that year Few met, apparently for the first time, the man who had become in J. B. Duke's later years his closest business associate and adviser, George Garland Allen. A native of Warrenton, North Carolina, who had taken a job with the American Tobacco Company as a very young man in 1895 and then risen through the ranks, Allen was destined to play major roles in both the Endowment and Duke University, not to mention the Duke Power Company. In June 1923 Allen was elected a trustee of Trinity College, thus beginning an association that would last until his death in 1960.

Alexander H. Sands Jr., a native of Richmond, Virginia, had also risen in the tobacco company to become the executive secretary for both J. B. and Ben Duke. Like Allen, he would be uniquely important in the ongoing operations of the various institutions and companies that J. B. Duke had established. In the autumn of 1923 Sands requested Few's assistance in obtaining a list of hospitals in North Carolina, with information about their operating costs and number of free-bed days, that is, the amount of charity work they did. Sands also wanted a list of orphanages, their per capita cost, capacity, and other relevant data. On the matter of the hospitals, Few turned to Rankin, and after providing all the assistance that he could, Rankin declared to Few: "Your idea of developing a large, adequate medical service for the State of North Carolina is one of the biggest conceptions of public service that I have heard of in many a day."[17]

When a newspaper story early in 1924 alluded to statements made by Rankin in what he had presumed to be an off-the-record gathering, he hastily apologized to Few. Rankin noted that when he had been asked why he did not push the idea of local hospitals in the state legislature, he had explained that "the problem was such a large one, one which eventually would require so much money, and one that as yet the public had not begun to think seriously about, that it seemed to me that it should be first undertaken by philanthropy rather than public funds, and that there was reason for believing that the idea might appeal to those who were financially able to begin the development." When someone in the group mentioned J. B. Duke's name, Rankin had stated that "if Mr. Duke would take the initiative in the development of such a system of hospitals . . . it would perhaps be best for the State to wait inasmuch as the right sort of program would require twenty-five years for its development."[18]

Rankin need not have worried, however, for the hints about J. B. Duke's plans that found their way into the newspapers were too incomplete and scattered for the public to pay much attention. Duke told one old friend that he was finding that making his money had been easier than trying to devise a means of giving it away wisely. Nevertheless, he proceeded as carefully and methodically in his approach toward philanthropy as he always had in his business affairs.

Someone who had always taken great interest and pleasure in construction work, J. B. Duke probably was, personally, more excited about the prospect of extensive building at Trinity College than in any other aspect of the development there. One of the most commendable aspects of the Dukes as benefactors of Trinity College had been, in fact, that they had never attempted to interfere in any way with the internal operation or academic aspect of the

institution. While their monetary gifts supported the whole college, in every
sense, their personal involvement had always been limited to buildings and
grounds — and especially the latter because of their penchant for horticulture
and landscaping.

As early as 1923 J. B. Duke picked the architectural firm that he wished to
design the new buildings he planned to give to Trinity, and the head of the
firm, Horance Trumbauer of Philadelphia, began corresponding with President Few. Few and one of his key advisers in the area of buildings and grounds
made a tour of eastern and mid-western college and university campuses in the
spring of 1924. Admiring the Tudor Gothic buildings they studied at Bryn
Mawr, Yale, Chicago, and elsewhere, Few and his associate conferred with
J. B. Duke and Trumbauer, and all agreed by September 1924 that the Tudor
or Collegiate Gothic style was their first choice for the new stone buildings to
be constructed in Durham.[19] "Personally, I have no doubt that Mr. Duke,
when he once makes up his mind definitely to go ahead, will see that a most
creditable job is done," George Allen assured Few in September 1924.[20]

Fortunately for the Carolinas, J. B. Duke finally had stopped concentrating
on building dams and generating electric power long enough to "go ahead"
with his philanthropic plans. In late October 1924 Robert L. Flowers, vice
president for finance at Trinity and Few's right-hand man in administration,
was in New York and began sending Few some interesting letters marked
"personal and confidential." Conferring at great length with Sands, Allen, and
Perkins, Flowers found that he faced a real challenge in explaining various
aspects of Trinity College to New York businessmen who were just becoming
acquainted with it. "I think everything is going all right," Flowers assured Few.
"From what they tell me, Mr. J. B. is right in behind the thing now. Mr. B. N. is
greatly interested." Later in the same day Flowers sent off another dispatch:
"Mr. J. B. is undecided how to have the trust fund administered." Up until that
time and during five years or so of the preliminary planning, the idea had been
to have the executive committee of Trinity's board of trustees administer the
fund. Now Flowers reported a highly significant new development: "They
have been to confer with the Rockefeller Foundation and at present they are
very much inclined to have fifteen trustees of the fund." Flowers thought it
might be unfortunate for Trinity to have the trustees of the foundation and
those of the reorganized college too widely separated. Still, the personnel for
the foundation's board would be the important thing, and both Allen and
Perkins, according to Flowers, were eager "to get in touch with the College."[21]

One of J. B. Duke's fellow millionaires, Andrew Carnegie, had written extensively to advise wealthy individuals to dispose of their fortunes carefully and wisely during their lifetimes. Ben Duke, unlike J. B. Duke who was not a reader of much beside business reports, may have read Carnegie's advice, and he certainly urged his younger brother to proceed expeditiously with his proposed philanthropy. Flowers reported that, thanks in part at least to Ben Duke and George Allen, "Mr. J. B. is pushing things just as fast as he can."[22]

Flowers proved to be quite correct about J. B. Duke's "pushing things" rapidly, for early in December 1924 Duke arrived in Charlotte with his wife, his daughter Doris, George Allen, W. R. Perkins, and his nephew-in-law, Anthony Biddle. They were soon joined at Duke's home in Charlotte by several top officers of the power company and one or two others. For an apparently brief part of the time, Few and Flowers joined the group. J. B. Duke announced that he had been working on his philanthropic plans for a number of years and that he now wanted the group to remain assembled until the job of polishing the indenture, the legal instrument that would create the perpetual trust, was completed. Stopping only for meals, the group reportedly met until well into the evening for about four days and discussed, section by section, the lengthy draft of the indenture that had been prepared largely by W. R. Perkins.[23]

Unfortunately, documentary evidence concerning what went on in this conference in Charlotte does not exist. Almost forty years after the event, one of the participants could recall no substantial alterations or additions that the group made. "Of course, Mr. Duke . . . was a positive man," this participant noted, "and when he made a positive assertion very few people controverted it."[24] If this memory was correct, and forty years is an especially long time where remembering accurately is concerned, the fact that J. B. Duke's associates did not scrutinize the indenture more critically was unfortunate, for, as will be discussed, there were a number of questionable matters and at least one major blunder, with immediately unfortunate consequences, that might easily have been avoided.

Since there is so little evidence concerning the conference in Charlotte, one can only speculate, but one possible explanation for the apparent lack of critical comment may have had to do with an idiosyncrasy of J. B. Duke's: over the years he had found that the quickest way for him to get at the hard-core essence of a business letter or report was to have Sands, Allen, or whomever was assisting him at the time read the document aloud to him, presumably skipping any prefatory or extraneous matter. Several of J. B. Duke's close associates noted that in that manner he could absorb and process information more rapidly than most people. So much did J. B. Duke like that procedure, in fact, that he memorialized it in the Endowment indenture by including the request, which has been faithfully honored, that the indenture creating the Endowment, which has long sections of numbingly legalistic language, be read aloud to the assembled trustees during at least one meeting each year.

That aural method of receiving and processing information apparently worked well for J. B. Duke. For many people, however, the eye works better than the ear for the absorption of complex, important data; and as any teacher knows, not a few people actually doze off if certain types of material are read aloud to them for any lengthy period of time. At any rate, one must certainly wonder if a person as intelligent and experienced as William P. Few was might not have caught certain unfortunate passages of the indenture concerning Duke University if he had gotten an opportunity to read the passages carefully and think about them.

At any rate, J. B. Duke had taken philanthropic action the likes of which the poverty-stricken South of that era had never known. He did not formally sign the indenture creating the Duke Endowment until December 11, 1924, at his legal residence in New Jersey, but news of it leaked to the newspapers two days earlier. While the nation at large paid ample attention to the development, the largest impact of the news was in the Carolinas where all of the beneficiaries were located. Securities worth approximately $40 million, mostly but not exclusively in the Duke Power company, were turned over to the trustees of the Endowment, and the annual income was to be distributed among four educational institutions, nonprofit hospitals and orphanages for both races in the two Carolinas, and the rural Methodist church in North Carolina. First of all, however, the trustees, after dividing among themselves 3 percent of the annual income as compensation for their services, were instructed to set aside 20 percent of the remaining annual income to be added to the principal (or corpus) until an additional $40 million had been accumulated. (This was accomplished in 1976.) The remaining 80 percent of the annual income was to be distributed in the two Carolinas as follows: 46 percent to four educational institutions, 32 percent to nonprofit hospitals for both races, 12 percent for certain purposes of the rural Methodist church in North Carolina only, and 10 percent for orphanages of both races.

Just as Trinity College had been the principal beneficiary of gifts from the Duke family from the 1890s onward, so was "[a]n institution of learning to be known as Duke University" designated as the recipient of 32 percent of the Endowment's annual income. Moreover, to help establish the new university, the trustees were authorized to expend $6 million from the corpus of the trust. Then in clumsy, legalistic, and superfluous language that immediately led to long-lasting misunderstanding, W. R. Perkins and J. B. Duke put this sentence in the indenture: "However, should the name of Trinity College . . . be changed to Duke University" within a three-month period, then the $6 million should go to that institution.

Journalists and others quickly seized on this section of the indenture and interpreted it, understandably enough, as a blatant case of J. B. Duke's "buying himself a university" or bribing a small college in order to memorialize himself and his family. Since the idea of organizing a university around Trinity and naming the enlarged institution "Duke" had originated with Few, the popular interpretation was hardly fair to J. B. Duke. Yet he and his lawyer were responsible for the clumsy language that inspired that interpretation. To no avail, Few issued explanatory statements and privately confessed that he was "sorry that the legal phrasing in the Indenture of Trust seemed to put Mr. Duke in a bad light."[25]

The sad fact, of course, is that truth seldom if ever catches up with error, especially if the falsehood may be turned to witty, amusing ends. H. L. Mencken's *American Mercury* magazine specialized in sophomoric attacks on J. B. Duke and his presumption in thinking he could build himself a university allegedly from scratch. Other journalists for many years ignored Few's patient efforts to set the record straight and kept alive the story of J. B. Duke's "buying" himself a university. An additional twist was soon added with the allegation that J. B. Duke had first tried to "buy" Princeton (sometimes Yale or some other college) but failing there, turned to a small college in the South that was unknown to so many in the East. Strangely enough, students and even some faculty members at Duke University itself have for many decades passed along the story about J. B. Duke and Princeton. (The story has also had a long, vigorous life at Princeton University.) Most of this silly, groundless myth-making arose out of ignorance not only about President Few's part in the naming of the university but more especially about the Duke family's long, close relationship to Trinity College.

The emphasis on the name change also obscured another important point. J. B. Duke had agreed to underwrite what Few called a "major" or "national" university. It was, in fact, to be a research university, and it was to be organized around, to have at its core or heart, as Few preferred to say, an older liberal arts college. That latter entity was to be the university's undergraduate college of arts and sciences, and it was named, and still is in the late twentieth century,

Trinity College. Understanding the truth, however, is often too much to ask of either some journalists or a portion of the public.

There were, in fact, even more serious problems in the indenture having to do with Duke University, but Few and his close associates would not come to perceive them until the late 1920s. Moreover, there is no evidence whatsoever that J. B. Duke lost a moment's sleep about the name-changing hullabaloo. He had long before developed a tough hide, possibly too tough for his own good, when it came to what journalists (and some politicians) had to say about him. He believed, whether rightly or wrongly, that he had more important things to do than worry about his image or misunderstandings on the part of the public.

While Durham, the home of Trinity College and Duke University, was at the eastern edge of the territory served by the Duke Power system, the other three educational beneficiaries were located much closer to the hub of that system. Given the largely Protestant and biracial character of the population of the Carolinas in the 1920s, the selection of the schools also reflected a gesture in the direction of ecumenism as well as racial liberalism. Davidson College, a Presbyterian institution near Charlotte, was to receive 5 percent of the annual income as was Furman University, a Baptist institution in Greenville, South Carolina. Johnson C. Smith University, an institution in Charlotte for African Americans, was to receive 4 percent.

The 32 percent of the net income that was earmarked for health care provided, at the "uncontrolled discretion" of the trustees, for aid to not-for-profit hospitals for both whites and African Americans in the Carolinas. At a time when Dr. Rankin and others calculated that, on average, it cost $3.00 per bed per day to provide ward service in Carolina hospitals, the trustees were authorized to pay $1.00 "per free bed day" provided by the hospital. Any residue of income left over after the provision designed to assist in free care was to be used to help those communities which wished to acquire and equip nonprofit hospitals, preferably in the two Carolinas but possibly in those states contiguous to them (Virginia, Tennessee, and Georgia) if surplus funds should be available.

As in the case of the name-changing clause of the indenture, a truly cautious participant in J. B. Duke's Charlotte conference early in December 1924 might well have questioned the wisdom of specifying the precise amount ($1.00 per free bed per day) to help toward hospital care for poor people. The assumption was, obviously, that $3.00 would remain the average cost for a ward bed for the indefinite future. While giving one-third of the cost was a significant boon for charity care at the time, what would happen if hospital costs began to climb, as they did so inexorably during and after World War II? The fact, however, was that J. B. Duke had spent his adult life in a period of marked price stability. True, there had been a sharp, unsettling burst of inflation in the United States from about 1918 into 1920, but it had receded more quickly than it had come after the national economic recession of 1920–21. J. B. Duke and his advisers apparently made the mistake of thinking that the dollar would retain a more or less fixed purchasing power in the long years ahead. The able staff of the Endowment's Hospital Section, however, with the backing of the trustees, would later have no difficulty in finding other creative ways to help in the health-care area even after both inflation and then the joint federal-state program of medical assistance for the poor (Medicaid) entered the picture in the 1960s.

While the Endowment's provisions in the health-care area represented J. B. Duke's relatively novel addition to the family's philanthropic pattern, the 12 percent of the annual income designated for the Methodist church in North Carolina harked back to the institution that originally inspired Washington Duke and then his sons to become philanthropists. To help build and maintain rural Methodist churches in the state, there would be 10 percent of the annual income, and the remaining 2 percent was to be used to supplement the church's payments to superannuated (or "worn-out") preachers and to their widows and children. For the institutions that served the white and African American orphans and half-orphans of the two Carolinas there would be 10 percent of the annual income.

Far back in 1893, Ben Duke had acted for the family in disbursing about $13,500 for charitable purposes. In 1924 J. B. Duke apportioned the income from a perpetual trust worth $40 million — and that amount would be vastly increased by the terms of his will. The striking point, however, is not so much the difference in the sums of money but the continuity in the purpose and nature of the giving.

The creation of the Duke Endowment was certainly not an inevitable development, for many rich individuals have found countless other ways to dispose of their wealth. J. B. Duke was perfectly free to dispose of his wealth as he might choose. The Endowment did have, however, a lot of family history behind it and was, as mentioned earlier, the culmination of a deeply rooted, long-standing tradition and pattern of giving that Washington Duke had begun, Ben Duke had largely supervised for many years, and J. B. Duke, after adding his own emphasis on health care, institutionalized for posterity on a princely scale.

J. B. Duke wanted the trustees to be a carefully selected, working group, the majority of whom he suggested should be either natives or residents of the Carolinas. He declared in his indenture that the trustees should "make a special effort to secure persons of character and ability" as their successors, that they should meet at least ten times each year, and, as stated, that they should be paid for their chores from a fixed percentage of the annual income.

He went on to explain in the indenture that he had carefully planned for much of the revenue from the power company to be used for the social welfare of the communities which it served. Therefore he recommended that the securities of the power company be "the prime investments for the funds of this trust," to be changed only in "response to the most urgent and extraordinary necessity." (As the only alternative to the stock of the power company, Duke approved certain types of governmental notes and bonds.) One reason for dropping the original plan to make the executive committee of Trinity's trustees also the trustees of the Endowment was made clear by Duke's next phrase, for he requested that the Endowment's trustees "see to it that at all times" the power company "be managed and operated by the men best qualified for such a service." In other words, he intended for the trustees of the Endowment, which would hold a controlling share of the power company's stock, to maintain a close, direct supervision of the actual operations of the power company. That was a task for which the trustees of a college or university might or might not be suited.

The close interweaving of a philanthropic trust and an investor-owned business was neither unusual nor frowned upon by governmental agencies in the 1920s. After World War II, however, the situation would change and finally reach a point where, for various reasons that will be explained, the Endowment's trustees would be forced to take legal action to modify J. B. Duke's plan.

J. B. Duke's obvious concern about and solicitude for the Duke Power Company also must be explained. The most important reason he wanted the best possible future for the company, aside from the fact that his perpetual philanthropic trust largely depended on it, was his profound belief that it was destined to play a major and crucial role in the industrial development of the Piedmont region of the Carolinas. In the first quarter of the twentieth century that development had already began to happen, and J. B. Duke, while by no means the only actor in the drama, was indeed a major player. He believed, quite correctly as later decades would demonstrate, that the Carolinas' escape from near-bottom-of-the-list poverty would come primarily through industrialization. He meant for the Duke Power Company to play a large role in helping that to happen.

If J. B. Duke had given all of his stock in the Duke Power Company, rather than just a majority of such stock, to the Endowment, his motivation could hardly be questioned. He did not do that, however, and chose to place a significant amount of the Duke Power Company stock in a trust for the benefit of his daughter Doris and other close relatives. He did this through the Doris Duke Trust, which he established at the same time he did the Duke Endowment. Two-thirds of the annual income of this private, family trust was to go to Doris Duke and one-third to J. B. Duke's nieces, nephews, and their descendants. Although Duke placed only $35,000 in cash and 2,000 shares of Duke Power stock in the trust at the time of its creation, by his will he added 125,904 shares of the stock. Temporarily this meant that the Doris Duke Trust actually held more shares of Duke Power stock than did the Endowment. That situation rapidly changed, however, and within a short span of time, by virtue of the restrictions on the Endowment's investments, its holdings dwarfed those of the Doris Duke Trust. By 1968 for example, the Endowment held 56.36 percent of the Duke Power Company's common stock and the Doris Duke Trust held only 8.73 percent. Since all of the trustees of the Duke Endowment (except for Doris Duke, who was to become a trustee upon reaching the age of twenty-one in 1933), also served as trustees of the Doris Duke Trust, it is clear that J. B. Duke had carefully made interlocking arrangements concerning the Duke Power Company, the Duke Endowment, and the Doris Duke Trust. One cannot argue, therefore, that J. B. Duke's concern about the Duke Power Company arose from completely disinterested or unselfish motives. Yet the fact remains that he planned carefully for the Endowment to own a much larger share of the power company's stock than would the trust for his daughter and close relatives.[26] In J. B. Duke's generosity toward his family, he was also following a tradition, one first established by Washington Duke and then practiced by Ben and J. B. Duke throughout their adult lives. Purists may well object, but the line between public and private (or family) beneficence was one that simply was not sharply drawn in the minds of this particular family.[27]

Toward the end of his indenture, J. B. Duke summarized his intentions in the Endowment: he had "endeavored to make provision in some measure for the needs of mankind along physical, mental and spiritual lines." Since his philanthropy was focused exclusively on the Carolinas, he admitted that he might have tried to extend aid to other causes and to other sections of the country. He asserted his own belief, however, that "so doing probably would be productive of less good by reason of attempting too much." He did not say, but certainly could have, that he had targeted two of the economically poorest states in the nation for his perpetual gift.

The twelve persons whom J. B. Duke selected as the original trustees of the Endowment were, in the order of their signing the indenture, Nanaline H. (Mrs. J. B.) Duke, George G. Allen, William R. Perkins, William B. Bell, Anthony J. Drexel Biddle Jr., Walter C. Parker, Alexander H. Sands Jr., William S. Lee, Charles I. Burkholder, Norman A. Cocke, Edward C. Marshall, and Bennette E. Geer. While two of these, Mrs. Duke and Anthony Biddle, were family members, all of the remaining trustees were business associates of J. B. Duke. Allen, Perkins, and Sands had long been key figures in the New York office of J. B. Duke and were also principal officers or directors of the power company. William B. Bell, as a young lawyer in Perkins's office, became associated with the American Cyanamid Company, in which J. B. Duke had a large interest, during World War I, and in 1922 J. B. Duke picked Bell to become president of that company. Parker, Lee, Burkholder, Cocke, and Marshall were all leaders in the Duke Power Company; and Bennette Geer was an educator and textile manufacturer in South Carolina with whom J. B. Duke, as the major stockholder in one of the larger mills managed by Geer, became closely associated. (An alumnus of Furman University and then a teacher there for a number of years before becoming a prominent textile manufacturer, Geer helped influence J. B. Duke's choice of Furman as a beneficiary of the Endowment.) One of the first actions of the original trustees was to elect J. B. Duke and Watson Rankin as trustees, with the latter put in charge of planning and launching the work of the Endowment's Hospital and Orphan Section.

J. B. Duke certainly did not consider the establishment of the Endowment as a stopping point, for he was keenly interested in the vast construction work that lay ahead for Duke University. Vigorous and apparently in good health at age sixty-eight, he also still had many dams to build in the Carolinas. In the spring of 1925 he and the other trustees of the Endowment met in Durham, in Ben Duke's home in fact, and made a number of important decisions concerning the location of the new Tudor Gothic buildings to be erected on Duke's new (West) campus and the eleven red-brick Georgian structures that were planned for the old Trinity (East) campus.[28]

As greatly interested as J. B. Duke was in the building and grounds at Duke (and he had selected the venerable Olmsted firm of Boston to design the grounds), he also had other large projects underway. In July 1925 he together with George Allen, W. S. Lee, and various officials of the Aluminum Company of America visited the Saguenay river in Quebec, Canada, to inspect the large dams and power sites there for which Duke had earlier received a one-ninth interest in the aluminum company. Duke and his party traveled on his private railway car, the "Doris," and Arthur Vining Davis, Secretary of the Treasury Andrew Mellon, his brother R. B. Mellon, Roy A. Hunt, who later became president of Alcoa, and other officials of the aluminum company went on another private car.

There was much visiting back and forth between the private railway cars, and when Andrew Mellon advocated investing money in art works, J. B. Duke reportedly replied that such a practice was all right for others, but he was more interested in "putting it into Duke University and in the [other] schools and helping out the people there in North and South Carolina." Roy Hunt at a much later date remembered Duke as alert and possessed of a sharp mind. Physically he kept up with the group in several days of fairly strenuous moving about in what was then a relatively undeveloped region. Hunt sized up J. B. Duke as a "soft-spoken" and "courteous Southern gentlemen" who seemed "very friendly and very keen."[29]

While J. B. Duke's Canadian venture had turned out well, his power company in the Carolinas encountered severe problems in the summer of 1925. Prolonged drought in the Piedmont region caused many rivers and reservoirs to fall to perilously low levels, so low that the company's coal-burning steam plants, which had been built for auxiliary or standby use only, had to be operated around the clock, seven days a week. By August the company had to call for curtailment of power consumption, at first only for those customers in certain zones and then for all customers. This crisis for Duke Power had not come with the dramatic speed of the devastating floods of 1916, but it was none the less acute.

J. B. Duke had grown increasingly aware of the need for additional steam plants even before the drought. His wife told a friend that for two years he had talked of nothing but steam plants, a subject that Mrs. Duke claimed not to understand. While that subject had interested J. B. Duke earlier, the summer drought of 1925 forced him to ponder it more than ever. Having visited Durham, Charlotte, and Canada in connection with his various projects, Duke joined his wife and daughter at his home in Newport, Rhode Island, in the later part of July 1925. Although he became ill from unknown causes at the time, he continued to confer regularly with Allen, Sands, Flowers, and others who made the trip to Newport; his wife initially believed that he seemed to improve and would gradually regain his health. When his illness gradually grew worse, however, he was carried on his private railway car to New York, and there his doctors discovered in September that he suffered from what they diagnosed as pernicious anemia, a disease for which there was no known cure at the time.

Despite his illness, however, J. B. Duke continued to make important decisions that vitally affected the power company, the Endowment, and Duke University. When his private nurse noticed his restlessness at one point and asked if he wanted something, he replied, "Please don't disturb me, I'm building a steam plant down South."[30] Sure enough, after studying blueprints and estimates, he authorized Norman Cocke and E. C. Marshall, who had come to New York to confer with him, to proceed with the construction of a large steam plant on the Yadkin river near Salisbury, North Carolina. With a proposed capacity of 70,000 kilowatts, it would be the first large-scale central-station-type steam plant in the Duke Power system and one of the first power plants in the country to utilize the new technology and equipment that allowed the burning of pulverized coal. J. B. Duke may or may not have realized at the time that the large steam plant would also be a benchmark in the transition of the Duke Power system from dependence on water to steam (or coal) as its primary source of power.

In one sense, therefore, even before J. B. Duke died, one of the ideas that originally led him to structure the Endowment as he did began to lose some of its validity or, put another way, to be significantly diluted. As Duke explained in his indenture, in his long involvement with the development of water powers in the Carolinas' Piedmont region he had "observed how such utilization of a natural resource, which otherwise would run in a waste to the sea . . . , both gives impetus to industrial life and provides a safe and enduring investment for capital." His ambition, he added, was "that the revenues of such developments shall administer to the social welfare, as the operation of such developments is administering to the economic welfare, of the communities which they serve." It was with these views in mind, he concluded, that he recommended the securities of the Duke Power Company as the prime investment for the Endowment. The power company's gradual shift after 1925 to an overwhelming dependence on steam plants, rather than on water power or hydro-stations, meant that the rivers of the Piedmont, the "natural resource" to which Duke had referred, were no longer the principal basis for either the power company or the perpetual philanthropic trust that was tied to it.

There was irony in the fact that J. B. Duke, up until the last days of his life, continued to display imaginative flexibility and the ability to change directions in response to changed circumstances. Yet in his indenture, because of his solicitude for the Duke Power Company, he mandated a highly restrictive, perpetual investment policy for the Endowment's trustees, a policy that actually denied the flexibility and the ability to adapt to changed conditions. Not until the early 1970s would the trustees succeed in gaining legal permission to modify the investment provisions of the indenture, and even then, as will be discussed later, there remained a formidable obstacle to the program of investment diversification that the great majority of trustees wished to pursue.

The power company was not, however, the only thing on J. B. Duke's mind during his final days. In his will, which he had signed in December 1924, when the indenture establishing the Endowment was also signed, he had provided under Item VIII that $10 million should be given to the Duke Endowment, $4 million of which was to be used to build and equip a medical school, hospital, and nurses' home at Duke University, with the income from the remaining $6 million to serve as an endowment for the university. His will further stipulated that the remainder of his estate, after all other bequests had been made, should be added to the Duke Endowment, and this would eventually turn out to be approximately $69 million, considerably more than the original $40 million given to the Endowment.

Despite these provisions in his original will, J. B. Duke continued to worry during his illness that he might not have provided enough money for the building program at the university. Accordingly, he summoned George Allen and on October 1, 1925, added a codicil (Item XI) to the will providing (1) than an additional $7 million be placed in the building fund for Duke University; (2) that 10 percent of the annual income from his residuary estate (the above-mentioned $69 million) should go to Duke University; and (3) that 90 percent of the annual income from the residuary estate should go to the Endowment to be used for "maintaining and securing hospitals."[31]

One should note that J. B. Duke was not just ill but a dying man as he made this last-mentioned provision for such lavish support of hospitals. If literally followed by the Endowment's trustees, it would have made the hospital-building program of the Endowment by far the largest beneficiary. The indenture, however, gave the trustees "uncontrolled discretion" concerning annual allocations of income (except where Duke University was concerned), and, as will be explained later, the trustees would decide within a few years following J. B. Duke's death that there was more income in this Item XI account for hospitals than could be properly and wisely used in the Carolinas and that they did not think it prudent to expand the hospital building program into states contiguous to the Carolinas. Accordingly, the trustees would proceed to make the four educational institutions, and especially Duke University, the prime beneficiaries of the Duke Endowment.

One should note that the Endowment's trustees, because of these provisions in Duke's will, would have to maintain an elaborate system of separate accounts. That is, what came to be called the "corpus account" dealt with the original $40 million as specified in the indenture, which was actually only $34 million since Duke had authorized the trustees to take $6 million from the corpus to use in the building fund for Duke University. Because of provisions in the will, the trustees would have to maintain a separate Item VIII account for the benefit of Duke University and a separate Item XI account for the benefit of the university and the Hospital Section of the Endowment. Annual income from these separate accounts, for which J. B. Duke had specified certain purposes, would not, therefore, fall under the distribution formula that Duke had mandated for the original corpus.

Soon after signing that last codicil to his will, Duke developed pneumonia, later lapsed into a coma, and died in his mansion on Fifth Avenue on October 10, 1925. He would have been sixty-nine years old on December 23. After a simple private service without eulogy or sermon in his New York residence, his body was carried by train to Durham. There, after services in Duke Memorial Methodist Church, he was buried beside his father in the family mausoleum in Maplewood Cemetery. Some years later, after the completion of the great chapel that he had wanted on the high ground and at the center of the Tudor Gothic buildings on the university's West Campus, the remains of Washington Duke, Benjamin Newton Duke (who died on January 8, 1929), and James Buchanan Duke were moved to three sarcophagi in a specially designed Memorial Chapel to the left of the chancel in the chapel of Duke University.

If J. B. Duke had lived longer, and death seemed to have taken him somewhat by surprise, he would, naturally, have exercised considerable power and influence in a variety of businesses and institutions but especially in the Duke Endowment, the Duke Power Company, and Duke University. As matters stood after his death, however, much of that power and influence were inherited by two individuals, George G. Allen and William R. Perkins. Nanaline H. Duke, J. B. Duke's wife, had no pronounced or sustained interest in either business or philanthropy, and Doris Duke, not quite thirteen years old when her father died, was too young to participate in such matters. Consequently,

Allen and Perkins, more than anyone else, would play large roles in carrying on J. B. Duke's multiple enterprises. They depended heavily on Alexander Sands, for he too had worked closely with J. B. Duke for many years and was both tireless and impeccable in his attention to matters large and small related to J. B. Duke's various interests. As for the Hospital and Orphan Section of the new Duke Endowment, however, all three of those key players yielded precedence to Dr. Watson Rankin. He became the chief architect of a most important, trailblazing part of the Endowment's activity.

2 ·

LAUNCHING

THE

ENDOWMENT

The Hospital and

Orphan Section

(Part I)

CLEARLY THE MOST INNOVATIVE aspect of the Duke Endowment was James B. Duke's provision concerning health care in the Carolinas. Philanthropic support for medical research and medical education, as shown, for example, in numerous Rockefeller-backed initiatives, had become commonplace by the 1920s. Through the projected medical school and hospital at Duke University, J. B. Duke also would be following that well established pattern. In the provision for aid toward the cost of hospitalization for the Carolinas' poor people and for the building and equipping of community hospitals, especially in rural areas, however, J. B. Duke trailblazed. Moreover, Watson Rankin seized upon those two elements in the health-care area of the indenture and used them in such a creative way as to increase vastly their social and medical significance, primarily and immediately for the benefit of Carolinians but also indirectly for the benefit of a larger national and even international constituency.

A leading historian of American hospitals in the twentieth century has pointed out that by the 1920s the policy of the American Medical Association—and one might more realistically call it a far-fetched dream at that time—was that every doctor should have access to a hospital. That access in turn, might help alleviate a major and widely recognized problem in the health-care area: the increasing shortage of doctors in rural areas. The very term "community hospital" enjoyed increasing popularity in the 1920s according to this historian, and the term carried with it general connotations of "community betterment and social action." This historian concludes that the "most sustained practical effort" in the 1920s to promote the establishment of community hospitals, especially in rural areas, was the program of the Duke Endowment in the Carolinas.[1]

The builder of that program, Watson S. Rankin, was born on January 18, 1879, in Mooresville, North Carolina. After attending Davidson College for two years, he obtained his medical degree from the University of Maryland in Baltimore in 1901, did postgraduate work at the Johns Hopkins medical school, and several residencies in Baltimore hospitals. He next taught for six years as a professor in and then the dean of Wake Forest's two-year, preclinical medical school, and made important investigations in the frequency of hookworm disease in North Carolina. Rankin became North Carolina's first full-time state health officer in 1909, and his long, highly successful tenure in that position was to furnish him the vast experience and many ideas that he brought to his new position in 1925 as the first director and actual creator of the Endowment's Hospital and Orphan Section.

Building on work that he had already done, Rankin cooperated with the Rockefeller Sanitary Commission from 1911 to 1916 in an intensive campaign against hookworm. Rankin believed that this campaign, more than any other single development, helped increase local interest in public health and led to the creation of full-time county health departments in North Carolina. He correctly regarded that as one of the most important achievements during his tenure as state health officer, and it attracted considerable national attention. Another important achievement, however, was his emphasis on public health education. This was carried on through the *Bulletin* published by the state health board, an organized newspaper service, and traveling exhibits. "We must do all we can," Rankin wrote another public health leader in 1930, "to shift the vested interest of the medical profession from ill health to good health." Since he wanted the physician to "become a health trainer and adviser as well as a healer," Rankin argued that the development of a sound basic medical service "must include provision for the practice of preventive medicine as a integral part of general practice."[2] Rankin's ideas and experience would profoundly influence the work of the Endowment's Hospital and Orphan Section.

As both a trustee of the Endowment and director of the Hospital and Orphan Section, Rankin had the primary responsibility of deciding where he and his section would be located. In the indenture J. B. Duke had merely stipulated that the trustees should establish a principal office, which might be changed from time to time, and that "the books and papers other than securities" should be kept at that office. The trustees, accordingly, had voted at their first meeting in December 1924, the meeting where J. B. Duke was elected as a trustee and chairman, to establish the principal office in the headquarters of the Southern (Duke) Power Company in Charlotte. Subsequently in February 1927 the trustees amended that regulation to provide for the Endowment's "books and papers" to be kept at the New York office, which had, since J. B. Duke's death in 1925, become the office of George C. Allen, William R. Perkins, Alexander Sands, and others.[3]

Rankin, while free to have his section's office where he wished it to be, announced in October 1925, shortly after J. B. Duke's death, that he had selected Charlotte as the best location for the office. As he explained to Sands, Charlotte was centrally located for work in both Carolinas, which would lessen the expense of the extensive travel in the field that would be an essential part of the work. (Rankin, like Sands and others in the Endowment, valued frugality and seemed always as careful about spending J. B. Duke's or the Endowment's money as he was about his own resources.) Furthermore, Rankin thought the presence of four other trustees in Charlotte (Burkholder, Cocke, Lee, and Marshall — all Duke Power officials) would facilitate frequent contact and conferences with them about the development of the section's work. Finally, there would be economic advantages in utilizing the office facilities available in the Duke Power building. He felt so sure about the trustees' approving his decision, he explained to Sands, that he was in the process of closing up his office in Raleigh and selling his house there.[4]

More important than the location of the offices of the Hospital and Orphan Section was the quality of the staff, for that would go far in determining the success or failure of what was inevitably to be a challenging voyage into uncharted waters. Enough has been said about Rankin to demonstrate that in him J. B. Duke had indeed chosen wisely. As matters turned out, Rankin himself made a brilliant choice when he selected a young North Carolinian named Graham L. Davis to be his assistant and, for a while, the only other staff member. Learning a great deal from Rankin as well as from his on-the-job experience in the late 1920s and 1930s, Davis was destined to play a major role in getting the section off to a most successful start and then later to become a national leader in the hospital world. As industrious as he was intelligent and creative, Davis turned out to be an ideal backup man for Rankin.

The son of a country doctor in Beaufort in eastern North Carolina, Davis entered the University of North Carolina in 1916 but withdrew in 1917 to join the staff of the first chief of the Army Air Corps. After serving in France for two years, he returned to the United States and continued his college work at George Washington University. Then he studied law at New York University before securing a job in J. B. Duke's New York office in 1924 to help make a survey of hospitals in the Carolinas. With only Davis and a secretary, therefore, Rankin began the work of the Hospital and Orphan Section in the Charlotte office early in 1926.

As a result of his long and highly successful career as North Carolina's top health officer, Rankin had become a past master at the job of educating the public. In his new position he not only had to do that but also had to make sure that the trustees of the Endowment fully understood the nature of the problem and the proposed course of action. In one of his early public statements entitled "A Million Dollars a Year for Hospitals," he proceeded to describe the medical problems of an average rural county in the Carolinas (which would also apply to much of the rest of the South) and to suggest how large a field of service lay open to the Hospital Section. Such a county would be 500 square miles in area, Rankin noted, with a population of 30,000. For each 1,000 people, 25, or a total of 750, were constantly sick to the point of being bedridden and of those, 75 were so sick as to need hospital care. During the year 720 women became pregnant (he wrote "confined"); the federal Children's Bureau estimated that they received about one-fifth of the medical care needed and that one-third of the mothers had no medical attendant when their babies were born; of the 720 babies, 61 died during the first year of life and 39 during the second year—a total of 100 deaths within two years of birth.

In this same average rural county, Rankin continued, there were constantly present 150 infectious cases of tuberculosis, with 30 deaths annually. There were 27 deaths during the year from cancer, and some 50 to 60 cases of cancer constantly present. Each year 400 to 500 children had the ordinary contagious diseases of childhood with 30 to 40 deaths. In the public schools there were 1,000 children with defective vision and between 200 to 400 who needed operations for adenoids and diseased tonsils. A large number of adults were impaired to the extent of from 20 to 40 percent of their efficiency because of such chronic and prevalent conditions as gall stones, kidney stones, hemorrhoids, hernias, and unrepaired injuries resulting from childbirth. There were many accidents and emergencies, such as acute forms of appendicitis, which required prompt surgical treatment.

In about one-third of the average rural counties, Rankin stated, there were no hospitals at all. In the remaining two-thirds, there were from one to one and a half hospitals beds for each 1,000 people, whereas modern medical authorities believed that five hospital beds were needed for each 1,000. Many of the hospitals in the rural counties were proprietary (privately owned), and therefore "closed" to most physicians. Also, while an occupancy of 75 percent of hospital beds was regarded as normal, only a bit more than 50 percent of the hospital beds in the rural counties were constantly used.

The modern hospital, Rankin went on to explain, had come to play an essential part not only in the practice of medicine but also in the distribution of medical personnel. Well-trained medical doctors could not satisfy their professional ideals if they were denied the use of modern equipment for the diagnosis and treatment of disease. Such equipment as the diagnostic laboratory, the x-ray, the electrocardiograph, an apparatus for the study of nutrition, a modern operating room, radium, various appliances for physiotherapy — all these were too costly and complicated for individual purchase and use. Such equipment, which was absolutely essential to the practice of modern medicine, was not and could not be made available to most physicians outside of a hospital. Thus it was that the American Medical Association and other important groups believed that the proper distribution of hospitals would go far in effecting a better distribution of doctors.

What remedial steps did the Duke Endowment propose to take? Rankin explained that J. B. Duke, "exercising the same careful and discriminating judgment in investing in humanitarian service that he had used in his business enterprises," had seen this great need of rural people and provided a sum for hospital purposes that would, at least initially, produce an estimated $1 million annually. Through the great medical school that was projected at Duke University and the income from the trust fund for hospitals, Rankin foresaw four distinct types of medical service that would be rendered to Carolinians. First, the Endowment would provide financial assistance in the form of $1.00 for each day a bed in a nonprofit hospital was occupied by a patient who was unable to pay. Rankin emphasized that this assistance would only go to community-supported hospitals, for if "a people can find no interest and take no part in dealing with a problem so large and urgent" as that previously described, then the Endowment could take no part. "The stimulating effect of this provision on the community conscience and capacity is self-evident," he added. About one-third of hospital patients in the nation were charity patients, with a slightly larger fraction in the Carolinas, but to the extent that there might be surplus funds beyond what was needed for the $1.00 per day maintenance fund (and there soon would be such a surplus), the Endowment would help in the construction and equipment of community hospitals.

Second, through the Hospital Section's record keeping, it would be able to provide valuable assistance to hospitals concerning their costs and professional services. Given the information that would enable a hospital to locate its problems, either in economy of operation or efficiency of professional services, the next step of finding a remedy would be made easier.

Third, the Endowment would assist communities in organizing their large but often latent and unorganized interests in the care of the sick. Since Endowment assistance would cover a third or more of the cost of charity patients, the remaining two-thirds would either have to be collected from private (pay) patients or contributed by the community's voluntary or governmental agencies.

Fourth, and finally, the Endowment, through the close association of its trustees with "a great central hospital and medical school" at Duke, on the one hand, and with many smaller community hospitals on the other, would encourage in every way open to them the development of cooperative and mutually advantageous relations.[5]

Privately, and primarily for the benefit of the Endowment's trustees, Rankin explained some of his ideas more fully and pointed to certain options the trustees had and decisions they would have to make. Thoughtfully conservative in the best sense of the term, Rankin thought it desirable in the preliminary stages of such a large and far-reaching development that there should be no hard and fast conclusion prematurely reached. Rather, the principles for the guidance of the trustees "should be a growth emerging from an accumulating experience in a new and heretofore untilled field of vast humanitarian service." The only fixed principles in the preliminary stage, he argued, were those from the indenture itself: (1) that the trustees might apportion $1.00 per free-bed day to not-for-profit hospitals in the Carolinas; (2) that they could use their discretion in determining whether all or a part of the not-for-profit hospitals which did charity work were entitled to assistance; (3) that if there were a surplus of hospital funds beyond what was needed to assist in the charity work, that surplus might be used in the construction and equipment of community hospitals in the Carolinas; and (4) that, under certain conditions, the trustees had discretionary power to apportion funds for hospital uses in other states, preferably those contiguous to the Carolinas.

As a second consideration, Rankin believed it important for the trustees, in exercising their discretionary powers in assisting hospitals, to "distinguish carefully and sharply between *stimulating* local interests and self help and *substituting* [for] local interests and self help." For example, if a grant to an orphanage or a hospital should be followed by a cut in funds previously provided by a church or a county, then "instead of developing the muscle, we are splinting the arm and providing for the wasting away of the natural agency." If, however, the trustees used Endowment funds to stimulate additional funds and help, they would be, and here Rankin resorted to the biblical language and parables that he often used, like "the trusted servants that multiplied their master's talents, the two into four and the five into ten, and not as the one who preserved the one talent which he did not put to such use as to make it two." Rankin added that he had already received ample indication from local leaders involved with both hospitals and orphanages that they thought it vital that Endowment money be used for leverage rather than substitution.

Rankin's third, and quite important, consideration for the trustees was that it seemed both desirable and necessary that there should be at least one condition that an institution, whether hospitals or orphanages, should comply with to become a beneficiary: the institution should file a report (it would soon be called the "Application for Assistance"), on forms furnished by the Endowment, which would indicate (1) the character of the business management of the institution, and (2) the character of its professional work. Only through the information contained in such reports, Rankin cautioned, could the trustees avoid substituting instead of stimulating local interests and responsibilities. (Rankin did not say, perhaps because at this early stage he could not fully realize, that it was through the data gathered from these "Applications for Assistance" that the Endowment would perform a significant national as well as Carolina-based service. While the assisted Carolina hospitals were the first to benefit from the rich comparative data that the Hospital Section soon began to assemble, it quickly became apparent that the assisted hospitals were the largest group in the nation employing uniform record keeping, which the Endowment required and which allowed the data to be truly comparative. The result was a treasure trove of information that was highly useful, not just in the Carolinas but for hospitals across the nation and for the medical profession at large. As will be explained, the achievement of the uniform record keeping required long, arduous effort by both the staff of the Hospital and Orphan Section and the record keepers of the beneficiary institutions.)

As a fourth consideration, Rankin noted that the trustees had to decide whether the appointment of maintenance support (the $1.00 per free-bed day) was to be a general distribution to all qualifying hospitals or a special distribution only to those hospitals that offered conditions for stimulating rather than substituting local interests and for improvements, both quantitatively and qualitatively, in service. In the beginning the trustees might make a general distribution and then subsequently "vary their apportionment per free-bed day in accordance with the provisions, equipment, and character of service being rendered by the hospital." Under the latter pattern, there could come into existence a loose classification of hospitals for the use of the trustees and perhaps not for publication. Such a classification, say into A, B, C, and D categories, "would have a far-reaching effect in stimulating hospitals to make continuous improvements in their services." Such a plan would also be strongly supported by such national organizations as the American Medical Association, the American Hospital Association, and the American College of Surgeons. (Rankin did not say, but the trustees surely realized, that there would be serious political or public relations problems with any such classification system.)

Rankin thought an advantage of a general distribution, however, would be the rapidity with which the work of the Hospital Section could start. Moreover, it would harmonize with "the good reasoning of starting with conditions as they are and gradually lifting them." There were, however, two disadvantages: (1) the danger of substituting instead of stimulating local interest and self-help, and (2) it would probably postpone that time when there would be a surplus of funds which could be used for assistance in the construction of community hospitals. And he happened to know already of some "outstanding opportunities" where a small grant of 25 percent of the hospital cost would be sufficient encouragement to counties to gain approval of bonds for hospital construction. Yet the special distribution would afford the trustees greater freedom of action, would be more stimulative of local interest, and would provide, almost from the beginning, funds for construction purposes.

Finally, Rankin explained that he would send to all hospitals in the Carolinas not operated for private gain the forms approved by the trustees. Those hospitals wishing to apply for assistance would use those forms and be asked to return them by February 1, 1926. During the following two months or so, the staff, that is Rankin and Davis, would carefully study and check them and compile data so that the trustees, perhaps at their April meeting, could decide which of the two courses of distribution they chose to follow. (The trustees would shortly elect to make a general distribution to all eligible hospitals.)[6]

While the trustees made the final decision, Rankin and Davis did the actual toiling; and since Rankin had to spend a great deal of his time visiting hospitals and orphanages and making speeches to various groups scattered over the

Carolinas, Graham Davis ended up with a mountainous task especially in the spring of the year.

In a personal letter to a friend and coworker in the Endowment's New York office, Davis gave a glimpse into the difficult task he faced in the early years of the section's operation. Life had been greatly complicated, he noted, by the introduction of a new accounting system to be used in 1927. "I feel like a professor of accounting," he declared "and, strange to say, I do not believe that any of these professional accountants know yet that I am not an accountant, or even a bookkeeper." He estimated that about 60 percent of the beds in assisted hospitals were already operating under the new system, and the remaining task would be to get the others switched over.

Since Rankin had also wanted something done about the orphanages, Davis explained that he called together representatives appointed by the orphanages' conference to secure their ideas and gain their cooperation about a record system. There were seven child-care institutions in the Charlotte area and they, he added, "hang on my neck for help all the time." He did "not mind the Junior League Baby Home so much because they send in very attractive young ladies." But he had had to spend three hours out at an orphanage in the Charlotte area helping them finish their application. "It is surprising how few records some of these institutions keep," Davis declared. This particular one had no records except a few cards and a much-used copy book, with pages falling out and jumbled up, that contained the minutes of trustee meetings. The orphanage had real difficulty in determining how many children it had cared for last year, and it was "largely a matter of guesswork as to dates when children were taken in and discharged." In many instances there were no records of the children's ages.

Davis went on to say that he had spent an entire afternoon with "a broken down preacher from South Carolina who runs an orphanage trying to get his financial statement to balance." Davis had finally told the superintendent to leave the books and after two hours of work "last night" he had found the errors and gotten the books to balance.

Since something like that happened almost every day, finding time to correct the applications from the hundred or so institutions was not easy. "I send every one [of the applications] back for an average of about twenty-five corrections after I go over it with a fine tooth comb," he explained. Davis thought the spirit of cooperation shown by the institutions as a whole, however, was "very fine and they are expecting great things from us in the way of increased efficiency, both financial and professional." The institutions were beginning to realize, he believed, that the money they received from the Endowment was probably not as valuable to them as the free service they got from the staff, and he wondered if the trustees were grasping the full significance of that aspect as rapidly as the hospitals and orphanages were.

Since Rankin was away more than half the time but kept the one secretary occupied even while away, Davis complained that he really had little or no help, and the files were in "miserable shape." He and Rankin simply had to talk with Alexander Sands about getting another person in the office.[7]

The plea of Rankin and Davis for additional help did not go unheeded, for in 1928 the Hospital and Orphan Section added two men to the staff who were to spend their entire careers with the Endowment. Marshall Pickens and George P. Harris were both recent graduates of Duke University. After receiving an A.B. and M.A. (in economics) from Duke, Pickens, the son of a Methodist preacher in the Western North Carolina Conference, had for two years headed the school operated by the Methodist Orphanage in Raleigh — and the superintendent there noted proudly that Pickens had fielded one of the best high school football teams in the state. Harris, after graduating, worked for two years as a bookkeeper and teller at a bank in Albemarle in central North Carolina. Not only did these two additions considerably lessen the load on Rankin and Davis, but both Pickens and Harris were also destined to play important roles in the Endowment's life. Initially, Harris took over a large amount of the necessary travel to widely scattered hospitals, and while Pickens also worked with hospitals, he assumed a primary responsibility for the orphanages.

Davis, Pickens, Harris — and several others like them who would come later — all became experts in many aspects of the construction, equipment, and operation of hospitals. All three learned a great deal from Rankin, of course, but their hands-on, day-to-day experience gradually gave them an expertise and fund of knowledge that not only made them extremely helpful to the assisted institutions but also highly respected leaders, first on the regional and then the national scene of the hospital world.

Graham Davis especially proved to be indefatigable, both in his work in the section and in his reading and thinking about many of the larger medical and social problems involved. As an example of his deep involvement with the detailed, technical aspect of his work, one might note his grappling over a period of several years with the problem of nomenclature. In 1927 he began corresponding with T. R. Ponton, noted author of a recently published book, *Nomenclature of Diseases and Operations,* and congratulated him on the fine service he had performed for the hospitals for the county. Davis went on to explain that in 1926 fifty-two general hospitals in the Carolinas had applied to the Endowment for assistance, and they ranged in size from 10 to 300 beds, with an average of about 67. The question that concerned Rankin and him, Davis continued, was whether they would be justified in imposing such an elaborate classification as Ponton had employed upon these particular hospitals in the Carolinas. "The necessity for some sort of check on the character of the professional work in these hospitals is obvious," Davis admitted, "but the difficulty is in getting this information so that one hospital can be compared with another or with hospitals in general." For example, since authorities in the field did not agree on the matter, Davis would like Ponton's definition, if he had formulated one, on postoperative death.[8]

Several years later Davis was still struggling with the problem, for he wrote an official in the American College of Surgeons that he was trying to simplify Ponton's *Nomenclature* so that the Hospital Section could get more reliable data on surgery from the smaller hospitals and at the same time give enough explanation with the terms to describe operations so that the average person who kept clinical records in a hospital would understand what it was all about. Was there help available from the library of the College of Surgeons?[9]

Rankin and Davis were attempting to achieve a larger purpose in dealing with what seemed to be an arcane matter of nomenclature: they were attempting to raise medical standards in the Carolinas. One way of doing this was to go to leading national authorities and organizations for advice and help, and then quietly, without a lot of counterproductive fanfare about "raising standards" and helping to lead the Carolinas out of regional backwaters, to introduce new ideas and approaches. For example, Davis, having done extensive study on the matter for several years, went public, so to speak, in 1933 with a paper on "Operative Nomenclature Problems" for the Tri-State (the Carolinas and Virginia) Hospital Association. He began by explaining that the indenture establishing the Duke Endowment permitted the trustees to assist hospitals that were "properly operated." While hospital operations could be conveniently divided into two separate but closely related functions — business administration and patient services — the latter was clearly more important, for it was the primary reason for a hospital's existence.

About three of every five patients who went to the hospital, Davis explained, had surgical operations of some kind, and, according to existing classification, approximately one of every four patients had major surgery. Of 25,000 major operations in assisted hospitals in 1932, Davis reported, approximately 20,000 were in the abdominal region. Surgery, therefore, played an important role in the activities of a general hospital, and the quality of the surgery was perhaps the most important test of the "proper operation" of a general hospital. For that reason, the trustees of the Endowment, differing from some other organizations that aided hospitals, had always insisted that they should know something about a hospital's surgery.

With no precedent as a guide, Davis continued, the Hospital Section began in the late 1920s to gather data on surgery that would reveal something of its quality. It was a difficult task, for surgery was advancing rapidly, and terminology was in flux. For an example, Davis noted that an operation for appendicitis had been reported with a half dozen or more different names. Aside from the lack of uniformity in nomenclature, some hospitals counted the number of operations (often multiple operations on the same patient) rather than the number of patients operated on, which invalidated the fatality rate. To avoid the difficulty, the Endowment asked the hospital to report only the main operation intended to relieve the primary cause of the trouble. For example, if a person suffered acute appendicitis and had to undergo surgery for the condition, that would be reported and other procedures performed at the same time would not be reported to the Hospital Section.

Davis candidly explained that his effort to find an authoritative source for nomenclature had had only mixed results. Partially adapting a model used by the Presbyterian Hospital in New York, he had divided the body into four operative regions: gastrointestinal; genitourinary; eye, ear, nose, and throat; and orthopedic and general — "for lack for a better terminology." The most difficult problem, however, was making a distinction between major and minor surgery. Defining major surgery as that involving not just a risk of fatality but a considerable risk, Davis argued that he would eliminate (from consideration as major surgery) all operations that had an ordinary death rate of less than 1 percent. He thought the tendency to introduce the factor of technical skill into the definition of a major operation was a mistake, for while a plastic surgeon, for example, had to have great skill to make skin grafts, there was not the same risk of life as in a craniotomy. After discussing various other technical problems, he concluded: "We [in the Hospital Section] realize of course that the fatality rate is not the only test of the quality of surgery in a particular institution, but it is one of the more important tests."[10]

Concerning the matter of hospital standards, Rankin in 1931 sent to a fellow trustee of the Endowment, W. B. Bell, who had inquired about the matter, the official statement of the American College of Surgeons. Rankin did not stop at that, however, for he proceeded to explain that standardization depended on three things: (1) accurate and complete clinical records for each patient; (2) the responsibility of a hospital's medical staff for and that staff's supervision over the professional work of each of its members; and (3) an inspection by an outside agency of the clinical records and work of the staff, as shown in properly kept minutes. Using language that Bell could quickly appreciate, Rankin suggested that complete and accurate clinical records served as a basis for a review of the work of doctors in exactly the same way as financial records served as a basis for an audit of the business management of a hospital.

Rankin hoped that the time was fast approaching when the Endowment would impose some professional standards upon the assisted hospitals. He explained that he had held several conferences with national authorities on the subject and hoped that perhaps in the next year he might have some recommendations to make to the trustees. (The worsening economic depression and its devastating impact on health and hospitals would, however, frustrate that hope.) He noted that in 1931 the American College of Surgeons had surveyed 122 general hospitals in North Carolina and approved only 50 percent. Of the nonprofit hospitals, it had approved 56.8 percent and of the nonprofit hospitals to which the Endowment contributed, the College of Surgeons had approved hospitals that contained 76 percent of the beds.[11]

While Rankin's efforts to raise standards and improve hospital efficiency through collecting a rich variety of data obviously required more thought and effort than a casual observer might imagine, J. B. Duke, again inspired by Rankin, had envisioned aid for the construction and equipment of community hospitals if and when funds should become available. Within a relatively short span of three years from the Endowment's establishment, it began to be clear that there was indeed enough money to proceed with that second aspect of the Hospital Section's mission. While the Endowment would help many communities convert preexisting proprietary hospitals into not-for-profit institutions, Rankin also foresaw the need for newly constructed hospital plants. Accordingly, he secured an appropriation for $7,000 from the trustees in 1926 to procure plans for various model hospital units, plans that might help communities if they chose to build new plants. Turning to an architectural firm in Cincinnati, Ohio, that specialized in such design problems, Rankin obtained layouts of drawings of the various departments and subdivisions that would normally be found in hospitals that contained twenty, thirty, and forty beds. Those drawings, together with various recommendations concerning site choice, parking area, and many other such matters were put together in a small booklet published by the Endowment and entitled *The Small General Hospital*. Subsequently revised and republished several times, it found a wide audience outside of the Carolinas as well as within them, for since many parts of the world especially in underdeveloped regions, faced hospital problems comparable to those of the Carolinas, requests for *The Small General Hospital* were still coming in from Brazil, India, and elsewhere as late as 1959. At the time of its first publication, one review hailed it as "the best presentation of the subject that has been made to the hospital field."[12]

Equipped, therefore, with some possible design plans if needed, the Endowment made its first appropriation for the construction or acquisition of thirteen community hospitals in March 1928. The procedure in this matter, as in almost all other cases of the payment of funds, was for the appropriate committee of the trustees to make a recommendation, which the full board of trustees normally accepted. Since the committee on hospital and orphanages then consisted of Rankin, the chairman, and Burkholder, Cocke, Lee, and Marshall (all Charlotte residents), Rankin generally succeeded in gaining trustee approval of whatever he recommended to his committee.

One early example of Endowment aid in the building of a new hospital, and one where the Endowment contributed a larger share of the total cost than it usually did, was the Berkeley County Hospital in Monck's Corner in South Carolina's low country. One of the state's largest and poorest counties, Berkeley had a population in 1930 of 23,546 that included over 17,000 African Americans, most of whom were tenant farmers and their families. The county had no hospital facilities of any sort, the nearest adequate hospital being thirty-five miles away in Charleston. In short, if the hospital should be constructed, it would be, as the Endowment's committee on hospital put the case, "in the state with the most inadequate hospital facilities of any state in the Union and in that particular section of the state where hospital facilities are most limited."

The proposed plan was for the county to come up with $35,000 and for that amount to be matched by the Endowment. The county had reached its goal through approval of a bond issue for $10,000; $7,000 through private subscription; and $18,000 from a New York businessman, Hugh S. Robertson, who also had a home in Berkeley county and who wished to help in the improvement of living conditions there and especially in providing more adequate medical services.

The county, obviously with Rankin's encouragement, wished to include in the hospital provisions for a certain number of cases of tuberculosis, there being in the area quite inadequate provisions for the treatment of that disease and especially among African Americans. Rankin's committee also pointed out that the American Hospital Association and other such national organizations recommended that provisions for the care of tuberculosis be included in general hospitals, partly because tuberculosis had been too much separated from the general problems of medicine and there were many complications with the disease where the presence of a staff interested in general medicine would be helpful in effecting a cure. The Endowment's trustees promptly approved the committee's recommendation of a $35,000 grant.[13]

Looking back on the Endowment's early program of helping communities either build or purchase small privately owned hospitals, Graham Davis in 1940 took a long-range view of the matter. He admitted that small-town hospitals suffered more by comparisons with metropolitan hospitals than did either small-town schools or churches. This was because the modern hospital had become such a relatively expensive institution to construct and operate. As for the quality of professional service, with the quality of the medical staff being of greater importance than the quality of the plant, he conceded that the shortcomings of the small hospitals were reflected in these comparisons: the American College of Surgeons approved 93 percent of the hospitals it surveyed with 100 or more beds and only 35 percent of the hospitals with from 25 to 49 beds, practically all of which were located in small towns and rural communities. (The College did not even survey hospitals with fewer than 25 beds, though there were 3,000 or more of such in the United States and Canada.)

Davis also noted that there was disagreement about the solution of the problem, for one well-defined school of thought opposed the building of more hospitals in small towns and rural areas. The argument was that because of the economic factors involved, sick people in those areas should simply go to urban areas for treatment. The Duke Endowment, Davis continued, obviously disagreed, and he mentioned three other foundations that joined the Endowment in promoting community hospitals even in rural areas: the Commonwealth Fund in New York had, beginning in the late 1920s, helped build a dozen or more demonstration rural hospitals scattered across the nation (though it did not require as much community involvement in financing as did the Endowment); the Bingham Associates of Boston focused on rural Maine; and the W. K. Kellogg Foundation was building rural hospitals in Michigan. Davis suggested that the attitude of these four foundations was best represented by the statement of the Endowment's Hospital Section in the Endowment's tenth annual report: the central object was not hospitals in themselves but "hospitals as an important element and influence in improving the medical care of the people." The approach was the hospital, but "the object was good medical service." The strategic importance of the hospital in providing medical service, especially in small towns and rural communities, was not in the number of beds or the number of patients but "in its influence upon the number and type of physicians that serve the community, the ten percent of the seriously ill who require hospital care and the ninety percent of the less seriously ill who are cared for in their own homes and in physicians' offices." In short, the Duke Endowment and the three other foundations operated on the theory that "the rural population is entitled to just as good medical care . . . as people in large cities."

Turning to the work of the Duke Endowment, Davis noted that the first hospital constructed with its aid was the Haywood County Hospital in Waynesvile, North Carolina, a town of 2,800 people in a comparatively poor and sparsely settled mountain county. Opening early in 1928, it had averaged 15.5 patients per day that first year and 49.2 patients per day during 1939. In 1928 it discharged 626 patients, plus 14 newborn infants; in 1939 it discharged 1,785, almost three times as many, plus 258 infants.

Davis explained that as of 1940, of the fifteen new hospitals that the Endowment had helped to build in towns of fewer than 10,000 people, all but two replaced inadequate structures, frequently old residences of frame construction. The two exceptions were the Berkeley County Hospital mentioned earlier and a hospital in Southport in Brunswick County on the southern coast of North Carolina. Both counties were among the poorest in the nation and with large African American, tenant-farmer populations.

Davis explained that because the Endowment's assisted hospitals had been on a uniform accounting and statistical basis for fifteen years, it was easy to tell what had happened to them with reference to business management and operating efficiency. To demonstrate more or less intangible improvements in service to patients, however, was not so easy. Yet Davis suggested that there was one measure: none of the thirteen hospitals that had been replaced with new plants were approved by the American College of Surgeons during the time they operated in the old plants. Now, however, thirteen of the fifteen new hospitals were on the approved list; one was too small to gain approval, and the other had a peculiar local situation — all of the doctors in town were on the hospital's board of trustees, the only instance in the group where there was such an arrangement, which was frowned upon by the College of Surgeons, the American Hospital Association, and other accrediting agencies.

Davis argued that the modern hospital plants had clearly played an important role in the hospitals' gaining the approval of the American College of Surgeons. He insisted, however, that wise planning in the hospitals with reference to the medical staff had been of even greater importance. He recalled that when he had assisted Alexander Sands in surveying hospital conditions in the Carolinas in 1924, he had discovered that, except for ten or twelve of the largest nonprofit hospitals in the larger cities, the balance of the hospitals approved by the College of Surgeons, practically all of which were in small towns, were proprietary institutions owned either by a surgeon or a group of physicians that included a surgeon. Of the 140 general hospitals then in the Carolinas, 93 were proprietary but, nevertheless, had been most cooperative in applying data for the survey. It had become quickly apparent, Davis explained, that the proprietary hospitals as a group, in places of fewer than 10,000 people, were in better shape financially and rendering better service than the nonprofit hospitals.

The difference between the two types of institutions, Davis argued, was in the surgery. In the proprietary hospitals surgery was limited, as a rule, to one or two doctors, who were frequently fellows of the College of Surgeons. In the nonprofit community hospitals, as a rule, there were no restrictions concerning surgery, and it was frequently done by a half dozen general practitioners with little or no special training in surgery. "The consequence was," Davis continued, "that the patients in these small nonprofit hospitals were either the sick poor, who had no choice . . . or people with a blind faith in the ability of their family physician as a surgeon." Most of the people with money to pay hospital bills and surgeons' fees went elsewhere for serious operations.

In the thirteen Carolina communities where inadequate hospitals were replaced by modern ones, Davis noted, the leaders carefully considered the problem of the surgical standard and worked it out in various ways. (Davis did not say, but could have, that Rankin and others on the staff of the Hospital Section quietly but effectively advised and helped in the working out of the problem.) In some instances the doctors agreed among themselves that major surgery should be limited to one or two well-qualified persons. In one instance, the experiment was tried of limiting surgery to fellows of the College of Surgeons in a well-established clinic some nineteen miles away. When that arrangement did not work so well, however, the trustees named a well-trained surgeon as medical director of the hospital and limited all major surgery to him. In three of these communities, where there were no trained surgeons, boards of trustees brought in young, well-qualified surgeons on a guaranteed-income basis.

Davis insisted that the results of attention to surgical standards spoke for themselves concerning the fifteen hospitals. From the marked reduction in the ratio (not the numbers) of free or charity patients and the increase in collections from patients, as well as a 130 percent gain in the number of patients, it was clear that pay (private) patients, who were going elsewhere before the new hospitals were built, began staying home and paying fees to local physicians. The reason clearly was the improvement in surgical standards, because the great bulk of patients in small hospitals were classified in general surgery or in one of the surgical specialties. When some hospitals had problems, Davis concluded, they were frequently rooted in low standards for surgery but, as the Endowment's experience clearly demonstrated, those problems could be remedied.[14]

Davis's earlier reference to the relatively large number of proprietary or private hospitals in the Carolinas during the 1920s, some of which hospitals were of high quality, touched on an important and tricky problem for the Endowment. J. B. Duke had, of course, restricted his medical benefaction to the not-for-profit hospitals. Rankin, Davis, and others on the staff of the Hospital Section were quite aware that proprietary hospitals had played an important, highly useful role in the past and that they continued to do so in much of the South even as they receded in importance in much of the rest of the country.

Although the general public was certainly not well informed or much concerned about the matter, the modern general hospital, as most of the twentieth century would know the institution, was an evolutionary creation of the period between about 1870 and 1920. Prior to around 1870, those few so-called hospitals that existed in the United States, mainly in metropolitan centers, were actually more like almshouses for the poor than medical centers. As one educated New Yorker observed in the mid-nineteenth century, the "people who repair to hospitals are mostly very poor, and seldom go into them until driven to do so from a severe stress of circumstance."[15]

The germ theory of disease gradually triumphed in the last half of the nineteenth century, however; the growing effectiveness of aseptic surgery, the advantages of the x-ray and clinical laboratory, the convenience of around-the-clock nursing, and attendance by the house staff — all these developments were making a hospital operating room the most logical, convenient place to perform surgery. "To many surgeons, in fact," as one historian has stated, "[the hospital operating room] was beginning to seem the only ethical place to practice an increasingly demanding art."[16] Accordingly, by the time of World

War I, middle-class Americans in many parts of the county and especially in urban areas had begun to consider hospital care a plausible option in cases of serious illness or medical problems.

Just as widespread, deep poverty caused the South to lag behind the rest of the nation in building genuine, effective public school systems, so too was the South behind in the development of modern general hospitals. In the larger southern cities, of course, such hospitals did get started, a few in the 1880s and more in the 1890s and after, but since so much of the South remained rural, most of the region continued to be woefully deficient in hospitals.

This is where the proprietary institutions entered the picture and why, for a time, they were so important. Rankin had, of course, closely observed the massive changes occurring in the area of health care throughout his adulthood and, as top health officer in North Carolina for fifteen years, appreciated the role that well-run proprietary hospitals had played. He likened them to the better private schools or academies that had flourished in the post–Civil War South, when there were no true public schools systems, and where those financially able to attend such institutions had received solid instruction along classical educational lines. As southern public schools began to grow stronger in the early twentieth century, however, most of those private academies began to disappear. Since Rankin deeply believed that health care should be the concern of the entire community, as public schools had become, he also felt that the proprietary hospital in the South needed to give way to another model. He was diplomatic enough, however, to be quite careful about what he said publicly on the matter.

Rankin's younger colleague and, in a very real sense, his student, Graham Davis, also was circumspect in his discussion of the private hospital. In a long, private letter in 1934 to a friend associated with a private hospital, Davis expatiated on why he thought North Carolina had such a high proportion of proprietary hospitals. He began by briefly mentioning certain points mentioned earlier, namely that there were few general hospitals in the nation before the 1890s and that earlier hospitals, mostly in the largest cities, had been patterned after Great Britain's charity (or voluntary) hospitals for the poor. "The idea of class distinction in hospital service did not set well with American traditions and ideas," Davis wrote, "and our general hospitals have developed largely as non-profit institutions . . . caring for rich and poor alike, everyone paying for service according to ability." (Rankin liked to say that any hospital exclusively for poor people was highly likely to be a poor hospital.)

Davis, who confessed to liking history and declared that he approached almost all problems by wanting first to know their history, pointed out that North Carolina had not been settled by Catholics or Episcopalians, both of which groups had a long tradition of supporting charitable institutions, first in Europe and then in America. "Shouting Methodists and hard-shelled Baptists and numerous other similar religious groups," he pointed out, "never had a well defined tradition of supporting hospitals that amounted to much more than lip service, probably because the Catholics and Episcopalians did have such a tradition." The Tar Heel state's itinerant Methodist preachers were, he charged, "more concerned with saving souls than with keeping body and soul together." Moreover, North Carolina was still and had been an overwhelmingly rural agricultural state, one with few cities of any consequence and few rich people to help build hospitals. The religious leaders, Davis alleged, had helped secure fine church buildings but tended to forget about Jesus' parable of the Good Samaritan who helped the battered victim of thieves after the pious folk had ignored him.

As for certain of North Carolina's proprietary hospitals established around the turn of the century, Davis expressed great respect for them and the high character and ability of their founders. Yet not all of the subsequently developed private hospitals he pointed out, came up to the standards set by the pioneering group, nor had many of the nonprofit hospitals for that matter. Davis noted that a friend of his in the national office of the American Medical Association, an expert in hospital matters, had told him that of the 576 hospitals which the American Medical Association had recently refused to register, most were privately owned, and that most of the hospitals that had collapsed during the depression were also in that category. That had not happened as much in North Carolina, Davis explained, because the Endowment had often come to the rescue and assisted communities to take over the hitherto private hospitals.

"The ethically operated private hospital has many good points about it," Davis conceded, "but it also has many limitations, the largest of which perhaps is the difficulty it has in getting adequate support from [county] tax funds or from charitable contributions to care for the 50 percent of the population in the South that cannot pay, under ordinary circumstances, for hospital care." In a survey the Endowment had made earlier in 1934, it had found that the average private hospital reported only about 11 percent charity work. Yet he believed that the Endowment and a heightened public consciousness had helped the situation concerning medical care for the indigent in North Carolina: in 1924 the state's general hospitals had averaged about 364 free patients per day, but in 1934 that figure had risen to about 1,345 — a gain of approximately 400 percent. Nevertheless, Davis guessed that there were as many patients who needed hospital care but were not getting it as there were those who got it.

Davis insisted that he and others associated with the Endowment would be the last persons in the world to do anything that might impair the remaining investment in the state's private hospitals, and, despite what certain critics charged, it had never been the policy of the Endowment to harm the private hospitals. On the other hand, there were prominent authorities in the hospital field who argued that within two or three decades every hospital in North Carolina (and elsewhere in the nation?) would be owned and operated by the state, "just like the public schools are operated now." After all, a majority of the hospital beds in the nation were already owned and operated by governmental units. The hospital authorities even argued that hospital service was "of far greater importance to the welfare and happiness of the people than education," that the public would eventually realize that fact, and that the existing system had simply failed to provide an adequate hospital service.

Davis, being almost as conservative in these matters as was his mentor, Rankin, confessed that he would hate to see a state-operated hospital system for many reasons. "In the first place," he insisted, "political control has a deadening effect on practically everything it touches, except petty politics and petty graft." Despite what he considered the stabilizing influence in North Carolina of the carefully nonpolitical Endowment, Davis asserted that there seemed always a political upheaval of some sort going on in the hospitals owned by counties or cities. "They frequently tend to become," he argued, "nothing more than glorified boarding houses for the sick poor." Moreover, the next step after a state-owned system of hospitals would "naturally be all physicians employed by the state on a salary basis." While Davis admitted that he did not at all like the idea, he suspected that when President Franklin D. Roosevelt's "brain trust" discovered that North Carolina had about half as many general hospital beds as the state needed, the New Deal administration would be quick to start trying to do something about the situation. Davis's advice to any owner of a private hospital would be to "get out from under as quickly and as easily as possible."[17]

Despite the efforts of Rankin, Davis, and their associates to proceed with the utmost circumspection concerning the private hospitals, the Endowment came under angry attack from a group of doctors associated with such institutions. While the group was not all that large, its spokesmen pulled no punches in criticizing the Duke Endowment and various of its policies and actions. James W. Davis (no relation to Graham Davis), a doctor in Statesville in North Carolina's western Piedmont and owner of a hospital there, emerged as the most prominent of the Endowment's foes. He may well have been hostile to the policies and purposes of the Endowment's Hospital Section regardless, but when it assisted in transforming another private hospital in Statesville into a community hospital, that, according to Graham Davis, especially aroused the owner of the Davis Hospital. At any rate, James Davis was no hypocrite or hidden foe, for he asserted in a conference with Graham Davis that he believed that "sooner or later it was coming to a showdown as to whether the medical profession or the Duke Endowment was going to control medical service in North Carolina." Subsequently, James Davis wrote Graham Davis charging, among other things, that the Endowment was furnishing "unfair and unjust competition for private institutions and very little has been said about it."[18]

Among the issues that aroused the ire of James Davis and some of his allies among the owners of private hospitals was an effort to raise the standards of nursing education in North Carolina. The primary movers behind this effort were the professional organizations of registered nurses and the North Carolina Board of Nurse Examiners, not the Endowment. Using the Hospital Section's abundant statistical data on hospitals in the Carolinas, however, Graham Davis in 1930 had come up with conclusions that had profoundly disturbing implications for the owners of certain small hospitals that also ran training schools for nurses. He studied twenty-four comparable, Endowment-assisted general hospitals (none of which were named in the study) that averaged fewer than twenty patients per day, twelve of the hospitals operating schools of nursing and twelve without them. Among other things, Davis found that the nursing schools in such small hospitals were uneconomical and generally failed to meet accepted standards. Moreover, he found that the hospitals without the nursing schools had a larger percentage of free (charity) patients; furthermore he suggested that the trustees of the twelve hospitals that operated the schools had a duty to the people who paid the operating deficits, from tax funds or otherwise, to make clear that a considerable part of the deficit was caused by the operation of the nursing schools. Davis also predicted that in a few years the North Carolina Board of Nurse Examiners would not permit the graduates of those schools to take the examination for registration, and already the graduates were not eligible for membership in national nursing organizations.[19]

The fact that an article in the *American Journal of Nursing* picked up on

Davis's study and reported its findings across the nation merely added insult to injury as far as some, probably not the majority, of the hospital-owning doctors in the Carolinas were concerned. The author of the article in the national journal concluded that "nurses who are interested in raising the standards of nursing education can help towards that end by becoming familiar with Mr. Davis' study" and then helping to spread the word to all nurses.[20]

All of this was, in one sense, just a phase in a battle across the nation about nursing education and standards, a battle that had begun much earlier and would go on for many years.[21] While some male doctors sympathized with the nursing reformers, many did not, wanting nurses primarily beside the patient's bed and at the doctor's side rather than in the classroom. James Davis obviously belonged in this latter category, for in 1937 he and a group of other, like-minded doctors organized, as a potential rival to the much larger North Carolina Hospital Association, the North Carolina Hospital and Training School Association. In a letter that went out to an unknown number of medical doctors in North Carolina, Davis and a colleague warned that the situation concerning training schools for nurses was bad. Some hospitals that should properly have had schools had been forced to close them, which might have been justified in a few instances, but many had been closed that should not have been. "There must be a different standard for the training schools," the letter argued. "More practical work and less theoretical work must be done." Moreover, the "training must be suited to the South and the ways and methods of Southern hospitals and Southern doctors. Adverse Northern influences have been brought to bear." One of the most glaring and unfair requirements for admission to the training school for nurses was, according to Davis and his associates, the requirement of certain subjects that were not even taught by all public high schools. Graduates of each and every high school in the state should be eligible for admission to any training school. The letter went on to complain about other things, such as the allegation that the annual dues of the North Carolina Hospital Association were too high and that the organization was too much dominated by laymen. What the letter did make explicit was that James Davis and a few others like him were totally unsympathetic with the idea of introducing national standards into various aspects of the health care field in North Carolina.[22]

If the reference to "adverse Northern influences" in the above letter was an indirect hit at the Duke Endowment, as it may have been, it was quite accurate in one respect: Rankin, Graham Davis, and others associated with the Hospital and Orphan Section, were all native-born Southerners, but then and for many years to come, they worked constantly and arduously to link the entire health-care field in the Carolinas with national organizations, national publications, and, above all, the latest and best of national thinking about health-care matters. They regularly attended the meetings of the American Hospital Association and certain other related national organizations and subscribed to a wide range of relevant national publications. The staff members of the Hospital and Orphan Section had an unstated but quite important objective: the doing of everything possible to help the Carolinas escape from historic provincialism and backwardness in those areas where the Endowment concerned itself. (Nor was it a coincidence, perhaps, that in the field of higher education, Duke University set itself on a similar course.)

The Endowment, through the Hospital Section, did everything it could, through grants and personal involvement of staff, to help strengthen the North and South Carolina Hospital Associations. Graham Davis, in fact, was such an ardent believer in what might be called the Hospital Gospel that in his free time, that is at night and on the weekend, he almost single-handedly launched a publication that helped to strengthen and galvanize the hospital associations not only in the Carolinas but ultimately throughout the South. Simultaneously he cultivated newspaper and radio contacts that helped reach an even larger audience with various messages about hospitals and health care.

The publication began as a mimeographed newsletter of the North Carolina Hospital Association (NCHA) in late 1933. Writing to a friend who had been elected president of the NCHA, Graham Davis enclosed an article he had written concerning the recent convention of the American Hospital Association. He explained that he had been pushing the NCHA for some time to publish a bulletin at least, as did the associations in New York, Pennsylvania, Ohio, and other states. "My only interest," Davis explained, "is to build up a strong Hospital Association that will take the leadership in establishing real hospital service in North Carolina." He suggested that the NCHA could send out the first half of the statement about the national meeting in October and then in November send the second half along with an article prepared by a certain hospital, which he named, that had managed to reduce its laundry bill by $1,200 per year. While Davis insisted that he wanted his name kept entirely out of the limelight (which was done), he offered to furnish all the supplies, cut the stencils, and run them off before sending the bulletin to the president for mailing.[23] Clearly Davis subscribed to the idea that there was no end to what one could accomplish if others got the credit.

The president of the NCHA accepted Davis's suggestion, publishing the full statement that the latter had prepared. Then in April 1934 Davis again wrote asking if it was not about time for another issue of "our famous bulletin." This time it could feature an article on National Hospital Day and, he suggested, a tribute to Florence Nightingale might be politic. "My impression is," Davis explained, "that the girls are not so hot for the North Carolina Hospital Association at present and it might make them feel better." The president could also take the opportunity to report on the high spots of the NCHA's meeting in Charlotte, the directors' meeting, the committee appointments, and other such matters. "If you let the folks know what is going on," Davis argued, "it removes a lot of suspicion that may arise as to what might be going on." After getting a go-ahead signal from the president, Davis sent him a draft of the next edition of the bulletin and added that he wanted to start sending it to all the trustees of the Endowment-assisted hospital, for they "need some educating, as I have found by experience." He noted that Rankin believed that the *Bulletin* of the North Carolina board of health had "done more to sell public health to the people of this State than any other one thing."[24]

Having been named the chairman of the NCHA's committee on community relations, Davis utilized that position as a base for expanding and strengthening not only the bulletin but also the whole public-relations program of the NCHA. Radio station WBT in Charlotte offered the association free time on the air to have talks about hospitals, and Davis figured that other radio stations in the Carolinas would probably do the same thing. Accordingly, he wrote the American Medical Association's director of health and public education requesting copies of their radio broadcasts. When permission to use them came through, provided the North Carolina Medical Society approved, Davis diplomatically seized the opportunity to forge a closer working tie with the organized doctors. When he asked the secretary-treasurer of the medical society if that organization would be willing to vet or censor the NCHA's radio talks, bulletin, and any other publicity that it might generate, the medical official quickly agreed that the three physicians on the medical society's own committee on public relations would indeed be willing to check over any publicity material of the NCHA. Well might Davis proceed so cautiously, for he alleged that doctors connected with private hospitals had long dominated the NCHA, but when they resisted efforts to standardize nursing education and even attempted to gain control of the standardization board, the nonprofit hospitals, having grown more numerous anyhow, asserted themselves and elected a layman who was a hospital superintendent, rather than a doctor, as president of the NCHA. Following a meeting in Raleigh with the executive committee of the medical society, Davis reported to the NCHA president that the doctors had been entirely cooperative. He had told them that, "We did not want to run the risk of saying something unintentionally that might offend the medical profession, and that we wanted to submit our publicity material to them for criticism before publishing it." Moreover, Davis argued, by submitting the NCHA material to the doctors, "we earn the right to ask to see their publicity material and if any doctor gets to criticizing hospitals . . . I shall take violent exception to what he has to say." But he really did not, he added, expect any difficulties.[25]

As for the bulletin, Davis negotiated with a firm in Charlotte that printed the accounting and statistical forms used by the Endowment. The firm, having found profitable the printing of a journal for the state's furniture industry, was willing to assume financial responsibility for printing an eight-page, letter-size bulletin if the firm could use about two-thirds of the back page to advertise itself and its printed forms. Subsequently, the plan was for additional advertisers (which Davis would scramble diligently to secure) ultimately to make the venture profitable. The printer was so enthusiastic, Davis reported, that, if Davis agreed to serve as editor and supply enough good material, he wanted to get out 3,000 copies and include doctors on the mailing list, but Davis suggested 2,000 copies to begin with, including the 800 or 900 doctors on the medical staffs of hospitals in the state. Since the printer wanted to put pictures of the NCHA's officers on the front page, Davis urged the president to send along his best picture by the next mail. "My idea is that the thing should be broader in scope than Hospital Management for example," Davis explained. "Our publication should interest the lay hospital trustee in hospital problems, because the South has about half as many hospitals beds as it needs to properly care for the people."[26]

When Wilburt C. Davison, dean of Duke University's medical school and close friend of Watson Rankin, encouraged Davis about the idea of a printed bulletin, Davis replied with a sketch of the project's history and noted that the national hospital publications, which were not widely subscribed to in the South anyhow, tended to concentrate on matters that concerned the larger, metropolitan hospitals and often in a technical fashion. Davis, who admitted to striving for a writing style in the bulletin that was inspired by *Time* magazine, hoped for a more general audience. He also mentioned a number of possible radio talks in the health-care area, including one by Davison on pediatrics, his specialty. Davis warned, however, that doctors "on the radio I am afraid will be inclined to talk in language that the average layman cannot understand."[27]

Although James Davis, who happened to be the vice president of the NCHA, vigorously objected to what Graham Davis was doing with and through the expanded bulletin, the overwhelming majority of the NCHA gave him a vote of confidence. Gratified by that, he reported to a coworker, "The Directors seemed to think that Dr. Davis represented the views of Dr. Davis only and perhaps two or three others."[28]

By this time Graham Davis began to implement a plan he had long been contemplating: transforming the monthly *Bulletin* of the NCHA first into *The Carolina Hospital* when the South Carolina Hospital Association joined in and then, finally, into *Southern Hospital,* so that many states could be included. To realize his plan, Davis, after easily securing the cooperation of the South Carolina Hospital Association, wrote the president of the Virginia Hospital Association and explained that an anonymous donor in Charlotte (who was probably someone connected with the printing firm) had given him $50 to pay for 100 subscriptions of the bulletin on the condition that the Virginia hospitals raised a similar amount. "To be perfectly frank about it," Davis wrote, "one reason we are anxious to include the Virginia hospitals in the Bulletin is to increase the circulation and make it easier to get advertising." The printer could not afford to continue printing the bulletin indefinitely at the loss he was then taking, and the hope was to increase the size of the magazine to about twenty pages, change its name, and make it a more attractive publication. Davis wanted the secretaries of the three hospital associations to be the official coeditors (and he would continue to be the offstage managing editor). Since the postage on the larger publication would be more than one cent, the yearly subscription rate of fifty cents, which would be included in the dues paid to hospital associations, would only pay the postage and cost of mailing.[29]

With Virginia roped in by early 1935 and because Davis foresaw the inclusion of additional southern states, he pushed for the bulletin to be renamed *Southern Hospital,* which was done in the issue of March 1935. Since the publication had earlier carried articles, with pictures, about the oldest hospitals in the two Carolinas, Davis set out to get a similar article about a Virginia hospital, for he planned to focus largely on Virginia in the March issue. With the advertisers finally beginning to come through, largely due to Davis's own efforts, he felt encouraged when there appeared to be sufficient advertisements in the March issue to pay for the cost of printing. Meantime he solicited articles from doctors, hospital superintendents, nursing officials, trustees of hospitals, and others, but always with the stipulation that the articles be written for a general audience and with some angle of human interest if possible. Another encouraging sign, Davis argued, was that additional hospitals were joining the NCHA—a dozen in the last half of 1934, with eight or ten more ready to join—and he doubted that there would have been "a single additional hospital without this Bulletin."[30] Speaking at a joint meeting of the Georgia and Florida Hospital Associations late in 1935, Davis soon had those states plus Alabama signed up for *Southern Hospital* and proudly reported that the December 1935 issue would go to over 600 hospitals in a half dozen states, to some 800 active staff physicians, and approximately 1,000 hospital trustees plus a miscellaneous group. He emphasized that it was a nonprofit venture sponsored by the hospital associations, that copy for the publication was provided by volunteers, and that no one received a salary or commission in connection with it. The associations, he summarized, simply hoped to use *Southern Hospital* "to build up a more cooperative spirit among hospitals to the end that we will eventually have an adequate hospital system that is best suited to the needs of the people and on a sound basis financially."[31]

By early 1936 Davis found that there was so much work in connection with the advertising and business aspect of *Southern Hospital* that he needed help. He found it in the form of an experienced newspaperwoman who undertook to solicit advertisements for the publication on a 15 percent commission basis. In 1936 Davis persuaded the president of the NCHA that he, Davis, had chaired the committee on community relations long enough and that from that point on his relationship with *Southern Hospital* should be in a purely advisory capacity. Letters of congratulations on and praise for the publication had come in from various national leaders in the hospital field, and Davis could take real satisfaction from the fact that by 1939, when he had managed to pass on much of the responsibility for the *Southern Hospital* to others, it had become the official publication for twelve southern states. Davis believed that the work of the hospital associations in the South had made great progress in the late 1930s, and he credited *Southern Hospital* with a significant part of that progress.

The executive director of the Florida Hospital Association wrote to Davis saying that he thought *Southern Hospital* was an "interesting cooperative enterprise," one that met "a real need of the several hospital associations." The Floridian graciously, and quite accurately, added that Davis had "acted as 'Southern Hospital's' godfather" and, in doing so had "made very heavy investments of time and energy in it at real personal sacrifice." Now would not Davis be interested in trying to use *Southern Hospital* to get a uniform policy on certain hospital problems in the twelve associations? Davis replied in a fashion that suggested that, while he was actually a glutton for work, he recognized limits. "My philosophy of life," he told the Floridian, "is to count at least twenty before I kick a sleeping dog, if he is a big dog and vicious I may decide not to kick him at all."[32]

Despite wariness of that particular "sleeping dog," Davis, like Rankin, managed to stay on the creative and often controversial battle front of many health-care problems of the day. One that deeply interested both men, and one with which they were grappling during the same years when *Southern Hospital* was born, had to do with the rising costs of health care and the problems which that development posed for the public as well as for hospitals and doctors. A prominent historian of hospitals points out that by the 1920s the capital-intensive institutions increasingly faced a dilemma: treating the growing number of poor and lower-middle-class patients threatened hospitals with unending deficits. Accordingly, hospital administrators sought as energetically as possible to maximize income from private patients. They, in turn, except for the truly rich, protested the rising costs of health care. "The hospital had become an indispensable element in American health care," this historian concludes, "yet just as it achieved that status experts decried its failure to provide optimum care at reasonable costs."[33] The idea of group hospitalization and prepayment (insurance) was about to make its debut on both the national and the Carolina scene.

Confronted with growing public protest about the rising costs of medical care and hospitals, the distinguished national Committee on the Costs of Medical Care, supported by grants from several foundations, began its work in 1927 and would continue for five years. Rankin served first as a member of the committee and then also on its executive committee. Given his earlier prominence in the public health field, Rankin served on numerous, important national commissions and committees throughout his quarter-century directorship of the Hospital and Orphan Section. Closer to home, he had long been interested in what was then a relatively unique arrangement for health care in Roanoke Rapids, North Carolina, in the northeastern section of the state. A physician there persuaded the six owners of local industries (mostly textile mills) to build a fifty-bed hospital in 1914 and give it to a nonprofit corporation with a self-perpetuating board of trustees representing the community. The employees of the mills, in turn, agreed to a payroll deduction of fifteen cents per week to support the hospital and pay for their use of it; the employers paid the salaries of the physicians in the hospital. When X-ray, laboratory facilities, and other improvements were added to the hospital, the weekly payroll deduction went up to twenty cents; and in 1928, when the original

fifty-bed hospital became overcrowded, the hospital borrowed $50,000 to
build a fifty-bed addition, and the employees increased their contribution to
twenty-five cents a week to help pay the principal and interest on the debt. At
the worst of the depression in the early 1930s, the mill owners decided they
could no longer afford to pay the physicians' salaries, and the employees voted
overwhelmingly to increase their contributions to fifty cents a week, the extra
twenty-five cents paying the salaries of five physicians.[34]

This pioneering arrangement at Roanoke Rapids profoundly impressed
Rankin and, through him largely, various other leaders in health care. When
President Few in 1927 selected Wilburt C. Davison, a young pediatrician and
assistant dean at the medical school of Johns Hopkins University, to become
the first dean and organizer of Duke University's proposed medical school, one
of Davison's first moves was to visit Durham, and Few arranged for Davison
also to meet and take a motor trip with Rankin. Davison may or may not have
realized it fully at the time, but his unusually close, lifelong friendship with
Rankin, whom Davison grew to regard as a beloved and respected father
figure, was to have a profound influence not just on Davison personally but
also on many aspects of the Duke University Hospital and Medical School. In
countless ways, the work of the Hospital Section would become interrelated
with that of the medical center at Duke. Of the numerous examples that could
be cited, perhaps Davison's early interest in a program to train hospital administrators (as well as record keepers and other such technical personnel) was the
best illustration of how the Hospital Section and the Duke Hospital worked to
benefit each other as well as the health-care needs of the region. After the first
visit and trip with Rankin, Davison wrote Few: "I saw more and more clearly
that the medical school by cooperating with the community hospitals will
have a tremendous opportunity for medical service."[35]

In addition to learning about the Roanoke Rapids plan, however, Davison,
as a Rhodes Scholar studying medicine in England in the years just before
and during World War I, had become familiar with England's voluntary,
community-based (rather than industry-based, as in Roanoke Rapids) prepayment plans for hospitalization. Consequently, in 1929, more than a year before the Duke Hospital would even open, Davison attempted to launch such a
prepayment plan in Durham. Although he failed in this effort, the idea remained very much alive.[36]

Just as Rankin clearly had a large influence on Davison, so too did he have
an equally great impact on his associate, Graham Davis. He, in fact, began
to pour an immense amount of his time and energy into the promotion of

group hospitalization, and it became a major theme of *Southern Hospital.* While Davis had not experienced at firsthand, as Davison had, the English community-based plans for group hospitalization, Davis had met and enjoyed talking with English representatives at a meeting of the American Hospital Association in 1929. As a result, he had subscribed to publications issued by the hospital associations in Britain and begun corresponding with several leaders in hospital work there. An Anglophile anyway, Davis also felt that the British, in refusing thus far to plunge into state-controlled medical care as various European nations seemed to be doing, had lessons about hospitals, and particularly their financial support, to teach Americans.

The 1930s, because of the depression and then the New Deal, brought profound changes to many areas of American life. With admiration for capitalism at a low ebb, confidence in the ability of government, and particularly the federal government, to solve the nation's major problems reached new heights. While card-carrying Communists remained relatively few, those who allowed their faith in government to carry them all the way to a passionate belief in democratic socialism were far more numerous. Yet, as a prominent historian of the nation's twentieth-century hospitals has argued, the voluntary hospitals were not fallback organizations that came into existence only because government had not acted. Rather, they "are instruments of America's version of the capitalist state — social structures established to maintain, interpret, and extend it, as essential in their way as business corporations." Moreover, this same historian points out that while the voluntary hospitals have had to behave as businesses, expanding and trying to produce income, they have also "simultaneously carried symbolic and social significance as embodiments of American hopes and ideals: not only of science, technology, and expertise, but of altruism, social solidarity, and community spirit." The "ideal of 'charity,' " according to this historian, "has been [for the hospitals] at least as important as the 'business of business.' "[37]

While Rankin and Davis lived and worked for hospitals long before the above words were written, they intuitively acted on the insights and principles that are well expressed in the historian's statements. When the distinguished Committee on the Costs of Health Care came out with its final, majority report in 1932 (and there was also a minority report), it carried, in the words of the above-cited historian, "the strong suggestion of universal (if not compulsory) health insurance."[38]

Rankin, however, when asked as a member of the executive committee to criticize an early version of the report, argued that it suggested "a larger participation of the government in providing medical care than I believe is justified or desirable." He though the implication of various statements in the report was that the government should regard the medical profession in a different light from other professions and should provide a tax basis for the practice of medicine. "Now in the first place," Rankin continued, "I am not sure that medicine has a right or that medicine would ask for special treatment at the hands of the government." In the second place, Rankin thought that other remedies for providing medical care without government participation had been passed over but should be considered. Unemployment insurance and old-age pensions, he suggested, should be utilized before the government attempted to use the taxpayers' money to cover the cost of medical care for a large portion of the population. "It is so easy to unload on the government," Rankin declared, "that it has become a pernicious and exceedingly dangerous line of popular thinking."

Concerning the report's references to the rural areas, Rankin spoke from great experience in suggesting certain revisions. First, he believed that the organization of medical service in rural areas would have its real beginnings in community hospitals of from thirty to fifty beds. A large number of rural counties already had such hospitals, and he predicted that the number would increase tremendously during the decade ahead. In such a hospital, he pointed out, were gathered the necessary medical personnel and equipment, and when dentists and pharmacists were added, one would have "assembled in one hospital all of the essential elements for group production [of health care]."

In the second place, Rankin maintained that the group purchase of health care in rural areas probably would not be as difficult as urban-minded students of the question might think. There were all sorts of functioning groups in the rural areas — civic, religious, and agricultural organizations — and a hospital or health council could easily work through such groups to achieve group purchase of medical care. Rankin seriously questioned the notion that tax support would be needed in rural areas, for the people in those communities were "perhaps less likely to unload their social obligations upon the tax payer and the government than industrial groups, and are more likely to find other resources for the relief of dependent sickness."[39]

Beginning in the early 1930s, therefore, Rankin and Davis, and through them the trustees of the Endowment, rallied enthusiastically behind the idea of group hospitalization or prepayment partly because the depression vastly increased the charity load (and therefore the deficit problem) of the community hospitals and partly because they did not want the federal government moving massively and directly into the area of health care. Various circumstances about the medical situations in the 1930s and 1990s vastly differed, of course, but it is also interesting that, in one sense, Rankin, Davis, and their contemporaries were grappling with many of the same problems that the American public continued to confront in the last decade of the century.

The campaign for group hospitalization in North Carolina got underway in 1933. In Durham, despite Davison's failure to get such a plan started in 1929, he joined forces this time with a wealthy businessman, George Watts Hill, and they together with some others secured a legislative charter for the Hospital Care Association in August 1933. Although supported by both Duke and Watts Hospitals, as well as Hill, the Hospital Care Association got off to a slow and somewhat shaky start. Moreover, that it ultimately intended to try to expand beyond its Durham base and become statewide was not clear at first. On top of that, it initially at least seemed aimed more at middle-class people interested in private rooms in hospitals than at poorer people who would be fortunate to obtain ward service. At any rate, Rankin, Davis, and finally the Duke Endowment had a different approach in mind and proceeded to help establish another organization based in Chapel Hill, the Hospital Savings Association. The unforeseen result would be that North Carolina would end up with two, competing, statewide hospitalization plans, an anomalous, often troublesome situation that would last for over thirty years (until 1968, to be exact) and that authorities in the American Hospital Association, which accredited the nonprofit "Blue Cross" plans that sprang up around the nation in the 1930s, did their best to end.

Graham Davis, with Rankin's full backing, became a dynamo of the movement for group hospitalization in the Carolinas. When the Tri-State Hospital Association met in Charlotte in April 1934, he managed to have a lively session on the subject and saw to it that the newspapers, both in Charlotte and across the Carolinas and Virginia, carried stories about it. The NCHA's *Bulletin* became an important vehicle for publicizing the matter, as would its successor, *Southern Hospital.* Sending a friend a copy of memorandum on the subject, Davis declared that it was "a social movement of the first importance to the health and welfare of our people." Davis added that he thought that "the unqualified success of the Roanoke Rapids experiment over a long period of years" seemed to prove that the British with their voluntary, community-based plans for group hospitalization were on the right track.[40]

Davis soon found an important ally when Isaac H. Manning, dean of the preclinical medical school at the University of North Carolina, gave his presidential address to the North Carolina Medical Society. Since Manning had taught, and was much admired by, many of the doctors in the state, he had considerable influence. He not only endorsed the idea of group hospitalization but also recommended that the physicians should encourage the NCHA to supervise the development of it in the state.

Unlike hospital administrators, the medical profession, in both state and nation, was initially divided on the subject of group hospitalization. While many doctors had come to see its advantages and timeliness, others disagreed. Morris Fishbein, editor of the *Journal of the American Medical Association,* declared in early 1934 that the association strongly opposed any scheme for the group practice of medicine or for health insurance as being "un-American." In North Carolina, an official of the American Medical Association urged the state's doctors to "resist vigorously all attempts on the part of laymen or politicians to socialize medical service."[41]

Some doctors, as Manning himself pointed out, did not object to prepayment plans if they could be limited to ward patients, but they strongly objected when it came to private, middle- and upper-class patients. The president of the American Medical Association reportedly asserted early in 1937 that while the majority of the members opposed any form of health insurance, either voluntary or compulsory, he personally opposed only the compulsory variety but preferred, in a columnist's words, the "old Robin Hood technique of charging fees based on 'ability to pay' and soaking the rich patients in order to give free or cheap service to the poor." This irreverent columnist in the *Charlotte Observer* proceeded to attack this argument on two grounds. First, because of the uneven distribution of wealth between regions of the country as well as between individuals, there were wide areas where there were not enough rich patients to allow "the boys with the black satchels to play Robin Hood." That meant that millions of people, not only in the South but in other regions also, struggled along with inadequate medical care or none at all. And, second, the columnist continued, the Robin Hood system made every doctor a "voluntary tax collector," and even the best of tax collectors made mistakes. Moreover, and here the columnist got mean, "there are doctors who think the Hippocratic Oath is a license to scalp patients." Historically considered, the acerbic newspaperman concluded, "the medical profession has opposed every important advance in the technique of healing—antisepsis and anaesthesia included," and it now presumed "to oppose a social advance calculated to make medical protection and care available to millions who lack it."[42]

Since many doctors, like Manning, lined up solidly behind group hospitalization, the columnist was unfairly overstating his case. But the conversion of many in the North Carolina medical profession, at least, came about partly through the publicity campaign orchestrated by Graham Davis. Starting in the summer of 1934, both the *Charlotte Observer* and the regional Associated Press office gave extensive publicity to the new movement. Davis went to Chapel Hill in July 1934 for the first meeting of the joint committee that had been named by the NCHA and the Medical Society to work out a statewide periodic payment plan for the purchase of hospital care. The *Charlotte Observer* carried the story, included information about the Roanoke Rapids plan, and quoted Davis as saying that while including hospital care in a family budget was a comparatively new idea in the United States, it was "a common practice in practically all of the other civilized nations of the world," either on a voluntary basis or by legal compulsion for people in low-income groups. A few months later the *Observer* editorialized that it had begun to be clear that plans for hospitalization for persons of moderate means, through the payment of small weekly sums, would materialize. "The movement has gained immense momentum," the paper noted, "since the embryonic idea was launched only a few weeks ago."[43]

One part of Davis's campaign to publicize the group hospitalization idea was to bring to North Carolina as a visiting speaker an Englishman who was prominent in his own country's voluntary contributory plans. When the general secretary of the Merseyside (Liverpool) Hospitals Council, Sydney Lamb, was scheduled to speak on group hospitalization to the annual meeting of the American Hospital Association in the fall of 1934, Davis arranged for the NCHA to sponsor an address by Lamb in Charlotte. Securing much publicity for Lamb's visit and speech, Davis reported afterward that the visitor had given a "new inspiration" to the proposed statewide plan for North Carolina. "He has a remarkable personality," Davis noted, "and after meeting him you can understand why group hospitalization on a voluntary basis has made such progress in Great Britain." Davis could only wish that "we had a similar personality to put the thing over in North Carolina."[44]

From the outset of the meetings of the joint committee that had been organized to come up with a plan for North Carolina, Graham Davis took a philosophical and idealistic approach that would ultimately prove to be one that the majority of the committee did not share. He did not know that at first, of course, and proceeded to make a powerful case for his position. In a memorandum to the joint committee early in its work, Davis began by emphasizing what he called the "social theory involved in group hospitalization." It was, he said, "a method by which the group acting collectively (and not as individuals)" protected itself against a hazard of life that could not be anticipated with any degree of certainty. He wanted, therefore, to emphasize the mutual-aid principle rather than a strictly businesslike insurance approach.

The health of the wage earner in particular, he argued, was of vital importance to the welfare and happiness of society, yet 25 percent of family incomes in the nation, in normal times, were less than $1,200 per year, and the percentage was much higher in the South. The low-income group could not ordinarily pay hospital bills, which was why over half the patients in North Carolina's general hospitals paid nothing for their hospital care—and the ratio was much higher in mental and tuberculosis hospitals. People were forced by circumstances to pauperize themselves by asking for charity, or, what Davis considered worse still, to make promises they knew they could not fulfill, which further destroyed their character.

The existing situation was intolerable from many angles, and "since the health of the people is 'suffused with a public interest' to a much greater degree than, for example, protection of property by fire insurance," the government in many civilized nations had stepped in and made health insurance compulsory. The approach to the problem in those nations, such as Germany for example, had been from the standpoint of society as a whole. Consequently, every individual in the group with an income was taxed on the same basis, regardless of the number of dependents, on the theory that the health of the group as a whole was of equal importance to the earning capacity, both present and prospective, of every member of the group. The health of the non-income producers, therefore, became the common responsibility of society.

Davis confessed that he would hate to get away from the above principle in North Carolina, though he also wanted to avoid compulsory health insurance. His solution to this dilemma, which solution derived largely from his understanding of the British experience with voluntary prepayment plans, was to argue for an appeal to the public based not on selfish individualism but on a "sense of Christian and social duty to make some contribution to a common fund that will provide hospitalization for everyone in the group who needs it." He believed that the lack of this broader, humanitarian appeal was a great weakness in the group hospitalization plans that were springing up around the country. Admittedly experimental, they had so far, he maintained, largely provided a means by which people of middle- and high-income groups, who paid their hospital bills anyway, could do so with less difficulty. Existing plans, in short, had not even "begun to scratch the surface of the real problem of providing hospital service for the forty to fifty percent of the people who cannot even in normal times pay for hospital service when they need it." Davis insisted that it was those poorer people whom the British contributory plans, like the plans at Roanoke Rapids and at one or two additional textile towns, helped. Davis conceded that, as a first step, it might be necessary to sell the idea first to the higher-income group.

Hospital charges, he reminded the committee, were unlike doctors' charges in that the former were not generally based on ability to pay but on the type of accommodation furnished. "The only excuse as I see it for the existence of our committee," Davis concluded, "is the fact that our hospitals now are over-crowded with patients who cannot pay for hospital care, that this condition constitutes a severe strain on the financial resources of our hospitals, that thousands of others who need hospital care are not getting it because they cannot pay for it and hospitals are not so financed that they can take them in for nothing, and that it is both socially and morally undesirable that this condition should continue to exist." The committee should direct its attention to the solution of that particular problem, and something like the Roanoke Rapids plan, with slight modifications, should be the ultimate objective for the whole state. Meantime, Davis advised his fellow committee members that an enclosed press release had gone out after the last meeting and had been carried by all the larger daily newspapers. "The editors appear to be strong for us," Davis noted.[45]

Aside from the larger, less tangible matter of philosophical tone and approach, the difference between Davis and the majority of the committee would narrow down to the question of what weekly fee should be charged to the purchaser of group hospitalization, which would determine how much money the hospitals would receive for each day of care. Strongly pushing for smaller amounts in both cases than the majority preferred, Davis would lose that fight also, but before that matter could be settled, there were other important questions that had to be answered. Perhaps the biggest was this: where was the capital that would be needed to start a statewide plan to come from?

The joint committee had decided to name the organization pushing the new statewide plan the Hospital Saving Association (after a similarly named organization in London), and Manning had agreed to serve as president, presiding over a board composed of some prominent business leaders in the state as well as physicians and hospital administrators. Because of the problems of financing, Davis informed Manning that he hoped they could incorporate the already existing Hospital Care Association in Durham into the new organization, but, as mentioned earlier, that was not to be.

As for procuring aid from the Duke Endowment, Davis was not sure that the indenture would allow it. Lawyers (meaning W. R. Perkins primarily?) would have to decide and would not go to the trouble without a concrete proposition before them. The trustees, Davis explained, were businessmen whose policy was "to help those who show an inclination to help themselves." If the hospitals got the project started in a small way and demonstrated its practicability, it was possible that the Endowment would then extend assistance "to get the thing going in a big way." The trustees were, he maintained, "very much interested in any movement that will improve hospital service in this State."[46]

Both Rankin and Davis had been, in fact, quietly educating certain trustees about the group hospitalization movement. In mid-1934 Davis wrote Alexander Sands explaining how group hospitalization might reduce the amount of free hospital service in North Carolina. Davis noted that the Roanoke Rapids hospital, which served a lot of tenant farmers in addition to mill workers, had reported only 13 percent of free or charity days in 1933 as compared with a 60 percent average for all hospitals assisted by the Endowment.[47] Sands hardly needed for Davis to explain that the less money the Endowment had to spend to assist with charity care the more it would have for the construction and equipment of hospitals.

Rankin took another angle in a letter to a fellow trustee. "Those of us who have been keeping in close touch with the larger trends of medicine," Rankin explained, "have a rather definite feeling that a voluntary spreading of the cost of medical care . . . over large groups of population and over periods of time must come if we are to be saved from a compulsory sickness insurance with a tax basis instead of a [voluntary] contributory basis."[48]

With such support from Rankin and Davis and after the latter helped prepare the application to the trustees, the Endowment in April 1935 gave $25,000, a significant sum in that era, to help get the Hospital Saving Association going. When Manning inquired as to whether the grant should be publicized, Rankin and Davis assured him that it should and that the press release should emphasize that the Endowment trustees wished to cooperate with the NCHA and the Medical Society in the improvement of hospital service in North Carolina by relieving the hospitals to a certain extent of "the enormous charity load they are now carrying." Thus the Endowment could increase its usefulness to hospitals by releasing money paid out for the care of charity patients and making it available for hospital construction and equipment. "Another factor of course that influenced the trustees," Davis added, "was the possibility of prevention of pauperization of people in the lower income groups." Davis also hoped that publicity concerning the Endowment's grant would "serve notice on the compulsory health insurance gang" in the state that the NCHA and the Medical Society proposed "to solve this problem without interference by the State."[49]

Encouraged by the significant boost from the Endowment, Manning wanted Davis to become the director or manager of the Hospital Saving Association. Davis, who had long wanted to study the British contributory plans at first-hand, said that *if* (and he carefully emphasized the if) he should decide to accept the position, one condition before he would even consider it would be that he and Manning should first be sent to England to study the group payment schemes. Would Manning get the directors of the Hospital Saving Association to request the Endowment to release Davis for the trip, with the idea that at the end of it they would decide definitely whether Davis was the right person to manage the Hospital Saving Association? "I am not particularly interested in another job," Davis added, "but I am interested in the Hospital Saving Association." And he was by no means sure that he was the best person to manage it.

Davis thought that the simplification of records that might be possible after the observation of British methods would probably save the Hospital Saving Association the cost of his and Manning's trip. Too, Davis said he was now wondering how the reaction of employers to group care was going to be affected by the new payroll taxes and deductions that would go into effect under the New Deal's social security provisions for unemployment insurance and old age pensions. He wanted to investigate British experience with those matters, too.[50]

Manning admitted that Davis's suggestion had great appeal but also wondered if the proposed trip were the best method. The business of group payment for hospital care was of such general interest, Manning pointed out, that some organization should be in a position to give dependable advice about its workings. "The Duke Endowment has undertaken to furnish plans for the building of small hospitals," he continued, and "has undertaken to introduce a uniform accounting system and [rationalized] other details of hospital management." Manning avowed that he knew of no other organization so specifically concerned with hospital management, so would it not be a fine thing "if the Duke Endowment could work out a plan of management . . . of group payment?"

He believed that the American Hospital Association or the American Medical Association, or both jointly, should have long ago worked out such a plan.

"Of course the A.M.A. has enough money," Manning declared, "but it is so lukewarm, if not really opposed, that I would question its work. I am disgusted with its attitude toward the whole problem."

As another consideration, Manning stated that if the Rosenwald Fund or any of the other foundations interested in "socialized medicine" programs were to undertake the task of providing a model plan for group hospitalization, "they would probably not stop with hospitalization, but would ride their pet hobbies." Manning wanted "someone who is not soaked in theories to make a business-like, unbiased study of the management of group payment plans and get it out of the experimental stage." He insisted that he knew of no one better qualified than Davis to do the job.

If the Endowment trustees thought that a small portion of their $25,000 grant should be used in such a way, Manning explained, then he would "be mighty glad to go along as your chaperon or in any other capacity, but I must say in conscience that I would be scarcely more than a part of your baggage." He did think that it "would be fine if we could set up a model system in North Carolina."[51]

Manning and Davis made the trip. Pushing hard to complete the drafting of the tenth annual report of the Hospital Section before leaving, Davis arranged for Marshall Pickens and George Harris to cover his responsibilities concerning *Southern Hospital*. Though Manning halfheartedly tried to back out at the last minute, Davis would not let him. As for Davis, Manning advised that the rest afforded by a sea voyage would be helpful. "You would be better looking and your wife will think more of you," Manning explained to Davis, "with an additional 25 lbs."[52]

In preparing for the trip, Davis arranged for the American Hospital Association to name Manning and him as official delegates to the British Hospital Association, which met at the end of May 1935. They planned also to attend the annual meeting of the British Hospital Contributory Schemes Association. Although Davis had been in correspondence with various British leaders in the hospital field for several years, he secured letters of introduction from certain American leaders to their counterparts in Britain as well as France, where Manning was interested in the government-sponsored plan for the payment of physicians.

Keeping meticulous records of their modest expenses, Manning and Davis conferred with a dozen or more different executives of the hospital contributory plan in England and also attended the annual meetings as planned. While Davis went highly predisposed toward the British approach to the problem, he apparently saw or learned nothing that changed his mind, although he did discover that there were many local variations in the plans and that they were still highly experimental despite the fact that 15 million members belonged to some 400 different organizations. Although the two were briefly in France, Manning decided that he would say as little as possible in his report on the trip about the "schemes to pay the doctors" since that was, at least for the time being, "a sensitive point."[53]

While Manning still urged Davis to take on the job of managing the Hospital Saving Association, Davis finally decided that it was not for him and successfully pushed for the appointment of someone else. Davis did not say so, but clearly one reason for his disinterest was that, despite his best efforts and arguments, the Hospital Saving Association had not actually turned out as he had hoped it would. The directors of the organization, responding to the thinking of hospital administrators as well as certain sympathetic physicians, opted eventually for a plan that would pay all participating hospitals $4.00 a day for ward service. (Those wishing private rooms could pay extra for them.) Since there was abundant evidence from the Hospital Section's statistical records that the average cost of ward service in the Carolinas was then close to $3.00 per day, Davis came privately to believe that the hospitals were ignoring their larger social obligations to poor people and using the new group hospitalization plan to maximize their income.

Early in the joint committee's deliberations, Davis objected to the idea of paying the same rate to all hospitals. From his experience over the previous ten years, he insisted that the quality of service was not uniform and even if it were, there would still be wide variations in cost. He cited, for example, the case of a fifty-bed hospital averaging forty patients a day, which could render the same quality of service at a much lower cost than would the same hospital averaging only ten patients per day. Davis asserted that "the poor devil who has to pay for hospital service has not been given the consideration he deserves so far in the deliberation of our Committee." Since he was the only member with no direct connection with the production end of hospital service, he thought he might have a more detached viewpoint of the matter.

Hospital service was of such vital importance to the public welfare, and especially to the low-income group, that all of the national organizations interested in the matter had emphasized that group hospitalization should not be commercialized. For that reason, Davis noted, he objected to paying a sorry hospital that had a low grade of service, and consequently a low per capital cost, $4.50 a day — or any other amount that would give it a profit. It would not only be unfair but would offer the institution no incentive to improve its service.

Both the American Medical Association and the American College of Surgeons, Davis declared, had urged that attention be focused on the quality of service and that only approved hospitals be admitted to participate in group hospitalization plans. Yet only 51 of 107 general hospitals in North Carolina were on the last approved list of the College of Surgeons, with the number expected to rise to 60 on a forthcoming list. Davis thought the joint committee should take the initiative in improving hospital service in the state by refusing to approve for group hospitalization any hospital that did not meet the minimum requirements of the American College of Surgeons.[54]

Davis accused one of the most prominent of the national leaders in the group hospitalization movement, C. R. Rorem, whom Davis claimed as a friend and with whom he frequently corresponded, of thinking that the new development was intended only or primarily for the middle class. Rorem, according to Davis, had "that middle class complex and apparently cannot get away from it."[55]

Davis, on the other hand, kept poorer people in the forefront of his thinking. One good, detailed illustration of that came in a long (five and a half single-spaced, typed pages) letter that Davis wrote concerning a particular hospital in Anson County, North Carolina, which is located in the south-central Piedmont just above the South Carolina border. He wanted the Hospital Saving Association, which was already largely committed to a uniform statewide plan, to take a flexible, experimental approach in Anson County.

The county had a population of 30,000, Davis explained, about half white and half African American, and was "practically all rural with no industry worth mentioning and one of the poorest in North Carolina." In the previous winter, it had had the largest proportion of its population on relief in the state, Davis added. The one hospital in the county, in Wadesboro, had averaged 25 patients per day in 1934, which gave it an occupancy rate of 62 percent, which Davis said was "rather high for a small rural hospital taking both white and negro patients." The average collection per in-patient per day in 1934 was only $1.27, with three of every five patients being free and the "ratio for the negroes ran up to around 90 percent." The average cost per patient per day was $2.48, but Davis expected the cost to gradually work back up toward $3.00.

Davis explained that he had just learned that the surgeon, who treated 71 percent of the patients discharged in 1934, was interested in group payment and had sparked some community interest in the matter. As the surgeon had tentatively worked out his plan, he would charge white families, regardless of the number of dependents, $12 a year and for African Americans he would charge half of that amount "because he says they cannot afford and probably will not pay more." One reason he was interested in the plan was "because he is not making a decent living," and knowing him and the circumstances, Davis said he believed the surgeon.

The Wadesboro doctor argued that an outside organization like the Hospital Saving Association could not come into the community and put the thing across nearly as effectively as the local hospital could "because the hospital is so well and favorably known in the community and the appeal could be made to the community to support its own local institution much more effectively than if they thought the money was going to support hospitals all over the State." Davis added that he had told the doctor that his own opinion was that "every effort should be made to conserve this local interest in the local hospital." The way the British sold the idea, Davis noted, it had a double-barrelled appeal, "as contrasted with the appeal when you sell it simply as insurance." When one became a contributor in Britain, "You are helping a very necessary local institution and also providing against a contingency that may wreck your financial resources or make you an object of charity." (Davis reported that he and Manning were impressed in Britain that even persons "on the dole," that is on the state relief program, paid their small weekly dues to the hospital contributory schemes.)

What all this boiled down to was that Davis wanted the Hospital Saving Association to tell the people in Anson county that only 10 percent of collections in the first year would be used for operating purposes. Then a local man could be employed as the organizing secretary for around $1,800 a year, with the local hospital to pay $600 of that salary for the man to serve as the business manager of the hospital with his office there and the Hospital Saving Association to pay the remaining $1,200. Then a campaign could be started to get at least 1,000 white families at $12.00 each and $9.00 for Negro families. It might be advisable to use a stamp system for weekly contributions, as was done in Britain.

The Hospital Saving Association should promise the Wadesboro hospital to pay $2.00 per day at the end of each quarter, and at the end of the year, if there were sufficient surplus left after deducting 10 percent for operating expenses, pay enough in addition up to the average cost per patient per day for the year. Any surplus would accumulate to the credit of the hospital to eliminate the 21-day limit or to provide additional hospital benefits.

Davis reiterated that he had never been happy about the decision to have the

Hospital Saving Association pay every hospital the same amount. If the quality of service rendered in all hospitals were the same, the principle of equal payment would be sound. The quality of service was not the same, however, and the difference was frequently reflected in cost. He thought the people of Wadesboro would laugh at the representative of the Hospital Saving Association if he went there and told them that the cost of operating the hospital should be at least $4.00 a day and that the contributory fund would be operated on that basis. The surgeon, the hospital trustees, and the community generally would, Davis insisted, "be delighted if they could collect $2.50 per day from the contributory fund." In fact, he thought they would be satisfied and could greatly improve the financial position of the hospital if they collected only $2.00 per day.

Davis believed that a better place than Anson county to start a rural hospitalization demonstration could not be found. "If the thing goes over properly," he surmised, "we could probably get someone from some foundation to develop a really comprehensive health program in cooperation with a full time county health department; in other words use group payment for hospital care as a constructive force in building up community health."[56]

Davis gradually came to believe that he and others who helped establish the Hospital Saving Association had, in one sense, made a mistake, for, as he wrote a friend who was a Blue Cross leader in New York, the existing statewide plan fitted conditions in only 70 to 80 percent of the state's communities. If he were starting over, Davis explained, he would recommend a federation for local community plans with only as much uniformity as was possible in the beginning. Then as experience developed and hospital service became more standardized as to cost and quality, a uniform plan would emerge from the process. By keeping some control in a central organization, many of the disadvantages of separated local plans would be eliminated; but at the same time certain advantages of a local plan, such as support of and community pride about a hospital, could be retained.

To offer what he admitted was an extreme example, Davis cited a mission hospital of modern, fireproof construction in the village of Banner Elk, North Carolina. The hospital, which served about ten sparsely settled mountain counties with extremely low per capita incomes, was fully approved by the College of Surgeons and the chief surgeon was a fellow of the College. The operating cost was $1.50 per patient per day, and the hospital leaders there would not consider at all the statewide plan that charged individuals 15 cents a week and paid hospitals $4.00 per day. Consequently, Davis said, he was trying to help the hospital develop its own plan.[57]

Though convinced that many of the group hospitalization plans that had sprung up across the nation in 1930s were focused too largely on the middle class, Davis by 1939 took a long view and remained hopeful. When a friend in Pennsylvania expressed fears about the plans' impact on hospitals, Davis replied that he and Rankin thought the worry was unnecessary. "My feeling is that this movement is going to both improve the quality of hospital services and promote more economical and efficient administration," Davis declared. The thousands of people in a community paying periodically for hospital care stimulated great interest in the hospital itself, the money paid in stabilized and increased income, and that in turn caused hospitals to improve the quality of service. The organized group demanded better service, and since they paid for it, they were entitled to it.

Davis conceded that his experience in the Carolinas had convinced him that a lot of the voluntary hospitals in the United States were wasting money because they were not efficiently managed. "When a large city hospital with a fairly modern plant and a reasonable bed occupancy operates at a cost of over $5.00 or $5.50 a day," Davis observed, "I become suspicious that there is something rotten in Denmark." He had found several like that in the Carolinas in 1925, he said, and in some instances "they were politically controlled institutions and there was more or less graft, in addition to sorry management." But by 1939 he had come to believe that, with two or three exceptions, from the 130 Endowment-assisted hospitals "the people of the Carolinas are getting more for their hospital dollar than in any other section of the country." The hospitals certainly were not perfect, for poor buying and collection methods continued to be serious defects in many hospitals.[58]

In a friendly, epistolary debate with another hospital leader in Pennsylvania, Davis confessed that the more he dug into "this problem of providing the low wage earner with adequate hospital care," the less sure he became of his convictions, for "there are so many uncertain factors." The Pennsylvanian wanted any hospitalization plan to pay full cost, but Davis countered that such an approach would limit the appeal to people with incomes large enough to make the corresponding contribution. He, on the other hand, would settle for a plan paying less than full cost and broaden the appeal to include almost every one with an income. In either event, he argued, the total income of the hospitals from patients would not be much different, but his approach would take part of the cost of hospitalizing a larger proportion of the population off the shoulders of the taxpayer and would preserve the self-respect of the low-income groups by making it possible for them to pay a substantial part of their bills.

Turning specifically to the Carolinas, Davis reminded the Pennsylvanian that the people in the two states got about half the hospital care they needed because they could not pay for it under existing conditions. About a half of South Carolina's population was African American as was about a third of North Carolina's and, Davis explained, "not over ten percent of the Negroes at present can afford to pay hospital bills." He did not believe that you could possibly enroll over 20 percent of the blacks in a voluntary plan paying full cost, for among the 135,000 people enrolled in the two North Carolina plans in the previous few years, there was only a handful of African Americans. "That would put the cost of adequate hospital care for eighty percent of the Negroes on the shoulders of the taxpayers," Davis continued, "and, knowing the economic and social conditions in the South as I do, it will be a long, long time before the Negro gets adequate hospital care under those conditions."

Davis said he had no objection to a tax-funded subsidy for ward beds for the low-wage group. He was much involved with the hospital and community leaders in Greenville, South Carolina, in working out a group payment plan, and the governmental authorities there had agreed informally to make up any deficit incurred by participating hospitals. Why should not that be done generally in the Carolinas?[59]

Graham Davis, as industrious as he was deeply informed about hospitals, probably overworked himself. At any rate, in the fall of 1939, feeling that he was "losing his pep and drive," he consulted doctors at Duke University Hospital, and they warned him that if he did not soon take a vacation voluntarily, he would "probably have to take it by compulsion." Turning down the chairmanship of the program committee for the Carolinas-Virginia Hospital Conference, Davis lamented, "There is so much that needs urgently to be done in the hospital field, but I cannot do it all."[60]

Not long afterward, Davis resigned from his position with the Endowment to become the director of the rural hospital program of the W. K. Kellogg Foundation in Michigan. He went with the blessings and encouragement of Rankin, but early in 1940 George Harris wrote Davis, obviously in jest: "We have let practically all of the hospitals know that we can give them very little assistance from the office this year on account of your leaving and they appear to be buckling down to real work." In a more serious vein, Harris added, "All of us feel that you have an ideal opportunity in your new field of activity in that you will have an opportunity there to get across many of your ideas to the national organizations dealing with health and medical services." Davis replied that his departure was probably a good thing for the hospitals in the

Carolinas, for they had "been coddled too much" and would now learn to do more for themselves. He reported that he was making plans for conferences with the hospitals in his new area, such as the Endowment held, and hoped eventually to get all the participating Michigan hospitals on a uniform accounting and statistical basis.[61]

Continuing the important work with various committees of the American Hospital Association that he had done throughout the 1930s and having a number of his articles published in leading professional journals, Graham Davis had established himself nationally as a leader in his field. One admirer wrote him that with "so much feeling in the hospital and medical fields regarding the competency of 'lay' administrators," Davis's continued success gave "courage to us who dare to follow."[62]

In 1946 Rankin and Marshall Pickens took the lead in organizing a successful campaign to have Davis elected president of the American Hospital Association. All of the Hospital Section's staff were on hand for the presidential address in 1947, and Davis informed Rankin that the latter's approval of the address carried greater weight than that of any other person of whom he could think. When Davis died on July 4, 1958, as the result of an automobile accident in eastern North Carolina, Marshall Pickens declared in a private letter, "I don't know of any individual who during his lifetime contributed so much to the upgrading of our hospitals and public health services as did Graham. He worked harder than anyone I know and apparently spent 24 hours of every day thinking and working to improve the health facilities in the United States."[63] Rankin and the Duke Endowment, too, deserved to be proud.

3 ·

LAUNCHING

THE

ENDOWMENT

The Hospital and

Orphan Section

(Part 2)

THE DEPARTURE OF GRAHAM DAVIS in 1940 obviously meant the loss of a singularly creative and industrious staff member for the Endowment, but there were ample backups. In addition to Marshall Pickens and George Harris, both of whom had joined the staff in 1928, James R. Felts Jr. became a field representative for the Hospital and Orphan Section in 1937. He had earlier attended the University of North Carolina and worked as an accountant for Duke Power for five years. After a stint in the United States Army during World War II, he returned to the Endowment and remained there for the rest of his career. Another longtime staff member, H. Carl Rowland Jr. came on board in 1951. A graduate of Davidson College who served in the United States Navy during World War II, Rowland worked as a hospital administrator for more than two years prior to accepting a position as field representative for the Hospital Section. From a staff of three in 1926 — Watson S. Rankin, Davis, and a secretary — the section had grown by midcentury to a total of nine persons. As had been the case with Davis, the combination of Rankin's influence and mentoring with the rich, firsthand experience in a large, varied group of hospitals in the Carolinas meant that Pickens, Harris, Felts, and Rowland all acquired considerable expertise in varying aspects of their work.[1]

The uniform system of financial and clinical records among the assisted hospitals ultimately became one of the great achievements of the Hospital Section, an achievement with a variety of national as well as regional benefits, as will be shown. The uniformity did not, however, come easily. In a couple of memoranda in 1937, which played a part in the addition of Felts, George Harris pointed out that during the early years, the section did not have a clear policy about field work, that is about direct assistance with the fairly elaborate records that Rankin wanted from the hospitals. Initially the Endowment had recommended the accounting system preferred by the American Hospital Association, with a few features borrowed from the system used by state-aided hospitals in Pennsylvania. It had quickly become apparent, however, that the system was designed for larger hospitals with experienced bookkeepers and auditors and was too complicated for the small hospitals that predominated in the Carolinas. Few of them, Harris noted, then employed experienced book-keepers or even had "anything that could be called a bookkeeping system." On the other hand, the larger hospitals that had been in operation prior to 1925 had their own systems and were reluctant to change. There were many mis-understandings, according to Harris, and the Hospital Section's annual ap-plication for assistance "came to be looked upon as a nightmare."

To end the confusion, Rankin and Davis had found it necessary to send field representatives (initially Harris and Pickens) to the hospitals to assist with their record systems, help train bookkeepers and auditors, and lend a hand with the applications for assistance. With fifty-two hospitals applying in 1925, and an average of eight new ones each subsequent year (with the largest number, fifteen, in 1929), the Hospital Section adopted a simplified account-ing system and recommended a cross-index system of diseases, operations, physicians, and surgeons. "There has been and always will be a large number of problems in field work," Harris concluded. Some hospital administrators did not realize the importance of accurate records, though there had been considerable improvement in that regard. Because a large proportion of the bookkeepers and record librarians were underpaid and overworked, the turn-over was high.

In addition to field trips by the staff, Harris thought the Endowment should consider establishing workshops or institutes for record librarians and book-keepers. That would enhance the consultative and advisory service rendered by the Hospital Section. Even if a hospital had no trouble with its record systems, Harris believed it was important for the Endowment to keep in close touch. "A word of explanation or encouragement now and then," he sug-gested, "is of assistance to the hospital which is striving to meet the requirements of the American College of Surgeons." For example, when a field representative explained the necessity and advantage of having all tissues removed during surgery examined by a pathologist, Harris had found that it frequently got results. In fact, the field representative could give advice about all sorts of problems that the hospital superintendent might not wish to get into lengthy correspondence about. By 1937, Harris found that 40 of the 123 assisted hospitals employed accountants and about half of the hospitals had experienced record librarians, who often served also as bookkeepers.[2]

Harris won his case for an expanded, regularized field service. In addition to personal visits and regional workshops, which the staff held in various locations scattered across the Carolinas for the hospital bookkeepers and record librarians, the Endowment in the late 1940s began holding summer workshops on the campus of Lees-McRae College in Banner Elk in the mountains of North Carolina. While the participants (or their hospitals) paid their own travel expenses, the Endowment paid all the costs of the workshops. When, after several years of concentration on the bookkeepers, the medical-record librarian got a turn, one of them commented after the workshop had ended, "Before coming here, I didn't even know what the word nomenclature meant, and now I'm planning to set up a disease and operation index the first of January." Aside from remarks about how ideal Banner Elk was for a summer conference, another participant noted that the week had been "the most valuable I've ever spent since being in record librarian work."[3]

While medical records are perhaps a bit arcane to the laity, Harris, in speaking to a group of the record librarians, argued that they might have as much to do with saving lives as a well-trained nurse or a skillful surgeon. Careful analysis of the monthly and annual statistical reports of the record librarian could reveal certain facts or clear trends which called for prompt and concerted action by the trustees of the hospital, the superintendent, or the medical staff. Perhaps the number of infections was on the increase or the number of autopsies declining. "Perhaps a change of technique, the purchase of a new piece of equipment, an increase in personnel, a word of advice or encouragement on the part of the chief of [the medical] staff to a younger physician, or perhaps the actual removal from the staff of a certain physician," Harris suggested, "any of these procedures may result in the better care of the patient, the decrease in the length of stay of the patient with the accompanying saving in money and time, together with the actual saving of lives." Without the reports of the record librarian, in short, a hospital could easily lose sight of its "clinical sins of omission and commission, just as without the reports of the bookkeeper or auditor, the hospital may be heading for a big deficit or even bankruptcy without the superintendent or board of trustees even realizing the danger."

In addition, Harris reminded the record librarians that the forms they filled out for the Endowment were the basis for the annual reports of the Hospital Section. Those reports not only went to hospitals and libraries throughout the United States and abroad, but they were also much used for reference and research. Consequently, he invited the help of the librarians in making any changes that would improve the forms.[4]

While Harris worked with the record librarians and also served as a principal liaison with nursing organizations in the Carolinas, Marshall Pickens, among other things, frequently advised hospital administrators and trustees concerning management problems. Just as the Hospital Section had published much-used bulletins concerning hospital design and accounting, its *Bulletin Number 4* dealt with "The Small General Hospital, Organization and Management." When a hospital administrator in Mississippi sought advice concerning the lack of regulations about the performance of major surgery in his hospital, Pickens suggested that the bylaws should be amended. Perhaps those already performing major surgery could be allowed to continue, but there should be strong restrictions as to the future. After writing at some length to indicate how the bylaw might be worded, Pickens also mentioned the need for a bylaw to prevent physicians and their spouses from serving as trustees or directors of the hospital. That caused problems with other doctors, and a better way of communicating was to have a committee of the medical staff meet with a committee of the trustees to deal with medical-administrative matters.[5]

Advising George Watts Hill Sr., a powerful trustee of Watts Hospital in Durham, Pickens stressed the importance to the medical staff of the financial protection of the hospital. It was to the financial interest of the doctors, Pickens explained, to have a well-operated and well-financed hospital to which they could send private patients. "If the medical staff selfishly insists upon getting their fees before the hospital is paid . . . , it is not in the best interest of the medical staff, the hospital, or the patient."

Pickens also noted that the medical staff needed to recognize the legal responsibility of the trustees for the operation of the hospital, including the medical service. The trustees, of course, could delegate certain aspects of the hospital's operation to the medical staff or to the administrative personnel, but final responsibility rested upon the trustees. The importance of having lay people, not physicians, on the governing board of community hospitals needed emphasizing. "Our physician friends must realize," Pickens declared, "that as the public puts more and more financial resources into hospital facilities, more and more public control will have to be the result." Pickens, an amiable conciliator himself, concluded that the doctor-hospital relationship "must be a team work proposition with mutual respect on the part of both groups."[6]

Like Graham Davis, Pickens also developed the ability to see the larger picture and to communicate aspects of it to the general public. In an article for the *Charlotte Observer* in 1951, for example, he pointed out that in 1924 only 49 percent of the beds in the Carolinas' general hospitals had been in not-for-profit institutions; but by 1950, however, 95 percent of the beds were in such hospitals. If one went as far back as 1900, Pickens pointed out, almost all the general hospitals in the Carolinas were privately owned but by 1950 only 5 percent were.

Without mentioning the Duke Endowment, which was at least a part of the story, Pickens explained the change by noting (1) that there was a better understanding on the part of the public about the need for hospitals and therefore more resources from public funds; (2) that the increased cost of such facilities made it difficult for individual physicians to provide them; (3) that there was a greater use of hospitals because of the change in the mode of living from rural to a more urban and industrial setting; (4) that doctors were trained in hospitals and needed the equipment to be found there as well as conserved time by concentrating their work there; and (5) that there had been an increased use of hospital insurance by large employers and the general public.

As an additional indication of what Pickens saw as progress in the Carolinas' hospital development, he noted that the number of hospital beds per 1,000 people had increased almost 84 percent since 1924. That rate of increase was almost exactly twice that which had been reported for a group of nineteen of the nation's states with roughly comparable rural populations.[7]

In an article in a national publication, *Hospitals,* that brought inquiries from across the country, Pickens compiled statistics for the ten years between 1940 and 1950, explaining at the outset that the uniform records kept by the Endowment-assisted hospitals were the basis for the study. (While hospital statistics, or any type of statistics, are certainly not an average person's favorite reading matter, they often can be illuminating and helpful to administrators, trustees, and makers of public policy.) At 130 general hospitals in 1940 the cost per patient per day averaged $3.92; by 1949 it had increased to $16.76.

During the same period, income per patient per day rose from an average of $3.14 to $9.44. In 1940 the full-pay patient paid in excess of cost an average of $1.02 per day, but in 1949 that had been cut to 49 cents. That is, with rising costs, the full-pay patient was not being overcharged to carry charity work but was paying an amount much nearer cost, and the cost of charity was being covered from other sources.

Salary cost per patient per day in 1940 was $1.66, but that figure had risen to $5.48 by 1949. Nursing cost rose from 82 cents per patient per day in 1940 to $3.11 in 1949, the largest single increase. Raw food cost increased 115 percent.

While charity days of care amounted to 37.4 percent of the total days in 1940, that had dropped to 18.7 percent in 1949. The cost of charity increased, however, from $3,279,000 in 1940 to $6,701,000 in 1949, and contributions for charity from public and private agencies increased 142 percent. In 1940 the excess cost of charity over contributions, which cost had to be covered by the hospitals, was 18.1 percent, but in 1949 it was only 3 percent, indicating better support by private as well as public agencies for indigent patients.

The average stay in the hospitals declined from 9.4 days in 1940 to 7 days in 1949. This shorter stay helped explain why the cost of care for the individual patient rose only 104 percent while the cost per patient per day rose 174.5 percent. The shorter stay also made available a greater bed capacity, for in 1940 each bed was used on average by forty patients, whereas that increased to fifty-two patients by 1949.[8]

As hospital costs began their upward spiral after World War II, Pickens and others on the staff tried to help keep the matter in perspective. One way of doing that, they suggested, was to relate hospital costs to those of comparable service industries. Statler hotels, for example, had seen salaries and wages increase 200 percent from 1937 to 1949, and in hospitals the increase had been 230 percent. Income for both the hotels and the hospitals had increased 200 percent, while the number of guests in hotels increased 100 percent and the number of patients in hospitals increased 95.6 percent.

The wholesale price indices issued by the Bureau of Labor Statistics showed that, with 1926 as 100, all commodities in April 1941 showed an index of 83.2; by April 1951 the figure had increased to 183.5. Food increased 138 percent and textile products 125 percent. The purchasing power of the dollar in 1941 was $1.20, but by April 1951 it had fallen to 54 cents. "Increased cost of hospital care," the Endowment's staff argued, "is not out of line with increases in the cost of other services and commodities."[9]

Carl Rowland, like his more senior colleagues, acquired expertise about hospitals in many different areas. In 1960, however, when the America Hospital Association sponsored an institute on hospital design and construction, Rowland signed up, explaining that his primary responsibility was to work with hospital consultants, architects, owners, and administrators in developing hospital, nursing home, and nurse-residence projects. Since this work involving building and equipment took him all over two states, Rowland noted, it was important that he keep abreast of the latest thinking and development in the field. As a result of his thus keeping abreast, Rowland acquired a certain national reputation in a highly specialized field. For example, when a group of hospital planners in Ohio learned that the Hospital Section had systematically studied mistakes made in hospital construction and equipment, the Ohioans invited Rowland to speak to them. According to the *Toledo Blade's* account, Rowland emphasized, among other things, the need for hospitals to provide privacy for patients, since it was unproven that multiple-occupancy rooms could be served more cheaply than single-occupancy ones. After stressing the need for employing a competent hospital-planning consultant, the importance of site selection and room for expansion, and the use of automation and electronic techniques to reduce personnel costs, Rowland was reported to have "delved deeply into details such as sanitation techniques, communication and illuminating devices, and construction material and practices."[10] Rowland refused to let the Ohio group pay him either a fee or expenses, explaining that the Duke Endowment was interested in the health and welfare of the nation as well as in the Carolinas.

When a northern hospital planner asked if the Endowment had any figures showing trends about laboratory procedures and how they might affect planning, Rowland promptly supplied the data. Basing his figures on 136 assisted general hospitals in 1949 and 172 in 1959 (after the Hill-Burton hospital-building legislation had made its impact), Rowland reported that laboratory procedures per patient discharged (not including newborns) rose from 6.6 per patient in 1949 to 9.4 in 1959. Such a rising trend prompted Rowland to sound this cautionary note: "Architects and hospitals consultants are too prone to place diagnostic departments in locations that cannot give them expansion without moving the entire department to a new location." Not only was that quite expensive but it also often moved the department from a desirable traffic flow to and from the areas served.[11]

In 1954 Harris, Felts, and Rowland got help when Billy G. McCall joined the staff as the fourth field representative. A native of North Carolina and a graduate of Clemson University, he was a hospital administrator for several years prior to his employment by the Endowment. He too became widely recognized for expertise about hospitals; this is perhaps best suggested by the fact that when the managing editors of the *Modern Hospital,* published in Chicago, asked an official of the American Association of Hospital Administrators to recommend the best person to write an article on the role of the controller in reducing hospital expenses, the official suggested McCall. He performed the task, as he would many others like it.

Perhaps enough has been said to make clear that the Endowment's Hospital Section was not simply disbursing annual payments toward the cost of charity care in the Carolinas and helping to build and equip community hospitals. Not only did the staff of the section enter into a more or less permanent ongoing relationship with the beneficiary hospitals, but the Charlotte office also became a clearinghouse on hospital matters for the Carolinas as well as for a much larger area. Since examples of this are quite numerous, only a sampling will have to suffice. That doctors who wished to practice in the Carolinas and communities who needed them would turn to the Endowment's Charlotte office was a natural development that began early and long continued. Likewise, hospitals in need of administrators and those who sought such posts found the office always willing to help — and very much in a strategic position to do so.

As mentioned earlier, Wilburt C. Davison, dean of Duke University's medical school, had learned from Rankin about the need for well-trained hospital administrators, a relatively new professional field. As a result, Davison instituted the first such graduate program in the county when the Duke Hospital opened in 1930. By the late 1930s the program had grown and begun to include a three-month internship with the Hospital Section and some of the hospitals that it assisted. With the Endowment paying the expenses of the students, Rankin assured the Duke Hospital official in charge of the program that the Endowment wished to be of the greatest possible help to the young men in the program. Rankin and others on the staff took considerable time with and interest in "these boys," as Rankin called them, and one of them wrote Marshall Pickens that he and his fellow trainees deeply appreciated the "complete unselfishness" of the Endowment and its staff. The young man added that he could not help but catch the "infectious enthusiasm for hospital service" displayed by George Harris and Jim Felts.[12]

In addition to the administrative interns whom the Hospital Section helped train, an impressive number of foreign visitors found their way to the Char-

lotte office. Many were steered toward the Endowment by the United States
Public Health Service, the Rockefeller Foundation, and other such agencies;
one key reason was that the community hospitals in the still rural regions of
the Carolinas were closer to what many underdeveloped regions needed and
wanted than were the larger metropolitan hospitals of the nation. Some
foreign visitors began coming in the 1930s but more came after World War II.
In 1950, for example, there were eight official visitors — from China, Venezu-
ela, India, and the Philippines — who spent from a week to two months in the
Charlotte office and visiting hospitals in the area. The next year there were
another eight — four from South American countries, three from Japan, and
one from Greece.

The staff worked out a standard procedure for orienting the foreign visitors
and trying to show them the size and types of hospitals in which they were
most interested. Moreover, both the foreigners and the student interns got a
sampling of southern hospitality when staff members had them as dinner
guests in their homes and showed them various other kindnesses beyond the
call of duty.

The Hospital Section did not, of course, limit its assistance to foreigners to
those who physically visited Charlotte. For example, health officers in the
Netherlands needed data concerning the number of bacteriological examina-
tions performed in university hospitals of various sizes so that proper allocations of space, equipment, and staff could be made in a renovated facility.
When the Dutch officials asked for assistance in the matter from the United
States Public Health Service, the latter organization turned to the Hospital
Section. Using data from the three teaching hospitals it assisted, the Hospital
Section promptly supplied the needed information. For another example of
foreign service, a medical official in Chile sent a hospital plan that was being
considered for use there and requested advice. Rowland sent a careful, detailed critique that included such matters as the necessity of having the doors
of inner toilets swing out so that patients who fainted could be removed; the
need for double doors that are double acting at the entrances to the surgical
and obstetrical suites, with no traffic through the suites so that they could be
kept as sterile as possible; the need for an emergency room and entrance separate from any public or service entrance; and various other such matters. The
list could go on, but the point is that the Hospital Section freely shared both its
data, which had long been relatively unique, and the expertise of its staff.

Two national leaders in health care visited the Hospital Section and certain
of the assisted hospitals in the late 1930s, and the visits had important

repercussions. In 1936 and 1937 Rankin gave Thomas Parran, surgeon general of the United States Public Health Service, and Vane Hoge, the hospital
director of the same agency, a careful introduction to the Endowment's hospital program and the philosophy behind it. Then the two visitors traveled with
Rankin through parts of the Carolinas to see certain of the Endowment-
assisted community hospitals at firsthand.

There were many other agencies and groups that played a part in the
enactment in 1946 of the Hill-Burton Law, the federal government's program
to assist states and communities to build hospitals where they were most
needed. Rankin's ideas and the Endowment's hospital program, however,
were clearly a major influence. The American Hospital Association joined
Thomas Parran and others in making the strongest case possible for such a
program, with much of the intellectual and ideological groundwork being laid
during the war years. Appropriately enough, the Kellogg Foundation in Michigan sponsored an innovative, influential hospital program directed by
Graham Davis, and he also happened during the war years to chair the
American Hospital Association's organizing committee for a national hospital
study by the commission on health care. As Davis later explained, the Hill-
Burton legislation assisted the states first to make an inventory of their existing
hospitals and a survey of their hospitals needs; then the federal government,
giving preference to low-income and rural areas where the need was greatest,
assisted the states and communities to build new hospitals. One purpose, as
Rankin had emphasized back in the 1920s, was to help get doctors and nurses
into rural areas by providing them with adequate facilities.[13] When Congress
enacted amendments to the Hill-Burton Law in 1949, an official in the United
States Public Health Service wrote Rankin, "The Duke [Endowment] philosophy has served as a pattern for us working for this legislation."[14]

While the Endowment, through its Hospital and Orphan Section, clearly
had an influence and usefulness far beyond the Carolinas, its primary focus
was always, as James B. Duke intended, on the two Carolinas. Since African
Americans made up approximately half of South Carolina's population and
approximately one-third of North Carolina's when the Endowment began its
work, they were, quite naturally, important beneficiaries. J. B. Duke, following his father's spirit of friendly helpfulness toward the black minority, had
carefully stipulated in the indenture that the Endowment should extend assistance to all of the Carolinas' not-for-profit hospitals "whether white or colored," and he mandated the same policy toward "white or colored whole or
half orphans" in the Carolinas.

During the Endowment's first decade, this biracial policy resulted in its contributing well over $1.5 million directly to African American hospitals, orphanages, and a university (Johnson C. Smith). In addition to the last-named beneficiary, money went to ten hospitals in North Carolina, nine in South Carolina, two orphanages in North Carolina, and three in South Carolina.

The actual sums for African Americans were much larger, however, because out of 115 general hospitals aided in 1935, 74 admitted both white and African American patients. Although for the first two years of the Hospital Section's operation the days of free-bed care were not broken down by race, the 115 general hospitals cared for 29,500 African American patients, over 20,000 of whom were in hospitals that admitted both races. Moreover, all or practically all of the 65 hospital construction projects that the Endowment assisted during its first decade contained accommodations for both races.[15]

Much more than most observers at the time, Rankin, Davis, and others in the Hospital Section were keenly aware of the enormous problems involved in health care for African Americans. In response to a query in 1927, possibly from an officer of the Rosenwald Foundation, Rankin requested the superintendent of the Roper Hospital in Charleston, South Carolina, the largest hospital then assisted by the Endowment, to divide his patient days on a racial basis. The superintendent soon advised that he had 40,078 days of care for African American patients during 1926; 2,827 of the days were full pay, 33 were part pay, and 37,018 were free. Rankin also noted that 53 percent of Roper Hospital's days of care were given to African Americans but only 42 percent of the patients belonged to that racial group. The reason for that, Rankin explained, was that the average stay for the African American was 18.5 days, while the average stay for the white patient was 12.3 days. "This is explained by the fact," Rankin added, "that the black man is not particularly fond of hospitals and he usually waits until he is half dead before he will consent to go to a hospital," with the consequence that it took him longer to convalesce. Rankin also emphasized that 71 percent of Roper Hospital's free days were given to African Americans and noted that he thought that pattern would be true throughout the Carolinas. "As a consequence, I should say," Rankin added, "that approximately half of our contributions to hospitals is for the care of free and part pay colored patients."

Rankin believed that the problem of hospitalization for African Americans was both financial and educational and that hospital facilities would be provided as fast as some way could be found to pay for the care of African American patients and to educate them to use hospitals. To illustrate the latter need, he cited the report of an official of Charlotte's Good Samaritan Hospital, one of the oldest African American hospitals in the nation, who declared that there were "still Negroes in Charlotte who would rather be sent to the chain gang than to the hospital." They said, the official reported, "if we go to the hospital we will die — and if we die, they will let the doctor cut us up." Rankin drew the conclusion, somewhat defensively, that "the Negro is getting a fair share of the hospital care in the two states." He added, however, that "some Yankees, who have not yet fully recovered from the Civil War probably will not agree with this statement."[16]

A glimpse into the wide and uneven variety of hospital facilities available to North Carolina's African Americans may be obtained from a memorandum, which was probably written by Rankin in 1929. He and W. C. Davison led a visiting officer of the Julius Rosenwald Fund and several others on a tour of inspection. The group's first stop was at the 100-bed Saint Agnes Hospital in Raleigh, which was operated under the auspices of the Episcopal church. Rankin pointed out that while the plant was not as good as that of some other African American hospitals, he considered it "the best operated Negro hospital in the Carolinas." With both white and black physicians on the staff, it was accredited by the American College of Surgeons and ran a training school for nurses. Since the hospital hoped to build a much needed residence for nurses, Rankin explained that the Endowment would help with that, and he hoped the Rosenwald Fund "might be interested to a like extent." Saint Agnes Hospital, according to Rankin, not only provided "a great humanitarian service for the Negroes of a large territory," but it also served "as an admirable training school for colored nurses and doctors."

After visiting an Endowment-assisted African American hospital in Henderson, which is north of Raleigh, Rankin led the visitors to Roanoke Rapids, the home of the then novel group-hospitalization plan that so much interested Rankin and others. Twenty or so of the beds in the 100-bed hospital, Rankin noted, were reserved for African Americans. In Rocky Mount, another eastern North Carolina city, the group visited a 75-bed hospital that had been privately owned until three years earlier when it was reorganized as a community hospital and became a beneficiary of the Endowment. The provisions for about eighteen African American patients were of special interest, for a "corridor running back of the hospital for about fifty yards had been constructed and at the end of the corridor is a one-story wooden pavilion consisting for the most part of wards, in each of which three or four beds could be placed." The hospital tried to use African American nurses in the separate pavilion, but at the time of the group's visit one white and one black nurse were on duty.

In nearby Wilson a two-story wooden hospital for African Americans had provisions for twenty or twenty-five beds but operated with an average of from two to five patients. "It is the poorest excuse for a hospital that one could probably find anywhere," Rankin declared. "There is an apparent total absence of the sort of community interest that the hospital needs." Three nurses not only did most of the professional work but also, for much of the time, did the cooking and cleaning. The next day Rankin and Davison led the visitors to Durham to see Lincoln Hospital, which Benjamin and J. B. Duke had much earlier given to the African American community, and the new buildings for Duke University that were not yet completed.[17]

Like Rankin, Graham Davis grew to understand both the enormity and the larger societal significance of the African American health-care problem. In fact, Davis privately argued what he labeled as his "pet theory": that the general economic level in North Carolina, as well as in the rest of the South, would never "be raised much until we pay more attention to the education and health of the Negro and make him a more productive unit in society." Davis believed that the presence of African Americans in large numbers, especially in the eastern counties of North Carolina, tended "to drag the whole economic structure down . . . and the social structure to some extent." Davis well understood that what he was arguing, while he believed it to be painfully true, was not politically acceptable to the white majority of the 1930s. He emphasized, therefore, that he spoke not for the Endowment but as an individual who had been studying Carolina health problems for seven years or so.[18]

One reason for Davis's passionate belief in as low-cost group hospitalization rate as possible was his conviction that the South simply had too many poor people, especially but by no means exclusively African Americans, who could not afford to pay much. When Davis drew up a group-hospitalization plan for Mississippi in 1937, a plan that various national leaders in the hospital field applauded but that was too advanced for the Mississippi medical and hospital officials, he referred again to his "pet theory." This time, moreover, he asserted forthrightly that "the only way we are ever going to build up the earning capacity of the people as a whole is to start with the Negro, a very difficult thing to do I admit." The only way to increase the African American's earning capacity, Davis argued, was "to make him as healthy as he was as a slave and educate him, both difficult problems."[19]

Thanks to J. B. Duke, then, the Endowment at least grappled with, even if it could not solve, some of the most intractable social problems of that as well as the present era. Another area of social concern, one that is perhaps even more prominent in the 1990s than it was in the 1920s, is that of child care, the nurture of children who either have no families or whose families either cannot or will not function as such. Having known the loss of his own mother when he was less than two years old and having grown up in a family that took a great interest in the Oxford Orphanage, J. B. Duke stipulated that 10 percent of the annual income of his original trust fund should be used for "the benefit of white or colored whole or half orphans" who were in "organizations, institutions, agencies and/or societies" in the Carolinas. At another point further on in the indenture, he explained that he had included orphans "in an effort to help those who are most unable to help themselves." Duke added that while it was his opinion that nothing could take the place of a home and its influences, "every effort should be made to safeguard and develop these wards of society."

Although the word "orphanage" did not appear in the indenture, neither the term nor the concept that lay behind it had gone out of fashion in the Carolinas when J. B. Duke established the Endowment. In other parts of the country, however, institutionalized child care was increasingly frowned upon by social workers, pediatricians, and others. The highly favored alternative to the orphanage, with its no doubt unfair but popular connotations of the grim institutions Charles Dickens had so memorably portrayed in his novels, was foster care. As one medical historian has explained, government officials and child-serving professionals in the early decades of the twentieth century "developed the foster care ideal as a calculated, carefully reasoned response to the perceived failings of the children's institution or foundling home. Pediatricians, together with other professionals in the child-care field, had come to believe that "institutions for children posed insurmountable physical and emotional obstacles for rearing children."[20]

In preparing to establish the Endowment, as mentioned earlier, J. B. Duke requested Alexander Sands in 1923 to make a study of the orphanages in the Carolinas. In doing so, Sands turned to officials in the Child Welfare League of Americas in New York. They in turn requested Kate Burr Johnson, the first North Carolina commissioner of welfare and a member of the executive committee of the Child Welfare League, to assist in the matter. Sands himself visited North Carolina to inspect several orphanages at first hand and to confer with various leaders in the field there.

The long memorandum which Sands subsequently wrote for J. B. Duke is interesting not only for the light it sheds on the Carolinas' child-care situation in the early 1920s but also for the ideas that Sands obviously borrowed from prominent national leaders in child care. Unfortunately, J. B. Duke and W. R.

Perkins apparently did not carefully study Sands's memorandum, for the indenture would prove, at least for a time, to be more limited and restrictive in its approach than certain of Sands's ideas suggested was wise.

While Sands included many statistics in his report, he noted that there were many things that statistics alone did not bring out. Not surprisingly, he found first of all that the great majority of the Carolina institutions did not keep proper records for obtaining desired information and that there was no uniformity in what few records were kept. Some institutions investigated applicants who applied for admission, while others failed to do so.

Sands discerned a tendency on the part of some of the orphanages to enlarge the scope of their activity. For example, some were building or hoping to build baby cottages in order to admit quite young children, a field which, Sands believed, should be covered only by a state institution when a child was mentally defective and needed institutional care. He thought that all normal, healthy children of two or three years of age and younger could readily be placed in private homes, either by some charitable agency's paying their board or by providing for their adoption. Such a course of action would not only be less expensive than institutional care, he suggested, but would also give the child a chance to have the benefit of home life.

Sands noted that he had conferred with the state superintendent of the North Carolina Children's Aid Society in Greensboro as well as with officers of the Child Welfare League of America and that they all advocated child placement in homes instead of institutional care for normal, healthy children. Sands suggested that this was "a fertile field for help" such as J. B. Duke proposed to give to "orphan or otherwise dependent children" in the Carolinas. Sands was also encouraged by the fact that Kate Burr Johnson supported the principles of child placement and mother's aid. Moreover, the Baptist Orphanage of Thomasville, North Carolina, had recently joined the Child Welfare League and began a department of mother's aid.

"Mother's aid," Sands explained, was the assisting of mothers with children whom they were unable to support properly; "under the old scheme of things," such children [often half orphan?] would be placed in an orphanage, but mother's aid allowed the home to be kept intact. "It can readily be seen," Sands argued, "that this should not only prove to be cheaper than institutional care but much more satisfactory."

Concerning standards for child-care institutions, Sands said he knew no better source than a pamphlet of the Child Welfare League. It suggested that for admission there should be an intensive investigation (by a trained social worker?) to determine whether admission was the proper course for the particular case. The availability of assistance funds for mothers and the recognition of the value of the child's own home had to be considered, and there should be proper records to measure accomplishments.

As for the standards of care within the institution, there were a large number of considerations: (a) those who supervised children should be persons of good moral character who would be good examples for children "even though they are serving in humble capacities"; (b) all buildings of two or more stories should have fire escapes; (c) adequate provision for both artificial and natural light; (d) children should sleep with windows open and should have sufficient clothing to keep warm; (e) proper water supply regularly analyzed; (f) play room with proper toys, books, and so forth; (g) dining room preferably with tables for not more than eight or ten children, with proper equipment; (h) single beds with sufficient linen and blankets so that they could be kept clean and changed often; (i) proper facilities for bathing, with separate towels, wash clothes, combs, toothbrushes, and so forth; (j) separate hospital and isolation quarters; (k) articles of clothing individually marked and preferably not uniform; (l) proper supervision of weight, height, health, and diet; (m) good food, plenty of water, and so forth; (n) whenever possible, children should go out to [public] schools rather than attend school within the institution, and the course of study should include vocational training and/or domestic science; while children should be assigned definite tasks within the institution and those varied from time to time, they should also be given a chance to play under proper supervision, and older children should be given a chance to earn something so that they may learn the use of money; (o) "natural punishment should be employed, accompanied in each case with a clear explanation of what the offense has been . . ."; (p) children should have proper religious training and be sent to Sunday school and church; (q) "The institutional life should conform as near as possible to a normal family home."

As for standards concerning discharge from the institution, a trained representative should carefully investigate potential foster homes and keep complete records. The homes should be visited at least three times a year and, additionally, whenever the needs of the children demanded.

In order to determine whether an institution was eligible for support from the Endowment, Sands thought—and he was far too optimistic and idealistic here—the orphanage should be required to answer a questionnaire which would indicate whether it met the above standards. This should be followed up by a personal visit to each institution. There should also be prescribed a uniform system of accounts and records, with a regular audit of same by a public accountant or someone representing the trustees of the Endowment.

Turning to the North Carolina orphanages, Sands called attention to the fact that 31.51 percent of all the children in them were full orphans. Since he had learned that the national average for full orphans in child-care institutions was around 9 or 10 percent, North Carolina seemed to be unusual in that respect. Some of the Carolina institutions were fortunate in being well supported by the church groups or other organizations that sponsored them; some had the capacity for more children than they had funds to care for; and some had long waiting lists.

Sands reported that a number of institutions in their correspondence with him had intimated that they would like to have funds for expansion. He understood, however, that it was "not part of your program to go into this phase of the matter, nor do I think it necessary if they would pay more attention to the matter of mother's aid and child placing." He urged support for the Children's Home Society of North Carolina, which covered the state. It maintained a temporary-care home in Greensboro for about fifty children and had on its board of directors prominent people from across the state. Having placed over 2,000 children since its establishment some two decades earlier, it employed four social workers who traveled over the state in Ford cars, visiting the various homes of 1,100 children at that time.

Sands wrote that he could go into detail about the stated needs of each individual orphanage, but he hardly thought that necessary in this particular report. After J. B. Duke had studied the statistics and selected "such as you would care to cover I would then make a more detailed report on each one, possibly after having made a personal visit to them."

As for the South Carolina institutions, he noted that there were fewer of them than in North Carolina. The general comments concerning the North Carolina orphanages, however, applied as well to the South Carolina ones. Too, the Child Placing Bureau of South Carolina's public welfare board had recently joined the Child Welfare League.[21]

Unfortunately, despite all of Alexander Sands's careful labors, J. B. Duke apparently never read the long memorandum. Many years later, someone who had been working in the New York offices of the Child Welfare League in 1923 recalled Sands's request for help and remembered that for two months or so league officials, including Kate Burr Johnson, exerted themselves to draw up a comprehensive proposal for J. B. Duke's consideration. Then months passed with no word from Sands until one day (late in 1924?) he telephoned in some distress to say that "he had not been able to get the old gentleman [J. B. Duke] to read" the memorandum before the indenture was all drawn up.[22]

One result of J. B. Duke's and W. R. Perkins' failure to study Sands's memorandum (and, possibly, related documents) was that the indenture seemed, at least for a while, effectively to restrict Endowment support to "white or colored whole or half orphans" in "properly operated" institutions or organizations in the Carolinas. The trustees were given here, as elsewhere in the indenture, "uncontrolled discretion" as to selecting the institutions or organizations and determining the amount of support. Rankin and the other trustees of the Endowment no doubt spent considerable time reading and rereading the section of the indenture containing the 10 percent for the full and half orphans. The entire paragraph consists of one quite long sentence containing no less than 149 words and is a good example of the legalese so beloved by W. R. Perkins and other lawyers of his era.

Despite the seemingly restrictive language, the trustees would gradually — too gradually in the case of at least one trustee, as will be discussed — move toward a more flexible or expansive interpretation of the indenture as far as the full and half orphans were concerned. Finally, at a later date, the section's name could quite legitimately be changed to Hospital and Child Care Section.

Ironically, the foster-care alternative to institutionalization that was so widely and strongly pushed in the early decades of the twentieth century has lost much of its appeal by the closing decades. The medical historian mentioned earlier points out that many professional groups that work with children have come to criticize the foster-care system rather severely. The lack of routine health care for children in foster homes, the inability for a child to develop emotionally in a rotating system of foster homes, the difficulty social workers face in providing adequate supervision of children in foster care, a long history of unsuccessful rehabilitation programs — all these and other problems have led to the widespread recognition, as the historian declares, that foster care "is clearly not working as its architects had hoped."[23]

At any rate, when the time arrived for the first distribution of payments in support of the orphans, Rankin and his fellow trustees opted for the simplest and easiest route: across-the-board payment of an equal amount in support of all institutionalized orphans and half orphans in the Carolinas. Not all of the orphanages, of course, were truly "properly operated," as Rankin well knew. But most were doing the best they could with the resources available; denying assistance to the weaker orphanages would certainly not help the children there; and Rankin's idea, which the other trustees obviously shared, was that the Endowment would simply try, as best it could, to help all of the institutions do better and, as in the hospital field, strive gradually and quietly to raise standards. In April 1926, therefore, Rankin reported that there were 4,767 whole and half orphans in institutions in the Carolinas and that there was about $63,200 available for distribution in their support. The trustees authorized Rankin to pay each institution $10 per orphan or half orphan and explain that a small additional payment might soon be made.

In the first two or three years of the Endowment's existence, Rankin and Graham Davis were obviously overextended, and the orphanage wing of the section probably did not receive full attention. The addition of Marshall Pickens to the staff in 1928 helped in that respect, and, while he was also involved with hospitals, he took over, under Rankin's general supervision, much of the work with the orphanages. Studying at one point at Columbia University's school of social work, Pickens soon joined various national organizations that dealt with child-related matters, such as the Child Welfare League and the National Conference of Social Work, and gradually acquired a certain expertise in the field, just as Graham Davis had done concerning hospitals.

Working with the assistance of national welfare agencies and in consultation with representatives from the Carolinas orphanages, Rankin and Pickens designed uniform business and social-service records that were used by all the assisted institutions. In other words, the Endowment used the applications for assistance from the orphanages to gather comparative data just as it did with the hospitals, although the orphanages obviously did not generate the type of valuable medical or clinical data that the hospitals did. Rankin and Pickens divided the orphanages into groups according to size, race, and type of care; this meant that the average cost of an individual institution could be compared with the average cost of the group. The reports allowed comparisons to be made of fourteen principal items of expense at an institution, along with comparisons of the cost during the current year with that of the previous year. According to both Pickens and Rankin, numerous directors and trustees of the orphanages stated that the comparative information was of even greater value to their work than the actual money received from the Endowment.

The money was not to be sneezed at, however, especially during the grim years of the Great Depression. In 1936 Pickens gave a broad overview of the Endowment's work with the child-caring institutions from 1925 through 1935 and began by admitting that the trustees had loosely interpreted the indenture's phrase concerning support for "properly operated" institutions. He insisted that by assisting practically every child-caring institution in the

Carolinas, the Endowment had helped those that were below standard to improve and had, in some cases, encouraged additional support from other sources. "Almost without exception," Pickens declared, "the standard of work has been raised in spite of adverse economic conditions."

To get at the quality of service rendered at an institution, Pickens and others in the section worked with representatives from the orphanages to design a method of evaluating the work on a numerical basis. Using 1,000 points as a total, the Endowment assigned 250 points for social service (meaning trained social workers), 125 to housing, 100 to food, 75 to clothing, 115 to education, 85 to health, 150 to moral and religious training, and 100 to financial records. Out of thirty North Carolina institutions in 1931, when the system was still new, the Endowment rated thirteen as having over 800 points; thirteen as having between 600 and 800 points; and three with fewer than 600 points. Of sixteen South Carolina institutions, it ranked nine as having over 800 points; four between 600 and 800 points; and three with fewer than 600 points. In North Carolina, only one institution, the Presbyterian Orphan's Home at Barium Springs, received the full 250 points for social service, and, though Pickens did not say so, that was probably one of the weaker areas for many of the other institutions.

The point should also be emphasized that the Endowment went to great lengths to avoid embarrassing any individual institution. While it shared group comparisons with all institutions in the group, the Endowment carefully avoided naming individual orphanages, just as was also done with the hospital data.

Basing assistance on the number of days of care given to orphan and half-orphan children, the Endowment, from 1925 through 1935, contributed a total of $1,294,150 to fifty-one child-caring institutions. Of these, thirty-three were in North Carolina and eighteen in South Carolina. The average annual contribution during the eleven years was $117,650, which Pickens figured to be the income from approximately $3 million at 4 percent interest.

The Endowment's contribution averaged 6 percent of the total contributions received by the institutions during the period, and the Endowment was the only organization from which all of the institutions received aid. In 1935 the Endowment contribution varied from 14 percent of the total contributions at the African American institutions to 1 percent at certain of the others. In 1933, when the total contributions to forty-six institutions were the smallest reported during the period, the Endowment's contribution was the largest and amounted to 10 percent, thus helping most when the need was greatest. In other words, Pickens explained, while the Endowment contributions were a small part of the money necessary for the operations of the institutions, the Endowment had helped to develop new services at some of them, and at others it had allowed services to be continued during the depression, services which might otherwise have been discontinued.

Pickens summarized the Endowment's first decade or so of service to the child-caring institutions in this manner: (1) the development of uniform financial and social records; (2) the establishment of a clearinghouse of information about the best practices in the operation of child-caring institutions; (3) the creation of tentative minimum standards of institutional child care; and (4) an annual contribution amounting to an average 6 percent of the total contributions received by the institutions from all sources.[24]

The record is by no means complete on the matter, but one person who apparently wanted to see the Endowment move more quickly to a broader, more flexible interpretation of the indenture's provisions for child care was Doris Duke. The minutes of the Endowment's trustees, as will be discussed subsequently, were designed primarily for lawyers and accountants, not for historians. That is, the minutes record action taken, appropriations made, and other such formal steps but give no information about discussion or possible dissension. There are clues, however, that point to an early and ongoing effort on the part of Doris Duke to bring about changes in the child care policies.

As J. B. Duke had requested in the indenture, on November 22, 1933, when Doris Duke became twenty-one years old, the trustees elected her a trustee. While she was present for that occasion, she apparently did not attend another meeting of the trustees, who met ten times a year, until June 30, 1936. That initial, long absence from the trustee meetings suggests one of the problems about Doris Duke's problematical relationship with the Duke Endowment: while in later years she would have occasional spurts of better attendance at meetings, she tended always to be rather spasmodic in her involvement. At least, that is what the bare facts of the minutes suggest. She was, however, a quite young woman in 1933, and, along with much socializing and travel, she married James Cromwell in February, 1935, and took off on an extended tour around the world. A few months after their return, Doris Duke Cromwell and her close friend and secretary, Marian Paschal, went in April 1936 on an automobile trip to the Carolinas. Traveling incognito, they visited several of the institutional beneficiaries of the Endowment, including certain hospitals, at least one orphanage (and possibly more), and Duke University, where they spent several days in a campus dormitory.

When Mrs. Cromwell again attended a meeting of the Endowment's trustees in June 1936, she reported, undoubtedly at the urging of Allen and Perkins, on her visit to the Carolina institutions. More importantly, she had even earlier begun independent efforts to try to shake things up a bit in the child-care field in the Carolinas.

Fiercely private despite the incredible amount of unwanted publicity she received throughout the 1930s, Doris Duke, even before she married Cromwell, set up her own carefully anonymous charitable organization, Independent Aid, Incorporated. (In the 1950s she changed the tax-free organization's name to the Doris Duke Foundation.) With Marian Paschal as the executive secretary, Independent Aid contributed to an unknown number of causes, but one important one was the medical center at Duke University. One of the urgent needs of the Duke Hospital in its early days was an adequate social service division, and Dean Davison in 1937 persuaded Mrs. Cromwell to provide an anonymous gift to get such a program started and sustained.

Exactly how or when one of the world's richest young women became interested in social work, particularly as related to child care, is not known. Moreover, she hid her tracks as carefully and completely as she could. Marian Paschal may have been one source of the interest, for when she died in the early 1950s, an anonymous donor, who was undoubtedly Doris Duke (who regained her maiden name after a bitter divorce from Cromwell in the early 1940s), gave a fellowship in Paschal's memory to Columbia University's school of social work. One of the interesting stipulations of the fellowship was that the holder of it should come from outside the New York metropolitan area and agree to work in a section of the country (such as the Carolinas?) where professionally trained social workers were most needed.[25]

At any rate, one institution which Doris Duke Cromwell and Marian Paschal visited in 1936 was the Connie Maxwell Orphanage in Greenwood, South Carolina. Of all the Endowment-assisted orphanages, Pickens in the early 1930s thought Connie Maxwell had the best social-service system. Even before 1936, however, an official in the Child Welfare League in New York, C. C. Carstens, wrote the superintendent of Connie Maxwell, and one can only wonder if Independent Aid may have inspired the letter. It argued, at any rate, that children's work in the Carolinas was not developing normally, except in certain unusually good spots (such as Connie Maxwell). Carstens feared that the Duke Endowment did not have the opportunity, because of its legal limitations and the almost exclusively institutional work in the Carolinas, to render the service that the League had hoped for from the Endowment.

He went on to say that many of the Carolinas' institutions contained a large number of full orphans, which fact suggested that many of them should be adopted into good homes; there were also large numbers of half orphans whose fathers were dead, suggesting that there was a need for the development of more extensive plans for mother's aid programs. Pickens had assured Carstens that there was no Endowment requirement that children should remain in institutional care and that the Endowment was interested in the most approved type of care for the orphans and half orphans. Carstens had replied that in that case, the League or some other agency might work with one of the "more progressive" institutions in the Carolinas to demonstrate what the development of a more complete program might mean, and he hoped to confer soon with the superintendent of the Connie Maxwell Orphanage.[26]

Doris Duke's marriage and world tour in 1935 may have interrupted the effort to produce some child-care changes in the Carolinas. Late in that year, however, the same officer of the Child Welfare League, C. C. Carstens, wrote North Carolina's director of charities and public welfare that he considered that the state's rate of institutional care of children, 94 percent, very high and, in fact, unbalanced. He stated that New Mexico was the only state with a higher percentage. The League's study had revealed, Carstens wrote, that North Carolina's institutionalized children included 25 percent full orphans and 47 percent whose fathers were dead but whose mothers were living. In contrast, Minnesota's institutions had only 6 percent full orphans and 11 percent whose fathers were dead and whose mothers were living; Wisconsin and Massachusetts both had 5 percent and 10 percent in the two categories.

Carstens noted that he had held further conversations with Marshall Pickens. While Pickens had been sympathetic, he explained that the Endowment's policy was to avoid trying to tell the beneficiary institutions what they should do and that a request for a demonstration of what social service could do for the children in institutional care would have to come from the institutions themselves. That would be fine, Carstens concluded, but he feared it was unlikely.[27]

Unlikely or not, Doris Duke Cromwell, when she once again turned her mind to the problem, set about to get things moving. The superintendent of the Connie Maxwell Orphanage, A. T. Jamison, was attending a summer institute or workshop for orphanage personnel at Duke University in August 1937. (It was one of a long, annual series of such workshops that the Endowment sponsored.) Dean Davison summoned Jamison and explained that Mrs. Cromwell had telephoned from her home in Somerville, New Jersey, and wanted Davison, Rankin, and Jamison to come there for a conference. They immediately went and spent a full day at Duke's Farms, the vast estate that J. B. Duke had begun creating in the 1890s, with her, Marian Paschal, and one other woman.

Jamison recalled that Mrs. Cromwell stated that she might, under certain conditions, help supply high-quality social casework service to any child-care institution in the Carolinas which might wish to have it. She referred several times to her visit to Connie Maxwell and explained that she wanted to help other institutions introduce "extramural care" of children. She requested Rankin to prepare a memorandum on the matter, which he agreed to do.

After returning to Charlotte, however, Rankin and Pickens decided that for the Endowment to lead in the matter was not desirable. Pickens, therefore, requested Jamison to secure a representative committee from the orphanages to shape the proposal, which he promptly did. He also turned to the Child Welfare League in New York for help, reporting that he had recently met with a group of seven executives of children's institutions and all approved of what Mrs. Cromwell wanted to do. Interestingly enough, the same group had turned down such a proposal from the league in 1934.[28]

In the 1937 memorandum prepared, as requested by Jamison, by the officer of the Child Welfare League, Carstens repeated various points that he had made in statements that have been discussed previously. There was an interesting new angle, however, concerning the Social Security laws that had recently been enacted. By means of Aid to Dependent Children, Carstens explained, there was now a new emphasis on keeping children in their own homes or those of a relative and in foster-family homes when other than their own homes were needed. The new laws were beginning to affect the populations of institutions in the Carolinas, for applications for children whose fathers were dead but whose mothers were living were beginning to fall off. The proportion of full orphans was also slowly declining since people tended to live longer as the century progressed. There were, however, additional children in the Carolinas who needed care, Carstens noted, since the Endowment had reported in 1936 that 1,451 children had been refused admission to child-care institutions and 959 children were on waiting lists.

Carstens went on to emphasize that a well-established principle for all child-care institutions and agencies was that they should be fully equipped with social service, that is social workers. They were important in the careful selection of those who needed to be provided for outside their own homes; for the light that could be thrown upon the individual child's development and his or her relationship to the family; and, eventually, for the children's proper read-justment back into their own families or into other homes in the community.

A proper social-service program in the Carolinas could be done on a limited, demonstration basis at first, he suggested, but might have a far-reaching effect. Carstens thought that the salary for the type of experienced social workers that were needed might run from $2,000 to $2,400 per year, and that, if there were three institutions selected in North Carolina and two in South Carolina, the program director's salary might range from $3,600 to $4,500. There should be an executive committee of five or so persons representing the institu-tions, and Mrs. Cromwell and Marian Paschal should be asked to serve on the committee. Carstens also suggested that a consultant from the Child Welfare League might be helpful. In all, he estimated that the cost for the five social workers, their automobiles, and clerical help would be about $24,000 and for the director and support staff about $8,450.[29]

Pickens, Rankin, Jamison, and others made slight modifications in Car-stens's draft, suggesting, among other things, that the participating institu-tions should pay at least a third of the costs. There was even correspondence between Marian Paschal and Rankin in October 1937 suggesting that Mrs. Cromwell was considering another inspection trip to the Carolinas. Unfortu-nately, however, the records in the Endowment archives stop abruptly at that point, and what, if anything, ever came of all the negotiations and plans for more social work and more "extramural care" is not known.

The main point, however, is quite clear: Doris Duke was particularly inter-ested in child care, clearly more than in other aspects of the Endowment's activity, and the focus of her concern was on the need for more social work and something beyond, or at least in addition to, institutional care.

The Endowment's trustees did, in fact, in 1944 begin a long, steady process of loosening or liberalizing its policies in the child-care area. Since W. R. Perkins, the vice-chairman of the Endowment and chief author of the inden-ture, became ill late in 1942, he steadily lessened his involvement with the Endowment from that time until his death in June 1945. One has to wonder, at least, if he may not have interpreted his 149-word, one-sentence paragraph concerning the provision for child care in the indenture to mean that funds could be given only in support of institutionalized orphans and half orphans. Others read the marathon sentence differently, but Perkins could be quite adamant in defending his viewpoint; moreover, as J. B. Duke's chief counsel, no one, except perhaps George C. Allen, could speak with greater authority about the donor's intentions.

At any rate, in May 1944 the trustees, acting in response to the report of Rankin and his committee, and after discussion on the matter in earlier meetings, voted to pay the same per diem amount for orphans and half orphans placed by and under the supervision of orphanages in foster or boarding homes as was paid for orphans and half orphans in the institutions themselves. Interestingly enough, Doris Duke, a member of Rankin's committee, was present for this meeting as she had been also for the trustees' meeting in March 1944.

In Rankin's report to the trustees he explained that 99 percent of the funds used in the Carolinas for the care of children outside of orphanages came from the combined contributions of federal and state-county agencies. This Aid for Dependent Children program, in other words, provided homes for dependent children either with a parent or close relatives. In addition, North Carolina provided an additional fund, contingent upon financial participation by the county, for the care of dependent children in homes other than the homes of relatives (i.e., foster homes).

Rankin noted that three of the forty orphanages assisted by the Endowment provided foster-home care: The Baptist Orphanage of North Carolina had eighty-three children in such a program, the Presbyterian Orphan's Homes in North Carolina had eleven, and the Connie Maxwell Orphanage in South Carolina had seventy-six. The superintendent of the Baptist Orphanage of North Carolina, according to Rankin, believed that the orphanages should venture further into the field of foster-home care and considered what his institution had already done along that line "the best welfare work we have done in recent months and years."

Some other superintendents disagreed with that viewpoint, Rankin admitted, but the superintendent of the Connie Maxwell Orphanage pointed out that the average institution had a shrinking number of children from reasonably stable homes seeking admission. "But we are faced in a tremendously serious way," this superintendent declared, "with the need to care for children from disrupted or unhappy home situations." Describing a condition that would grow more and more widespread and serious as the years passed, this superintendent noted that frequently one or both parents were living but were "utterly inadequate and unable to carry on in a decent way in the matter of supervision and care of the child." This meant that many of the children who came to the orphanages were "more difficult to care for" and had "so frequently been damaged in their basic security in life that they are inclined to strike out at the world which has hurt them."[30]

While the Endowment's work with the orphanages lacked the medical dimension and technological complexity of the work with hospitals, human lives were just as much involved, albeit in a different way. Yet the trustees faced a difficult task in conveying to the public precisely what the Endowment, particularly in the Hospital and Orphan Section, was all about. From the beginning, unlike many later, less reputable and less conscientious tax-free foundations, the Endowment published a full, carefully prepared annual report that disclosed in detail the appropriations that had been made and the source of all available funds. In other words, the trustees of the Endowment ran a tight ship, and full public disclosure of the financial records and activities was the norm from the beginning.

Yet the annual reports, often highly statistical, were not exactly easy or light reading, and the larger issues involved in health care or child care were generally obscured or not even addressed. Too, by its very nature, the annual report covered one year's activities, and that made it difficult for a reader to discern long-range trends or even to see the larger picture. The bigger daily newspapers as well as the smaller weekly papers regularly carried stories about the appropriations made by the Endowment, but these tended to be repetitious recitals of sums given to various beneficiaries.

The trustees believed that having the public understand what the Endowment was all about was important, and especially so in the 1930s. Since tax-free charitable organizations had uniquely flourished in the United States after 1900 or so as a byproduct of capitalism, it followed that, when capitalism fell under attack from various quarters as it did during the 1930s, so too were the appropriateness and efficacy of the private foundations questioned. Many powerful people, especially in Franklin D. Roosevelt's New Deal administration, deeply believed that the federal government, sometimes acting in cooperation with state governments and sometimes acting alone, could do a better, fairer job of solving social problems with the taxpayers' money than could the tax-free charitable organizations.

Aside from this general, somewhat philosophical but nevertheless quite real matter of the intellectual climate, there was a particular problem in the 1930s about investor-owned public utilities. Looking back from the 1990s, one can see that the Tennessee Valley Authority, the Roosevelt administration's giant foray into government-owned and taxpayer-funded electric-power generation (among many other aspects of the TVA) turned out to be something of a solo venture or an exception. In the 1930s, however, that was by no means clear, and the trustees of the Endowment, which was the principal owner of the

Duke Power Company, joined other investor-owned utilities in anathematiz-
ing the TVA and its architects.

The Duke Endowment became even more directly involved in a battle with
the Roosevelt administration when Greenwood County, South Carolina, applied to the Public Works Administration for a loan of $2.6 million in order to
build an electric-power plant on the Saluda River. Since that was in the heart
of territory served by the Duke Power Company, George Allen, W. R. Perkins,
Norman Cocke, and others who controlled both the Endowment and Duke
Power were understandably irate when they learned through the newspapers
that the Board of Public Works, chaired by Secretary of the Interior Harold
Ickes, had voted four to two in favor of making the loan.

Allen immediately wrote to Ickes protesting the loan and requesting that
Duke Power be given at least a hearing. Perkins informed the Endowment
trustees about the matter at their meeting in June 1934 and argued that
the loan created a precedent for the granting of similar loans by the Public
Works Administration to every municipality that might apply; that the Duke
Power Company, which had to pay taxes, could not compete with municipally
owned and operated power plants that could borrow government money at
low rates of interest and pay no taxes; and that the consequent reduction of
income of the Duke Power Company would reduce the amount available for
distribution to the beneficiaries of the Endowment. The trustees, therefore,
authorized Allen and Perkins to advise all the beneficiary institutions about
the matter and to take such steps in opposition to Greenwood County's application as they considered wise.

In Allen's letter to the beneficiaries and a similar letter to the *New York
Times,* which gave considerable coverage to the matter, he began by quoting
from that portion of the indenture where J. B. Duke explained his plan to have
the revenues from the water-power development (Duke Power Company) used
for the "social welfare" of the people in the territories served just as the developments themselves promoted their "economic welfare." Allen noted that
since the Endowment's establishment, it had paid over $19 million to the bene-
ficiaries, nearly 58 percent of which had come from securities of Duke Power.
"The Federal Government," he warned, "is pursuing policies which, unless
abandoned, will seriously cripple, if not destroy, the Duke Power Company."

Allen then gave the background of the Greenwood County matter and
stated that various officials and boards in Washington had refused to give the
representatives of Duke Power a hearing prior to the approval of the loan
application by Ickes's board. After protest from Allen, Perkins, and others,

however, Ickes finally consented to have his committee on electric power hear the representatives of Duke Power. "Unfortunately, however, we cannot feel sure that the merits of the matter will prevail," Allen continued. "We say this because of the well-known views of the element in the present Administration which is positive and outspoken in the belief that the government should own and operate the utilities."

Allen's letter went on to argue, as Perkins had to the trustees, that no private utility could compete with a government-backed utility that had ample, cheap capital at its disposal and which functioned without the burden of taxes and code restriction (referring to the codes of the National Recovery Act). "Therefore, government can easily use its revenues to destroy private utilities," Allen declared, "if it chooses to do so." He wondered why the government should use its revenues from taxpayers to duplicate and thus ruin private businesses in whose securities immense private funds had been invested. "Such a course is destruction," he insisted, "which makes for depression, not recovery."

Allen pointed out that electric rates were regulated by commissions chosen by the people in the various states. Why, then, was there a need for government ownership in the utility field? Conduct of the utilities by the government, he warned, would only augment bureaucracy and increase the public debt and taxation. Then in conservative words that would probably find a larger and more appreciative audience in the 1990s than they did in 1934, Allen concluded by saying that government ownership "kills private initiative, which alone accomplishes true permanent progress and prosperity." Did not history reveal that such had "been the record of all nations which have thus enhanced government by the suppression of the individual?"

In Allen's letter to the *New York Times,* he also pointed out that some 30 percent of the federal funds for the Greenwood County project would be given outright while the balance would be lent at long term at 4 percent interest. While the Greenwood project would pay no taxes, out of every dollar collected by Duke Power in South Carolina, twenty-seven cents were paid out in taxes. Moreover, Duke Power, in response to the depression, had voluntarily abandoned contract minimums for large industrial users of its power and made rate reductions at an annual aggregate cost of $2.5 million. "But existence, not rates," Allen insisted, "is at stake."[31]

J. B. Duke in the indenture had failed to indicate that not all, just a large majority, of the profits from the Duke Power Company would be used for charitable purposes. While the Doris Duke Trust would end up owning a great deal less of the Duke Power stock than did the Endowment, the private trust for J. B. Duke's daughter and close kinfolk did own a sizable block of the stock. Allen, following J. B. Duke's lead, also failed to present the full story, and this lack of complete candor played into the hands of Harold Ickes and his allies.

In 1935, as the controversy about the Greenwood County power plant filled the newspapers and led to a marathon legal battle, Ickes authored *Back to Work: The Story of PWA* and devoted several pages to his version of the matter. Casting all operators of utility companies in the mold of the notorious Samuel Insull, whose utility empire had crashed in 1932 in one of the largest corporate failures up to that time, Ickes declared that if private utility operators were having a difficult time during the depression, they had "only themselves to blame." They were all "greedily selfish," he charged, and lacking in intelligence. "And if the people can protect themselves from corruption and subversive influences and at the same time supply themselves with power at rates equal to or lower than those charged by private utilities," Ickes asked, "what reasonable argument is there against the right of the public to own and operate their utilities?" (The Duke Power Company, incidentally, was not involved in Samuel Insull's mammoth scheme.)

Turning to the Greenwood County matter, Ickes saw the controversy as "typical of the resistance put up by the private companies to public ownership of the utilities." He noted that the city of Greenwood, the largest in the county, owned its own distribution system but purchased electricity from a Duke Power subsidiary. The rural areas were without electricity (though that would soon be changed by the New Deal's Rural Electrification Administration), and the local textile companies obtained power from their own steam plants. Only 21 percent of the total power proposed to be sold, according to Greenwood County's application, was then being furnished by Duke Power. The political leaders in South Carolina, including the two Democratic senators, had endorsed the project. Suddenly, however, "the Duke Endowment began a noisy protest, asserting, in effect, that the modest Greenwood County project would bring starvation and ruin to the hospitals, schools, orphanages, and churches supported in part by it in both South and North Carolina."

Ickes explained that the "Endowment leaders' devastating picture of impending doom" led the Public Works Administration (PWA), which had earlier approved the application, to send the project to the electric power board of review for closer study. There, he claimed, it was discovered that the Duke Endowment, the Doris Duke Trust, and the Duke Power Company "were so inextricably tied together that only a lawyer of unusual ability could unravel the legal skein into which they have been so skillfully intertwined." On the surface, Ickes argued, "it appeared that only the finer humanitarianism of the Dukeites was pained by the prospect of lower rates to the people." George Allen had led the protest in his capacity as chairman of the Duke Endowment not as president of the Duke Power Company and was simply playing a "Jekyll-Hydeian role." (That Ickes would compare the presidency of a business corporation with the fiendish side of Robert Louis Stevenson's famed character is interesting.)

If Ickes had limited his attack to the fact that the profit from Duke Power did not, in actuality, all go to charitable purposes, he would have scored a point. That was not sufficient for him, however, and he distorted the truth by declaring that only "a relatively small amount of the power profits goes to charity" and that the Doris Duke Trust owned more Duke Power shares and thus received more dividends than did the Endowment. The Duke Power Company, Ickes concluded, "was making a practical application of the old adage that 'Charity covers a multitude of sins.' " Hiding behind "the flimsy skirts of its own philanthropy," Duke Power was raising "a tremendous fuss" over the potential loss of an insignificant amount of its business.

Although the board of review, as Allen had feared, approved the PWA grant-loan, it did require that Greenwood County should gain clearance from the South Carolina courts to issue revenue bonds for the purpose of building a power plant. When the state's top court, rejecting the arguments of the Duke lawyers, gave the go-ahead signal to the project, the Duke interests asked the federal courts for an injunction, and Ickes's account ends with the statement that the "courts have not yet decided this question."[32]

Duke Power did, as a result of its efforts in federal court, gain temporarily the injunctive relief it sought in 1935, but the United States Supreme Court late in 1936 ordered that the case be retried in the lower courts. The whole matter dragged on until December 1937, when the case was again before the Supreme Court. "Bare of legal technicalities," as the *New York Times* reported, the point of the case was "whether the [federal] government was legally entitled to finance municipal power plants in competition with private business." Restating arguments that Allen and Perkins had earlier made, the counsel for the Duke interests, W. S. O'B. Robinson, was described as "waving his arms and shouting," when Chief Justice Charles E. Hughes leaned forward and said with a smile, "Will you restrain your voice? It will help your argument." Although Robinson reportedly spoke less vehemently thereafter, that did not, in the end, help his case, for the Supreme Court ruled unanimously against the arguments Robinson had advanced and in favor of the government's program to lend and grant money to municipal electric plants even in competition with private enterprises. Secretary Ickes happily declared that the Court's action had ended a three-year fight and released $109.7 million to sixty-one projects being held up by injunctions in twenty-three states.[33]

Even though Supreme Court decisions were not made in response to public opinion, the Endowment's trustees clearly felt the need to inform a larger audience as to what the Duke Endowment was all about in the early years of the New Deal. Accordingly, in 1934 the trustees contracted with a well-known filmmaking company, Pathé News, to make a movie about the work of the Endowment. Although the Pathé people estimated that an appropriate film could be made at a cost of from $15,000 to $18,000, the trustees authorized the committee on public information to spend up to $25,000 if necessary on the making and showing of it.

Watson Rankin appeared as the chief narrator in "The Trail of the Circuit Rider" and, with the probable help of Graham Davis and others, may have been the person who arranged the story. It was inspired by oft-quoted words of J. B. Duke: "Whatever I amount to in life is due to my old daddy and he always said whatever he amounted to was due to the [Methodist] Circuit Riders." With "The Bells of St. Mary's" as opening music, the film began with a voice-over introduction by George C. Allen. He explained that several generations ago preachers on horseback visited country churches and homes to preach the gospel, emphasizing that their hearers should "Bear ye one another's burdens." Allen added that, while the pioneer circuit riders had passed from the scene, "there has sprung up in the trails which they blazed, churches, hospitals, schools and orphanages, ministering to the needs of the human race."

No professional actors were used in the film, but as a device to move the story along and link the various portions together, Marshall Pickens, then still a young and handsome ex-football player, played the role of the silent preacher on horseback. In the film, he rode up to the modest, frame farmhouse which Washington Duke had built in 1852, later known as the Duke Homestead, and Rankin briefly explained how Washington Duke had returned home penniless from the Civil War and soon proceeded to launch his family into the home manufacture of smoking tobacco. The focus shifted quickly to the youngest child, J. B. Duke, his rapid rise in the tobacco industry, then his dominant role in the creation of the Duke Power Company, and finally his establishment of the Duke Endowment.

Appropriately enough in light of the family's early involvement with the

Oxford Orphanage, the circuit rider next went there, where the superintendent presented Rankin to five children whose mother, left penniless when her tobacco-farmer husband was killed in an accident, had requested the admission of the older children so that she could try to take care of the two youngest children. Then Rankin (and the camera) looked in on a "mother's aid case" where the orphanage sent regular aid and a social worker to a widowed mother with five children. After scenes of orphans at breakfast, in school, at various daily tasks, and at play, the circuit rider proceeded to a hospital.

At the hospital in Banner Elk, North Carolina, which had been built a few years earlier with Endowment assistance, Rankin invited viewers to compare the scene of two doctors performing major surgery with an earlier shot of surgery being performed in a mountain home. A map showed the distribution of the hospital's 900 bed patients from thirteen mountain counties in 1933, and another map showed the distribution of 2,300 ambulatory patients in the outpatient clinic. Rankin pointed to an inscription on one of the hospital's walls, "For the sick without regard to race or creed," and he suggested that the chief lesson he hoped the viewer would learn from the Banner Elk hospital was this: a hospital did away with the need for the doctor to travel in order to take care of the sick and enabled "two physicians to do what ten physicians could not do half as well without a hospital."

Then the circuit rider led Rankin to a community quite different from Banner Elk. In Allendale, South Carolina, in the state's low country, Rankin met a couple of local citizens in an aging doctor's office. One of the citizens, a woman who was the county welfare officer, noted, "There are a number of dependents in this county who could be partially or completely relieved if they could be given good medical care." The doctor, who had practiced in Allendale for more than forty years, stated that each day he found "a greater need for a local hospital," and another local citizen pointed out that the nearest hospital was fifty miles away. Using data that Rankin may have supplied, the citizen noted that there were 800 cases of seriously ill people who needed hospitalization during the course of the past year, but only 53 actually received hospital care in other counties. Of the 400 charity cases among the 800 persons needing care, only 12 received treatment in hospitals or other counties. He admitted that the people of Allendale could not undertake to care for all who needed treatment, but he thought it was their "imperative duty" to make a beginning effort. "Now, Dr. Rankin, we have made our appeal for assistance through you to the Trustees of The Duke Endowment," the citizen concluded, but he wanted to let some of the local sick people speak for themselves.

The doctor then introduced one of his patients: "This is Lucy Warner. A burn on her foot three years ago, imperfectly treated on account of the limitations of her home." Lucy Warner: "Bad, real bad — so raw places — raw just like this and holes busted all in my leg here and everywhere." The doctor added, "All of this suffering and infirmity would have been prevented if she could have been treated for her burns in a hospital." Another patient, a thirty-two year-old African-American woman, had a uterine fibroid. The doctor's comment was that the case had been operable and curable a year and a half earlier but was "not curable now." After various other sick persons were briefly interviewed, the male citizen explained that often in dramatic situations, such as automobile accidents and gunshot wounds, the victims were moved quickly by ambulance. "But these chronic conditions, where neither severe pain nor impending death require decisive action," he explained, "are allowed to remain and accumulate until local interests and a local hospital bring them relief."

Rankin then took the Allendale group to Monck's Corner in Berkeley County, South Carolina, where the Endowment had recently helped to build a much needed hospital. A doctor there took Rankin to see an African American couple who had fourteen children; the mother became ill after having the thirteenth child, and when the doctor took her to the hospital, they found she had a thirty-two pound tumor. Then a year and some months later, she had not only recovered but had delivered their fourteenth child. When the doctor asked the father what he fed so many children, the father replied: "Feed them on cornbread and clabber [curdled milk] one day and clabber and cornbread the next and that's about out now. Crops is all burned up with the drought."

When Rankin asked the Berkeley County doctor how many of the approximately 650 charity cases in the county were treated in the new hospital last year, the doctor replied that 413 were. Then the camera moved to a scene in a hospital where a laboratory and an x-ray machine saved a man, suffering acute abdominal pain and other symptoms, from surgery when the x-ray revealed a kidney stone. "We'll give him a good dose of morphine to relieve his pain and relax the muscular coat of his ureter," the doctor explained, "and the stone will probably pass."

Then the circuit rider proceeded to the campuses of Furman University, Johnson C. Smith University, and Davidson College for brief statements from the presidents of the institutions. At Duke University, President Few spoke briefly about the church-related beginnings of Harvard, Yale, and Princeton but particularly emphasized the relationship with various churches of the Endowment's four educational beneficiaries. After outlining the main components of Duke University, Few concluded his appearance with an idea that he frequently reiterated: "When religion and education can everywhere be brought to join wholeheartedly in their common task to make a better world, then we may expect a steadiness in the progress of the race instead of the . . . spiritual ebb and flow that is so conspicuous in the records of mankind."

The movie ended with a picture of J. B. Duke under these words from the indenture: "I have endeavored to make provision in some measure for the needs of mankind." To summarize the Endowment's work, a narrator explained, presumably in voice-over, that the Endowment provided for orphanages the equivalent of one meal each day for 5,800 orphans in the two Carolinas; for hospitals, the equivalent of the cost each day of 1,000 charity patients in Carolina hospitals; and for education, the equivalent each year of the total cost to 1,400 students in Carolina universities and college. "And last but not least," the narration concluded, "many thousands of dollars annually for religion, so that the work of the Circuit Riders may go on and on." Just as the movie had opened with music, it ended with a well-loved, old Protestant hymn, "I Love to Tell the Story," played on the carillon of Duke University.[34]

Put on 35-millimeter film for showing in regular movie houses and 16-millimeter film for use with portable equipment, "The Trail of the Circuit Rider" received a wide showing in the Carolinas. For the rural communities still without electricity, the trustees authorized $1,000 for the purchase of a special truck equipped with a generator so that the movie could be taken wherever a church, civic, or hospital group wished to show it. By September 1937 an estimated 99,000 people had seen the film in 165 showings in North Carolina and 69 in South Carolina. Although no attendance figures for showings outside the Carolinas are available, hospital groups particularly showed the film in a number of other states and even at some of the national meetings of hospital people.

There were some interesting and varied reactions to "The Trail of the Circuit Rider." The "Colored Ministers Union" of Anderson, South Carolina, reported that the film had favorably impressed an African American audience at the local high school. "We think the showing of this picture," the preachers declared, "is a potent factor in arousing the people to the needs of 'mercy' and in promoting wholesome Race Relations."[35]

An ardent, young New Dealer, Jonathan Daniels, however, took a different view of the film. He admitted that the movie was "perhaps more effective because of the obviousness that the men and women and children acting and talking were not finished actors but the people who are actually helping and suffering in the social drama of the Carolinas." Having conceded that point, Daniels then proceeded to ignore the true purpose of the film, which was to show the work of the Endowment, and to write as if "The Trail of the Circuit Rider" were a film biography of James B. Duke. Daniels, clearly continuing in the anti-Duke footsteps of his father, Josephus Daniels, thought it a "vast pity" that the story of J. B. Duke had fallen into the hands of those "who are afraid, as Buck Duke was not afraid, of the strong meat of his life." Attempting "to force the drama of a Napoleon into the pattern of a Saint Francis of Assisi," the filmmakers, Daniels charged, had good intentions but seemed "intent on perpetuating the memory of the man" by "destroying the man who lived."

J. B. Duke's story, as young Daniels saw it, was that of "the America in which he lived, of the South in which he was born," where "strong and ruthless men rose to power and wealth, and in rising built vast corporations and huge factories and sought and found world markets and millions." Whether a reign of ruthlessness or creation, Daniels argued, "it was a reign of the strong, of men of the strength and single mindedness who have always made history's and drama's greatest protagonists." Daniels asserted that J. B. Duke had "a right to live, not merely as the dim shade in a circuit rider's shadow . . . but also as one of those men, great and few and terrible, who take the world for their orange and are not afraid to squeeze."[36]

Although the Endowment's movie was primarily about its work and only incidentally about J. B. Duke, Daniels's robber-baron interpretation was in great vogue among intellectuals in the 1930s. Just how the portrait of the ruthless orange-squeezer might fit with the creation of the Duke Power Company, not to mention the Endowment, was obviously a matter that did not concern Jonathan Daniels.

If Daniels attacked "The Trail of the Circuit Rider" for its alleged sanctification of J. B. Duke, an official in the office of Inter-American Affairs in Washington, D.C., rejected the movie for another reason altogether. The official had hoped to use a Spanish-language version of the film for Latin-American audiences and, after viewing it, admitted its excellence and social value. He decided, however, that the film could not be used because much of the material dealt "with people in the lowest income brackets and the problem of caring for our orphans, educating our youth and supplying medical care for citizens regardless of their economic situation." Such subject matter was too often misunderstood by foreign audiences, he feared. "Although the picture points out the progress in meeting our problems," the official concluded, "the picture of the plight of many of our citizens is hardly flattering to the United States."[37] The Washington official certainly did not mean to compliment Rankin and the others responsible for "The Trail of the Circuit Rider," but in a way the rejection was a tribute to its truthfulness in portraying certain painful realities in the depression-era South.

Just how Rankin felt about his leading role in the Endowment's foray into film-making is not known. A modest man, he probably took it quietly in stride and proceeded about his business. Having reached the age of seventy-one in 1950, Rankin resigned as director of the Hospital and Orphan Section in June of that year. "Few men have been privileged to devote themselves to so large and so congenial a service as has been my good fortune," he wrote Alexander Sands, "and perhaps fewer still have enjoyed the understanding, encouraging, and sustaining interest of their associates and employees in the degree that has been my happy lot."[38]

Marshall Pickens succeeded Rankin as director of the section, but Rankin continued to serve as a consultant to it and as an active trustee of the Endowment until he resigned in 1965. He died on September 8, 1970. J. B. Duke had formed a generous idea about helping out with health care and child care in the Carolinas, particularly for those poorer folk, black and white, who most needed help. Watson Rankin had seized upon that idea and transformed it into something infinitely more medically and socially valuable as well as long lasting.

4 ·

THE

ENDOWMENT

AND THE FOUR

EDUCATIONAL

INSTITUTIONS,

1924–1960

JAMES B. DUKE'S INDENTURE gave the trustees great discretionary power even as the same document also provided careful and explicit guidelines for the proportions of annual income that were to be distributed to the various beneficiaries. The key to this apparent paradox lay in the seventh paragraph of the indenture's third section. While this is another of William R. Perkins' mind-boggling and excessively long sentences — this one with 232 words — the meaning is fairly clear: "As respects any year or years and any purpose or purposes for which this trust is created (except the payments hereinafter directed to be made to Duke University) the trustees in their uncontrolled discretion" were empowered to withhold all or a part of payment to any of the other designated beneficiaries. While more will be said later about the special protection given to Duke University in the above formulation, the important words for the present analysis are "uncontrolled discretion." The marathon sentence goes on to say that the trustees may dispose of any funds so withheld in one of four ways: (1) use the withheld money, or any part of it, at a later time for the original purpose for which it was designated; (2) add all or a part of the withheld money to the corpus of the trust; (3) use the withheld money for one of the other designated purposes of the trust; or (4) use all or part of the withheld money "for the benefit of any such like charitable, religious or educational purpose" in the Carolinas "and/or any such like charitable hospital purpose [not necessarily in the Carolinas]," which at least three-fourths of the trustees might select. Thus J. B. Duke bestowed considerable power upon the trustees of his Endowment and denied to the Endowment's beneficiaries, except Duke University, an absolute assurance of continual, annual support.

The four educational institutions named as beneficiaries in the indenture were together to receive 46 percent of the annual income from the original corpus, and only 32 percent was designated for hospital purposes. This meant that higher education was obviously the top priority of the indenture in terms of monetary support. By a codicil to his will, however, J. B. Duke ordered that the residue of his estate (not otherwise disposed of by other provisions) be given to the Endowment. Moreover, the trustees of the Endowment were authorized (1) to spend $7 million of this residuary estate to help build and equip Duke University; (2) to spend 90 percent of the income from the remainder of the residuary estate "for maintaining and securing hospitals"; and (3) to spend 10 percent of the income in support of Duke University.

This portion of J. B. Duke's residuary estate turned out to be, when the dust had settled several years after his death, around $69 million. He had directed that $6 million of the $40 million he originally placed in his trust be used to help build Duke University, so that $69 million was more than twice the amount ($34 million) that the trustees originally had to work with as the so-called corpus. Moreover, the 90 percent (of approximately $62 million, after the $7 million for Duke University was deducted) for hospital purposes changed the priorities of the indenture and placed hospitals ahead of educational institutions in terms of monetary support.

While this may seem like Oriental water torture to some readers and old home ground to lawyers, one additional aspect of the indenture needs to be explicated. In the portion of the indenture concerning the 32 percent of the annual income for hospital purposes, J. B. Duke stipulated that if in any year the money available for hospital purposes should be "more than sufficient" for the designated purposes, then the trustees in their "uncontrolled discretion" could use the surplus funds for similar hospital purposes "in any other State or States, giving preference, however, to those States contiguous" to the two Carolinas. This meant, as mentioned earlier, that if there should be surplus money for hospital purposes, J. B. Duke preferred that the trustees use it in Virginia, Tennesse, and Georgia — or, in memory of W. R. Perkins, perhaps one should say Virginia and/or Tennessee and/or Georgia.

Although there is no record at all in the trustees' minutes of any discussion of this matter—after all, no positive action was taken, only what might be termed a highly important inaction or failure to act—the trustees apparently decided not many years after J. B. Duke's death that they had no interest in carrying the Endowment's hospital work outside the Carolinas. One clue pointing to this conclusion is Rankin's statement in a private letter to a Georgian in July 1927 that the Endowment's activities would "be confined for many years to come to the States of North Carolina and South Carolina."[1]

This confinement to the Carolinas was not inspired by a shortage of funds for hospital purposes, for in December 1929 the trustees exercised their "uncontrolled discretion" in a highly significant fashion: when the treasurer of the Endowment reported a sum of $3,352,021 in hand (over $3,228,000 of which came from funds in estimated excess of requirements for maintaining and securing Carolina hospitals), the trustees voted to withhold the money from the object to which it would otherwise be distributed and keep the sum plus interest from it in a separate reserve fund to be allocated as the trustees might wish.[2]

Much of this particular withheld money, as it turned out, the trustees used to build the great Tudor Gothic chapel at Duke University. Alexander Sands Jr. had spent a week at the university and prepared a careful survey of the cost of operations and a tentative budget covering its expenses for the next three years. Moreover, in January 1930 George G. Allen reported to the trustees that he and Perkins had spent a day with William P. Few and Robert L. Flowers going over the university's budget, and all agreed that an adequate program could be carried out without the use of the $2 million for the proposed chapel at Duke University. Accordingly, the trustees voted to appropriate that amount for the building, exclusive of the architect's fees, the stained-glass windows, the pipe organ, and the carillon.[3] This provision for the chapel, however, was an ad hoc disposition of reserve funds and not necessarily an indication of the trustees' intentions concerning the Endowment's long-range priorities. They would not be finally revealed, as will be discussed shortly, until 1934.

Just why the trustees chose not to extend the hospital program outside the Carolinas is not known. There was probably not enough money in the hospital account, even with the 90 percent from J. B. Duke's residuary estate, to extend the program into all three contiguous states, and on what possible basis could only one or even two of the three states be selected? One must remember, too, that the Endowment did not just assist with indigent care and help communities build hospitals, but, under the system Watson S. Rankin had devised, the

Endowment entered into a long-term ongoing relationship with its hospital beneficiaries. A relatively small staff managed to carry out this program in the Carolinas, but if it should be extended beyond those two states, then there would have to be a significant and costly expansion of the staff. Moreover, there was a certain symmetry, which was rooted in geography and history, between the work of the Endowment in the Carolinas and its close ties with the Duke Power Company.

The trustees may simply have decided, in an informal manner that left no record in the minutes, that they preferred the priorities of the indenture to the shift that could occur under the codicil that a critically ill J. B. Duke added to his will not long before his death. If that was the case, however, it would not become clear until five or so years after the private, completely unpublicized decision not to expand the hospital program beyond the Carolinas and, instead, to keep the educational institutions as the top priority in terms of monetary support.

In the Endowment's relations with its educational beneficiaries down to about 1961, there was a striking contrast: with Davidson, Furman, and Johnson C. Smith, the Endowment maintained a completely hands-off, somewhat distant policy even as it supplied annual income that immeasurably strengthened the three institutions. With Duke University, on the other hand, the Endowment became just as entangled and involved as it was with the Duke Power Company. Duke University, unlike the other three institutions, owed its very existence to J. B. Duke's princely gifts and his provisions in the indenture, and for many years the annual contribution from the Endowment covered approximately half of the university's budget.

In the long run, the conclusion is inescapable that the symbiotic relationship between the Endowment and Duke University worked out to the great and lasting financial advantage of the latter institution. There were certain serious problems, however, and, as will be discussed, the autonomy of the university was compromised at several important junctures. The climax of the Endowment's questionable involvement in the university's operation would come in the late 1950s, ending in a major crisis in 1960. Then in the years after that, and especially after about 1970, the Endowment would, quietly and again without any public announcement, continue to support the university most generously, even creatively, but without also attempting to have a decisive voice in running it.

While Trinity College's President Few, in a more limited way than he no doubt preferred, had collaborated with J. B. Duke in the planning for the Endowment, the presidents of Davidson, Furman, and Johnson C. Smith received total and blissful surprises when the newspapers announced the creation of the Endowment in December 1924. The news came at a particularly opportune time for Davidson, since the college was coping with some especially difficult problems in the early 1920s. In fact, D. Grier Martin, who would later become the president of Davidson, declared in 1957 when he was its treasurer that "except during the Civil War, there has been no period in the history of the College when there were more problems" than in the early 1920s.[4]

Begun by Presbyterians in 1836 as a college for young men, Davidson, like the Baptists' Wake Forest and the Methodists' Trinity, struggled to survive in the nineteenth century. Since almost three-fourths of all the colleges established in North Carolina before the Civil War did not survive, one can easily see that permanence was by no means guaranteed to educational institutions, no matter how well-intentioned their founders may have been. Yet Davidson not only managed to survive, it also resisted the temptation of trying to become other than what it was: a liberal arts college for undergraduates. Although countless suggestions cropped up over the years about Davidson's adding this or that professional school, it immeasurably strengthened itself and increased its integrity by staying focused on its one, central task of giving a solid education to undergraduates.

The great loyalty of a small but devoted body of alumni proved to be one of the major sources of Davidson's strength. While the enrollment was increasing after World War I, the financial resources of the college were not, and when Chambers Building, the heart of the college, burned in 1921, the college was able to rebuild only a small part of a new Chambers. With an endowment of only $671,000 and a student body of 627, the college had only twenty-nine faculty members, or one teacher for twenty-two students. According to Grier Martin's later testimony, the Davidson salaries were not only low but also considerably lower than in some neighboring, competing institutions. There was relatively little support from the church and virtually none from other sources for current expenses. A campaign in 1924–25 to rebuild Chambers raised $262,000, but there were expenses of $100,000.

Everything done at Davidson after 1924, Martin continued—and since he was addressing the Endowment trustees he should probably be excused for exaggerating the Endowment's role and failing to mention other sources of support—had been done directly with funds from the Endowment or indirectly by relieving the need at another point and thereby making funds available. As early as 1929, President W. J. Martin, Grier Martin's father, had pointed to five areas where the Endowment had been most beneficial: the faculty had increased from twenty-nine to forty-five; salaries had been raised; a retirement program for faculty and staff had been established; many campus improvements had been made; and the raising of money for Chambers Building and other purposes had been made possible because of the help for operating expenses that came from the Endowment.

By 1957 Grier Martin could point out that a new library was the only building constructed since 1929 that was not paid for at least in part with Endowment funds, and two buildings, the Duke dormitory and the Martin science building, had been built with funds exclusively from the Endowment. The faculty had grown to number sixty-three, and the salary scale, maintained without reduction during the depression (which was indeed a rare distinction among colleges and universities), had been increased about 100 percent.

Martin suggested that one of the greatest contributions the Endowment had made to Davidson was to inspire confidence in the stability and future of the institution among alumni, friendly individuals, corporations, and foundations. That same confidence, he believed, had enabled Davidson to attract outstanding leadership among its trustees, administrators, faculty, and student body. Pointing out that Davidson by 1957 already ranked among the top colleges in the nation in the percentage of its graduates in Who's Who and among Rhodes scholars, Martin did not say, but certainly could have, that Davidson was well on its way to becoming not just a premier liberal arts college in the South but among the best in that category in the nation.[5]

If survival in the nineteenth century was a triumph for Davidson, it was even more so for Furman. Begun by South Carolina Baptists as the Furman Academy and Theological Institution in 1826, the school was intended to train ministers and had an average enrollment of about ten students — with funds equally scarce; it closed and moved three times before settling in the Piedmont town of Greenville, South Carolina, in 1851. There it became Furman University and, while keeping its theological seminary, expanded into a college of literature and science. According to a lively and refreshingly candid history of Furman, however, most of the institution's first century of existence was "marked by a fitful search for identity." Even after the theological seminary was separated from the college and finally moved to Louisville, Kentucky, in 1877, many ardent Baptists in South Carolina, even into the twentieth century, according to the historian, refused to concede that Furman "should be more than a denominational training ground."[6]

Closed during the Civil War like so many other Southern colleges, Furman reopened in 1866 but remained, according to the above-mentioned historian, "an insignificant institution, barely alive, more like a high school or junior college than a full fledged senior college."[7] Then between about 1881 and 1925, thanks to effective leadership and other developments, Furman finally defined itself as a true liberal arts institution. When William J. McGlothlin became president of Furman in 1919, he vigorously set about strengthening the institution in many ways. Determined that it should be accredited by the Southern Association of Colleges and Secondary Schools, he achieved that goal in 1924. With a Ph.D. himself from the University of Berlin in Germany, McGlothlin found only one other holder of the Ph.D. on Furman's faculty, but he acted to change that situation in a hurry. He wanted and got a number of new buildings but saw them "only as instruments to the greater goal of academic excellence." J. B. Duke probably did not realize it, but when he included in the indenture "that little college located in Greenville that Ben Geer is such a fool about," he had hit upon an institution much in the process of improving its performance and raising its aspirations. "Mr. Duke's gift has changed the whole face of things for us, so far as endowment is concerned," McGlothlin declared to Furman's trustees. He thought that Furman was "now probably the richest educational institution among Southern Baptists" and, in light of the "absolute freedom" that the board had in using the Endowment money, he suggested that the unexpected gift and the freedom "lay upon us grave responsibilities and afford us great opportunities."[8]

The Endowment annually supplied Furman much needed money but did not, as mentioned earlier, cultivate any particular or close relationship with it. The economic slump that especially distressed southern farmers in the 1920s, some years before the crash of late 1929, indirectly affected Furman, for it found itself burdened with a debt of $160,000 by 1928. With the state's Baptists giving pitifully small amounts to the institution, enrollment began to decline seriously in the late 1920s. By late 1928 McGlothlin advised the trustees that only the income from the Endowment was keeping Furman from total "collapse" and that even that money might be withheld if indebtedness got out of hand. He did not say, but perhaps he well understood, that "properly operated" was a frequently used phrase in J. B. Duke's indenture and that the Endowment's trustees had "uncontrolled discretion" to withhold payments to all beneficiaries except Duke University.

Sure enough, Alexander Sands, the secretary of the Endowment as well as its de facto executive director, reported to the trustees in late 1931 about Furman's indebtedness, slipping enrollment, and the fact that for the past three years the income received from the Endowment had been greater than that received from tuition. The trustees thereupon authorized Sands to advise McGlothlin that they would appreciate a full report on the matter. Furman's president soon reported, in response to the no doubt alarming request from Sands, that the school's trustees had acted to balance the budget for 1931–32 by, among other things, materially reducing salaries for faculty and staff. To keep the budget balanced in the future, the trustees had voted to abolish the law school, which Furman had long coveted but not opened until 1921. In addition to increasing the number of students, McGlothlin noted that Furman planned a campaign to liquidate the school's debt and increase its endowment. One sure way of increasing the enrollment became clear the following year when Furman opted for a coordinate-college arrangement with Greenville Women's College, also a Baptist-sponsored school.

When McGlothlin died from injuries suffered in an automobile accident in 1933, a divided board of trustees finally elected Bennette E. Geer as Furman's new president. Aside from being a former teacher, dean, and treasurer at Furman as well as a longtime trustee, Geer had enjoyed marked success as a textile manufacturer. Though he was not a scholar, the fact that he was an original trustee of the Endowment and had first interested J. B. Duke in Furman also played a role in his election as president. Although a historian of Furman notes that Geer's five-year administration was "the stormiest of any Furman president," he also credits Geer with implementing "the most ambitious, forward-looking program ever tried at Furman up to that time."[9]

All of that, however, is part of Furman's rather than the Endowment's history, and perhaps the central point here is that Endowment money played a major role in helping Furman establish its identity as an ambitious liberal arts college, one that would grow steadily stronger as the twentieth century proceeded.

Like Furman, Johnson C. Smith University also long had a problem about its identity, except that in Johnson C. Smith's case the problem was seriously compounded by a geographical anomaly, which itself was rooted in historical circumstances. Established in Charlotte in 1867 as a missionary enterprise of the northern Presbyterian church for the newly emancipated African Americans, the institution was first known as the Henry J. Biddle Memorial Institute. The name honored a white Union soldier who was killed during the Civil War and whose widow, a Philadelphian, gave nearly $2,000 to help start the school. Its primary purpose was to educate young African American men and train them to become Presbyterian ministers. (Actually, Presbyterians were scarce among African Americans as compared to Baptists and Methodists, but the Presbyterian church, unlike the two larger denominations, had always emphasized the importance of an educated clergy.) Although most of the white people of Charlotte probably looked askance at the "Yankee intrusion," a local white citizen, W. R. Myers, did give eight acres of land that became the nucleus of the campus. With several white Presbyterian alumni of Princeton University prominent among the small faculty, the "Colored Princeton of the South," as it proudly considered itself, offered preparatory work (high school) as well as college-level work and three years of theological training. Soon becoming Biddle University, the pioneer institution acquired its first African American president in 1891 when the Board of Missions for Freedmen of the Presbyterian Church (USA) named a former slave from South Carolina, Daniel J. Sanders, to the post.[10]

Biddle University was obviously a source of great pride in the African American community, but unfortunately and through no fault of its own, it was isolated from the larger white community of Charlotte and the state. Not only were most of the trustees residents of the North, but since Biddle's business office was located in Pittsburgh, Pennsylvania, its payroll and even its bills had to be handled from there. This anomalous situation would change in the 1960s, to the great benefit of the institution, and the Endowment would be significantly involved. Before that happened, however, there were other important developments.

After an interlude when industrial education was pushed, Biddle returned to an emphasis on training preachers and teachers to serve among African Americans in the South. The school reported in 1908 that it had served some 8,000 students since it opened soon after the Civil War. While the great majority of the students had never graduated, even from the lower school, of the 307 graduates holding bachelor's degrees, only 16 were reported to have left the South.[11]

A fire in 1921 destroyed Biddle's theological dormitory as well as one or two less important structures. With an estimated $45,000 needed to replace the lost buildings, the Board of Missions for Freedmen (in Pittsburgh) reported that only $2,000 had been received toward the replacement cost by the end of the year. The number of theological students continued to decline, but there was an increase in the collegiate department. Biddle, in other words, faced serious problems in the early 1920s.

At this juncture, skies brightened when a wealthy, white widow in Pittsburgh, Pennsylvania, Mrs. Johnson C. Smith, learned of the school's plight and gave the funds, in her late husband's memory, to replace the theological dormitory. She subsequently visited the campus and ended up contributing over $700,000 to the school by 1929. In gratitude for such generous support, the trustees and mission board of the Presbyterian church decided in 1923 to change the institution's name to Johnson C. Smith University.

When J. B. Duke included the school in his benefaction late in 1924, Johnson C. Smith instantly became relatively unusual among voluntarily supported colleges and universities for African Americans at that time: it had what amounted to a real endowment, a dependable source of a significant amount of unrestricted annual income.

When the Endowment published its first yearbook, which covered the period from December 1924 through December 1928, it asked the presidents of the four educational institutions to prepare brief statements. H. L. McCrorey, the president of Johnson C. Smith, gave a short sketch of the school's history and then noted that in the previous eight years, the enrollment in the collegiate department had increased from 75 to 268; that the high school department was about to be eliminated; and that the North Carolina state board of education had given the collegiate department an "A" rating in 1924. McCrorey reported that the annual income from the Endowment had enabled the school to add faculty, raise salaries, repair buildings, pave walks, plant shrubbery, and make other permanent improvements. He concluded by noting that there had been four significant gifts in the school's history — two in the early period, from H. R. Myers and Mrs. Biddle, and two in the more recent period, from Mrs. Smith and J. B. Duke. The first two donors, McCrorey suggested, "made their gifts to the institution on faith, not knowing the capabilities of the Negro to acquire education, nor how he would use it after acquired." The last two donors, however, "based their gifts on evidence of what education has done and can do for Negroes, by the product sent out from this institution during its past history of more than half a century."[12]

Admitting women students to its junior and senior classes in 1932, Johnson C. Smith became fully coeducational in 1941, and shortly before that James B. Duke Memorial Hall, the first on-campus dormitory for women, was dedicated. Thus, while the school continued to strengthen its collegiate program during the 1940s and 1950s, the enrollment in its theological seminary remained small, even though the seminary consumed a significant portion of the institution's resources. The geographical anomaly of the school's being situated in one area of the country but having its business office as well as most of its trustees in another region also continued. The Endowment would successfully collaborate with Johnson C. Smith's president and key faculty members to help change both situations in the 1960s. The result would be a clearer, more focused identity for a school that belatedly developed strong and steadily more rewarding ties with Charlotte and North Carolina.

Like Furman and Johnson C. Smith, the new research university that began to be organized around Trinity College late in 1924 also faced the task of establishing its identity. Fortunately for the new Duke University, both J. B. Duke and W. P. Few strongly agreed on the main points: (1) that, while the multifaceted university should, as the indenture stated, strive to achieve "a place of real leadership in the educational world," it should also preserve an emphasis on the teaching and character strengthening of undergraduates; (2) that the university should try to be of the utmost possible service to the people of its own state and region as it simultaneously welcomed faculty and students from other parts of the nation; and (3) that the historic ties between Trinity College and the Methodist church, ties that were friendly without being constrictive, should be maintained by the new university.

In specifying that the Endowment's trustees, in their "uncontrolled discretion," could withhold annual payments from any of the designated purposes of the trust "except the payments hereinafter directed to be made to Duke University," J. B. Duke signaled that he obviously considered the university to be in a special, protected category. The special treatment afforded Duke University in this portion of the indenture constituted, in effect, J. B. Duke's acknowledgement of the fact that the Duke family's long involvement with Trinity College and his own desire to "do something big" for this institution were, in fact, the original inspiration for the Endowment. If J. B. Duke had left the matter of the university's relationship with the Endowment as it was put in that third section of the indenture, the following decades might have been easier, less problematical ones for the university.

From the university's standpoint, however, it was highly unfortunate that in the fifth section of the indenture, in another of W. R. Perkins' heroic sentences, J. B. Duke partly stripped away the special protection for Duke University that he gave it in the third section. That is to say, the trustees were empowered to withhold all or any part of the 32 percent of the annual income allotted to Duke University if it should "incur any expense of liability beyond provision already in sight to meet same, or in the judgment of the trustees under this Indenture be not operated in a manner calculated to achieve the results intended hereby." The first phrase hinting at fiscal prudence, balanced budgets, and avoidance of expenses that could not be covered was probably a quite salutary warning that the university should be "properly operated" from a business standpoint. The second phrase concerning the university's operating "in a manner calculated to achieve the results intended hereby" was, on the other hand, a vague, subjective nightmare.

What "results" did J. B. Duke intend for Duke University to achieve? Presumably, as certain trustees would later point out, that was spelled out in the seventeenth section of the indenture where J. B. Duke declared:

> I have selected Duke University as one of the principal objects of this trust because I recognize that education, when conducted along sane and practical, as opposed to dogmatic and theoretical, lines, is, next to religion the greatest civilizing influence. I request that this institution secure for its officers, trustees and faculty men of such outstanding character, ability and vision as will insure its attaining and maintaining a place of real leadership in the educational world, and that great care and discrimination be exercised in admitting as students only those whose previous record shows a character, determination and application evincing a wholesome and real ambition for life. And I advise that the courses at this institution be arranged, first, with special reference to the training of preachers, teachers, lawyers and physicians, because these are most in the public eye, and by precept and example can do most to uplift mankind, and, second, to instruction in chemistry, economics and history, especially the lives of the great of earth, because I believe that such subjects will most help to develop our resources, increase our wisdom and promote human happiness.

Taken literally, and lawyers could no doubt argue until Kingdom come just how the phrases should be taken, J. B. Duke might be understood as requiring the trustees of the Endowment to pass on or give their approval to the various curricula of the university's multiple schools; after all, he had expressed clear notions about the "courses at this institution" and his preference for "sane and practical" education as opposed to "dogmatic and theoretical." Since he had described various attributes he considered desirable in administrators, trustees, and faculty, were the Endowment's trustees to have a voice in their selection? Likewise, he, wisely it must be admitted, preferred that the university admit only those students whose previous records showed "character, determination, and application evincing a wholesome and real ambition for life." Were Endowment trustees to sit on the university's various admission committees? Obviously, J. B. Duke intended no such extreme outcomes as are suggested above. Yet the language about the Endowment trustees' being empowered to withhold money from Duke University if the university should not be operated "in a manner calculated to achieve the results intended hereby" was an incredible murky invitation to trouble.

One result that obviously was both intended and achieved by granting the Endowment trustees the power to withhold payments to Duke University under certain conditions was to greatly increase the power of the Endowment's trustees in the university's operation. Certain events would make this increasingly clear in succeeding years, but not until 1960 would the general public, or that part of it interested in Duke University, become fully aware of the matter.

If President Few initially had any worries about the above-mentioned portions of the indenture, the record does not reveal them. A voluntarily supported college or university needs an endowment for many reasons, but the principal one is, as Grier Martin had indicated, to inspire confidence about the permanence and stability of the institution. Few, like the public in general, seemed to assume that J. B. Duke had given Duke University, in its 32 percent share, all the assurance of permanence that it needed. Before the decade of the 1920s was over, however, Few would be forced to face discomforting realities about the relationship of Duke University and the Endowment.

Before that transpired, however, the trustees of the Endowment — and especially Allen, Perkins, and Sands — did everything they possibly could do to help make the J. B. Duke-W. P. Few vision of Duke University come true. When J. B. Duke died in October 1925, the trustees of the Endowment, as another indication of the university's special place, elected Robert L. Flowers, the university's veteran vice president for finance, to fill the vacancy on the board. Allen subsequently explained that the university's special relationship with the Endowment was the justification for Flower's election and that a similar arrangement with other beneficiaries was not to be expected.

One of the principal activities of the Endowment between 1924 and the end of 1932 was to oversee the giant building program at Duke University.[13] J. B. Duke had given about $19 million to be used in the rebuilding of the old Trinity campus (East Campus), the construction from scratch of the Tudor Gothic structures on the new campus (West Campus), and the purchase of about 5,000 acres of forest and farm land. It was a vast undertaking, for only a few colleges or universities up to that time had ever had such a large part of their physical plants constructed at one time, much less with the architectural harmony that would characterize the Georgian buildings on East

Campus and the Tudor Gothic ones on West Campus. (When someone once suggested to Few that too much of the university's money had gone into buildings, he quickly replied that it was not the university's money but J. B. Duke's money.)

J. B. Duke had selected the architectural firm that he wished to design all the new buildings and, in consultation with Few and others, had chosen the type of architecture to be used on the two campuses. Since the plan was to rebuild East Campus first and then start on West, work on the former had barely begun when J. B. Duke died in October 1925. He had seen and approved various plans but did not live to see a single one of the many new buildings he was giving to the university. The Endowment, therefore, and particularly Allen, Perkins, and Sands, became the surrogate representatives of J. B. Duke in the physical building of Duke University.

For such a huge project, one that stretched over about nine years and required close collaboration between the Endowment group on the one hand and Few and his associates on the other, it was accomplished with remarkably little friction in so far as surviving records reveal. There were tough decisions that had to be made too. For all of J. B. Duke's generosity, there actually was not enough money to do everything that he had envisioned. The size of various buildings, particularly on West, had to be reduced and, as mentioned earlier, when the time came to start building the towering chapel that J. B. Duke had particularly wanted as the centerpiece and dominant structure of the Tudor Gothic campus, the Endowment trustees had to do some scrambling to come up with an extra $2 million.

By 1932, when the chapel was almost completed, the great project, at least in its initial stage, was finished. While Few exulted in the beauty and harmony of Duke's two plants, George Allen and his key associates in the Endowment had every reason to be proud of their accomplishment. Appropriately enough, Allen would continue as chairman of the university trustees' building committee into the 1950s and would receive the deserved honor of having the last of the Tudor Gothic buildings to be erected (1954), the one that completed the entire ensemble, named the George C. Allen Administration Building.

From the long-range point of view, a more serious matter than a shortage of funds for the building program began gradually to become apparent to President Few after J. B. Duke's death: the university, for all of its reported (and highly exaggerated) wealth, did not have the monetary resources to do well all that it was undertaking to do. Few had envisioned an elaborate design for Duke University—two undergraduate colleges and at least three professional schools (Divinity, Law, and Medicine), with several others as possibilities. The whole idea was to have a high-quality institution, to go first class or not go at all. J. B. Duke had accepted Few's entire plan and incorporated it without significant change in the indenture. The 32 percent of the Endowment's income had the potential, of course, of becoming a larger and larger amount of money as the years passed, but Few's task was to staff and equip a complex research university and to start doing so in a meaningful manner from 1925 onward.

Whether Few or J. B. Duke — or both — was responsible for underestimating the amount of money actually needed to start staffing and equipping a first-rate research university is not known. There is a story, possibly apocryphal, that at some point in the early 1920s J. B. Duke had asked Few how much money would be required to build and endow a first-class university. Few replied, according to the story, "About $100,000,000." J. B. Duke, taking Few's reply as a joke, is said to have chuckled and, upon seeing Few subsequently, remarked teasingly, "Here comes the hundred-million dollar man."

The truth is that Few probably did not know just how much money would be needed to expand and strengthen the faculty of arts and science while simultaneously recruiting faculty members for the professional schools and providing the libraries and laboratories that would be required. Few, with good reason, had always been wary of the enormous expense involved in establishing and maintaining a four-year medical school with its necessary teaching hospital. He had persisted in reminding J. B. Duke about that particular matter, and the result was that shortly before Duke's death he added a codicil to his will which, among other things, provided for $4 million to be expended in erecting and equipping a medical school, hospital, and nurses' dormitory at Duke University.

With that final gift targeted toward the physical construction of the medical center, Few and the university were committed to the inclusion of a medical school in the plans. The question of whether it would be a four-year school or merely provide the last two years of clinical training (both Wake Forest and the University of North Carolina provided two-year, preclinical training) remained open and would not be finally settled until late in 1929.

Few had long enjoyed a friendly and helpful relationship with the Rockefeller-funded General Education Board (GEB). Its officers began advising him about the costs involved in a medical school as early as 1916, and in the early 1920s, when Few unsuccessfully attempted to have Trinity College and the University of North Carolina cooperate in establishing a four-year medical school, the GEB had warmly encouraged Few. Few decided in 1926 to make his first step toward the establishment of Duke's medical school the selection of a dean who could then take the lead in planning and staffing. He turned again to the GEB, whose officers arranged for Few to meet with the leaders of the Johns Hopkins Medical School in Baltimore. That meeting eventually resulted in the appointment of Wilburt C. Davison in 1927 as the organizing dean of Duke's medical center.

The GEB, as one of its foremost leaders explained, had as one of its major undertakings "the revolution of American medical schools."[14] Given that fact and in light of Few's past dealings with the GEB, he naturally turned to it in seeking help to provide a separate endowment for Duke's medical school. Writing to Abraham Flexner, author of the famed 1910 report on American medical schools and one of the GEB's principal officers after 1913, Few explained in 1926 that he sought help in establishing an initial endowment for the projected medical school (the buildings themselves having already been provided for) of $6 million. While J. B. Duke's residuary estate had not yet been settled, Few noted that enough was already known for him "to say definitely that if the medical school is otherwise endowed we shall then have for the support of the other departments an endowment of not less than $25,000,000." Moreover, J. B. Duke had believed, according to Few, that the provisions of the indenture would lead within a dozen years or so to an endowment for the university of around $40 million. (No one knew, of course, that a major economic downturn, such as happened after 1929, might alter such a timetable.) Flexner and his associates already knew, Few concluded, that, "We are committed to the policy of trying to do well what we undertake to do — trying to build up a university which while adapting itself to the conditions and needs here in the South will at the same time . . . keep in line with the best educational standards and ideals of our time."[15]

Despite Few's eloquent appeal and after additional conferences and letters, the GEB in March 1927 refused his request. Not only was Few disappointed, but he also now grew profoundly worried as he gradually learned that the officers had made their negative decision for two reasons, one more important than the other. The lesser reason, and the one Few could not argue with too much in light of his knocking on the GEB's door, was that the officers believed that Duke University did not have adequate financial resources to do all that it was attempting. The more serious reason was that they were skeptical about the university's system of governance because of the division between the two boards of trustees. That is, while the university's board presumably controlled the university, the Endowment's board controlled the money necessary for the university's operation.

For the first time apparently, Few had run head on into the university's immense problem arising from the fact that it had no absolute guarantee of annual support from the Endowment. For the next seven or eight years this would be at the heart of what Few regarded as the most serious problem with which he had to grapple — and in organizing a major research university there were, of course, problems galore. As for the immediate problem of help with the medical school, Few, never one to give up easily where he believed the welfare of Duke University was concerned, patiently and persistently set about to convince the officers of the GEB that they were wrong. Working as closely with Allen and Perkins as the busy New Yorkers would allow, Few proceeded to draft two documents, both of which he ultimately had printed for private distribution, one on the history and the various charters of Trinity-Duke and one on the relationship between the university and the Endowment.

The latter pamphlet proved to be the crucial one. In it Few, after quoting the scattered provisions in the indenture concerning the university, argued that the trustees of the Endowment were "in a very real sense . . . also trustees of Duke University, providing as they do, a large part of the income and responsible as they are for seeing that the University keeps true to the purpose for which it was founded." After elaborating on his confidence in the trustees of the Endowment and in their whole-hearted devotion to the university, Few declared that they would "never under any circumstances be a menace to the educational integrity of the University."

Perhaps the most important part of Few's pamphlet was his explanation that as president of the university, he had adopted the policy of presenting to the trustees of the Endowment (meaning Allen and Perkins) for their consideration "all proposals, before the proposals are fully adopted and made effective, if they call for the expenditure of money by the University or involve changes of importance in the operations of the University and come under the terms of the Trust Indenture establishing The Duke Endowment." Few, in short, meant that he already was giving and expected to continue giving a veto power over most matters of large policy and planning concerning the university to Allen and Perkins.

Few concluded by noting that the above procedure had been approved by all concerned, was working well, and would most likely be recognized by all as "a safe procedure that is apt to become permanent." Since both boards were self-perpetuating and not apt to be "subject to violent changes," there was every likelihood that the described procedures would pass on from one generation to the next.[16]

While Few chose not to say so in his pamphlet, he privately advised Allen and Perkins that he thought that within a year or two there should be worked out in the university's charter from the legislature an addition which formalized and made permanent the arrangement that he had described to the GEB. Perkins, replying for both himself and Allen as was usually the case, seemed wary of Few's idea and suggested that it might be best "to let the harmonious cooperation [between the university and the Endowment] that has existed continue until it becomes a course of procedure by experience and lapse of time."[17]

After the GEB again declined to assist with Duke's medical school, Few sent them his pamphlets and a strongly worded letter in which he said, among other things, that he considered it "of the first importance that the officers of Duke University and of the General Education Board go through to the end of this matter," for "under all the circumstances, a failure of the General Education Board to give recognition to Duke University would be, in the judgment of time, a reflection on the administration here or there." Few added that he felt "this deeply and I know you will not mind my saying it to you."[18]

Few's strong letter, coupled with his pamphlet on the relationship of the Endowment and the university (the GEB requested twenty-five additional copies) and a conference which he and W. C. Davison had with GEB officers in New York in early November 1929 — all these finally won the day. Later that month the GEB made a grant to Duke University of $300,000 to be distributed on a diminishing basis over a five-year period, thus guaranteeing that Duke could open a four-year medical school on schedule in the fall of 1930.[19]

As pleased as Few was about finally securing the monetary assistance of the GEB, he considered the stamp of approval that the GEB had given to Duke University and its unusual system of governance infinitely more important for the long run. Believing, therefore, that the governance matter was more or less settled, except perhaps for some tinkering with the university's charter, Few tried to focus the attention of Allen, Perkins, and other key friends of Duke on the critical need for additional endowment for the nonmedical components of the university. Duke's medical school, Few advised Perkins, was "better set up than any other one department of the university." But on the overall picture for Duke, he candidly spelled out some gloomy forebodings:

But the simple fact is, without increased endowment we cannot possibly build a great university. Indeed, unless we get a great deal more endowment Duke will drag indefinitely, just as Cornell dragged for twenty or thirty years until a new generation came with reinforcements and put that university at least within the running of the greater universities of the country. Johns Hopkins, except in its School of Medicine, still drags. What we all, of course, want to do is to put Duke across in our generation, as was done at Chicago and so insure Duke's "attaining and maintaining a place of real leadership in the educational world."[20]

As Few launched his private campaign to increase the university's endowment, he, like most Americans at the time, was unaware that an unprecedentedly severe economic depression was getting underway. No reference to "unfavorable" business conditions appeared in his correspondence until June 1930. Raising large sums of money for additional endowment was about to be quite problematical. Moreover, the governance problem, which Few had seemed to put on the back burner, was about to reappear in a more serious and potentially dangerous form than ever. Few and Duke University would ultimately ride out a series of crises, but at a price, and resolving them required all the skill, diplomacy, and patient effort that William P. Few could muster.

While Allen and Perkins clearly wanted to carry out what they perceived J. B. Duke's vision of Duke University to have been, they were, in the last analysis, native-born southerners who had become well-to-do New York businessmen. There was much about academia and universities that they neither understood nor sympathized with. The centrally important concept of academic freedom, for example, was but one crucial area where they were quite tone deaf. If their relationship with Duke University had been comparable to that which they had with the three other educational beneficiaries of the Endowment, their incomprehension of academic freedom would hardly have mattered. Such was not, however, the case.

Few did his best, of course, to educate Allen and Perkins about university values and procedures. On one occasion, for example, when Few was worried about possible repercussions from the more or less forced resignation of a prominent member of the medical faculty, he tried to explain to Allen why it was essential for Duke to avoid any problems with the American Association of University Professors. Few enclosed with his letter a leaflet concerning the principles that governed academic freedom and tenure. He admitted that businessmen might think certain academic traditions and principles unwise, but it was necessary to remember, Few continued, "that all this has grown out of centuries of educational history. Many a good man has been dropped from provincial colleges because it was unpopular . . . to teach evolution, historical criticism of the Old Testament, free trade, tariff and so on." Allen merely replied briefly that he was not at all keen about "what I consider the excessive lengths to which so-called academic freedom" were being carried.[21]

The issue that gradually led to a hidden crisis in the governance of Duke University was not, however, a conventional tenure dispute but really more a matter of free speech on a university campus. Since what might be called the Norman Thomas affair at Duke has been described at length in *The Launching of Duke University,* it need not be elaborated upon here. Suffice it to say that when the famous Princeton-educated, Presbyterian minister and Socialist spoke on Duke's campus late in 1930, completely unbeknownst to Few who was out of town, Allen and Perkins exploded and requested an explanation from Few. In the correspondence that ensued, Few patiently and eloquently defended the idea of the university campus as a place where ideas could be — indeed, had to be — freely exchanged and that it was "the business of Duke University to hear both sides of all questions that are fairly debatable."[22]

Such arguments made no impression at all on Allen and Perkins. They insisted that they accepted the principle of free speech — but not about socialism or one or two other matters, such as advocacy of slavery — and that they considered it just as much Few's responsibility to protect the minds of Duke's students from such a vile doctrine as socialism as it was to protect their bodies from impure food and water. After the exchange of additional letters that got nowhere, Perkins finally resorted to J. B. Duke's indenture and particularly cited (1) his words about "education, when conducted along sane and practical, as opposed to dogmatic and theoretical, lines" being, "next to religion, the greatest civilizing influence"; and (2) his giving the trustees of the Endowment the authority to withhold funds from Duke University if it was not "operated in a manner calculated to achieve the results intended hereby."[23]

Few, at this juncture, stopped writing letters and went to New York. An infinitely patient man when he had to be, he had no intention of jeopardizing the future of Duke University. Unlike so many Americans of a later era, Few did not regard litigation as a desirable solution of the problem. A more hot-tempered or more egotistical person, when confronted with the obstinate obscurantism of Allen and Perkins, might well have thrown up his hands and said, "To hell with it, and let the chips fall where they may." Few, however, went to New York determined to make peace and, for a time at least, succeeded in doing so. Exactly what was said in the New York conference, is not known, but in all probability Few promised that in circumstances where university officials might properly have a say concerning speakers who were to be invited to the university (and who would be using a university auditorium or other space), great care and discretion would be exercised. At any rate, such became Duke's policy, as it was at many other similar institutions in that era.

The specter of Norman Thomas, however, would not disappear. In the presidential election of 1932, a number of North Carolinians, including some faculty members at both Duke and the University of North Carolina, signed a petition to have Thomas's name placed on the ballot as the candidate of the Socialist party. In doing so, various faculty members explained publicly that while they were not necessarily supporting the Thomas candidacy, they believed the voters of the state should have the opportunity to express their sentiments.

Once again, Allen and Perkins demanded to know how Duke faculty members could possibly lend even indirect support to a man who wanted the government to take over all public utilities and thereby rob the university of the major portion of its income. Once again, Few found himself in a correspondence where sweet reason batted zero and another peacemaking trip to New York became necessary.

By that time, that is 1933, Few had turned again to the matter of a basic change in the legal basis for the governance of the university. The tensions and dangerous confrontations that kept occurring concerning Norman Thomas (whom a group of "older students in the School of Religion" again invited to the campus) renewed Few's zeal to try to protect the university. His plan was to alter the university's charter from the state legislature so that it would require that at least three of the persons who sat on the seven-person executive committee of the university's trustees be also trustees of the Duke Endowment. Since the executive committee met monthly (whereas the full board of trustees then met twice a year) and exercised most of the same powers that the full board possessed, it was the single most important body in the actual governance of the university. Such an arrangement, Few argued, "would still leave the actual work of governing the University where I think it ought to remain, in the hands of the Executive Committee," but it "would let the Endowment trustees in on any fundamental changes in the University; and just that opportunity for them is what I am personally anxious to protect for the long future." Few thought he could get such a change through "without a jar."[24]

Few proved to be mistaken when he avowed that he could secure the change in the charter "without a jar." Few usually got whatever he wanted from the trustees, but the aging chairman of the university's board, John F. Bruton, a trustee since 1901, balked at the idea of the proposed change in the charter.

Bruton informed Few that he had tried to see the matter as Few did and had
"earnestly prayed over it," but all he could see in it were "results embodying an
almost unpardonable mistake and irreparable injury to Duke University."[25]

Faced with such strongly felt—and quite rare—opposition, Few dropped
his idea of changing the university's charter and settled instead for the much
less complicated procedure of changing the university's bylaws in order to
guarantee that the Endowment would have three of its trustees on the university's executive committee. Bruton opposed even that move, arguing that it
would be "full of mischief" and that already there was a feeling on the part of
some of the university's trustees that they were "regarded as mere figureheads." Despite the chairman's fears and misgivings, Few finally won him
over, and in March 1935 the university's trustees unanimously adopted the
bylaw that Few regarded as so essential. Allen, Perkins, and another trustee of
the Endowment, William N. Reynolds of Winston-Salem's tobacco family,
were soon members of the executive committee.

Few's plan worked well for the remainder of his presidency and life (he
died in October 1940). For entirely different reasons, as will be explained, it
worked out reasonably well in the 1940s and into the 1950s. During the late
1950s, however, the "mischief" that the university trustees' chairman had
feared in 1935 began to become a reality, and a serious, profoundly embarrassing and demoralizing crisis would befall the university in 1960.

One possible consequence of Few's dogged determination to work as closely
as possible with Allen and Perkins and, finally to assure them a formal, authorized voice in the governance and operation of Duke University was that the
Endowment trustees finally made clear in 1934 that the educational institutions (and especially Duke University) rather than hospitals were to be the
prime beneficiaries of the Endowment. That decision may have been made
earlier, say in the late 1920s, but if so the record does not reveal it. The trustees
of the Endowment had clearly decided in the late 1920s that they did not
choose to expand the hospital program beyond the Carolinas and that a sizable portion of the then-accumulating funds in the hospital accounts (and a
relatively small amount from the fund for building rural churches) should be
placed in a reserve fund. In other words, the Endowment might be said to have
not dropped the other shoe about its priorities until 1934.

It did this in an unpublicized and therefore unnoticed resolution passed
by the Endowment trustees in June 1934 whereby they created, in effect, mini-
endowment funds earmarked for the four educational institutions. Since these
funds were added to the corpus of the Endowment, the resolutions—and there

were twelve separate ones between June 1934 and November 1959 — became known as the "additions to corpus resolutions." As a result of them, the Endowment by the end of 1959 carried a special account (or endowment) for Duke University that had a book value of approximately $15,000,000; accounts for Davidson and Furman with a book value of nearly $1,560,000; and one for Johnson C. Smith of nearly $606,000. Each institution received 100 percent of the annual income from its account, and the income was unrestricted as to its use, just as was the income under the 32-5-5-4 percent formula.

It should also be noted that none of the money that was appropriated by these "addition to corpus resolutions" came from funds that were designated for the educational institutions, orphanages, or retired Methodist preachers and their dependents. In other words, the funds that were withheld (and then subsequently appropriated) came overwhelmingly from the hospital account and to a quite small degree from the church-building account.

The trustees of the Endowment never offered any formal or official explanation for their having finally chosen the educational institutions as the prime beneficiaries of the Endowment. Since Duke University benefited most of all from this decision, one can only surmise that Allen, Perkins, and Sands, with the concurrence of the remaining trustees, decided that if J. B. Duke had lived to realize that Duke University was actually underfunded for what it was attempting to do and to be, he would have concurred in the decision. In these matters, no one had a stronger or more legitimate claim to represent J. B. Duke's wishes and intentions than Allen, Perkins, and Sands. President Few had his share, perhaps more than his share, of problems with Allen and Perkins, but he also seems to have influenced and educated them in a manner that greatly redounded to the financial benefit of Duke University.

When Few died in late 1940, the executive committee of the trustees promptly named Robert L. Flowers as the acting president of the university. In view of Flowers's long service to Trinity and then Duke (he had joined Trinity's faculty in 1891) and his great popularity among the alumni and even many of the faculty, this appointment as acting president was a well-deserved and widely applauded recognition of Flowers's key role in the institution's history.

When the executive committee acted as its own de facto search committee, however, and named Flowers as the regular president in January 1941, that was highly unfortunate, perhaps for Flowers himself and certainly for the university. If Flowers had been in robust health, the fact that he was seventy years old when he became president might not have mattered. But, in fact, he had long had some health problems that prompted him to take refuge in Florida during the late winter months. Moreover, Flowers, unlike Few, was not a scholar. Again that, in and by itself, was not necessarily a fatal flaw, but there is strong evidence that, for all his amiability, Flowers was not completely at ease among serious scholars and perhaps did not truly understand certain fundamental truths about research universities and their faculties.

During World War II, Duke, like so many other universities, had to more or less forget about institutional advancement and concentrate on contributing to the war effort. In that situation, Flowers functioned adequately. In the years immediately after the war, however, the university faced a host of difficult problems as well as certain challenging opportunities, and Flowers was simply not up to the task even though he clung to his position. There would be, in short, a serious leadership crisis at Duke University in the late 1940s.

In all likelihood, Allen and Perkins were the dominant figures on the university's executive committee when it chose Flowers as the regular president. They had worked closely with Flowers, who had become a trustee of the Endowment in 1926, for many years, and he probably never sounded off about academic freedom and other such troublesome matters. He was in fact, as events would soon reveal, a regular pussycat as far as Allen and Perkins were concerned. In a brief biographical sketch of George G. Allen prepared by his daughters some years after his death, they note that their father had been "credited with supporting a particular individual for the presidency of Duke University when others felt that the man was unqualified for such a responsible position." Then they go on to say that the individual in question was "considered by many today to have been Duke's strongest president."[26] This clearly refers to Flowers, despite the debatable nature of the phrase about the "strongest president."

That Flowers tended to roll over when Allen and Perkins barked is best illustrated by something that happened fairly soon after Few died. The details need not be presented again here, but the incident not only reveals the power that the Endowment trustees exercised in university affairs but also the way they employed the executive committee to bypass, even to ignore, the great majority of the university's trustees. This same pattern would be repeated in the late 1950s.

Late in 1936 William Hayes Ackland, a native Tennessean who had become a wealthy cosmopolite and art lover, informed Few that Duke was one of three institutions he was considering for a benefaction: he wished to have his estate used to erect a memorial art museum that would house his collection as well as his mausoleum, and whatever excess funds there might be were to serve as an endowment for the museum. Since Duke was seriously deficient in the field of art history and that was already something that Few and others were working on, Few responded warmly and quickly. After Ackland visited Duke as the personal guest of President and Mrs. Few in May 1937, he definitely picked Duke to receive his gift, and Few proceeded to have the university's architects prepare plans which Ackland liked. These plans included the mausoleum, which did not seem to faze Few in the least.

From the beginning of the long-drawn-out negotiations, Few kept Allen and Perkins fully informed, and the latter, while saying nothing about the mausoleum, did raise serious and legitimate questions about control of the art museum if Ackland left his estate in trust, that is in the hands of trustees. Sharing this concern, Few, over a period of three years or so, did his best to persuade the aging and none-too-robust Ackland to make his gift while he was alive and let the university pay him an annuity. Influenced by his financial advisors, however, Ackland failed to follow Few's advice and died in February 1940.

Few, determined to carry out Ackland's wishes, both for Ackland's and the university's sake, set about trying to cooperate with Ackland's representatives. They informed Few that the estate, exclusive of the art collection (which turned out to be mostly reproductions and somewhat humdrum), amounted to around $1,300,000 and that money for the museum at Duke should be available by the end of 1940. As for the matter of the ownership or control of the museum, the Ackland trustees and their counsel assured Few that they fully understood the situation and would cooperate with Duke in every way to obtain a declaratory judgment from the proper court giving Duke University complete ownership and control of the museum and the endowment fund.

There were other legal complications, but despite that, one may conclude that if Few had not died suddenly of a coronary thrombosis in October 1940, the Ackland Museum may well have been eventually built at Duke. As matters stood, however, Perkins, who was backed in the matter by Allen, was determined that the Ackland bequest not be accepted by Duke. In September 1941 the executive committee — without informing the full board about the matter — officially declined to accept all of the provisions of the Ackland will concerning Duke University.

Completely shocked by the receipt of this news, the attorney for the Ackland estate in Washington, D.C., promptly telephoned Perkins and, among other things, repeated the promise that a court order would be expeditiously obtained and would make it clear once and for all that the art museum and endowment fund belonged exclusively to Duke University. Thereupon, Perkins finally let the cat out of the bag by declaring that (despite all of his previous arguments) there actually was a more serious matter than the question of control, and that was "the erection of a mausoleum with a recumbent state of Ackland on the Duke campus." Perkins asserted that he "would oppose to the very utmost" any such arrangement and that "there never had been a time when even Dr. Few could have gotten the sanction of the Trustees for the project set up in the will of Mr. Ackland, as much as Dr. Few was admired and respected." Flowers, upon reading Perkins' account of his conversation with the attorney for the Ackland estate, promptly advised Perkins, "I approve heartily of what you said."[27]

What Perkins had never quite screwed up the courage to say during Few's lifetime was made clear finally, at least to a very few insiders, in September 1941. That is to say, since there were already recumbent statues of Washington, Benjamin N. Duke, and J. B. Duke on top of their sarcophagi in the university's vast chapel, the proposed mausoleum for Ackland would bring, in Perkins' eyes, simply one recumbent too many to the Duke campus. And he persuaded Flowers and the other members of the university's executive committee to go along with his view.

Perkins, Flowers, and others associated with Duke would have been happy if the whole matter of the Ackland will could have quickly been forgotten. Such was not the case, however, since certain prominent alumni of Trinity-Duke in Washington, D.C., began to raise embarrassing questions. Moreover, newspapers in North Carolina began to gossip and speculate about the unusual case of Duke University's turning down a bequest. Finally, Chairman Bruton informed Flowers that certain trustees of the university thought that the full board should have a say in the Ackland matter. Bruton wanted Perkins to make a comprehensive statement on the subject at an upcoming meeting of the full board and perhaps also make a "delicate reference" as to why the executive committee had felt it necessary to act on its own rather than bring the full board into the discussion.

Perkins, as it turned out, proved unable to attend the meeting of the full board. He sent a statement, however, that recapitulated his version of the Ackland affair and that notably deemphasized his objection to the mausoleum while concentrating on the question of ownership and control. If Perkins had been present, he would have vigorously opposed and probably blocked a resolution that the trustees present passed without objection: that Duke University (i.e., Flowers) should issue a public statement explaining its position in the Ackland affair.

Perkins emphatically disagreed with the idea of the university's issuing a statement. It would fan the flames of public controversy, he argued, and produce even greater trouble than already existed. Allen assured Flowers that Perkins was "eternally right," and though Bruton chimed in that many trustees were troubled and that the "attitude of 'the public-be-damned'" was a dangerous one, Flowers ended up siding with Perkins and Allen. Despite the trustees' resolution, no public statement was ever issued.[28]

Thus neither the public nor most of Duke's trustees, for that matter, ever learned exactly why Duke declined the Ackland bequest. Thanks to an earlier will of Ackland's that mentioned the University of North Carolina as one of three possible sites for the museum and after many years of complex litigation, the William Hayes Ackland Art Museum of the University of North Carolina was dedicated (complete with mausoleum and recumbent statue) in 1958. The building and its equipment cost approximately $955,000; there was about $285,000 in an accumulated income fund immediately available for the purchase of art objects; and there was a permanent endowment fund of about $1,450,000. Duke would not acquire its much-needed art museum until the late 1960s and then only in a part of a partially renovated building on East Campus. The possibility of one recumbent too many — at least in the eyes of the powerful and combative Perkins — proved to be costly for Duke University.

Perkins, as mentioned earlier, died in 1945. Alexander Sands then joined George Allen as the most active and influential Endowment trustee as far as Duke University was concerned. A much less combative person than Perkins, Sands had long played a quiet but highly important, useful role in university affairs. After the war, for example, Sands worked closely with certain leaders at Duke to begin educating the faculty, alumni, and other friends of the university about the fact that the Endowment's resources were limited; that it had numerous obligations other than those to Duke University; and that in a period of escalating prices and costs the university was going to have to broaden the base of its support.

Unfortunately, President Flowers's advancing age and deteriorating health increasingly marginalized him. While there proved to be money for various new buildings, which were admittedly much needed, faculty salaries stayed stuck at prewar levels even as the cost of living escalated. Quite a few important members of the faculty began to leave Duke for better-paying jobs elsewhere, and recruitment of new faculty, except at the beginning level, began to be more difficult.

As Duke faced a profound crisis in leadership after World War II ended, the election of a forceful, dynamic chairman of the board of trustees in the spring

of 1946, Willis Smith, helped the university gradually to work its way out of a
sad, serious situation. (Bruton, who had for so long and faithfully served
Duke, died in his eighty-fourth year in March 1946.) An alumnus of Trinity
College's law school, Smith was a prominent attorney in Raleigh who was
serving as president of the American Bar Association when he was elected
chairman of Duke's board. Though he had long been a trustee, his national
prestige became important in his service to Duke, for he was not a person to be
easily intimidated or overawed.

Smith, working closely with Sands and certain leaders at Duke, set about
reinvigorating the board and tackling a wide variety of problems that need not
be discussed here. One of them, however, was to persuade Flowers, ever so
gently, that he should give himself a rest and, while remaining in his university-
owned house and drawing full pay, occupy a new position (largely honorary)
that had been especially created for him, that of chancellor of the university.
This meant that finally, in early 1948, the university could set about the task of
finding a new president.

Smith, supported by Sands and others, followed a different procedure than
that used in 1940. While the search committee itself was composed of trustees,
Smith invited a strong, representative committee of the faculty to play a consultative role in the search. When that committee polled the faculty about the
matter of a new president, it turned out that a strong majority of those who
responded preferred that an outsider be brought in for the post. Precisely why
the majority took that position is not known, but one probable reason is that
most of the faculty feared precisely what the Endowment trustees wanted: that
Wilburt C. Davison, dean of the medical school, be named president.

An enormously popular and likeable person, Davison had certainly been
highly successful in playing a key role in the building from scratch of what
quickly became perhaps the strongest, most nationally respected component
of the university. Among his many admirers, none were more enthusiastic
about him and his role in creating the medical center than the Endowment
trustees. Perhaps they could understand what Davison and the medical center
were all about better than they could, for example, the graduate school of arts
and sciences.

The nonmedical faculty, however, worried about some matters that apparently did not concern Allen, Sands, and other Endowment trustees. For example, while no one questioned Davison's prowess as a medical dean, many had
good reason to wonder about his understanding of or respect for liberal arts
education. Davison had ardently championed a plan whereby premedical stu-

dents could be admitted to medical school after only two years of college work, and this hardly connoted any deep concern about a broad, liberal arts education for those who were to become medical doctors. In a more mundane area, many nonmedical faculty believed, with good reason, that the university had constantly to guard against letting the medical tail wag the dog, especially where financial resources were concerned. The fact that the university had to cover the virtually chronic deficits in the budget of Duke Hospital meant that there was less money available for other purposes in the university. This became an increasingly serious matter after World War II, for as the hospital deficits soared, the medical facilities and staff kept growing. There was no one, however, to blow the whistle on Davison and his colleagues. Even before a new president was found, Willis Smith and others managed to have a new comptroller and business manager named at Duke, Alfred S. Brower, and his first task was to try to rein in Davison. "I cannot stress too strongly that it will be impossible for the University to continue to increase its allocation from its endowment revenue for the purpose of the Medical School and Hospital as it has in the past," Brower informed Davison in 1948, "and you may expect this action to be typical of that which will necessarily follow in future years." Brower went on to note that there had been little increase in income from endowed funds in recent years, and the rate of return on the funds had gone steadily downward. Yet the medical school had "increased its draft upon the income of the University in an almost steady progression from $296,000 in 1939–40 to $456,000 in 1947–48." The result, Brower noted, was that the medical area had come to absorb more than half of the university's entire income from the Duke Endowment.[29]

Against such a background, the nonmedical faculty's wariness of Davison becomes both reasonable and understandable. Although Sands certainly grasped the larger picture and all the implications concerning the medical center's relationship with the rest of the university, that did not deter him or the other Endowment trustees from pushing hard for Davison to be named president. Although there is no known evidence to support the idea, there is the possibility that another reason that the Endowment leaders were so pro-Davison was that they saw a Davison presidency as a feasible way of interesting Doris Duke in the university. After Few's death, Davison became the one person at Duke with whom the heiress maintained close, friendly relations.

Despite the faculty's preference for an outside appointment, the Endowment leaders might well have succeeded in ignoring faculty opinion except for one thing: Willis Smith, plus some other university trustees, did not want

Davison to be made president. Smith, as suggested earlier, was not one to be easily intimidated. After a meeting of the trustees' search committee where the division of opinion became clear—and it was probably a tense meeting—Smith avoided a formal vote because, as he explained to Allen, he agreed with Sands that the committee's nomination should be unanimous. There is even a story, which is probably true, that at some point in the proceedings, Sands hauled out the big gun and said something about the Endowment trustees' power to withhold payments to the university. Willis Smith is said to have snapped back briskly, "Well, you just go ahead and do that."

Tempers calmed, and Smith and other university trustees managed to prevail about an outside appointment. After not one but two near misses, when attractive candidates seemed on the verge of accepting the post only to withdraw their names at the last minute, the search committee in the fall of 1948 selected and the trustees quickly appointed A. Hollis Edens as the university's third president. Born in a Methodist parsonage in rural Tennessee, Edens had been forced to scramble for an education but managed to graduate from Emory University at age twenty-nine. After teaching in a secondary school and serving as principal for several years, he received a master's degree from Emory and began to hold a series of administrative posts there while he also began graduate work in public administration at Harvard. After the war, he advanced rapidly through several administrative posts at Emory and at the University of Georgia before accepting a position with the General Education Board in New York. That was where the Duke search committee found him, though Edens had to delay actually moving to Durham for several months while he completed his doctoral dissertation. So while Edens came to Duke with a Ph.D., he was not primarily a scholar, and his fast-changing career had actually been in administration. The fact that Edens was never the Endowment's first choice may have been a factor in trouble that began developing several years after he assumed the presidency.

Since Edens was an outsider, Smith as well as many others at Duke believed that the new vice president for education (the former one, William H. Wannamaker, had been gently removed along with Flowers) should come from the ranks of the Duke faculty. Consequently, Edens, acting on the advice of Smith and others, soon selected Paul M. Gross as the vice president for education. A chemist who had come to Trinity College in 1919, Gross had made the department that he chaired one of the stronger ones in the university; had established a solid reputation in his field, especially as an administrator and academic statesman; and had always taken a comprehensive, broad view of the mission of Duke University. Like Few, and even more so in one or two small but important ways, Gross understood well what a research university was all about. While he shared Few's understanding about the importance of the undergraduate colleges and the teaching that occurred in them, Gross was equally concerned about graduate education and became dean of the graduate school of arts and sciences in 1946. While one or two people suggested him for the presidency in 1948, the preferences of the faculty majority and of Willis Smith for an outside appointment precluded any careful consideration of Gross for the job.

The Edens-Gross team quickly began in 1949 straightening out a lot of accumulated problems at the university. In many ways they made a strong duo, for Edens was especially adept at cultivating strong, friendly relations with the alumni, the Durham community, and the Methodist church. A large, ruggedly handsome man of forty-eight (five years younger than Gross), Edens looked presidential and, without being a backslapper, had a great knack for putting people at ease and inspiring confidence in him. Gross, on the other hand, brought rich experience, great administrative skill, and a keen insight about proper priorities to his job.

The many ways in which Duke seemed to be strengthening itself in the 1950s need not be described in detail here.[30] As a recently established Loyalty Fund began to bring in increasingly significant sums from the alumni for the annual support of the university, Duke's first real development campaign ended in 1952 and raised $8,650,000. Extra help from the Duke Endowment came in numerous areas, such as the money to establish endowed chairs for distinguished members of the faculty — the first group of James B. Duke professors was named in 1953 — and later on support for the James B. Duke fellowships in the graduate school as the top awards to attract and support the best graduate students. There were also a number of important new buildings, but now they were accompanied by annual raises in faculty salaries that gradually began to rectify a sad situation in that area right after the war. Needless to say, faculty morale rose, not only in response to the better salaries but also because of the fact that the academic quality of undergraduate applicants to Duke, especially in Trinity College for men, began to show marked improvement. (The smaller Woman's College, with much less competition then than Trinity faced, had never had problems about quality.) Grants from the Ford Foundation, totaling nearly $6 million and ranking Duke tenth among the many institutions receiving Ford grants, also brightened the university's prospects. There were still some serious problems at Duke, of course, such as inherited but inadequate administrative structure as well as certain inherited administrators. On the whole, however, students, faculty, alumni, trustees — all of the important, diverse groups that make up a university — seemed to think that Duke was well headed in the right direction.

One person increasingly disagreed, and that was Paul Gross. In early 1955 he wrote a long, careful letter to Edens — rather than walking down the hall to talk matters over with him — and expressed his concern about and dissatisfaction with certain administrative arrangements at Duke. Among other things, Gross stated that he had felt increasingly over the past several years that his participation in "overall financial decisions" had been less than it should be if he was to carry out his responsibility effectively. Another matter of great concern to him, Gross explained, was that he did not believe that the educational program of the university received "wholehearted cooperation from some of the other divisions of the University." As a specific example, he pointed to the business division and to A. S. Brower, who, according to Gross, did not seem to realize that the whole purpose of the university was, above all else, education. Gross mentioned various other matters, some less important than others, and in many respects, he had a strong case.[31]

The crux of the matter was not what Gross was arguing for but the manner in which he proceeded to try to achieve his goal. There is no question that Gross had correctly diagnosed a weakness in Duke's administrative structure; moreover, his call for long-range planning in order for the university to begin moving more rapidly and systematically toward its goal of "a place of real leadership in the educational world," as J. B. Duke's indenture stated, was exactly on target. Instead of working openly to sell Edens and the university's trustees on his ideas, however, Gross chose to connive with his close friends from the Endowment who, in effect, controlled the executive committee of the university's trustees. This carefully hidden strategy would ultimately backfire and precipitate the crisis in 1960.

The role of the Endowment in the governance of the university was never more obvious than in the 1950s. When Willis Smith died in 1953, the university trustees elected Norman Cocke as their chairman. An original trustee of the Endowment, who had attended the University of North Carolina, Cocke had long been a key figure in the Duke Power Company and had succeeded George Allen as its president. Although both Allen and Sands continued to serve on the university's executive committee, Allen turned eighty in 1954 and, while still wielding great influence, was not as active in the affairs of either the Endowment or the university as he had been earlier. A younger man,

Thomas L. Perkins, gradually inherited much of the power that had for so long belonged to George G. Allen.

In many respects, Tom Perkins seems to have resembled his father, William R. Perkins, not so much physically perhaps as in temperament, manner, and a zest for combat. After graduating from Phillips Andover Academy, the younger Perkins worked on the stock exchange for several years before attending the law school of the University of Virginia, where he graduated in 1940. Joining his father's law firm in New York, he served for a time as legal counsel to Doris Duke and became a trustee of the Endowment in 1948. In 1958 he became a trustee of the university and soon thereafter replaced Allen on the executive committee. Perkins, like all the other above-mentioned Endowment figures, became associated with Duke University not as an alumnus but via the Endowment. Back in 1935, Chairman Bruton had warned Few that the plan to mandate that at least three Endowment trustees also be members of the university's executive committee was full of potential "mischief." A quarter-century later Tom Perkins, as much or more than anyone else, proved Bruton absolutely correct.

The unhappiness of Paul Gross about what he saw as unnecessary limitations to his own effectiveness and authority as well as about the alleged inadequacy of Edens as president reached a new high by late 1957. He therefore wrote a highly confidential, unsigned memorandum meant only for the eyes of certain members of the executive committee, though one of them would eventually show the document to Edens. After making a number of sagacious comments about where Duke stood as a university and how it should proceed to get where it wanted to go, Gross got down to specifics concerning the administration. He wanted the appointment of several younger persons as assistant or backup officers, and his suggestions here were subsequently followed after negotiations among Edens, Gross, and certain trustees. But the proposed change that Edens would not accept when he learned of it and that finally helped bring about his resignation was this: Gross suggested that "someone with intimate knowledge of all segments of the University's operation, who would be alert to the opportunities and needs for growth of the educational and other programs of the University," should be appointed as chancellor of the university. (Flowers, for whom the post had been created as a sinecure in 1947, had died in 1951.)

Gross saw the chancellorship not as a largely honorary post but as "a position somewhat similar to that of Executive Vice President in a business organization," and "that the incumbent should be charged with, and given responsibility for, overall supervision of the university's operations relating to education and the initiation, development and growth of the broad problems in this area." Gross declared that the chancellor should have real authority delegated to him; should work in cooperation with the president and the governing bodies of the institution; and should have direct access to the governing bodies alongside the president. The president, according to this plan, would continue to represent the institution before the public and also deal with broad policy decisions. During a transition period, Gross thought it would be wise for the chancellor to have also the title of vice president for education, although another title that Gross already had, dean of the university, might be assigned to someone else. That would relieve the chancellor vice president from certain onerous duties (connected with departmental budgets, new appointments to the faculty, promotions, and so forth) and allow more high-level concentration on long-range planning.[32]

Edens knew nothing of the above memorandum, but when he went to Charlotte late in November 1957 to confer with the chairman of the trustees, Cocke steered the conversation to the matter of the university's administration and suggested that Edens needed an executive vice president. Edens later recalled that he replied that the idea might be worth thinking about and that "it might be wise to bring in a man from the outside of an age bracket to succeed me in the years ahead." When Cocke promptly responded that Paul Gross would never stand for that and moved the conversation away from the subject, Edens began privately to wonder about what might be going on.[33]

A few days after Edens's talk with Cocke, both Cocke and Sands were on the Duke campus for a meeting about the Endowment's rural-church program, and Edens recalled that he thought that he detected that something was on the minds of the men. When Sands dropped by at the end of the day to say goodbye, Edens just asked him directly what was preoccupying him. Somewhat reluctantly, Edens remembered, Sands asked him if Cocke had talked with him about what "we have in mind." Edens replied that Cocke had opined that Duke needed an executive vice president. Expressing surprise, Sands said, "No, the title we have agreed on is Chancellor," and then took from his pocket "a memorandum which proved to be a rough draft of a pre-written minute [resolution?] of the Executive Committee which was to meet the following week, outlining a proposal which he was expected to make electing Vice President Gross as Chancellor, with the duties defined as general executive in charge of the total university operations on the campus." Edens recalled that he "expressed surprise and grave concern over the fact that this proposal had been agreed upon and apparently discussed with Vice President Gross without any participation on my part." Sands countered that Edens could at least try the arrangement for a year or two, then if he found it unsatisfactory, he "would just 'have to get out and do something else.'" After declaring his own friendly feelings toward Edens, Sands noted that such changes sometimes had to occur in large organizations and mentioned a large business corporation with which he was associated where the chief executive had been "kicked upstairs."[34]

Now truly worried, Edens decided to talk with Bunyan S. Womble, an alumnus of Trinity College, longtime trustee of Trinity-Duke, a member of the executive committee, and a prominent attorney in Winston-Salem. Womble was not only friendly toward Edens but was also sufficiently older than the president that he could and did offer candid, even fatherly advice. After Womble informed Edens that Sands had reported confidentially about administrative problems at Duke and that the two top men (Edens and Gross) had reached a demoralizing impasse, Edens gave him his view of the matter. He admitted that he had made certain administrative mistakes and that the relationship between him and Gross had become strained because he found it difficult to get the vice president to discuss matters freely.

As for making Gross chancellor, with the job described in the above-mentioned manner, Edens declared, "I could not agree to it under any circumstances." Edens went on to explain that Gross had gained the ears of two or three powerful trustees and obtained an agreement behind the president's back whereby he "expected to increase his authority . . . and that I refused to submit to such operations." Then Edens defined his position, one from which he refused to budge, despite considerable pressure, during the next two years: "I would be glad to move out of the presidency if the Board of Trustees wishes, but would not move over."[35]

Tense negotiations and conferences among Cocke, Womble, Edens, and Gross began in late 1957 and continued into 1958. Neither the great majority of the university's trustees nor the faculty, not to mention the public at large, knew anything at all about the university's administrative problems, for the matter was carefully confined to the executive committee. Finally in March 1958 a workable arrangement or détente seemed to have been hammered out. While Edens would not agree to a change in Gross's title, he tried to clarify the extent of the vice president's authority and fully agreed with the principle that "the academic function of the university is its reason for being." Relieving Gross of his job as dean of the university, as he had requested, Edens balked at naming the person whom Gross wanted for the position. Instead, Edens proposed a compromise candidate, Marcus Hobbs, who was an undergraduate as well as Ph.D. alumnus of Duke. In fact, Hobbs had received his doctorate in chemistry under Gross, established a strong record as a teacher and scholar, and succeeded Gross first as chairman of the chemistry department and then as dean of the graduate school.

Gross also gained additional changes that he wanted. The administrative committee of the university was enlarged to include W. C. Davison of the medical school, and two able young backup administrative officers joined the staff.

Perhaps the most important development of all, however, was that Edens named Gross as chairman of a newly established long-range planning committee. This meant that Gross finally had the opportunity to undertake exactly the sort of ambitious and broadscale planning for the future that he had long urged and for which he was superbly equipped. With Paul H. Clyde, professor of history and director of the summer session, as executive secretary of the planning committee, Gross led an able group in undertaking what would be the most careful and systematic examination up to that time of the university's strengths and weaknesses as well as its priorities for the future.

Working assiduously throughout the year and enlisting considerable help from the various departments and schools, the long-range planning committee produced its first progress report in 1959. Impressive for both its depth and specificity and exciting in its ambitious plans for the future, the report got an enthusiastic reception from the various constituencies of the university as well as from President Edens.

The details of the report need not be presented here, but to achieve the goals that had been spelled out, Gross and his colleagues proposed that the resources of the university had to be enlarged by $76 million by the end of the following decade. Making detailed projections of expenditures and income, including a series of tuition hikes, the committee called for $38 million of new endowment for salary projections; $24 million for new construction; and $14 million for the enrichment of the educational program. The explicit salary goal was to make Duke competitive with the fifteen best universities in the nation.

Edens, in a speech to the faculty and then in his published report for 1958–59, hailed the projected plans as "the most ambitious dream presented for the University since the dream which created it." He especially praised the historical portion of the progress report for its excellent assessment of Duke's heritage and emphasized that Few and J. B. Duke, as well as those who worked with them, had "not set out to build a provincial university, though they were in sympathy with the need to render special service to the South." They had fully understood, Edens asserted, "the exacting demands in teaching, scholarship and research on a national basis."[36] Both the strong support that Edens gave to the planning committee's program and his understanding of Duke's intertwined purposes of national and regional service should be carefully noted. Gross and his allies would later distort the record concerning these matters.

As 1960 began, optimism and enthusiasm characterized much of the Duke community and the university's constituency. Behind the scenes, however, and known only to the same small group that had been cognizant of the administrative trouble since 1957, the basic problem remained unresolved: Gross and his Endowment allies on the university's executive committee were not satisfied with the leadership and administrative operations of Hollis Edens.

By late 1959 Tom Perkins had replaced George Allen as the Endowment's chief representative on Duke's board of trustees and its executive committee. Perkins lost no time in making his presence felt and his views known. Inviting Edens to Charlotte for a conference, Perkins and Cocke, with the former "in charge," boldly confronted Edens with a new idea: why should not he move "up" into the chancellorship, defined now more as it had been for Flowers in 1948? Details of the conversation are not known, but Edens subsequently informed his assistant, Earl Porter, that it had occurred and that Perkins had a news release ready and planned to push the change quickly through the board of trustees. Edens, who may or may not have been surprised by the proposal, would only agree to think the matter over, although Perkins pressed him in a subsequent telephone call for a fast decision.

Since Edens eventually removed all documents relating to his conflict with Gross from his files and, as far as is known, destroyed them, one can only conjecture about what went on in his mind from December 1959 until mid-February 1960. At one point, according to Earl Porter, he considered fighting, for Edens knew that he had extensive support among the trustees as well as other key groups. On the other hand, he deeply wished to avoid hurting the university and feared that a knock-down-and-drag-out battle between the executive committee and its Endowment trustees on the one hand and the full board on the other might do serious, possibly irreparable, damage to the university. Other than confiding in his wife, his assistant, and Bunyan Womble, the harassed president kept his dilemma to himself. A proud, sensitive person, Edens probably felt many, conflicting emotions but one of them was almost certainly embarrassment or even humiliation. At age fifty-nine, healthy and vigorous, widely admired in North Carolina and respected in educational circles across the nation, he faced the prospect of ending his career in an unimpressive fashion, to put the matter mildly.

Since Gross also removed all papers concerning this matter from his files, how much he knew about the efforts of Perkins and Cocke to force Edens into the chancellorship is not known. That may well have been Perkins's own idea, though he and Gross had long been close friends. At any rate, in early February 1960 Edens went again to Charlotte to confer with Perkins and Cocke, and, as Edens told his assistant, it was a "real pressure meeting" with strong, candid talk. Edens noted also that he thought the two men's ideas about educational aspects of the university — especially Perkins's ideas — were "incredible."

Edens and the Endowment group agreed to meet again shortly in New York, this time with Sands present and Allen fully briefed. There they reached an agreement: Edens would announce his resignation from the presidency and remain in the position only until his successor could be named and take office. He would give as his reason for resigning the fact that, since Duke was about to launch an intense, ten-year development program, he believed that some-one who could remain at the helm throughout the decade should take over. (Edens favored a policy of having administrators resign at age sixty-five.) Moreover, he would say that, after eleven demanding years as president, he welcomed the opportunity to cultivate "the fine art of serendipity."

With Eden's letter of resignation in hand, Cocke called a special meeting of the executive committee in Charlotte on February 12, 1960, with Edens not present by mutual agreement. The committee members promptly voted to accept the resignation and took steps that indicated a hope of having a new president chosen with remarkable speed: they named a search committee, consisting of three trustees and two veteran faculty members, and asked it to look for a president within the ranks of the Duke faculty and staff and, if possible, to report the name at a meeting of the full board of trustees on March 23, 1960. Whether the Endowment group believed that the search committee, limited as it was in both the geographical scope and duration of its mission, would turn naturally to Gross as the next president is not known. Alternatively, the idea may have been to have the committee select someone who was acceptable to Gross and amenable to his guidance.

At any rate, as of mid-February 1960 only a small handful of people knew of Eden's resignation. It became public knowledge, however, when Edens wrote each member of the full board and then called a special meeting of the faculty to announce his plans. Understandably under the circumstances, most of the trustees as well as the great majority of the faculty, not to mention the alumni and students, were totally surprised and puzzled. Aside from the unexpectedness of the development, the reasons that Edens gave for his resignation were not too convincing. Even before the rumors of administrative friction began to appear in the newspapers, the faculty, after requesting its representative body (the University Council) to prepare appropriate resolutions expressing appreciation for Eden's service to Duke and regrets about his resignation, called on the University Council "to see to it there occurs that wide and effective consultation with this Faculty in the election of a new president that is consonant with the best accepted canons of good academic procedure." Accordingly, the council shortly afterward warned against undue haste in the search, expressed doubt about the likelihood of a decision by March 23, and called unwise the restriction of the search to Duke faculty and staff members. Just as the faculty showed its dissatisfaction with the procedure proposed by the executive committee, so also did a number of trustees. Consequently, the executive committee promptly withdrew the instructions that limited the search committee to persons at Duke and urged the committee to take whatever time it needed to find the proper person.

Those modifications, however, failed to halt the storm that was brewing among the trustees. One of them wrote Edens that he felt as if he had been "hit with a sledge hammer right between the eyes." Being proud of the honor of being a trustee, he declared that he felt "almost sick at heart to be notified about such a tremendous shakeup and never have been warned that such a possibility was imminent." This trustee insisted that "Eden's enthusiasm about the big development campaign" had been contagious, just as his "personal enthusiasm for the University's success has always caught fire with me, and I'm sure that it has with the rest of the alumni." The trustee hoped, in vain, that Edens would withdraw his resignation.[37]

Estelle Flowers Spears (Mrs. Marshall F. Spears), sister of the former president of the university and the first woman to be a Duke trustee, was also caught by surprise. Though she lived in Durham, only a short block from East Campus in fact, she thought it "incredible" that "a situation could have been building up over a period of time that made the President's position so intolerable that he saw fit to resign, and yet the Board as a whole should not be cognizant of it." Noting that she had promptly advised Norman Cocke that she disapproved of the limitations put on the search committee, Mrs. Spears insisted that to "find a man who will carry on the traditions of this institution and its spiritual heritage in the fine way in which Dr. Edens has done it will be exceedingly difficult."[38]

The newspapers, particularly in North Carolina's Piedmont cities, early began playing a role in the trouble at Duke, for other than members of the executive committee, virtually no one knew the full story or background. Vague rumors first appeared in the press, but investigative reporters in Winston-Salem and Greensboro moved beyond the rumors, talked with unidentified trustees and faculty members, and began to get at the complicated facts of the story, albeit in an incomplete and partial manner.

Although Edens, hoping to spare the university embarrassment, remained steadfastly silent as the controversy swirled around him, Gross chose to give an interview to reporters from the *Durham Morning Herald* on the day before the trustees were to meet. To say that Gross was practicing what a later generation would call "spin control" on a complex, controversial matter might be an exaggeration, but, at the least, he and the reporters managed to give an interpretation that was both inaccurate and unfair to Edens. Yet, ironically, Gross's interpretation would become the most widely accepted explanation of the conflict in future years.

The Durham reporters in their story on March 23, 1960, correctly predicted that the meeting of the Duke board that day would be lively, and they quoted one trustee as saying that, "The fur will fly." The centerpiece of the interview and story, however, came in several paragraphs that began with such phrases as "Gross feels" or "Gross would have." There was no question about the emphasis on the point that Gross had "pressed strongly for transforming Duke into a 'national type of university' along the lines of a Princeton, a Harvard, or a Columbia." That was quite true, as were other portions of the story that gave various details about Gross's aspirations and plans for Duke.

The trouble arose from the story's assertion that there had also been a great deal of pressure to keep Duke in the status quo — that is to say, "a very strong, but regional university," which was said to be "the Edens view." Moreover, the story claimed that there was "some strong feeling on the board of trustees to keep Duke at the regional level and to avoid catapulting the university into the ranks of a handful of strong national universities." In other words, Gross collaborated with the Durham newsmen to transform the long-building administrative fight into an alleged struggle between those who championed the idea of a national university and those who were said to prefer merely a strong regional status and identity.[39]

Since both Edens and the board of trustees had enthusiastically embraced the ten-year development campaign called for by the long-range planners, the grounds for accusing them of opposing Duke's national aspirations are hard to find. Edens and Gross had certainly disagreed about various details of timing and administrative procedure, but there is no evidence that either Edens or the great majority of the trustees felt any less ambitious for Duke than did Gross and his Endowment allies. Whether Gross might have suffered the same eventual fate at the hands of the trustees even if he had given no interview to the Durham reporters is not known. What is clear is that the story in the Durham newspaper increased the anger that the majority of the trustees felt toward Gross, and unfortunately for the university, not many hours after reading it the trustees would translate their anger into action.

No one could have been surprised that the board meeting of March 23 was a tense and ultimately explosive affair. P. Huber Hanes Sr. of Winston-Salem had become a trustee emeritus before 1960, but he kept in close touch with Duke affairs through his son, P. Huber Hanes Jr., who was a trustee, and through various others with important Duke connections. About a week before the board meeting, the senior Hanes wrote a strong, candid letter to his old friend Sands. After expressing shock upon learning of Eden's resignation, Hanes noted that he had been a member of the search committee that selected Edens and asserted his belief that Eden's record over the preceding eleven years had demonstrated the wisdom of the choice. "I think the Executive Committee exceeded its authority in accepting the resignation before having presented it to the Board," Hanes declared, and he thought there had "been some maneuvering, for how long I do not know, to force his resignation." Hanes thought the whole matter was "going to take years to overcome in the eyes of the public" and stated that, while he had not attended a board meeting since joining the ranks of the emeriti, he certainly planned to be there on March 23.[40]

Hanes undoubtedly knew that a group of trustees, including his son and Bunyan Womble, among others, had carefully planned their strategy for the board meeting. The group met first in Greensboro in late February, then in Winston-Salem on March 13. On the eve of the board meeting they caucused again in Durham and figured they were sure of at least twenty trustees, which was more than a majority, and thought it likely that three or four others might join them.[41] While their unhappiness was understandable in the circumstances, sober second thought might have suggested to them that quiet moves to persuade Gross to relinquish his administrative post would have been wiser than a carefully planned, semipublic "execution." While a small group of faculty members knew bits and pieces of what had been going on for several years, the vast majority of the faculty knew nothing until Edens announced his resignation. A member of the political science department probably spoke the plain truth when she stated, "The great majority of the Duke faculty has held both Dr. Edens and Dr. Gross in high regard."[42] That being the case and in light of Gross's widely acknowledged, faithful service to the institution for four decades, the manner of the demotion that was about to take place was bound to provoke a strong reaction among the faculty.

Before proceeding with the agenda, Chairman Cocke opened the meeting on March 23 with an unusual statement: he noted that an article in the day's *Durham Morning Herald* deserved some comment because it contained "many incorrect statements" and reflected "unfairly on Dr. Edens, and unjustly." After reading Edens's published and oft-repeated endorsements of the work of the long-range planning committee and the projected development program, Cocke added that Edens had cooperated throughout about the planning and "has at all times encouraged and supported the Development Program." After Cocke had finished, Womble pointed out that the publication of the allegation that Gross favored a national university while Edens and some of the trustees wanted only regional status for Duke had, he thought, done "great harm." Womble added that, while he did not know the purpose of publishing such a story, he had "never heard a word to substantiate that statement from the Trustees or Dr. Edens."[43] Since the board was meeting in executive session, those statements by Cocke and Womble were not published, although a release prepared by Duke's news bureau reported Cocke's denial of there having been clashing visions about the university's future. Many faculty members as well as alumni, students, and others, however, seized on the interpretation offered by Gross in his interview as the clearest explanation for what seemed a baffling series of events. Moreover, in later years, to the extent that there was on the campus any understanding of the great blowup of 1960, Gross's version of a clash between national and regional visions for Duke became the "standard" explanation. The only trouble was that it was not true.

After the trustees disposed of several routine items on the agenda, they turned to the matter of the president's resignation, and Edens read a short statement that he had prepared. He first noted that the reasons he had originally given for resigning had been and were still valid, but he now admitted that there had been "many converging reasons" that had gone into such a personal decision. "Subsequent to the announcement," he continued, "it has become evident [from newspaper stories] . . . that there were unannounced factors involved in the decision, factors which I had hoped to avoid discussing — as I do even now." Edens, obviously not wishing to elaborate on his long conflict with Gross and the Endowment trustees, then added that he did not believe there was "an indispensable man, at any level, in any large organization, certainly not in a university." He thought Duke was "strong enough and vital enough to gather its strength to move ahead into larger usefulness" and that the board of trustees was "competent and willing to assume its responsible role in seeing that that happens."[44] Edens then offered to retire from the meeting to allow more freedom of discussion, but various trustees asked that he remain. One of them, in fact, formally moved that the board request the president to explain all of the circumstances and facts as to why he had resigned. After the motion carried, Edens finally spoke extemporaneously on the subject that obviously pained him and that he had hoped to avoid. Mrs. Christine Kimball Mims, the president's chief secretary as well as secretary to the board of trustees, had a keener sense of obligation to history than did some of the major figures, for in addition to the traditional bare-bones, formalized minutes that she normally wrote up, she made and transcribed a complete stenographic record of the entire meeting, including Edens's off-the-cuff statement.

Edens began by reiterating his personal preference for not discussing the matter but added that, since he considered himself "subject to the command" of the board, he could not refuse to elaborate a bit. "Now, first I seek poise, restraint, good judgment and a sense of fairness to all concerned," he explained, "as I try to make such a statement." He pledged that he would avoid, as much as possible, "the calling of names or the making of charges or accusations" and would "try to remain within strict bounds of limited facts." Returning to his original explanation that he was resigning to make way for someone who could lead throughout the ten-year development program, Edens defended that widely publicized statement on the ground that it seemed "in the best interests of the University to select a valid reason that was as simple as could be made and let it rest there." Then the newspapers got into the act, though he noted that he had "constantly refused to be involved in any exchange with the press even when apparently an attempt was made to needle me into a provocative statement." The welfare of Duke being at stake, he insisted, "I took my action in what I believed was in the interest of the University" and "was unprepared for the uncontrollable stir which has come since."

Edens then briefly summarized the efforts beginning in late 1957 of "some members" of the executive committee to have Gross made the "chief executive of university operations," under one of several possible titles, and his (Edens's) refusal to accept that arrangement. Admitting that there had been differences in administrative judgments between Gross and himself, Edens failed to mention the concessions and administrative changes that he had agreed to in 1958. Then in late 1959, he noted, some members of the executive committee had urged that he "accept the position of Chancellor and vacate the presidency for a different type of leadership, with the belief that my role as Chancellor would be more effective, with those duties defined in general terms in the public interest of the University." Since the announcement had already been made that there was to be a study of the university's administrative structure, Edens stated that he felt it would be awkward for him to accept a new position before the study had been made. "Quite apparently," he added, "there are some members of the Board who feel that I am not the man to lead the University in the years ahead."

Rather than precipitate a fight in the full board of trustees and "stir up disaffection," Edens continued, "I chose to get out." Concerning his critics on the executive committee, Edens, after conceding his own fallibility, declared that "they are men of integrity and I must give them credit for standing up for what they believe to be the best interests of the University." Turning to his personal situation, he concluded:

> So, I felt that I ought to remove myself from the controversy and I ask you to allow me to do it. I have tried to reach back honestly and fairly and yet with restraint, without charges, recriminations and bitterness. I shall leave this University with good feeling, I shall continue to be available in any way I can serve, I shall have only lovely green memories of 11 years that have permitted me to, in my opinion, reach the crest of my career. . . . I shall not seek another high executive position, it would be an anticlimax after working with this wonderful University.

Almost as an afterthought or postscript, Edens referred to the statement that Chairman Cocke had made at the beginning of the meeting. "I am not aware of any conversation, or argument personally with Dr. Gross, or the Administration or the Executive Committee which has set a provincial local concept of the University over against [that of] a great national University," Edens avowed, and "I think it would be a mistake for you to argue around this fiction."[45]

After Edens then excused himself from the meeting, one trustee, clearly caught up in the unfolding drama, observed that if he had "ever seen a more perfect scenario for a moving picture, or a play on Broadway, than has developed here," he did not recall it. Moreover, he felt anxious about handling the situation so that "the University will have done everything it can and should to the end that our skirts will be clean and the press will have something to go on to clear the minds of the people, especially the alumni."

Womble interjected that he was not interested in personalities but in Duke. "I am not only an alumnus myself," he explained, "but all six of my children came to this University, and I have been a member of the Board, I expect too long, since back in 1915, and of the Executive Committee 10 years or more." Now he was concerned about Duke's future and the minimizing of the damage from what he considered "a terrible mistake." After other remarks, the trustees reached a consensus that Edens had clearly meant for his resignation to be final, and the motion that it be accepted, with appropriate resolutions of regret and appreciation, carried.

After disposition of several other matters on the agenda, one of the trustees moved, according to the prearranged plan of the pro-Edens caucus, that, "in view of the intolerable situation that prompted the resignation of President Edens and the impossibility of harmony under the administration of the Vice President in the Division of Education," Paul Gross should be relieved immediately from his duties as vice president and as chairman of the long-range planning committee. His role could be performed by the dean of the university (Marcus Hobbs) until a new vice president had been elected by the board.

In the tense discussion that followed this motion—a shock perhaps only to the Endowment trustees and one or two others—the first question was whether the board should hear Gross himself. "It is unthinkable that Dr. Gross be removed without a chance to be heard," Tom Perkins declared. Another trustee asked Cocke if the facts of Edens's statement were correct, and the chairman tersely replied, "Yes." "If that be so," the trustee asserted, "while it may be rather precipitate for us to act so promptly, I cannot see what purpose would be served by discussing charges with Dr. Gross." After a few more exchanges about the matter, Womble urged that Gross, who was in his office down the hall, be advised of the motion and invited to make a statement to the board if he wished. After due authorization, Womble marched down to inform Gross and bring him to the meeting.

Whether Gross was prepared for such a contingency is not known, but he may well have been. After thanking the trustees for the opportunity of speaking, Gross read the letter that he had written to Edens in 1955 wherein the vice president had pointed to what he regarded as various administrative problems and deficiencies. "The matter I was concerned about did not get better, but worse," Gross continued, "and I then went to Mr. Cocke and other members of the Board." He noted that then and on two subsequent occasions he put his resignation in Cocke's hands. Gross explained that in the first half of 1958, conferences among Edens, Cocke, and himself had resulted in the clarification of many issues, and he read a letter of his to Cocke of March 1958 (with a copy to Edens) and Cocke's reply.

Gross did not mention the various changes of title first for himself and then later for Edens that had been involved in all the discussions, but after he concluded his statement, he asked if the trustees had any questions. There was only one, when a trustee asked, "Dr. Gross, did you or did you not spend two hours with a newspaper reporter yesterday?" Gross replied, "I did," and added that he thought that some of the newspaper stories touching on him had bordered on libel. He therefore felt it necessary to defend and clarify his position. After again thanking the board for the opportunity to be heard, he left the room.

Chairman Cocke, after emphasizing the many contributions of Gross to the university and his national prominence in the scientific community, stated: "I think this resolution [to remove Gross from administrative offices] would have an unfortunate effect in the University, in the faculty, and I sincerely hope it won't be adopted at this time. We have a meeting in about two months and I think the atmosphere should clear itself." Womble replied that he feared that "if we do not accept Dr. Gross' resignation today the alumni and others will be greatly upset and I cannot help but believe that if we are to accept the resignation of one man we must have the resignation of the other." Another trustee suggested that the trustees as well as the public knew from the newspapers that Edens's resignation had been "brought about by the actions of certain individuals." Therefore, if the trustees took no action with reference to the other party, everyone would know that "one small group is directing Duke University and the Trustees as such are just a set of figureheads."

When another trustee asked about probable faculty reaction, Cocke asked Womble to comment. The latter then explained that he had spent a full day on campus in late February and, without even seeing Edens, had interviewed faculty members and others. Admitting that he might be wrong, the venerable attorney declared that he had gotten the impression that, while the faculty members were quite enthusiastic about the development program, "a large majority of them would not object to seeing Dr. Gross relieved of his authority with respect to the faculty." Unfortunately for the university, neither Womble nor the trustees realized that he had, no doubt unconsciously, probably spoken largely with a group of senior faculty members whose views and sympathies tended to coincide with his own and that the manner in which Gross was "relieved of his authority" would be crucially important.

Noting that Gross had mentioned proffering his resignation on three separate occasions, a trustee declared that if Cocke had it, it should be accepted. When others agreed with that idea, Cocke explained that he had heard Gross say he would resign but that he (Cocke) had no letter of resignation. "If I did," Cocke added, "I would accept it." Two trustees sympathetic with Gross urged that the dismissal of a faculty member from an administrative post should come as a recommendation to the board from the executive committee. An Endowment trustee, a member of the committee, favored "allowing this to come through regular channels and allowing Dr. Gross to submit his resignation and present it to the next meeting and acting upon it at that time."[46]

The trustee majority, perhaps fearing more dodging and maneuvering by an executive committee that appeared to be controlled by the Duke Endowment group, would not listen to the calls for caution and more normal procedure. After voting twenty-six to five in favor of requesting the resignation that day, the trustees assigned Womble the grim task of walking down the hall again to inform Gross and procure the desired letter of resignation. After Womble had done as directed, the trustees passed a motion that in the future, after each meeting of the executive committee, a copy of the minutes should be sent to each member of the board.[47]

Even before a carefully prepared news release appeared in the next morning's newspapers, many members of the Duke faculty became considerably disturbed and angry. Not knowing the full background of the dramatic and unprecedented action of the trustee majority and with Edens still adamantly refusing to make a public statement, most faculty members could only see that someone from their own ranks, a person highly senior and respected, had been treated in a harsh, humiliating manner. Now it was the turn of the faculty, or at least of a group of prominent faculty members, to react angrily and perhaps injudiciously. Several days before both Gross's newspaper interview and the board meeting, the University Council issued a statement expressing regret that an impression had been created that there were "serious divisions within the Faculty." The council insisted that there were "no major differences of opinion on the campus concerning the proper course of development for Duke University." Interested not in personalities but in the policies that were best for Duke, the council maintained that for orderly progress Duke needed a strong president, administrative restructuring, and increased communication among faculty, administrators, and trustees.[48]

Whatever the faculty leaders on the University Council may have earlier claimed about there not being "serious divisions" within the faculty, after the dismissal of Gross that was certainly not true. A relatively small group of senior professors who knew at least parts of the full story continued to defend Edens and to try to explain and justify the board's action concerning Gross. Before March 23 the most active and passionate defenders of Gross had also been a rather small group, chiefly in administrative posts, but the board's action brought a ground swell of faculty sympathy for Gross.

Passions ran high at a specially called meeting of the full faculty on March 25. Edens presided at the meeting as the ex officio head of the faculty and first announced that Marcus Hobbs, as dean of the university, would temporarily assume the responsibilities of the vice president for education and chairman of the long-range planning committee. Then, after considerable discussion, the faculty passed a resolution expressing to the trustees "their profound conviction that the appointment and dismissal of major University officers without prior broad and effective consultation with the Faculty is detrimental to the welfare of the University."

Turning to the newspaper stories about an alleged conflict between national and regional aims for Duke, William B. Hamilton, a professor of history and longtime faculty leader, introduced a resolution that echoed the views of former president William P. Few as well as of Edens and a number of trustees. It also succinctly explained why the national-versus-regional issue was essentially a false one, one that could all too easily become a red herring. Among other things, the resolution declared that the "aim of creating a university which will rank with the best is in no way in conflict with the special opportunities and obligations we acknowledge to the area in which we live." Duke, the resolution concluded, "could perform no better service to this region than to erect a university second to none in those fields in which its resources permit it to operate." After also passing that resolution, the faculty turned to a more controversial matter.

Since Gross had been immediately ousted from his administrative post and Edens was still occupying his and would until his successor had been named by the board, a group of Gross partisans pushed for a resolution urging the trustees to name a president pro tem immediately after commencement, if a permanent president had not been named by that time. That proposal stirred up the troops, but after much discussion the motion was tabled by a vote of 255 to 116, thus suggesting that faculty sympathy for Gross did not necessarily equate with antipathy toward Edens. Yet the faculty concluded the meeting by passing resolutions praising Gross for his many, varied services to Duke.[49]

The faculty, speaking collectively through a relatively rare full meeting, had acted carefully and with moderation. But a self-appointed group of thirty-two prominent faculty members, who were chairmen of departments or deans of some of the professional schools, obviously felt dissatisfied with the outcome of the faculty meeting and wished to issue a stronger rebuke to the trustees. Accordingly, on March 27 they signed and transmitted via Edens a petition to the trustees; they also sent copies to the president and to George Allen, chairman of the Duke Endowment. The letter also soon appeared in the newspapers. Addressing themselves primarily to the manner of Gross's dismissal, the petitioners charged that the trustees had "gravely damaged the morale of the faculty" and "damaged the University in the eyes of the academic world generally." They assailed the board's action against Gross as "ill-considered and destructive" as well as "irresponsible and not in the spirit of the trust assumed by the members of the Board in accepting their high office." The irate group noted that both faculty and trustees had been "mindful of a need for reorganization" of the university's administration. "We respectfully submit," they concluded, "that the time has also come for a reconstitution and reorganization of the Board of Trustees of Duke University so that, in the face of inevitable change, it may cope more adequately and efficiently with the ever-increasing complexity of the University's affairs."[50]

Just to round out the participation in Duke's donnybrook, the trustees of the Duke Endowment decided to get into the act. In a letter to the self-appointed committee of administrative faculty, a letter that also promptly appeared in the state's leading newspapers, the Endowment trustees declared that they agreed fully that the university board's action concerning Gross had been "precipitous and not in the best interests of Duke University." Quoting relevant passages from J. B. Duke's indenture creating the Endowment, its trustees emphasized their power to withhold funds from the university if it should not be "operated in a manner calculated to achieve the results intended hereby." Those results intended, the trustees explained in another quote from the indenture, were the "attaining and maintaining a place of real leadership in the educational world." After expressing their earnest hope that they would never be required to act under the above provision, the Endowment trustees joined the faculty group in calling for a reorganization of both the trustees and the administration at Duke.[51]

Here, for all who cared to see, was the Duke Endowment publicly blasting away at the university's trustees and threatening to use its very big stick of financial control. As old-timers used to say, William Preston Few was probably rotating wildly in his grave, for the unthinkable had happened: an angry split and feud between the two groups on whom the university depended for guidance and support had not only occurred but also become public knowledge. The Raleigh *News and Observer* asserted editorially that the Endowment trustees were not only "making an improper threat" in threatening to cut off funds to Duke, but "they were just talking nonsense." They might possess the legal right, the newspaper noted, but they "would make only a spectacle of themselves if they withheld [J. B.] Duke's money from the university which is his chief monument." The sad truth was, the editorial concluded, that "a great educational institution has already been made to seem confused and uncertain by all the undercover rowing within it which has inevitably become public."[52]

Amidst all the rancorous confusion, George G. Allen in New York telephoned Edens to express concern about the state of affairs "down there." Still clinging to a pet notion that the Endowment trustees had pushed unsuccessfully back in 1948, Allen wanted to know if Edens would be willing to step aside and let the medical school's Dean Wilburt Davison be named acting president. Refusing to do that, Edens told Allen what he had already stated on several occasions: he "would abide by the Board's wishes and leave at any time, but he . . . would not participate in the naming of his successor and that would include the acting president too."[53] In a telephone conversation some days later, Alexander Sands reportedly told Edens, "Well, we tried to run it [the university], and they didn't like what we did. Now let them run it."[54]

The first steps toward healing, which would be slower perhaps for certain individuals than for the institution itself, came in April 1960. Encouraged by Earl Porter to "try to heal things," Edens did make telephone calls and friendly overtures to Sands. The most significant step, however, came on April 21, 1960, when the board met again and the presidential search committee submitted the name of Julian Deryl Hart to serve as acting president.[55] Chairman of surgery in Duke's Medical Center since its opening in 1930 and one of its chief builders, Hart, who was nearly sixty-six, had the respect of all of the diverse factions in both the faculty and the trustees. After the full board quickly approved the appointment and Hart assumed the acting presidency on July 1, 1960, the mending process was well under way at Duke. In fact, Hart, with valuable administrative help from several outstanding faculty members who had managed to keep a safe distance from the earlier acrimony, performed so well that the trustees later dropped the "acting" and named him the university's fourth president.

Although the costs had been high, needed changes and improvements at Duke resulted from the Gross-Edens affair. As a number of people began to observe even while the drama unfolded, President Few's plan of entrenching three Endowment trustees on the university's executive committee had given that group too much power over the university. While the various individuals involved — George G. Allen, William R. Perkins, Alexander Sands, Tom Perkins, and one or two others — certainly had in mind the university's best interests, as they perceived them, their control over such vast sums of money simply endowed them with too much power and led to hubris. They provided a perspective that was often valuable, but they were essentially New York businessmen. Not only were they not alumni of Duke, but they also were occasionally insensitive about the institution's North Carolina roots and obligations and were unnecessarily wary about its historic, friendly connections with the Methodist church. When the Endowment's leaders began themselves to realize that it might be best if Endowment trustees not also serve as trustees of beneficiary institutions, the way was clear in 1965 for the elimination of Few's bylaw addition of 1935.

Within the university, the administrative restructuring that all had finally come to regard as desirable resulted in a number of changes. Perhaps the most important was the creation of the office of the provost, the top academic officer beneath the president and chief aide in maintaining university-wide authority over academic affairs. Taylor Cole, a distinguished political scientist, would be the first person to hold the post and fully demonstrate its usefulness.

Hollis Edens, after taking a much needed rest, accepted a position with the Mary Reynolds Babcock Foundation in Winston-Salem. Later he retired in Atlanta and died there at age sixty-seven on August 7, 1968. Gross returned to his post as the William H. Pegram Professor of Chemistry until his retirement in 1965; he also served as a paid consultant on educational matters for the Duke Endowment until his death at age ninety-one on May 4, 1986. In December 1968 the trustees of the university, remembering President Few's assertion that Duke always cherished the memory of those who had served the institution, took evenhanded action: they named a handsome new complex of dormitories on the West Campus the Arthur Hollis Edens Quadrangle and, at the same time, named the first architecturally interesting building to be erected on Science Drive the Paul M. Gross Chemical Laboratory. While the Gross-

Edens affair remained a painful memory, the university at least memorialized both of its leading participants.

The Endowment would, of course, continue to play an important, even essential, role in the life of Duke University. It would not again, however, attempt to place itself in such a dominant position in the governance of the university and to bulldoze, if not ignore, the university's own board of trustees. As a result, the way ahead would be clearer for Duke University after the early 1970s.

5 ·

IN

REMEMBRANCE

OF THE

CIRCUIT RIDERS

The Endowment and the

Methodist Church in

North Carolina, 1924–1960

ALTHOUGH THE INVOLVEMENT of Washington Duke and his family with Trinity College was what might be termed the starting point or nucleus of the Duke Endowment, they would never have become interested in the college if it had not been a Methodist institution. In one sense, therefore, the true fountainhead of the multifaceted philanthropy embodied in James B. Duke's charitable trust lay in North Carolina Methodism.

The lifelong devotion of Washington Duke to the Methodist church need not be again detailed and emphasized here. That he raised his children to attend regularly the same country church services that meant so much to him would be expected. He had first attended Sunday school at Mount Bethel Methodist Church near his home in the northern portion of Orange (later Durham) County, and at age ten, in 1830, he joined the church during a revival service there. Washington Duke's older brother, William J. ("Uncle Billy") Duke also exerted a large influence, for he was an exhorter or lay preacher. In the late 1830s he built a large arbor near his home where outdoor services and camp meetings could be held. Later he built a log church called Mount Hebron and more familiarly known as Duke's Chapel, where Washington Duke and his family also frequently worshipped. It was "Uncle Billy" Duke who once sent up a memorable prayer, one that still resonates with farmers and gardeners: "Oh Lord, send us some rain. We need it. But don't let it be a gully-washer. Just give us a sizzle-sozzle."[1]

Washington Duke and his family also attended services at another Methodist chapel, Orange Grove, that was near their home. In 1860 this church moved to the hamlet of Durham where a few dozen families had settled around a station on the new railroad. It was this church, which eventually became Trinity Methodist, where Washington Duke long served as a church officer and where his two youngest children, Ben and "Buck," had their own conversion experiences and joined the church in their early teenage years.

All of these Methodist churches with which Washington Duke and his family were involved were both small and poor in a monetary sense. That was why they could not afford to support a regular preacher who could hold weekly services on Sunday as well as midweek prayer meetings. They therefore shared a preacher who rode the circuit, preaching in one of the churches the first Sunday of the month, another the second, and so on. Especially devout lay Methodists such as Washington Duke often had to ride the circuit also if they wished to attend religious services more than once or at the most twice a month. In a hardworking farming community where diversions were scarce, the churches played an important social as well as spiritual role. Dinners-on-the-ground and weeklong revival meetings were important events that helped relieve the monotony of a hardscrabble existence.

"My old daddy always said," J. B. Duke often told his close associates, "that if he amounted to anything in life it was due to the Methodist circuit riders who frequently visited his home and whose preaching and counsel brought out the best that was in him. If I amount to anything in this world I owe it to my daddy and the Methodist Church."[2] Having grown up knowing well the vibrant but struggling country churches of North Carolina Methodism, J. B. Duke chose to include them as an important beneficiary of his philanthropy.

In the indenture, J. B. Duke allocated a total of 12 percent of the annual income from his original trust to Methodist causes in North Carolina. There were, however, three different parts of this allocation. From the time that Washington Duke began to enjoy a respectable income, which was probably in the 1880s, "worn-out" Methodist preachers and their dependents aroused his sympathy and became objects of his concern. Ben and J. B. Duke also began regularly in the 1890s to contribute money for this purpose, and in 1915 J. B. Duke began making an annual contribution of $10,000 to supplement the funds of the two Methodist conferences in North Carolina for their superannuated preachers and the widows and orphans of deceased preachers.

He requested Trinity College to make the annual disbursement, a task that President Few performed happily and gracefully just before Christmas each year and that brought in many heartwarming letters of thanks.

Accordingly, in the indenture, J. B. Duke stipulated that 2 percent of the annual disposable income from his trust should be expended by the trustees "for the care and maintenance of needy and deserving superannuated preachers and needy and deserving widows and orphans of deceased preachers" who had served in one of the two conferences of the Methodist Episcopal Church, South, in North Carolina.

Also in 1915 J. B. Duke had begun giving $25,000 annually to the Board of Church Extension of the Methodist Episcopal Church, South; he earmarked $15,000 of this for assistance in building rural churches and $10,000 to help with the current expenses of such churches. In 1920 J. B. Duke requested Trinity College to administer these funds also and explained to the Board of Church Extension that he made the change not through any dissatisfaction but simply because, "I have always been very closely identified with Trinity College, and not only would like for them to handle it for me, but think it would help the college by its so doing."[3]

Picking up these two benefactions in the indenture, J. B. Duke specified that the trustees should use 6 percent of the annual disposable income to assist in building Methodist churches in North Carolina; in no instance, however, should the trustees provide more than half of the needed funds. Moreover, "only those churches located in the sparsely settled rural districts" of North Carolina, and not in a town having a population in excess of fifteen hundred people, were to be eligible for aid in building. In other words, since a great many rural Methodist churches in the 1920s were still served by circuit readers, albeit increasingly in automobiles rather than on horses, J. B. Duke clearly meant to confine this building fund to those churches. And for the maintenance and operations of those same rural Methodist churches, J. B. Duke designated 4 percent of the annual available income from his trust fund.

As in other areas covered by the indenture, all of these payments for the benefit of the Methodist church in North Carolina were placed in the "uncontrolled discretion" of the trustees with respect to the "time, terms, place, amounts and beneficiaries." J. B. Duke also suggested that so long as the arrangement was satisfactory to the Endowment's trustees, these payments to the Methodist causes should be made through Duke University.

Unlike the aid for hospitals and orphans, therefore, there was already in existence when J. B. Duke established the Endowment a tradition of and mechanism for the assistance to the Methodist causes. Just as President William P. Few had played a key role in the matter when Trinity College served as J. B. Duke's agent prior to 1925, so would Few continue to do the same thing when Duke University became the agent. This meant that the work of the Endowment in the area of the North Carolina Methodist church was long based at Duke University and particularly in its School of Religion or, after 1941, its Divinity School.

The Endowment's annual supplement to the meager pensions that the Methodist church then paid its retired preachers or their surviving dependents was a fairly simple, even mechanical matter. The amount available for disbursement varied from year to year, but in 1932, for example, the payment to the superannuates from the Endowment was 34 percent of the pension paid by the church conference. That is, if the superannuate received $100 from the conference, he got an additional $34 from the Endowment. It was a warm, quite humane gesture and one that President Few enjoyed. Just how he managed to carry on all the correspondence that was involved, however, as he simultaneously played the key role in organizing and staffing a complex research university, is almost beyond comprehension. He had no formally designated assistant and probably placed a heavy burden on his secretary, but he got the job done, gracefully and always on schedule.

In the Endowment's first yearbook, which covered the period down through December 1928, Few reported that beginning in 1926 when funds became available down to the end of 1928, the Endowment had made 768 donations to superannuates for a total of $66,250. He added that the two Methodist conferences in North Carolina were making special efforts to build up their funds for the superannuates; with the aid from the Endowment and the church's conferences, the hope was that there would soon be an adequate pension system. Few explained that this was important for many reasons, but one in particular related to the church's work in the rural areas. As "preachers became less active [and older]," Few noted, "they are promptly sent to the country circuits and for lack of sufficient retiring allowances they are often kept there when they are very inactive." An adequate pension system, therefore, was an essential step in improving conditions in the rural churches. "All these things are coming in North Carolina," Few declared, "and the [Methodist] denomination in the great open spaces of the country is to have an opportunity rare among men to carry forward the causes of the Kingdom of God."[4]

When the Endowment's income shrank at the peak of the Great Depression in the early 1930s, all of the beneficiaries suffered reductions accordingly. Few wrote the same sort of pre-Christmas letter to the superannuates or their dependents that he had been sending out since 1915 but added a few sentences about how "very anxious" J. B. Duke had been that his trust fund "be built up through the years and kept available for the purposes it was set to serve." Yet conditions in recent years, Few continued, had tended to decrease the income from the fund. "Speaking for all concerned about it," Few added, "I can say that we have done the best we could to protect it. All of us regret that it is not larger but we distribute it with great good will and praying Heaven's richest benedictions upon you and yours now and always. Affectionately yours, W. P. Few."[5]

In response to this letter with its enclosed check, one of the recipients wrote Few that she was writing her first letter of the New Year to thank him and the Endowment. "The tone of your official letter to the beneficiaries of the Foundation," she explained, "is always so warm and personal, that I feel I must make a personal response." She added that she was especially grateful for the check that winter, for it made it possible for her "to lay in a supply of coal."[6]

While total amounts of money paid to the "worn-out preachers" and the average amounts paid hardly suggest the richly human element of the matter, the Endowment's annual report in 1950 offered an interesting summary of what had happened in the quarter-century of the Endowment's operation. The $605,191 contributed by the Endowment to the superannuates through December 1949 meant that for each $100 contributed by the two Methodist conferences, the Endowment had given $22.85. The growing realization of the need in this field, which J. B. Duke had envisioned in 1915, was well illustrated by the manyfold increase in allotments by the conferences over the years. In 1915 there had been 118 claimants; conference allotments totaled $18,711, which, when supplemented by J. B. Duke's $10,000, gave an average of $243 per claimant. In 1949 there were 418 claimants, and the conference allotments totaled $333,568, which, when supplemented by $29,500 from the Endowment, resulted in an average per claimant of $868. While there were in 1949 more than three times as many claimants as in 1915, the average payment per claimant had been trebled, and the conference allotments increased to fifteen times the earlier amount.

Not only were the funds for aid in building rural Methodist churches larger than those for the superannuates (6 percent of the income as compared with 2 percent), but the administration of the building fund posed greater problems. Poverty had been so endemic in the rural South for so long that there was a deep-seated cultural bias toward "making do" as best as one could under harsh circumstances. While the small churches scattered so liberally over the countryside were centrally important in the spiritual as well as the social lives of the congregations that gathered in them, the buildings themselves often tended to be indeed spartan if not downright ramshackle. The Endowment, in collaboration with leaders in the Methodist church, hoped to rectify that situation, but it would be a gradual, ongoing, and sometimes tricky proposition.

For one thing, church officials and the Endowment strongly favored the use of an architect in the erection or extensive renovation of a church structure. Many local congregations, however, were hard pressed to raise enough money to purchase necessary building materials and often regarded the use of an architect as an insupportable, unnecessary luxury. While selling the idea that an architect could actually save a congregation money in the long run was not easy, the Endowment, always acting in conjunction with church officials, gradually helped bring about a new era in the design and construction of rural Methodist churches in North Carolina.

President Few had worked with a committee of six Methodist clergymen (three from the older North Carolina Conference and three from the Western North Carolina Conference, and always in cooperation with the presiding elder and local pastor) in dispensing J. B. Duke's funds during the decade prior to the establishment of the Endowment. In 1926 the Endowment's trustees voted to continue that arrangement, with their own committee on the rural church working in close cooperation with Few's "Durham committee." For the church-building program in particular, the trustees adopted six general principles or guidelines: (1) the building should meet the needs, both existing and prospective, of the congregation to be served; (2) it should serve as an example for other congregations to follow and usually should provide at least three rooms (for Sunday-school purposes) in addition to the church auditorium or sanctuary, with the building plans to be approved before the commitment of any Endowment funds; (3) the structure should be a permanent one and constructed of brick or stone if possible; (4) the building site should be a good one and, if in the open country, should have plenty of land, say five to ten acres; (5) the churches should be strategically located, in communities that were apt to grow and at points where weaker churches might easily be consolidated; and (6) the Endowment should make the amount of money appropriated for a church building (which was never to exceed half of the total cost) larger or smaller depending on how a particular congregation met the preceding conditions as well as on its financial ability and only after a careful study and personal inspection by a member or members of the Durham Committee.

To illustrate how the Endowment proceeded to help rural Methodists improve their physical facilities for worship, one might take the case of the church in Macon, North Carolina. The village had in 1927, 150 white residents and 50 African Americans and was located six miles from Warrenton in the eastern part of the state. The Methodists there proposed to remodel their existing building (valued at $2,000) and add Sunday-school rooms. With a total estimated cost of $11,500, the congregation requested a grant of $3,000 from the Endowment. Few's committee endorsed the request, recommending that the Endowment appropriate $2,500, with $1,000 to be paid when a third of the total cost had been raised; another $1,000 when two-thirds had been raised; and the final $500 when, with that amount, the improvements could be completed and the church turned over to the congregation free of debt. When the Endowment's committee on the rural church — which then consisted of R. L. Flowers, Alexander Sands, and Norman Cocke — endorsed Few's recommendation, the full board of trustees voted the appropriation. With subsequent variations about the staggered payments, this would long remain the pattern for the Endowment's assistance in building rural Methodist churches.

The fact that Few actually knew a large number of the Methodist preachers in the state made him especially valuable in the Endowment's church work. He had either taught or known some of them at Trinity College; moreover, he faithfully attended Methodist meetings at all levels — local, district, conference, and general conference. Too, he had an extensive, deep knowledge of North Carolina communities. For example, when a Methodist church in Atlantic, North Carolina, applied to Alexander Sands in early 1925 (soon after all the initial publicity about the creation of the Endowment), Sands sought help from Few. Atlantic, Few reported, was an isolated fishing village of about 1,000 people. "It was originally hard shell [Primitive] Baptist and primitive in every way," Few noted, but it was changing. There was now an excellent public high school, which sent a number of its graduates to college, including some at Trinity. The Methodist church at Atlantic cost $7,000 or $8,000, had about 100 members, and was on a two-point circuit. "The whole eastern part of the state is in a rather bad way financially," Few explained, "and you may be prepared for a flood of applications like this one." Few added that Trinity College held annually a two-week summer session for North Carolina's rural Methodist preachers, and in connection with that, he and certain of his colleagues at Trinity tried to collect as much firsthand information about the rural churches as they could. He hoped soon to have a comprehensive survey of the state's rural Methodist churches.[7]

The survey to which Few referred would be the work of Jesse M. Ormond, who gradually relieved Few of much of the day-to-day responsibility in the rural church work, although Few continued to chair the Durham Committee. After graduating from Trinity in 1902, Ormond later (1910) received his divinity degree from Vanderbilt University. After serving a number of Methodist churches in North Carolina, he briefly taught pastoral and practical theology at Southern Methodist University before joining the Trinity faculty in 1923. Ormond soon became a specialist in rural church work and an important link between Duke University's School of Religion and the Endowment. In June 1926 Few informed the presiding elders and others that all inquiries and applications for assistance from the Endowment should go to Ormond and all questions concerning payments and settlements to the university's assistant treasurer, Charles B. Markham.

Just as Watson Rankin had early seen the need for model plans for small community hospitals, Ormond, probably at Few's suggestion, set out to obtain "modest sets of plans and specifications" for small rural churches. Ormond negotiated with the Methodist Board of Church Extension in Louisville, Kentucky, and first requested plans and specifications for a frame church with a seating capacity of 200 and costing around $7,500. Subsequently, he asked for two other types of plans, one in the range of $12,500 and one of $17,500. "This will give us a range from the cheapest possible church," Ormond noted, "to that which should be considered a maximum price for rural churches in poorer communities." He figured that any church planning to build a structure costing more than $17,500 should be able to do so unassisted.[8]

Soon equipped with his sets of church plans, Ormond strove diligently to raise the standard of architecture for the country churches. The initiative for improved facilities often originated in the Methodist Ladies Aid Societies, especially after publicity concerning the Endowment's program appeared in the *North Carolina Christian Advocate,* the Methodist newspaper. "We do not feel inclined to spend money on old houses which are simply one-room buildings," Ormond informed one Methodist woman. "We are anxious to see all our houses so thoroughly equipped that the most modern Sunday school and church work may be done, and if you all really mean business and want to have adequate equipment and are willing to make some sacrifice in order to get it, then I think I can assure that the Duke Commission will be greatly interested in your project."[9]

In response to an inquiry about possible assistance toward a new roof for a rural church, Ormond explained that the Endowment was not eager to help congregations just patch up an inadequate facility and make do. If the congregation wanted to think about remodeling, however, and make provision for the addition of a Sunday-school unit providing for at least three departments, then a new roof for the original structure could certainly be included in the plan.

While the Endowment's trustees certainly preferred brick or stone church buildings, the reality in much of the state was that the congregations were lucky if they could raise enough money for frame structures. A Methodist woman in a remote region of the North Carolina mountains wrote Ormond that she had not been able to attend church services in two years. The reason was that the nearest Methodist church with regular services was nine miles away, and she lived in a community that was two miles from a good road and seven miles from the railroad. Was there any chance of help from the Endowment? Ormond sent the woman the name and address of the presiding elder in her district, urged her to start with him, and assured her that the Endowment was eager to help when and where it could.

Widespread poverty in the mountains was matched by similar conditions in much of the eastern portion of the state. The presiding elder in the Wilmington district informed Ormond in 1929 that he wanted to build a small, new church in a community some seventeen miles north of Wilmington. "I should like to make it a sort of model building of this sort," the church leader explained, "so that other congregations in the district might pattern after it." He expected to have a considerable part of the building material contributed and for the church to cost around $3,500. The auditorium should seat about 135 persons, and there should be Sunday-school accommodations for 60 to 75 people. "No provisions need be made in the building for toilets," he explained, "as [piped] water is not available in the village."[10]

Ormond responded enthusiastically to the presiding elder's plan, despite the fact that it was perhaps more modest than the Endowment trustees had originally hoped for. "I am convinced that in many of the eastern counties as well as in the extreme western counties," Ormond declared, "some, new, adequate, cheap country churches must be built." He hoped the energetic presiding elder would show people just how to do that.[11]

Despite the severe economic slump that had hit North Carolina's farmers in the 1920s, some years before the entire nation encountered the depression, many preachers and their congregations kept trying to secure better church buildings. The Methodist minister in Plymouth, another farming community in the east, informed Ormond that his congregation had talked for years about a new church, and he was now determined to help them do something about it.

"Methodism hangs on a better church here," the preacher avowed. The existing church building had been erected before the Civil War and was a frame structure 33 by 66 feet; the balcony had been enlarged and glassed in to serve as a Sunday-school department. "Our church is the worst building in town used by any race of people," the minister insisted. When he requested Ormond to send his architect down for consultation, Ormond explained that there was no charge involved when the architect was consulted in Durham, so the minister and one or two of the leading lay members should take advantage of the service.[12]

The architect to whom Ormond referred was H. N. Haines whom the Endowment helped bring to Duke in the fall of 1929 from the Board of Church Extension. With an office near Ormond's in the School of Religion's building, Haines became available both for field trips when requested and for consultation on the Duke campus. Few, Ormond, and others involved in the program gradually learned that good intentions on the part of the ministers and their congregations were not enough. Not only were architectural plans and an architect's supervision required for assistance from the Endowment, but also church officials, before receiving any part of an Endowment grant, had to sign an affidavit that all conditions of the grant had been met and that the project was progressing in regular order. The idea behind this arrangement was to try to forestall misunderstandings on the part of congregations and to ensure that the original plans, on which a grant had been based, were carried out.

After Haines had been at Duke for two years, Ormond reported that the architect had visited 125 church-building sites, prepared seventy-five sketches for preliminary surveys, and made thirty-two working drawings and specifications. He had given full architectural supervision for practically all of the larger church structures. Ormond also made many field trips as well as received numerous delegations in his office.

As the depression worsened in the early 1930s, however, the building of churches necessarily slackened. Ormond noted that there were fewer requests for assistance in 1930 and 1931, and the average cost of assisted churches fell from almost $11,000 in 1929 to a bit over $8,000 in 1930 and 1931. The average donation from the Endowment was down from approximately $1,670 in 1929 to around $1,435. Yet, oddly enough, Ormond also reported that an increasing proportion of churches were being built of brick or stone.

At the height of the depression as far as the Endowment was concerned, when its own income had drastically fallen, the trustees, understandably enough, became quite cautious about encouraging congregations to undertake building projects. When a presiding elder early in 1932 pushed Ormond for a commitment from the Endowment of 50 percent of the cost for a desired project, Ormond insisted that the Endowment could not sustain such a large percentage, which he believed would be "disastrous to the country church itself as well as to the fund." The trustees had instructed him to say, he continued, that it was not a promising time to build churches. With banks closing, merchants declaring bankruptcy, and farmers without money, the trustees had come to believe that something of a moral question was involved in the consideration of building projects. Quite a few churches were already mired in embarrassing debts, and the trustees wondered if "it would be more moral for us to give aid to the distressed churches already projected than to encourage new projects at this time." Yet, Ormond added, if a congregation could show resources to cover up to 75 percent of cost, that would make a good talking point in presenting the application from such a church.[13]

Religious fervor did not, of course, fluctuate in synchronization with the economy. In early 1932, as the Endowment's trustees felt more and more cautious about helping to build churches, a circuit-riding Methodist preacher reported to his presiding elder in Wilmington that the members of one of his churches on the charge desperately wanted to remodel, but he thought the presiding elder had better consult with Ormond first. "Things are beginning to take on a new life on the circuit," the preacher reported. "On the fifth Sunday we have a circuit-wide prayer meeting at Carvers Creek. The object . . . is to meet in one big body and sing and pray and confess, and lay plans for a great awakening on this Circuit." He was having good crowds at the services and planned to organize an Epworth League for the young people at one of his churches on the following Sunday night.[14]

In Kitrell, a community north of Raleigh, also early in 1932 the preacher informed Ormond that the members at one of his churches greatly needed an assembly hall for Sunday school and social purposes. "Our folk are like the rest of the world—Bank Rupt," the preachers explained, so they were considering building the hall with plain logs. Since the preacher hated to see his congregation put materials and effort into something that would not be permanent, he wondered if Ormond could help if the preacher persuaded the congregation to use lumber and build the hall in keeping with the rest of the church. Counting the cash on hand, which was $125, and materials and labor pledged, the preacher believed they could raise $600 or $700.[15] Ormond replied that the Endowment would be glad to help, though it urged great caution at that time.

In fact, in 1932 the entire amount that the Endowment gave for church building was only $5,200, whereas in earlier years it had averaged around $50,000. Perhaps it was not altogether a matter of the Endowment's not having more money that could have been made available, but rather that the congregations simply did not have and could not scrape together the resources that they needed.

Aid in the worst years of the depression went in small amounts to the neediest places. One example of this came in 1935 when a graduate of Duke's divinity school reported to Ormond from the Old Fort circuit near Asheville. He had four churches on the circuit, all on good roads, and believed that he had found "one of the greatest possible opportunities here for real constructive building of the Kingdom" that he had ever found anywhere. The circuit, he thought, had been "fearfully neglected, as is the case with entirely too many of our rural churches." But the people were "eager for something they haven't had." The zealous minister reported that none of his four churches was equipped for Sunday-school work. In fact, all of them were "just big, old, open, cold sort of barns where little children, men and women gather and try to worship." The hopeful thing, in the preacher's view, was that the people were not satisfied with their situation and were ready to do something about it. He hoped to help them build two new churches and remodel another.[16]

Given such a case as this, Ormond replied encouragingly. He also cautioned, however, that it was unwise to have more than one project from the same circuit at one time. The preacher should, therefore, pick the most pressing case and fill out the application form only for it.

By 1936–37 Ormond was back in regular business and with even more money available than in the late 1920s. By 1950, when the Endowment had operated for a quarter of a century, it had provided nearly $1,180,500 to 673 rural Methodist congregations in North Carolina. Requests for assistance were arriving in growing numbers, so much so that beginning in 1949, instead of considering applications when they were received, the Durham committee required that all preliminary applications for projects in any one year had to be in hand by a certain date. This allowed the committee to appraise the relative merits of the proposals and to make a more equitable distribution of the limited funds.

Jesse Ormond, after his pioneering efforts in the life and work of the rural church, retired in 1949 and was replaced by A. J. Walton as director of field work and associate professor of practical theology. A West Virginian who had extensive experience as a Methodist minister before receiving his doctorate in divinity from Morris Harvey College in 1935, Walton served there as a dean before becoming the director of evangelism in the extension division of the Methodist Episcopal Church, South (1935–39) and then, after the reunification of the Methodists, superintendent of town and country work in the United Methodist Church prior to his appointment at Duke.

Described by one observer as a "human dynamo," Walton, like Ormond before him, counseled churches concerning their building projects, inspected and approved plans, and visited churches across a sprawling state. Not only was the task too much for one person, but various Methodist leaders, including prominent bishops, believed that the officials of the church needed to be brought more closely and formally into the process. Accordingly, Randolph E. DuMont, the longtime treasurer of the Endowment who took a special interest in the church-building program, consulted with the two bishops who presided over the North Carolina conferences. This resulted in an important meeting at Duke University in the spring of 1957 that was attended by the bishops, various other church leaders, Endowment officials, and, significantly, a large contingent of North Carolina architects.

After giving a brief history of the Endowment's church-building program, DuMont explained that after several years' experience with an architect based at Duke, it had become apparent that unless there could be a local architectural service available, such services would not be widely used and local contractors would continue to do double duty as architects. Since the Endowment's rural church program was one of assistance, in order for it to be effective there had to be a close working relationship between the Endowment and Methodist officials at the conference, district, and local level. DuMont assured the group that the Endowment had no desire to force any particular set of plans or the employment of any particular architect upon a local congregation. Nor did the Endowment insist upon any specific type of architecture or construction.

DuMont noted that the largest part of the cost of a church building was paid by the local congregation, with Methodist boards at the conference level making grants or loans. Often local labor as well as materials were donated. Endowment appropriations, therefore, ranged from only 5 percent of the cost of some large projects to 25 percent of smaller, more rural projects where the need was greatest. Approximately 75 percent of the Endowment's grants were for projects costing less than $40,000.

DuMont admitted that the Endowment considered an architect's service as desirable, but it also recognized that such service had to be a matter resting solely between the local congregation and the architect. J. B. Duke had demonstrated the importance he placed upon the appearance and location of a church building when he directed the architect of Duke University to have its Tudor Gothic chapel dominate the new West Campus. Likewise, the Endowment, DuMont explained, wished to encourage local congregations to build churches of pleasing appearance, but it also recognized "the beauty in simplicity."

In the Endowment's early years, DuMont suggested that the top priority had been to provide sanctuaries or auditoriums for worship. In the 1950s, however, many local churches, looking to the future, were building on a unit-plan basis, with educational units often being built before the erection of a sanctuary.

DuMont concluded by noting that the bishop of the North Carolina Conference, Paul Garber, had agreed to appoint a Bishop's Committee on Architecture composed partly of lay persons who were architects in the various areas of the conference. The members of the committee would be paid for their services but would be responsible to the bishop and in no way under the jurisdiction of the Endowment. The idea was to request the bishop of the Western North Carolina Conference to name a similar committee so that a joint committee would cover the entire state.

The Endowment, DuMont added, would be happy to pay for a collection of working plans with specifications for churches of varying sizes. The plans could provide for unit construction, and the use of donated labor and materials would also have to be taken into account. There might even be a prize competition for the best church plan.[17]

The upshot of the meetings that DuMont had helped arrange was the appointment by each of the bishops of the Bishop's Committee on Architecture consisting of architects, church officials, and lay representatives. Since the conference reported that at least one-fourth of rural Methodist churches were still one-room buildings, or nearly so, the committee had plenty of work to do in the years ahead.

DuMont himself was elected as a trustee of the Endowment in 1960 but died at age fifty-nine the following year. The North Carolina chapter of the American Institute of Architects had elected him an honorary member more than a year before his death, and he was memorialized by the Randolph E. DuMont prize awarded by the Endowment through the North Carolina chapter of the American Institute of Architects to the most outstanding design for a rural Methodist church.

The Endowment's program for assistance in helping to build rural churches, despite facing certain problems, had a more clear-cut, definable objective than the third and final portion of J. B. Duke's gift to Methodist causes in North Carolina—the 4 percent of the annual disposable income "to maintain and operate" the rural churches. As the Endowment got underway in 1926, a presiding elder in the eastern part of the state wrote Few that he had about six "weak, struggling charges" in his district that paid the pastor about $1,400 to $1,500 a year. Most of the churches were in "the old time one room" buildings. "As you know," the presiding elder noted, "it is impossible to develop weak charges by supplying them with weak men who are underfed and underpaid." If he could get the bishop to appoint "well equipped young men" to these charges, what sort of salary help might be obtained from the Endowment?[18]

In replying to this query, Few confessed to being worried and uncertain about the matter. He declared, "The wise expenditure of the Duke Fund for the maintenance of church work in the country creates for me one of the most difficult problems I have ever encountered." Few added that he would have to take some time to investigate and consult, but if the presiding elder wished to submit quite definite suggestions with complete information about the needy circuits, then the request would be carefully considered.[19]

The presiding elder probably received assistance, but Few had made his dilemma clear. There were probably two aspects to it. First, the 4 percent of the annual disposable income would certainly not be sufficient to help all of the needy Methodist circuits in North Carolina, and on what basis could distinctions be made and recipients of aid selected? Second, J. B. Duke's whole approach to philanthropy was based on the idea of helping people and institutions help themselves. Or, to put the matter another way, neither Few nor the Endowment's trustees wanted to create dependency in people or institutions. In the phrase they used, they believed that would "pauperize" those who came to expect handouts. A proud, even if sometimes painful, tradition of Protestant churches was that the members of a church paid the preacher's salary.

Caught in this bind, Few, and in subsequent years those who succeeded him in administering the maintenance fund, compromised: half of the available funds went to supplement salaries paid to preachers serving on the neediest circuits, especially in the mountainous areas and in the eastern portion of the state, and the other half went for a highly innovative program to be discussed below.

Thanks primarily to efforts of the Methodist congregations and the church leaders, with help also from the Endowment, the salaries of rural Methodist preachers in North Carolina were gradually increased. While the salaries remained far from adequate, they did compare favorably with the national average for all denominations and with the urban average as well. In 1939, for example, the regular pastors of rural Methodist circuits that were assisted by the Endowment received an average annual salary of $1,555. The national average for all denominations that year was $407 for rural preachers and $1,154 for urban preachers. (That compared with a national average in 1939 of $959 for teachers in rural schools and $1,955 in urban schools.)[20]

The innovative program that the Endowment's church-maintenance funds supported was the brainchild of W. P. Few. As he pondered the question of how to use the maintenance funds wisely, he also grappled with problems surrounding the establishment of Duke University's new School of Religion. Not only was it to be the first of the university's professional schools to be organized, but it also was to embody high standards, admitting only college graduates for work toward the divinity degree. The significance of that is highlighted by the fact that a survey of Methodist preachers in the South in 1926 revealed that only 4 percent had graduated from both college and a theological seminary; 11 percent were college graduates; and over half (53 percent) had only a high school education or less. Peter Cartwright, a famous circuit-riding evangelist of the early nineteenth century, had boasted that uneducated Methodist itinerants (such as himself) had set America on fire religiously before educated ministers had been able to light their matches. Overthrowing the vestiges of that tradition, perhaps once suited to a raw frontier society, was one of the chief purposes of President Few and Duke's new School of Religion.

There remained, however, a problem about money since divinity schools traditionally charged no tuition and also usually offered stipends to cover the students' basic expenses of living. Trinity College had long given full tuition scholarships to preministerial students, but now that Duke University was moving to a higher level of theological training, there was a critical problem about stipends or scholarships for the students in the School of Religion.

President Few came up with the idea, which the Endowment's trustees promptly endorsed, of having Duke's theological students serve summer apprenticeships in North Carolina's rural Methodist churches. While the work would be a valuable learning experience for the students, the churches could benefit from the vitality and fresh ideas of the apprentice preachers. Since local churches would be expected to furnish room and board for the student, the students would be paid for their services in this fashion: the university advanced to each student in the program $200 per semester to cover room, board, and other basic expenses, and the Endowment repaid the University when the summer apprenticeship had been served.

Starting with only five students in 1927, the summer program for ministerial students had grown to sixty-seven students by 1931. Since it was for many years the only source of scholarship aid in the School of Religion, the program was a crucial one and helped make the School of Religion one of the outstanding places in the nation for rural church work. Jesse Ormond, director of the school's rural church department, headed the program and conducted a noncredit seminar in which he tried to alert the students to possible problems and pitfalls.

The students, working as assistants to regular pastors and as directors of religious education, plunged quickly into all sorts of challenging situations. In the summer of 1931, for example, two students assigned to rural churches in the eastern part of the state reported that they had conducted a twelve-day revival meeting with two preaching services daily and a Bible school for about fifty children every morning at 8:30. Encouraged by the "splendid crowds" at the small church, the students added that they had "visited in practically every home" and were especially pleased that "eighteen new members were brought into the church on profession of faith." They were proceeding next to open another revival meeting at another church on the same circuit.[21]

Reports of similar exertions came pouring in, but there were also problems. Despite Ormond's best efforts, students fresh from their classrooms at Duke were not necessarily primed for functioning well in all circumstances. An experienced preacher in the mountains of western North Carolina reported on his dealings with a summer assistant from Duke and insisted that "when you are dealing with mountain people you are up against circumstances that are different from those to be found at any other place." The Duke student assigned to him, he declared, had argued with him since arriving, and though he had warned the student not to get "off on a tangent on the idea of Pacifism and the Racial question," the student had done exactly that in his evening sermon. When the minister warned again, the student avowed that "unless he could preach [on] those two things that he could not preach."[22]

President Few had spoken about Duke University's having a "duty of mediation" between the South's religious conservatism and the intellectual ferment of the era. No doubt Ormond and other professors in the School of Religion had a more immediate, literal task of "mediation" between their students and older Methodists, lay as well as clerical, in the state. At any rate, the summer program, despite occasional problems, proved to be a valuable mainstay of the school's scholarship support as well as a pioneering experiment in training young ministers for work in rural churches. By the end of 1949, the Endowment had spent $558,080 in support of the summer apprenticeship program and had appropriated only a bit more, $573,258, to help with salaries on rural Methodist circuits.

Washington Duke's deep gratitude to and appreciation of the Methodist circuit riders of his youth and middle years were fittingly, indeed marvelously, memorialized by his youngest son's benefaction to the several Methodist causes in North Carolina.

James B. Duke and his almost-seven-year-old daughter Doris in a photographer's studio in Newport, Rhode Island, in the summer of 1919. (*Special Collections, Perkins Library, Duke University*)

James B. Duke (fourth from the left, front row) and a group of his business associates aboard a merchant vessel belonging to a company largely owned by him. George G. Allen is on Duke's left, William R. Perkins stands between and just behind them, and Alexander H. Sands wears dark glasses on the top right. (*Duke University Archives*)

J. B. Duke Villa in Beautiful Meyers Park, Charlotte, N. C.—28

Two views of White Oaks, James B. Duke's home in Charlotte, North Carolina, where he and his associates gave a final review to the indenture creating the Duke Endowment in early December, 1924. (*Special Collections, Perkins Library, Duke University*)

Top left: George G. Allen, who succeeded James B. Duke as chairman of the Endowment and president of Duke Power Company late in 1925. (*Duke Endowment, Charlotte, North Carolina*)

Top right: William R. Perkins, chief legal advisor to James B. Duke and principal author of the indenture creating the Endowment. (*Duke University Archives*)

Bottom left: Watson S. Rankin, the primary creator and long the director of the Hospital and Orphan Section of the Endowment. (*Duke Endowment, Charlotte, North Carolina*)

Bottom right: Graham Lee Davis, indefatigable and highly creative assistant to Rankin in the Hospital and Orphan Section. (*American Hospital Association*)

Top right: Alexander H. Sands, executive secretary to both Benjamin N. and James B. Duke before becoming an original trustee of the Endowment and its long-time de facto executive director. (*Duke Endowment, Charlotte, North Carolina*)
Bottom left: Marshall Pickens, who succeeded Watson Rankin as director of the Hospital and Orphan Section and who served briefly as chairman of the Endowment. (*Duke Endowment, Charlotte, North Carolina*)
Bottom right: Wilburt C. Davison, first dean of the Duke University Medical School, who worked closely with Watson Rankin and the Endowment even before being himself named as a trustee of the Endowment. (*Duke Endowment, Charlotte, North Carolina*)

Top: Thomas L. Perkins, son of William R. Perkins, who succeeded George G. Allen as chairman of the Endowment and who was named chairman of the board of Duke Power Company. (*Duke University Archives*) Bottom: Richard B. Henney, who held several offices in the Endowment before being elected as a trustee and the first, official executive director. (*Duke Endowment, Charlotte, North Carolina*)

Doris Duke, who, as her father had directed, became a trustee of the Endowment when she became twenty-one in 1933. (*Duke Endowment, Charlotte, North Carolina*)

Archie K. Davis, who chaired the Endowment in the 1970s and, among other things, led in moving the Endowment's New York office to Charlotte. (*Duke Endowment, Charlotte, North Carolina*)

Mary Duke Biddle Trent Semans, James B. Duke's great-niece, Benjamin N. Duke's granddaughter, and the first chairwoman of the Endowment. (*Duke Endowment, Charlotte, North Carolina*)

Top left: John F. Day, who, after holding various offices in the Endowment, succeeded Richard Henney as executive director. (*Duke Endowment, Charlotte, North Carolina*)

Top right: Billy G. McCall, who, after long service to the Endowment, succeeded John Day as executive director. (*Duke Endowment, Charlotte, North Carolina*)

Bottom left: Jere W. Witherspoon, who held various posts in the Hospital Section and served as executive director of the Endowment after McCall's retirement. (*Duke Endowment, Charlotte, North Carolina*)

6 ·

TRANSITIONS

AND

TROUBLES

IN THE

1960s

AND 1970s

EXCEPT FOR THE ENDOWMENT'S involvement in the stormy Gross-Edens affair at Duke University in early 1960, one could justifiably say that the first thirty-five years of its existence had been relatively calm. With George Allen as the single most powerful trustee, after the death of William R. Perkins in 1945, and Alexander Sands as the hardest-working and most effective trustee — the de facto executive director — there was conspicuous continuity and stability in the operations of the Endowment down to 1960. Both of those veteran leaders died in that year, however, and a new era necessarily began in the Endowment's life. Thomas L. Perkins' succession of Allen as chairman of the Endowment signaled the transfer of power from the men who had known and worked closely with James B. Duke to a younger generation.

While that change in personnel was important, the main reason that the 1960s and 1970s brought serious problems and changes for the Endowment was that the tight interlocking relationship between it and the Duke Power Company came under heavy attack from some powerful Democrats in Congress. Beginning in the early 1960s, Representative Wright Patman, a Texas Democrat, launched an all-out crusade against alleged abuses of tax-exempt foundations in general, not just the Endowment, and his efforts finally culminated in the Tax Reform Act of 1969. Even before that, however, the Endowment's trustees had to begin to face up to the painful fact that J. B. Duke's Grand Design, in so far as it linked together the Endowment and Duke Power, had become a source of serious trouble.

Soon after becoming chairman of the Endowment, Tom Perkins in 1961 became chairman of Duke Power's board of directors. Because J. B. Duke's indenture had stipulated that the Endowment could invest its funds only in the securities of Duke Power or in certain types of government bonds, the Endowment's holdings of Duke Power common stock had climbed steadily over the years. By June 1968 the Endowment held over 56 percent of the company's common stock, and the Doris Duke Trust held almost 9 percent. The trustees, for various reasons that will be explained, were determined to try to get the courts to modify the indenture so that they could diversify the Endowment's portfolio, that is, invest in something besides Duke Power securities and government bonds. It would be a long, hard battle, but one that the trustees would ultimately win.

By 1961, of the original twelve trustees named by J. B. Duke in 1924, only two remained on the board—Bennette E. Geer and Norman Cocke. Geer died at age ninety-one in 1964 and Cocke, after resigning as a trustee in 1971, died at age eighty-nine in 1974. J. B. Duke's widow, Nanaline Holt Inman Duke, had been an original trustee but resigned because of her age and failing health in 1957. (She died in 1962 at age ninety.) In so far as available records indicate, she had never taken any sustained interest in the work of the Endowment and rarely attended the board meetings. In the early years, she chose to attend those once-a-year meetings where the indenture was read aloud, as J. B. Duke had requested, but that was obviously meant as a memorial gesture to her late husband's memory.

In resigning, Nanaline Duke wrote an interesting letter to the other trustees, a letter that was probably both inspired and drafted by Tom Perkins, who read it to the board. "I definitely feel that the time has come for me to step out and to pass on my responsibilities to younger people," she explained. "I know that only by constantly bringing into our group of Trustees young people with fresh ideas can we continue to properly keep The Duke Endowment the live, modern institution, wholly capable of carrying out its responsibilities in an ever-changing world, that my husband envisaged."

Mrs. Duke noted that her regret in resigning was tempered by the fact that "a member of our family is in my opinion fully qualified to step into my shoes." Mary Semans lived in Durham and, Nanaline Duke wrote, was "raising a fine family there." An alumna of Duke University, she was "deeply interested in Duke University which is certainly the most important of the beneficiaries of The Duke Endowment." She was also interested in hospital and other charitable work in Durham and North Carolina and, Nanaline Duke argued, "for all these reasons would, in my opinion, add a great deal of firsthand knowledge and enthusiasm to the Endowment affairs." Mary Semans was thirty-seven years old, which Mrs. Duke suggested was a good age for a trustee. "With the passage of time," she concluded "we must not forget that my husband appointed two Trustees who were younger than this [Anthony Biddle and Alexander Sands] and that the average age of all of the Trustees that he appointed was considerably under 50."[1]

Following Nanaline Duke's (and Tom Perkins'?) lead, the trustees promptly elected Mary Semans, who was destined to play an important role in the Endowment. Born to Mary Duke Biddle and Anthony J. Drexel Biddle Jr. in 1920, Mary Duke Biddle II married Dr. Josiah C. Trent, and the young couple had four daughters. Following Dr. Trent's untimely death, his widow subsequently married Dr. James H. Semans, and they had three children, two daughters and a son. In addition to her responsibility for a large family, Mary Semans was indeed, as Nanaline Duke suggested, very much in the same mold as her grandfather, Ben Duke, and her great-uncle, J. B. Duke, as far as concern for Duke University and charitable and civic activity in general went. Energetic, idealistic, and buoyantly optimistic, Mary Semans no doubt brought something new and distinctive into the ten meetings per year of the Endowment trustees. She was, however, enough of a diplomat and politician to know how best to proceed among a group of predominantly aging, well-to-do males.

An assessment of the role played by individual trustees of the Endowment, particularly during its first thirty or so years, cannot now be made because of the limitations of the sources. The bare-bones record in the minutes of the trustees' meetings indicate actions taken and appropriations made, but there is nothing that reveals the ideas of the trustees or their particular interests and aversions. Scattered letters in the files of the Endowment do suggest that William Brown Bell, one of the original trustees, took a lively interest in various phases of the Endowment's work, particularly in connection with Duke University's medical school. Bell had become associated with J. B. Duke during World War I through Duke's large interest in the American Cyanamid Company, of which Bell became president in 1922; he remained in that position until his death in 1950 at age seventy-two.

In the indenture, J. B. Duke had suggested, but not required, that the majority of the trustees be either natives or residents of one of the Carolinas.

In this, as indeed in all respects, the trustees scrupulously followed J. B. Duke's wishes.[2] This led to the election in the early decades of such prominent business leaders in the Carolinas as, to name only two, William N. Reynolds (1931) of the Winston-Salem tobacco family and J. Elwood Cox (1926), prominent manufacturer and banker in High Point, North Carolina. Aside from business leaders, the trustees elected a number of longtime Endowment officers to the board, such as Phillip B. Heartt (1951), Marshall Pickens (1951), Randolph E. DuMont (1960), and others who came later. For many years, Robert L. Flowers was the only full-time educator on the board, and after his death in 1951, aside from Bennette Geer, there was no trustee from the educational world until the election of Wilburt C. Davison in 1961, following his retirement as dean of Duke's medical school.

As will be explained subsequently, the election of Archie K. Davis as a trustee in 1972 turned out to be highly important, for he would play a key role in reinvigorating the Endowment. Associated with the Wachovia Bank and Trust Company from 1932 and chairman of its board from 1956, Davis was a mover and shaker not only in North Carolina but also in the national business scene. A former president of the American Bankers Association and chairman of the board of the United States Chamber of Commerce, he long served as chairman of the Research Triangle Foundation in North Carolina and held numerous other civic and business positions.

There is no question that the Endowment secured many talented people, mostly businessmen, to serve as trustees. As Nanaline Duke's letter suggested, however, there was a problem about lifetime tenure on the board and the obstacle that sometimes posed to the introduction of new ideas and younger trustees. That the trustees themselves worried about this was indicated in November 1961, when they adopted a resolution stating that all trustees elected henceforth would be asked to agree to tender their resignations at the end of the calendar year in which they turned seventy-five. Then in 1979 the trustees voted to require those elected as trustees subsequent to October 1979 to agree to tender their resignations at the end of the calendar year in which they became seventy. Just as these age-based policies were being adopted, however, the idea that people could be discriminated against on account of age (along with race, gender, etc.) was gaining ground, and the Federal government passed legislation to prohibit it. Accordingly in April 1983, after a committee had studied the matter and consulted legal counsel, the trustees of the Endowment voted to rescind the earlier regulations concerning mandatory retirement and revert to the concept set forth in the indenture whereby trustees could serve so long as they lived and continued to consider themselves mentally and physically capable of performing the duties of a trustee. The indenture gave the trustees the power, by a three-fourths affirmative vote, to remove any trustee "for any cause whatever," but that power has never been exercised.

Resignations, at least during the Endowment's first forty years, were rare. In fact, prior to Nanaline Duke's resignation in 1957, only one other trustee had resigned, and that was Anthony J. D. Biddle Jr. in 1930. (J. B. Duke had named him as an original trustee primarily because he was married to J. B. Duke's niece, Mary Lillian Duke, and when the couple divorced, Anthony Biddle ended his association with the Endowment.)

The trustees tended to remain on the board, for a variety of reasons, until they died. One was that, despite the ten meetings each year, the job was basically a pleasant one. The staff of the Endowment bore the brunt of the detailed, tedious chores, and the meetings of the trustees tended to be relaxed, semisocial affairs. They knew each other well, either enjoyed or tolerated each other's company, and undoubtedly gained satisfaction from knowing that they were helping to carry out J. B. Duke's generous plans for philanthropy in the Carolinas.

Then, aside from the prestige of being a trustee, there was money, a significant amount of money, paid as a commission. As wealthy persons anyhow, many of the trustees clearly did not actually need the pay; some were not truly wealthy, however, and probably either needed it or felt that they could put it to good use. Regardless, J. B. Duke had stipulated in the indenture that each trustee should "be paid at the end of each calendar year one equal fifteenth part of three percent" of the income from the trust property.

There is a story that one of the original trustees protested to J. B. Duke, perhaps as the draft indenture was being considered in early December 1924, that it really was not necessary to set aside as much as 3 percent of the total income for the purpose of compensating the trustees. J. B. Duke is said to have laughingly replied that the protestor had best kept quiet or he would make it 5 percent. Legally, of course, he certainly could have done that, since trustees of property placed in trust were legally allowed such compensation.

Although the matter of the trustees' compensation was never a secret — any one who took the trouble to read the widely reprinted indenture could hardly miss the matter — it was not widely noticed or even commented upon until the 1960s. Then, however, as Congressman Patman's crusade received increasing attention from the news media, the Endowment became the target of criticism because of the trustee-compensation feature. A study by the staff of the House of Representatives' banking committee suggested, among other things, that foundations should assert new leadership in "developing appropriate charitable levels for administrative expenses." Then the report specifically cited the Duke Endowment, which at the time was worth $629 million, for paying its trustees $43,000 each in 1968. Other news stories pointed out that the Ford Foundation, by far the largest in the nation, then paid its trustees $5,000, and the trustees of the Carnegie Corporation, which distributed more than $12 million annually, received no pay.[3]

While the Endowment's leaders were embarrassed by this unaccustomed and unflattering publicity, they nevertheless stood firm on the fact that they were simply doing precisely what J. B. Duke had stipulated in the indenture that they should do. Moreover, they pointed out that the Endowment was not a typical foundation but a charitable trust; not only were the trustees charged with responsibility for carrying out the provisions of the indenture in a manner that was not the case with many other foundations, but also the Endowment's trustees personally paid for expensive liability insurance.

The trustees actually had more serious problems to worry about as the 1960s began than the matter of their generous compensation. Their greatest concern now focused on what they had increasingly come to perceive as the unwise, possibly even dangerous restrictions placed by the indenture on the Endowment's investment policy.

The Duke Endowment, like most of the nation's older and larger foundations, was never guilty of the irresponsible and unethical, if not downright illegal, activities that Congressman Patman and his staff began to uncover and attack in the early 1960s. Some of the newer foundations, for example, had never published any type of report on their operations; the Endowment had scrupulously published full, detailed annual reports from its beginning. Some tax-exempt foundations, while accumulating additional funds each year, were not distributing any income from those funds. The list of abuses, which were committed by a relatively small fraction of the hundreds of foundations, went on.

The Endowment was vulnerable to attack, however, on the grounds that it was tightly linked with a profit-making business, the Duke Power Company. The fact that numerous other foundations, such as the Kellogg Foundation, were in a similar situation hardly lessened the seriousness of the matter. As the *Wall Street Journal* reported in the summer of 1962, Patman wanted Congress to enact new legislation for the regulation of foundations. He charged that too many of them had wandered far from charitable activities and were engaging in commercial activities where, because of their tax-exempt status, they allegedly enjoyed unfair competitive advantages. Patman believed that Congress should consider the money-lending operations of foundations (and the indenture specifically authorized the Endowment to lend its funds to the Duke Power Company), the alleged conflicts of interest involving the trustees and officers of foundations and the business they controlled, and the use of foundation money for business purposes.

Patman conducted his one-man war against the foundations in another era, the 1960s, that was much like the 1930s in so far as popular confidence in the federal government's ability to solve socioeconomic problems was concerned. Accordingly, Patman believed that the government should force foundations to pay taxes — provide a new source of federal revenue — so that Congress rather than private or voluntary agencies could address various social needs and problems. The Federal Revenue Act of 1950 had prohibited the "unreasonable" accumulation of funds by foundations, but Patman asserted that the prohibition was being ignored. An even more serious matter, he argued, was the increasing concentration of economic power in foundations through their ownership of stock in business enterprises. He pointed to a study made by the Small Business Committee of 522 large and small foundations; it revealed that 106 foundations owned more than 10 percent of the stock of one or more of 252 corporations as of the end of 1960.[4] The Endowment, in 1957, held over 57 percent of Duke Power's common stock and 76 percent of its preferred shares.

Aside from the mounting political pressure, there were other reasons why the trustees of the Endowment had decided that the time had come to seek legal permission to alter certain aspects of J. B. Duke's Grand Design. When he had created the Endowment in the 1920s, there were few regulations concerning the operations of the stock market; consequently, investing money in equities could be a most problematic affair for the unwary. Furthermore, in an era without inflation and when the gold standard helped protect the value of money, government bonds were an attractive, quite reasonable investment as an alternative to stock in a utility company such as Duke Power. The stock market crash of 1929 followed by early New Deal legislation, such as that establishing the Securities and Exchange Commission, had, however, totally changed the game as far as investing money in stocks and bonds was concerned. And the chronic inflation that developed following World War II made fixed-income securities, such as government bonds, much less attractive than they had been in the 1920s, especially for a tax-exempt organization.

For a variety of reasons, therefore, the Endowment late in 1962 entered the Superior Court of Mecklenburg County, North Carolina, to seek permission to alter the investment policy mandated by the indenture. A series of expert witnesses contributed to the Endowment's case. John J. McCloy, chairman of the board of the Ford Foundation, testified that the Ford Foundation at one time had 90 percent of its assets in the stock of the Ford Motor Company but had managed thus far to reduce the amount to only 46 percent. "A foundation should not be dependent on the fortune of one company or industry," McCloy declared.

The chairman of the committee on trust management of the Morgan Guaranty Trust Company in New York, Charles D. Dickey, informed the court that the Duke Endowment had "too great a concentration" in its investment and "definitely would be safer with greater diversification." Another expert witness, R. J. Saulnier, was a professor of economics at Columbia University and former chairman of President Dwight Eisenhower's council of economic advisers. He explained that "The whole direction of public policy at the present time rather encourages increases in prices [i.e., inflation]." Moreover, the costs of hospitals and higher education, two areas of prime concern to the Endowment, tended to increase considerably faster than general price levels, and he thought that trend was likely to continue. Saulnier pointed out that if a person had invested $1 million in bonds in 1924, he would have gotten $50,000 in interest then and about $45,000 in 1961. The $45,000 in 1961, however, would have paid for the same amount of educational services that $9,000 would have bought in 1924. Furthermore, he noted that if the $1 million had been invested in a hypothetical, diversified portfolio of stock in 1924, it would by 1961 have been worth $10.3 million and would produce annual dividends of about $309,000.[5]

One line of argument that the Endowment's lawyers advanced was dubious and probably a mistake. Philip B. Heartt, a longtime officer and trustee of the Endowment as well as a director of Duke Power, testified that the power company had probably reached maturity and could not be expected to grow in the years ahead as it had in the previous two or three decades. Actually, of course, Duke Power was on the verge of quite significant expansion, and the real problem for the Endowment arose from the fact that changed political circumstances made it increasingly difficult if not impossible for the Endowment to help facilitate that expansion.

Hindsight is, of course, marvelously wise and all knowing. One argument that the Endowment's lawyers did not make in 1962 — but one they would emphasize a decade later — was that J. B. Duke himself, despite the rigidity of certain aspects of his Grand Design for philanthropy, was nothing if not pragmatic. Throughout his long and spectacularly successful business career he had been quick to change course if circumstances demanded that. In other words, an impressive case could have been made that if J. B. Duke had been alive in 1962, he would have been the first to call for a modification of the Endowment's investment policy.

Even without that argument, however, the Mecklenburg County court ruled in favor of the Endowment and granted its request to modernize, that is to diversify, the Endowment's investment policy. Both the Endowment and the state attorney general's office, however, wanted the North Carolina Supreme Court to have the final say in the matter, and on appeal in the spring of 1963 the Supreme Court reversed the ruling of the lower court. One of the more telling points in the Supreme Court's majority ruling, which was written by Associate Justice William B. Rodman, was that, "Mr. Duke had as much right to name the securities in which the funds should be invested as he had to name the beneficiaries."

As for the alleged "maturity" of the Duke Power Company, Justice Rodman conceded that it had been "a mere adolescent" in 1924 and may have reached maturity some thirty years later. Yet he argued that there was "nothing in the record tending to indicate that it [Duke Power] is approaching decadence." The Supreme Court's majority believed that a comparison of the value and income derived from the Duke Power stock when it was originally placed in the Endowment with the value and income of the same stock in 1962 well illustrated the wisdom of the trustees' faithful compliance with J. B. Duke's specifications concerning investments. Furthermore, the result demonstrated "Mr. Duke's wisdom both as to a source for income and the human agencies selected for its efficient operation." The ruling concluded in words that praised J. B. Duke but gave scant comfort to his trustees of a later generation: "Past adherence to the trust agreement has, as Mr. Duke wished, promoted the economic as well as the social welfare of this and our sister state. The evidence fails to establish facts necessary for an order authorizing the trustees to disregard this express provision of the trust indenture."[6]

The North Carolina Supreme Court's ruling naturally disappointed the officers and trustees of the Endowment. After conferences with the Endowment's lawyers in both New York and North Carolina, however, Tom Perkins informed the trustees that the consensus was that "nothing could be gained by any further proceedings and in fact such proceedings could have a damaging effect in strengthening the decision against us."[7]

As the Endowment tried in vain to anticipate and escape, or at least mitigate, some of the problems that loomed larger and larger on the horizon, Congressman Patman and his allies continued their campaign for fundamental reforms concerning the foundations. Patman used his House subcommittee on small business to hold hearings in the fall of 1964; his purpose, he explained, was to probe the impact of tax-exempt organizations on the economy and alleged problems facing small businesses as a result of competition from these organizations. Then early in 1965 the United States Treasury Department, after a year-long study, published a report that had been requested by the Senate Finance Committee and the House Ways and Means Committee. The report recommended that Congress legislate a number of changes to eliminate the alleged abuses practiced by some tax-exempt private foundations. Specifically, it urged Congress to (1) generally ban dealings between a foundation and its donors, officers, or trustees; (2) limit foundations to owning less than a 20 percent interest in any ordinary business; and (3) bar foundations from speculating in stocks and commodities and narrowly limit their borrowing and lending. There were other reforms that were also proposed, but some of the strongest measures that had been considered were not recommended. For example, one rejected proposal would have required every foundation to cease existence after a specified time, say twenty-five years, and another called for the creation of a new federal agency to regulate foundations. Predictably, Patman declared that the proposals did not "go far enough," and a prominent Democrat in the Senate said that many of the report's recommendations amounted to mere "wrist-slapping."[8]

As foundation-bashing gained steam in the 1960s, the trustees of the Ford Foundation issued a philosophical statement of principles. Not only because the Ford Foundation was the nation's largest but also because some of its controversial grants had supported social and political activism, it became a particular target of criticism. The Ford Foundation's trustees, however, took to high ground: "The private philanthropic foundation is one among a rich diversity of public and private instruments evolved by American society for advancing human welfare. It reflects fundamental principles in the American system. One of these is the diffusion of responsibility for social, cultural, and educational affairs among private and governmental institutions. Another is the tradition of private, voluntary action to identify and treat these charitable needs."

The Ford trustees went on to argue that the nation's foundations had a record of nearly a century of "inestimable contributions to the well-being of American society." They had been responsible for uncommon advances in the nation's health, education, and social welfare, and they had established and nourished essential community institutions. Moreover, the trustees insisted that the foundations in the 1960s continued "to break new ground and demonstrate imaginative approaches to many of the most profound and complex challenges confronting American society."[9]

Although the Duke Endowment did not generate any broad, philosophical statements comparable to that issued by the trustees of the Ford Foundation, the Endowment's work after 1924 certainly illustrated one major point that the Ford trustees had made: thanks to J. B. Duke's (and Watson Rankin's) creative imagination, the Endowment had pioneered in assisting in the building and maintenance of community hospitals and in the medical care of the indigent. That the federal government itself later moved to help in those areas, with the Hill-Burton hospital-building act of 1946 and the Medicaid program of the 1960s, merely underscored the point that the Endowment, like other foundations in other areas of societal need and concern, had blazed a trail.

When Tom Perkins and Marshall Pickens appeared before the House Ways and Means Committee in October 1965, they strove to respond to the Treasury Department's report on private foundations from the standpoint of the Endowment and its particular nature. With assets having a market value of a bit over $672 million (as of August 1965), over 80 percent of those assets were represented by over 13 million shares of common stock of the Duke Power Company. That holding represented approximately 57 percent of the company's outstanding stock, and Perkins quoted from the indenture to explain why J. B. Duke had wanted the Endowment thus tied to the power company.

He went on to note that the North Carolina Supreme Court had favorably ruled on and approved the above arrangement in 1963. Perkins added that the Endowment was not a private foundation in the usually accepted meaning of that term. "In its broadest sense," he explained, "it might be considered a public trust for the benefit of the citizens and residents of the States of North Carolina and South Carolina."

Perkins expressed gratification that the Treasury Department report did not suggest a time limit on the life of private foundations, for the "needs of the beneficiaries served by the Duke Endowment will, as far as we can see, continue indefinitely." There were other aspects of the report's impact on J. B. Duke's indenture on which Perkins commented, and on the crucial matter of the Endowment's owning 57 percent of the Duke Power stock, he reiterated its centrality to J. B. Duke's overall plan and the express approval given that plan by the North Carolina Supreme Court. Furthermore, Perkins argued that considerations which might make it undesirable for a foundation to control a private business were not present, he believed, when that business was a highly regulated public utility subject to the control of both state and federal commissions and that an exemption might properly be made for foundations owning more than 20 percent of public utility companies.

Perkins explained that under the terms of the indenture, the Endowment's trustees could only invest its funds in Duke Power securities or in certain types of government bonds. The North Carolina Supreme Court had refused to broaden those investment provisions. The power company, he noted, had steadily paid annual dividends since 1926 and had increased its dividend each year for the previous decade, to the great benefit of the beneficiaries. Government bonds, on the other hand, would be fixed in value and would eliminate any hope of future growth to match the continued growth of the needs of the beneficiaries. To illustrate that last point, he pointed out that the budget of Duke University had increased almost 500 percent in fifteen years — from almost $9 million in 1950–51 to an estimated $44 million in 1965–66.[10]

In addition to testifying in Washington, Perkins and Pickens made sure that all congressmen from the Carolinas received the Endowment's annual report, and they also arranged to pay personal calls upon them. Then in 1969 as the tax legislation finally ground its way through the House and Senate, the Endowment's officers and lawyers, alongside countless other representatives from other foundations as well as the myriad other interests affected by the far-reaching legislation, went into high gear. Acting for the Endowment, Richard E. Thigpen, an attorney in Charlotte and trustee of Duke University, arranged for Senator B. Everett Jordan, Democrat from North Carolina, to accompany him on calls to the legislative counsel of the Senate's Finance Committee; to Senator John Sharpe Williams, Democrat from Delaware and member of the Finance Committee; and to Representative Wilbur Mills, Democratic chairman of the House Ways and Means Committee. While the Endowment had many concerns about the pending legislation, one particular matter had to do with the indenture's requirement that 20 percent of the Endowment's annual income was to be added to the original corpus of the trust until the sum of $40 million had been added. This "mandatory accumulation" feature was somewhat unusual and also problematic in light of the threatened legislation. As of the end of 1968, almost $26 million had been added, and the indications were that this provision of the indenture would be fully satisfied in less than ten years. (It was.) The upshot of the Endowment's efforts was that an amendment to the proposed legislation allowed the "mandatory accumulation" to continue if legal efforts to eliminate it failed, as they later did.

A detailed analysis of the complex Tax Reform Act of 1969, as it finally emerged from the conference committee of the House and Senate and was signed into law by President Richard Nixon, would require another book — and a different author. A former commissioner of the Internal Revenue Service noted in 1972 that prior to 1969, provisions of the IRS on exempt organizations covered from ten to fifteen pages. With the passage of the Tax Reform Act of 1969, however, the provisions extended to approximately one hundred pages, with new regulations and proposed regulations covering hundreds of additional pages.

As far as the Endowment was concerned, the principal results of the legislation, and admittedly there were quite a few additional but less important results, were these: (1) in order to avoid draconian penalties, the Endowment had to refrain from buying any additional common stock of the Duke Power Company and, within a ten-year period, manage to get its holding of the stock to be less than 25 percent of Duke Power's outstanding common stock; (2) the Endowment would have to seek legal permission to modify the indenture by adding a provision permitting invasion of the corpus to the extent necessary to comply with the distribution requirements of the 1969 tax law; and (3) the Endowment, like all the other foundations in the nation, had to pay a 4 percent tax on its annual income.

This 4 percent tax, while not as painful as the 7.5 percent that had first been proposed, remained a sore point with all foundations, including the Endowment. Since all of the Endowment's beneficiaries, like those of other foundations, were tax-exempt institutions and organizations, the tax on the foundations, in lessening the payments to their beneficiaries, was actually a tax on the beneficiaries. In 1972 the president of the Carnegie Corporation mailed a check for over $521,000 to the IRS in payment of the 4 percent tax; he then wrote a letter to the secretary of the treasury pointing out that instead of going into the general revenues of the federal government, the money could have been given in its entirety to colleges, universities, medical schools, and other charitable institutions. He suggested that the tax was discriminatory in that it was not imposed on other tax-exempt organizations and therefore represented a dangerous precedent to the entire charitable field. "The principle of pluralism, which holds that a strong society is one with vigorous private as well as public institutions," the Carnegie president declared, "has served the American people well and is a principle in which most citizens continue to believe." Yet the growing financial plight of private, voluntarily-supported institutions threatened that principle. "A tax on foundations strikes at the very heart of pluralism by shifting resources from the private to the public side of the ledger," he concluded. "If pluralism is good for Americans, a tax on foundations cannot be."[11]

Part of the rationale for the tax on the foundations was that it was meant to cover the costs incurred by the federal government in auditing the financial records of the foundations. In 1974 a spokesman for the Endowment pointed out that it was paying about $1 million annually in tax but paid its own, independent auditor about $15,000 for a complete audit of the Endowment's books. Accepting the idea of a more modest tax, the Endowment's representative agreed that the larger foundations should pay more than the smaller ones but suggested that there should be a ceiling on the tax of $50,000 or $100,000. That suggestion was not followed, but in 1978 the tax was finally lowered from 4 percent to 2 percent, which resulted in an estimated $40 million increase in the funds available to the beneficiaries of foundations.

The federal tax on foundations was not, however, the most important effect of the Tax Reform Act on the Endowment. The most crucial problem the Endowment faced after 1969 was the prohibition on its purchase of additional common stock in the Duke Power Company. Caught between the new federal tax act on the one hand and J. B. Duke's indenture on the other, the Endowment was, in truth, trapped between the proverbial rock and a hard place. Clearly, the Endowment had no choice but to seek relief once again in the North Carolina courts. Unlike the effort in 1962 to modify certain provisions of the indenture, this one would succeed.

Two persons in the Endowment's New York office who played important roles in preparing for the new round of litigation were Richard B. Henney and John F. Day. A wounded veteran of World War II, Henney graduated from the University of Virginia in 1950 and joined the Endowment in 1953. After serving as assistant treasurer and then treasurer, he also became secretary and was elected a trustee in 1961. In 1971 Henney was named to a newly created post in the Endowment, that of executive director. John Day, after graduating from Williams College, received a master of business administration degree from Harvard and accepted a position with the Endowment in 1958. He would serve as treasurer and/or secretary from 1966 to 1986, and he succeeded Henney as executive director following the latter's death in 1979.

Henney and Day worked closely with the Endowment's legal team, which was ably led by John Spuches in New York and Russell M. Robinson II in

Charlotte. Having learned certain things from the Endowment's abortive legal effort of 1962, Robinson and Spuches carefully prepared a formidable case, which again was heard first in the Superior Court of Mecklenburg County in the fall of 1971.

Since the Tax Reform Act of 1969 was excruciatingly technical in many respects, the Endowment's petition to the court had also to deal with certain arcane matters that, while quite important from a legal point of view, need not be dealt with here. The single most important objective for the Endowment was to gain permission from the court to broaden the trustees' authority over the Endowment's alternative, non-Duke Power investments. That is to say, since the Tax Reform Act prohibited the Endowment from buying additional Duke Power stock, the trustees' only alternative investment under the indenture was in certain categories of government bonds. Given the reality of chronic inflation and the consequent limitation on the attractiveness of such fixed-income securities as government bonds, the Endowment requested permission to change its investment policy on the grounds that "due to changes in conditions which could not have been foreseen by Mr. Duke, the purposes of the Endowment will be defeated in whole or in part if the investment powers are not modified, and Mr. Duke would modify them if he were here."[12]

In dealing with "the purpose of the Endowment," Robinson and Spuches made an illuminating analysis. Clearly one of the principal purposes, and perhaps the principal purpose, was to provide income for the beneficiaries, income that would increase over the years as the needs of the beneficiaries grew. The lawyers quickly admitted, however, that the Endowment also had important nonincome purposes. One was that J. B. Duke intended for the Endowment to control the Duke Power Company. That purpose, however, had been defeated by changes in public policy as expressed in the Tax Reform Act of 1969.

Another nonincome purpose of the Endowment was to assist in the development of water power (hydroelectric power) in the two Carolinas. The lawyers suggested that this purpose had been well served in the early years of the Endowment but by the 1970s had been defeated or diminished by changing circumstances beyond the control of the trustees. The hydroelectric potential of the Piedmont area of the Carolinas had been fully developed, with no more conventional water-power sites available there. Although by the early 1970s only 4 percent of Duke Power's revenue came from hydroelectric developments, the lawyers declared that it could "forever be said that whatever income the Endowment receives now or in the future was originally produced in largest measure by the utilization of water power in accordance with Mr. Duke's ambition." In the conclusion of this portion of their argument, Spuches and Robinson asserted that no reasonable person could maintain (as the North Carolina attorney general tried none too convincingly to argue) that any of the nonincome purposes of the Endowment could be achieved by forcing the trustees to operate under the unamended indenture and invest the non-Duke Power portion of the portfolio in government bonds.

To show how the indenture's restrictions on investments had harmed the Endowment and penalized its beneficiaries — even before passage of the Tax Reform Act of 1969 — the lawyers pointed to a large block of aluminum stock that J. B. Duke had given to the Endowment. (He got the stock when, not too long before his death, he swapped his interest in a gigantic hydrostation in Quebec, Canada, for a one-ninth interest in the Aluminum Company of America.) Already overloaded with Duke Power stock and anticipating political trouble because of that, the trustees were not attracted by the idea of investing more in government bonds. Consequently, they felt that they had no alternative but to hold on to the aluminum stock despite the fact that there were market signals that it was a good time to sell the stock. In early 1960 the aluminum stock was worth almost $110 million. By the end of November 1971 it had fallen in value to a bit over $40 million. That was a loss of almost $70 million, or about 63 percent of the value of those aluminum stocks. The lawyers pointed out that if the aluminum stocks alone could have been sold and invested in a diversified portfolio with an average growth rate of about 6 percent a year, which was a reasonably modest expectation, the non-Duke Power portion of the Endowment's portfolio would, by 1971, have been worth about $235 million instead of the $67 million it actually was worth. (The lawyers did not explicitly say but certainly implied that this was a classic demonstration of how J. B. Duke's plan of having different purposes for the Endowment had ended up seriously harming its income-producing purpose — much to the detriment of the beneficiaries.)

In view of the changed situation produced by the Tax Reform Act of 1969, therefore, Spuches and Robinson hammered away at the point that the principal purpose of the Endowment was to serve the needs of the beneficiaries. Those needs were served by the non-Duke Power portion of the Endowment's portfolio, which would increase in importance because of the Tax Reform Act, as well as by the continuing massive investment in Duke Power. The costs of the beneficiaries' needs had risen steadily and showed every sign of continuing to rise. The income of the non-Duke Power portfolio would not rise adequately if it had to be invested completely in fixed-income securities. Therefore, if the Endowment had to continue operating under the "outdated investment standards of 1924," the remaining principal purpose of the Endowment would be defeated.

But would J. B. Duke have agreed with this analysis if he had been alive in 1971? On this point, which had not been developed in the 1962 lawsuit, Robinson and Spuches had no difficulty in suggesting an emphatically affirmative answer. First, they reminded the court of Duke's outstandingly successful business career, which had been characterized by pragmatism and adaptability to fast-changing market conditions. The clincher for the argument that Duke changed course when circumstance dictated such a necessity was his response to the unprecedented drought that afflicted the Carolinas in the summer of 1925. J. B. Duke had envisioned the Duke Power Company as dependent upon water-power developments; the indenture, signed some six months or so earlier, contained several pivotal references to that ambitious plan for giving back to the people who owned the rivers of the Piedmont a significant portion of the profits made from harnessing them to produce hydroelectric power. But just as the great floods of 1916 had temporarily disrupted the Duke Power system, the unprecedentedly severe drought during the summer of 1925 played equally serious havoc with it. J. B. Duke's response, less than a month before his death, was, after conferring with the officers of the power company, to authorize them to build the company's first large-scale central-station-type steam plant, that is a coal-burning facility. It, and the many more like it that would be built in subsequent years, would not be seriously affected by floods or droughts, and Duke Power would become less and less dependent on water power as it steadily shifted to coal and steam. After describing this pragmatic response of J. B. Duke to the "contingencies of nature," Spuches and Robinson concluded that if J. B. Duke had been alive in 1971, he would have been the first to respond to the circumstances that had changed so much since 1924 and would authorize his trustees to diversify their investments in the non-Duke Power portfolio.

This portion of the lawyers' brief concluded with the assertion that there was "no reason or purpose to be served by refusing to allow the trustees to follow a sensible investment program for the non-Duke [Power] portfolio." All of the beneficiaries in the years ahead would be injured, if the change should not be allowed, because their benefits from the Endowment would be substantially lessened. The states of North and South Carolina would be injured because the Endowment's payments for private education, hospitals and child-caring institutions absorbed expenses that would otherwise burden the taxpayers. "And perhaps most important of all, Mr. Duke's plan and purposes would be injured because he established the Endowment to serve the growing educational, medical and religious needs of his native area, not to become a dwindling force as those needs increase."

All in all, John Spuches and Russell Robinson had made a masterful case for the relief that the Endowment sought. It is not surprising, therefore, that the Endowment prevailed, first in the Mecklenburg County Superior Court and then, on appeal, in the North Carolina Supreme Court. At long last, the trustees were free to diversify their investments of the Endowment's funds.

While that major objective of the authorization to broaden the investment power had been achieved, the supreme court refused to grant a less important request of the trustees. As mentioned earlier, starting in 1934 and continuing down into 1959 the trustees had passed a series of resolutions whereby they took funds from the Endowment's reserve fund (funds that had largely come from the hospital account) and added the funds to the corpus as mini-endowments for the four educational institutions. In other words, through these "addition to corpus" resolutions the trustees held, by 1971, securities worth nearly $15 million (book value) that were earmarked for Duke University; nearly $1,560,000 for Davidson and the same for Furman; and nearly $606,000 for Johnson C. Smith. Annual income from these mini-endowments went as unrestricted income (like the income under the 32-5-5-4 formula) to the four institutions.

Why the trustees had chosen to add these funds to the corpus of the Endowment rather than give the funds outright to the institutions, which could have been required to add the funds to their own endowments, is not known. One possible reason is that the trustees then wanted to keep the money invested in Duke Power stock. Just as likely the trustees simply wanted to help the corpus of the Endowment grow as much as possible on the good old American premise that bigger is better. And, of course, adding the funds to the corpus protected the power of the trustees.

Whatever the original motivation, by 1971 circumstances had, as the Endowment's lawyers kept emphasizing, indeed changed, and the trustees requested authorization from the court to transfer title to these mini-endowment funds to the four educational institutions. In making this request, the trustees and their lawyers were not altogether candid, for the reason they gave for making the request was that they wished to save for the educational institutions the sum of approximately $115,000 per year, which would have to be paid as the federal tax under the Tax Reform Act of 1969. While the tax-saving argument was true enough, a more substantial, though not stated, reason for the request was that, under the Tax Reform Act, the Endowment had to reduce its share of the outstanding Duke Power stock to 25 percent or less by 1979. Since most of the securities in the four mini-endowments consisted of Duke Power stock, transferring title to them would help the Endowment move toward its 25 percent target.

The trustees, at least those trustees who had unanimously voted for the "addition to corpus" resolutions between 1934 and 1959, were, however, hoisted by their own petard. The North Carolina Supreme Court ruled that J. B. Duke's indenture made no provision for the invasion of corpus — other than the $6 million (of the original $40 million) that the trustees were authorized to spend in the construction of the new buildings for Duke University. By adding the mini-endowments to corpus, the supreme court declared, the trustees lost the power to subsequently take them out.[13] Although the Endowment's trustees and lawyers apparently did not fully realize the matter in the early 1970s, they actually would not need to get rid of the Duke Power stock in the mini-endowments in order to reach the 25 percent target by 1979. Developments in the Duke Power Company itself would take care of the problem.

Concerning Duke Power, one point needs to be most emphatically stressed: the problems growing out of the Endowment's close relationship with it had absolutely nothing to do with the quality of performance of the power company. Rather, changes in the nation's political and economic climate after World War II made the close relationship increasingly problematic. It is sometimes said that in the long run, Duke University turned out to be the most conspicuous monument to J. B. Duke. One could also say, however, that, in the business world of the Carolinas, the Duke Power Company is an equally conspicuous monument. If J. B. Duke were alive, one would have to believe that he would be generally gratified by both monuments — and would be the first to point out that William P. Few, William S. Lee, and a host of others played indispensable roles in building them.

J. B. Duke had requested in the indenture that his trustees "see to it that at all times these [Duke Power] companies be managed and operated by the men best qualified for such a service." George Allen, W. R. Perkins, Tom Perkins and the other trustees who served during the Endowment's early decades took this request seriously, for by various measurements Duke Power was clearly one of the best-managed utility companies in the nation. Although the situation is changing fast in the last decade of the twentieth century, the original understanding about electric utilities, in the Carolinas as in other states, was, as a distinguished political economist has explained, as follows: "For most of the century the electric industry operated under an arrangement that gave the local utility companies regional monopolies and the promise of a fair opportunity to recover their prudently incurred costs in exchange for regulatory limitation of their profits and their assumption of an obligation to make whatever investments are required to ensure that the power comes on whenever anyone flicks the switch."[14]

The careful reader will note that the above sentence is somewhat like a juggler with, say, a half dozen balls in the air. If one focuses, however, on the phrase about the power's coming on whenever the switch is flicked, the honest observer would have to concede a basically important economic fact about the Piedmont region of the Carolinas: the power has come one, faithfully and regularly, at one of the lowest rates in the region (and even in the nation) throughout most of this century. Furthermore, the availability of that relatively cheap, dependable power has played a centrally important role in the industrialization that has helped transform the region.

This is not the place, of course, for even a mini-history of the Duke Power Company, but it should be obvious that anticipating a fast-growing economy's power needs is not an exact science. Skillful, experienced managers simply do the best they can. Furthermore, since state regulatory commissions cannot be operated in sterile environments, old-fashioned politics has often complicated the matter a great deal. Despite these problems, all shared with the utility companies in other states, Duke Power has managed to stand out. In 1973, for example, with efficiency ratings based on reports filed with the Federal Power Commission by all operating companies in the nation, Duke Power for the second straight year was honored as having the most efficient steam-electric generating system in the nation. Duke Power's largest generating plant at that time earned the unprecedented distinction of being the nation's most efficient steam-electric station for the seventh consecutive year. As if all that were not enough, the Edison Award, the electric utility industry's highest honor, was presented to Duke Power in April 1973 for its accomplishments in planning the vast, new Keowee-Toxaway development.

Following the pattern set by J. B. Duke, the company, unlike some others in the nation, employed its own engineering and construction personnel who designed and built its plants. While this "do-it-yourself" policy clearly contributed to the outstanding record for efficiency, it also played a part in the company's esprit and high morale. Aside from the fact that Duke Power's rates were approximately 20 percent below national averages in the late 1970s, the company took pride in the fact that its commitment to protecting the environment in its service area had begun in 1923, when it established its own environmental health department, headed by a physician specializing in public health, and set out on a massive program to control or eradicate mosquitoes around the company's many lakes and reservoirs. From that, the company had moved on to a full range of environmental activities ranging from erosion control to research in air and water quality.

Duke Power also felt good about the fact that its lowest-paid employee in the 1970s had the same fringe benefits as the chief executive officer — and the latter's salary was one of the lowest of any major public utility. That Duke Power tried to be a "no frills, no-nonsense" company was illustrated, according to its annual report in 1978, by the fact that it owned no company airplane and no automobiles larger or more expensive than Fords, Chevrolets, and Plymouths. In short, from many standpoints Duke Power was an outstanding winner, and the Endowment and its beneficiaries, for many of the early years, had benefited from that fact.

Yet, paradoxically enough, Duke Power — and consequently the Endowment — had more than its share of troubles in the early 1970s. While virtually all other electric utility companies in the nations were also in varying degrees of trouble at the same time, the Endowment, like the people of the Carolinas' Piedmont, dealt only with Duke Power. That much of the trouble arose from circumstances completely beyond the control of Duke Power was also true. Regardless, Carl Horn Jr., who advanced from being the president of Duke Power to the chairmanship of its board of directors in 1975, later declared that "the most critical, frustrating time we ever faced at Duke Power was the 1973–74–75 period."[15]

Because the Piedmont's economy was growing so rapidly in the 1960s, Duke Power was under constant pressure to keep expanding its production of electric power. This meant that the company required enormous amounts of capital, and after passage of the Tax Reform Act of 1969, the Endowment could no longer help supply that much-needed capital. Even if the Endowment could have continued to buy Duke Power stock, the company's capital needs were so large that the Endowment's share of the total outstanding Duke Power stock would have shrunk considerably. As matters stood, however, with the company forced to sell more and more stock to finance its expansion and the Endowment barred from buying any of it, by mid-1975 the Endowment's share of Duke Power stock had fallen below 25 percent of the total, and the

Endowment was thus in compliance with that aspect of the Tax Reform Act. In other words, by not buying Duke Power stock (rather than by selling any of its large holding), the Endowment solved one of its problems.

The power company's problems, however, continued to be grim, and they were rooted in the larger problems of the nation's economy. Inflation had begun to increase in the late 1960s; it grew worse in the early 1970s and, simultaneously, unemployment increased as the economy slipped into recession. The combination of inflation and recession, or "stagflation," was something new in the economic world, and Duke Power, like so many other key players in the troubled economy, faced unanticipated trouble.

The Arab oil embargo of late 1973 only made a bad situation worse. As oil prices soared out of sight and Americans for the first time had to face the consequences of their long-accustomed reliance on abundant and cheap energy, inflation rose into the double digits by 1974, and the economy sagged into what many called the worst recession in four decades. Fortunately for Duke Power, unlike many utilities especially in the Northeast, it used very little oil in its generation of power, but that was one of the few bright spots for the company.

A particular problem about inflation for Duke Power, like other electric utilities, was that rate increases were not only distinctly unpopular with the public, but they also were sometimes painfully slow in being allowed by the state regulatory commissions. Since timing was crucial in the volatile world of business, a regulatory commission's delay in granting a rate hike, even though the increase might have been fully justified on economic grounds, could cost a company millions of dollars. In the 1960s Duke Power had requested and gotten a series of rate *reductions,* which mostly benefited the company's large industrial and commercial customers. In the early 1970s, however, in a quite different economic climate, the company was forced to request a series of rate increases.

Duke Power's bond rating dropped during a four-year period in the early 1970s from AAA to plain A, and, as Carl Horn later explained, "There was a period in 1974 when you couldn't sell a single-A utility bond at any price. We had to sell those horrendous 13 percent, five year capital notes to protect our single-A rating."[16] While the company's earnings per share of common stock increased to $1.90 in 1973, up 12 percent over the $1.69 per share for 1972, the earnings still fell far below what the regulatory commissions had found to be just and reasonable as well as below what the electric industry had earned generally. Put another way, Duke Power's return on stockholders' equity was

9.7 percent whereas the electric industry on average had been earning about 12 percent on common equity.

Horn explained further that in 1973 only 6 percent of Duke Power's generation had come from oil and natural gas. The great majority of the company's kilowatt-hour production (84 percent) had come from coal-fired plants, with nuclear and hydro each accounting for about 5 per cent of the 1973 output. As the company during 1974 brought large, new nuclear and coal-fired units into operations, the figures would shift to 69 percent coal, 26 percent nuclear, and 4 percent hydro.

While the company continued to pay dividends on its stock throughout its ordeal in the early 1970s, the value of the stock plummeted. At 43.25 in the late 1960s, it fell to 29.50 in 1970 and a low of 10.75 by 1975. This meant, of course, that the value of the Endowment's huge stake in Duke Power declined right along with the price of the stock.

As if these various problems growing out the economy's general malaise were not enough, Duke Power inadvertently walked into a hornet's nest when in 1970 it purchased two coal mines in Harlan County, Kentucky, "Bloody Harlan," made famous by labor violence during the 1930s. Watching the company's coal inventory dwindle from an eighty-day supply to a twenty-two-day one during the coal crunch of 1969, the managers of Duke Power hoped to gain some protection and control over its coal supply. Since the company had no expertise in coal mining, it hired an experienced mining engineer to head a new subsidiary corporation, Eastover Mining Company. In 1971 Duke Power purchased a third mine in adjoining Bell County, Kentucky, and the hope was that when the three mines were fully developed, they would furnish about 25 percent of Duke Power's coal requirements.

The first two mines that Duke Power had purchased, Brookside and High Splint, had contracts with the Southern Labor Union, and Eastover (the Duke Power subsidiary) took over those contracts. The top rate of pay had been $18 per day, but when Eastover began operations the top rate was $28 per day; by 1974 the top rate had risen to $48 per day. That, as Carl Horn explained to the trustees of the Endowment, was "more money than the average Charlotte school teacher, policeman or top Duke Power Company servicemen or lineman earned in 1973."[17]

When the contract with the Southern Labor Union expired at the Brookside mine in mid-1973, the miners voted, in a contested election, to be represented by the United Mine Workers of America. (The contracts with the Southern Labor Union at the other two mines would not expire until mid-1975.) The president of Eastover and his local attorney negotiated with the UMW representatives through most of the last half of 1973. Since Eastover's wage rates, as a whole, were higher than the UMW rates, money was not an issue in the negotiations, though the Brookside miners under the old contract had worked an eight-hour day whereas UMW miners worked a seven-and-a-half-hour day.

The negotiations stalemated because the UMW insisted that Eastover would have to sign the same three-year contract that the UMW had made with the Bituminous Coal Operators Association in 1971. Eastover balked at these features of that contract: (1) it would cover all operations of the employer on any properties where the employer mined coal; (2) it lacked a no-strike clause; (3) promotions would be based on seniority regardless of ability; (4) it lacked a management-rights clause; and (5) it gave the UMW's safety committee the unilateral authority to shut down the employer's mine.[18]

There is no point in attempting in this study to trace the tortuous trail of this labor dispute as both parties filed charges with the National Labor Relations Board, administrative law judges got into the act, and violence again broke out in Harlan County. The point here is that the UMW, capitalizing on Duke Power's relationship with the Duke Endowment, waged a masterful public relations war against Eastover, and in the process considerably, and also perhaps unfairly, embarrassed both the Endowment and some of its beneficiaries. The UMW played a type of "hard ball" that neither Duke Power nor the Endowment had ever before experienced.

Shifting away from the actual issues that divided the two contestants, the UMW launched an all-out "humanitarian" campaign that essentially blamed Duke Power for not having solved historic socioeconomic problems in Harlan County that had existed for decades. In a letter to all of the trustees of the Endowment, Arnold Miller, the president of the UMW, explained that he was writing because the Endowment was the major and controlling stockholder in Duke Power. "So I know you will be disappointed to learn that in Harlan County, Kentucky," the UMW leader declared, "Duke Power Company has shown a callousness to human needs and suffering that flies in the face of everything the Duke Endowment stands for." While the Endowment was concerned about child care, the letter continued, in Harlan County Duke Power housed the children of its coal miners employees in "ramshackle coal camp houses with no indoor toilet, running water, or central heating."[19]

The long letter (five single-spaced pages) went on in this vein, but to take only the matter of housing, the truth was a bit more complicated than the UMW president suggested. When Duke Power acquired the two Harlan

County mines, there were, as Carl Horn explained, a large number of ramshackle, company-owned houses. Duke Power, or rather its subsidiary, Eastover, demolished a hundred of those run-down houses at Brookside mine and another hundred at the other two mines. The company then spent several thousand dollars for roofing, screening, and paint on the remaining forty houses at Brookside, and the improvement was sufficiently impressive that Harlan County gave Eastover its annual award for beautification. It was also true, however, that of the forty remaining houses at Brookside, only fifteen had indoor plumbing. The others were scheduled for demolition, to be replaced by a mobile-home park with sewage facilities. In other words, Eastover had acted and was continuing to act to rectify an admittedly deficient housing situation, one that had long existed in a generally depressed region.

"I was horrified to hear of the appalling conditions at Brookside camp," Doris Duke wrote the president of the UMW. She noted that she was only one of the fifteen trustees of the Endowment and had "very little influence," but she had telephoned her fellow trustee and cousin, Mary Semans, who had also received the UMW letter. "She too was extremely distressed to learn of these conditions," Doris Duke continued, "and said they planned to have one of the Board Members of The Endowment meet with you for a personal inspection tour." Doris Duke concluded by stating that she had been assured that she would be kept informed as to what progress was made "to alleviate this situation."[20]

Doris Duke claimed to have "very little influence," but, for many reasons, that was certainly incorrect. Carl Horn soon wrote to assure her that he would be happy to meet with her at a time and place of her choice to discuss the labor situation at Duke Power's mines in Harlan County. He believed that some recent developments suggested the possibility of a settlement, for he had met with the UMW president and hoped that negotiations would soon resume. Even if a settlement were reached, Horn thought Doris Duke would be interested in the company's long-range plans for improving the miners' living conditions. Duke Power had bought into "an economically depressed area," he noted, and while it had "improved the economy of the county, much remains to be done, particularly in the areas of housing, medical care and family planning."[21]

Duke Power would have been quite happy if the UMW had confined itself to letters to Endowment trustees and other prominent people associated with the Endowment, but such was not the case. With a sizable war chest, the UMW was determined to win the contest with Duke Power as a necessary step toward vanquishing its rival in eastern Kentucky, the Southern Labor Union.

Accordingly, the UMW launched an intensive attack on Duke Power, not only in the Carolinas, where the company was struggling to gain an essential rate increase, but in the nation at large. In the Carolinas, the UMW took out full-page advertisements in various newspapers opposing Duke Power's requests for rate hikes and charging that its refusal to sign a contract with the UMW was somehow responsible for the company's financial dilemma. Some student activists, no longer focused on Vietnam, were quick to join in the fight against Duke Power, and the UMW, working through the students' Public Interest Research Group (PIRG), a nationwide organization inspired by Ralph Nader, soon had placard-carrying students assailing Duke Power and protesting against rate hikes at various strategic locations throughout the Carolinas.

The president of the UMW took the fight to Wall Street. In a letter to the head of New York's First National City Bank, Arnold Miller began by stating that he wanted to register his concern about the bank's holdings of stock in Duke Power. After giving the UMW version of the Brookside mine matter, the letter went on to explain that, aside from the social implications of being a large stockholder in Duke Power, the bank should know that there was widespread citizen opposition in both Carolinas to Duke Power's pending rate increases. Nine or more different organizations in North Carolina and ten in South Carolina were said to have formally intervened to oppose the rate increases, and the UMW had retained a public utility consulting firm in Washington to provide expert testimony on behalf of the intervenors.

The UMW's nationwide informational campaign against Duke Power stocks and bonds, Miller explained, had brought results: fifty-two national labor organizations and four national church denominations had pledged to dispose of holdings in Duke Power and not to buy more until the Brookside strike was settled. The sixth largest stockholder in Duke Power, the Ohio Public Employees Retirement System, had informed the company that it, too, would purchase no more Duke Power securities until the strike was settled. "I am sure that the American labor movement would welcome the news — as the United Mine Workers would," the letter concluded, "that your company intends to reevaluate its position as a major shareholder in Duke Power."[22]

This kind of well-publicized pressure finally got to certain leaders of the Endowment, and its executive director, Richard Henney, urged Carl Horn to do more "publicity-wise to get our side of the story before the public." Henney explained that he was "convinced that this [UMW attack] is starting to have an effect on the financial community and we have to do something to counteract it."[23]

Even before Henney expressed his concern, the UMW had struck a telling but legally dubious blow at Duke Power. In March 1974 the company filed a registration statement with the Federal Securities and Exchange Commission concerning five million additional shares of its common stock to be offered for sale the following month. On April 16, 1974, as Carl Horn was about to go to New York to negotiate the terms of the stock offering with the underwriters, he received a telegram from Arnold Miller saying, in effect, that if Duke Power did not immediately (i.e., within the next day or so) agree to settle the strike at Brookside, then the UMW felt it had the "responsibility to inform potential investors and the general public about the long-term implications of the strike, our participation in the upcoming hearing" on Duke Power's request for another rate increase, and the company's financial condition. "We are taking the necessary steps to proceed in the public forum," Miller's telegram concluded, "steps which we will feel forced to take in the absence of an immediate good faith response by you to this telegram."[24]

When Horn and other Duke Power officials met with the New York underwriters, the latter recommended that the offering be reduced to four and a half million shares, and it was agreed that the sale should proceed despite Miller's telegram. On April 17, 1974, the UMW took a full-page advertisement in the *Wall Street Journal* attacking Duke Power not only about its position in the Brookside affair but also about its allegedly unsound financial position. Unfortunately for Duke Power, the UMW advertisement used out-dated data and failed to offer information that considerably brightened the picture for the company. The crux of the matter was that late in 1973 and early in 1974 the regulatory commissions in both of the Carolinas, despite the loud protests of the PIRG students and others, had granted rate increases. If the comparative statistics used in the UMW's advertisement had reflected those rate increases, Duke Power's financial condition would have placed it near the top of the list of 110 utility companies. The 14 percent return on common equity made possible by the rate increases would have placed Duke Power as the 20th out of 110 utilities rather than as the 107th, as shown in the UMW's advertisement. There were many other such distortions and inaccuracies, and Duke Power's lawyer summarized the matter thusly: "The situation described above is a unique and novel development in the law of federal securities regulation. What has occurred is that a union, in an effort to obtain its objectives in a labor dispute, published false and misleading statements about an issuer [of stocks] at a time when the issuer was offering a very substantial amount of its securities to the public and [was] thus severely limited in its ability to respond to such allegations." If this action of the UMW should not be challenged, according to counsel for Duke Power and the Endowment, then a major objective of federal securities laws — the sale of securities to the public in an orderly fashion upon the basis of full and fair disclosure — would be defeated.[25] Although Duke Power, through its lawyers, did protest to the Securities and Exchange Commission, nothing could be done about the after-the-fact situation. The company's stock offering of April 17, 1974, was successfully issued despite the UMW's advertisement.

The UMW was nothing if not resourceful. In late June 1974 both Richard Henney, the Endowment's executive director and a trustee, and Russell Robinson, the Endowment's chief counsel in Charlotte, received similar letters from a Maryland attorney who had been retained by the UMW to advise concerning the shareholder implications of the Brookside strike. The attorney explained that his initial concern related to the financial impact of the strike on Duke Power shareholders, and his study of the matter suggested that "the cost of the strike cannot be justified by any legitimate business purposes." Duke Power's refusal to settle was an "apparent abrogation" of its responsibility to its shareholders and only benefited certain other coal operators in Kentucky who wanted to end the organizing efforts of the UMW. (Why would Duke Power want to benefit other coal operators?)

The UMW's lawyer went on to say that in the course of his study of all the varied data, it had become apparent to him that the Duke Endowment, the principal shareholder of Duke Power, "has been in a fundamental conflict of interest since the passage of the 1969 Tax Reform Act." He argued that the Endowment owed a fiduciary obligation to its various beneficiaries; as the principal shareholder in Duke Power, the Endowment also owned a fiduciary obligation to all other shareholders of Duke Power stock. After the passage of the Tax Reform Act, however, the Endowment's obligations were in direct conflict. The lawyer continued his analysis by noting that the Tax Reform Act placed two primary obligations on the Endowment: (1) within ten years the Endowment had to reduce its holdings of Duke Power common stock to 25 percent or less of the total outstanding; and (2) the Endowment was obligated to pay out (distribute) a minimum percentage each year beginning in 1972.

The lawyer noted that he had discussed these matters with staff members of Representative Patman's committee in Washington, and they had informed him that most foundations (which faced the problem of owning too much stock in one business or company) had chosen to comply with the 25 percent requirement by making a secondary offering or by a trade with other foundations and institutions. The Duke Endowment, however, had taken the "totally unique" route of benefiting from an alleged "dilution" of Duke Power stock (i.e., the vast expansion of the amount of the company's stock necessitated by its capital needs). The UMW lawyer charged that the Endowment caused this dilution or knew of the plan to dilute, and, in either case, the Endowment benefited from it while other shareholders were hurt by it. At the same time and in part, at least, as a result of the dilution, the market value of the Endowment's holdings began to decrease so that a $570 million portfolio in 1969 was, by 1974, worth less than $200 million. That was a decline of over 60 percent, and that compared poorly with the Dow Jones average, which declined 14 percent during the same period. As a result of the decline in the value of the Endowment's holdings, in 1975 the beneficiaries of the Endowment would be entitled to receive only $9 million under the Tax Reform Act, whereas had the Endowment maintained its portfolio at the 1969 level, its beneficiaries would have been entitled to receive more than $30 million.

The trustees of the Endowment, the attorney charged, had managed to hurt its beneficiaries as well as the other shareholders and customers of Duke Power. He thought it was also clear that the power company's financial position was so precarious that its existing dividend levels were being seriously threatened. Against such a background, Duke Power's "refusal to negotiate a settlement of the strike simply adds to the abuse of trust."

The attorney then noted that several persons associated with the UMW, who also owned stock in Duke Power, had asked him to pursue the matter further — to litigation if necessary. Thus he had drafted a formal complaint (petition) to the federal courts, a copy of which was enclosed, "that charges all individual directors of Duke [Power] and [Duke] Endowment with stock manipulation, misrepresentation, and unlawful use of inside information." In addition, the complaint alleged that Duke Power's handling of the Brookside strike was "a gross abuse of trust to the shareholders."

All of the issues raised in the complaint, the attorney avowed, were "legitimate *bona fide* issues." Once raised in court, they would have to be prosecuted to their fullest extent. Moreover, the necessity of a court-approved settlement and widespread publicity would make any remedies immensely more complicated. "Therefore, I am genuinely hopeful," the attorney concluded, "that we can open up discussions to settle the issues raised in this letter and the enclosed draft complaint before filing." If Duke Power's attorney did not believe that such discussions would be appropriate, then they should consider the letter a formal demand on behalf of a stockholder of record, whom he named, that

Duke Power and the Endowment should take the action requested in the prayer for relief of the enclosed draft complaint. And he requested a response by mid-July 1974.[26]

On July 12, 1974, Russell Robinson informed the UMW attorney that discussions concerning the above matters might be appropriate. As Robinson later explained, the acknowledged principal purpose of the threatened action was to force the management of Duke Power to settle the Brookside strike and sign a contract with the UMW. The threatened law suit was a derivative action; that is, it was threatened by a plaintiff/shareholder on behalf of all the (non-Endowment) shareholders of Duke Power. In his discussions with the UMW lawyer, Robinson stated that he had made it clear that he and his associates did not think the threatened action had any merit whatsoever, but he had also emphasized that any settlement of the labor dispute would be made only with "the express understanding on the part of the prospective defendants [the trustees of the Endowment and directors of Duke Power] that the threatened lawsuit would not be instituted."[27]

The draft of the complaint, which the UMW lawyer sent to Robinson as well as to all of the prospective defendants, was never filed in court, and, according to Robinson, was incomplete in certain respects. Nevertheless, it was an interesting document and one that highlighted some of the trouble that had befallen Duke Power in the early 1970s. As the complaint stated, during the period from 1969 to 1973, Duke Power's earnings for common stock had increased by more than 50 percent. Despite the increase in earnings, however, earnings per share had declined; dividends had remained constant ($1.40 per share); and the price of a share of common stock had dropped 63 percent. While those facts were correct, the complaint ventured on to highly speculative, debatable ground when it suggested next that the decline in the value of the stock had resulted from a planned "dilution" of the common stock and other measures "which were not motivated by business judgments; which harmed . . . the shareholders, and which were never disclosed or approved by the shareholders." The complaint alleged that the plan began in 1969 and was designed to continue through 1979.

In 1969, as the complaint brought out, the Endowment owned 56.3 percent of Duke Power's outstanding common stock. Its price was 43.5, and the dividend had just been increased to $1.40, a yield of 3.2 percent. The Tax Reform Act of 1969 required, among other things, that the Endowment had to reduce its holdings in Duke Power to 25 percent of the total by 1979. The act also required, in effect, that the Endowment earn a rate of return on its holdings of a bit over 4 percent in 1972, with gradual increases up to 6 percent by 1975. In order to comply with the investment-yield requirements of the Tax Reform Act, the price of Duke Power stock, assuming that the dividend remained at $1.40, could be no higher than 24 by 1975. In summary, and without any discussion of other matters raised, the complaint alleged that the Endowment chose to comply with the Tax Reform Act by causing Duke Power to "dilute" its stock and decrease the price of the stock so that the Endowment could increase its investment yield (and decrease its percentage of Duke Power stock) to the newly prescribed levels. Put more succinctly, the complaint alleged that from 1969 on the defendants had grossly mismanaged the business of Duke Power because decisions had been "tainted by a design to reduce [the Duke] Endowment's holdings to 25% and increase its yield to 6% so as to be in compliance with the Tax Reform Act of 1969."[28]

Since this matter never proceeded to litigation, there is no way of knowing just how Russell Robinson and John Spuches would have answered the allegations. Regardless of what the Endowment's lawyers might have argued, any historian knows that "conspiratorial interpretations" of human events abound. Equipped with twenty-twenty hindsight and reading backward from outcomes in order to explain causes and motivations, various people have presented a staggering variety of "conspiratorial interpretations" about a large number of matters, ranging from the assassinations of Presidents Abraham Lincoln and John F. Kennedy to the Japanese attack on Pearl Harbor. While the UMW lawyer dealt only with a mundane matter of a utility company's management, the lawyer built his case in the classic manner of a "conspiratorial interpretation."

The crucial flaw in this particular application of the conspiracy theory lay in a matter of timing and sequence. Correctly anticipating the remarkable economic growth of the Piedmont region of the Carolinas, the management of the Duke Power Company, which did indeed include several Endowment trustees, made plans at least as early as 1967, if not earlier, for a significant expansion of power-generating facilities, both steam and nuclear. While the latter was quite expensive in the short run, it held out great promise for long-range savings. In other words, Duke Power managers knew perfectly well, long before the Tax Reform Act of 1969 was passed, that the company would have to raise an unprecedented amount of capital in the years immediately ahead.

What they did not know, of course, was that the American economy, as mentioned earlier, would be hit hard by both inflation and recession—and that the Arab oil embargo of late 1973 and early 1974 would further exacerbate an already dismal economic situation. In other words, unforeseen events and unanticipated contingencies drastically effected outcomes, as they always do in human affairs. To read backward from those outcomes and claim that fallible mortals "should have known" them or "might reasonably be expected to have anticipated" them long before they actually occurred has always been the disingenuous technique of those who push "conspiratorial interpretations."

At any rate, Duke Power settled the thirteen-month strike at Brookside and signed a contract with the UMW in late August 1974. The fatal shooting of a young miner involved in the strike several days prior to the settlement probably impelled Duke Power to take the step, and while it did win a limited no-strike clause, reportedly the first the UMW had agreed to since the early days of World War II, it lost some other bargaining points. (Some years later Duke Power sold its coal mines in Kentucky.) As far as the Endowment was concerned, the entire sequence of events concerning Duke Power after the passage of the Tax Reform Act of 1969 undoubtedly suggested to the trustees that a reduction of the Endowment's still massive holding of Duke Power stock would be the wise and proper course of action—if it could be accomplished.

Financially, Duke Power got out of the doghouse in the last half of the 1970s. An analyst from one of the leading investment banks studied the company in 1976 and concluded that because of an improvement in the regulatory climate and in internal cash generation, the company's earning performance was expected to improve over the next several years. The analyst also thought that Duke Power had "one of the most favorable fuel mixes in the industry." In 1974 coal supplied 77 percent of fuel requirements, nuclear power 15 percent, and hydro, oil and gas the remainder. By the early 1980s, however, the nuclear power component was expected to rise to 50 percent or higher, which would enable the company to achieve substantial economies in fuel cost. In short, the analyst believed that Duke Power represented "one of the most attractive issues in the electric utility groups" at that time.[29]

Another indication that there had been a marked change in Duke Power's (and therefore the Endowment's) fortunes came in late 1977 when *Electric Light and Power,* a leading magazine of the industry, named Duke Power the nation's outstanding electric utility for 1977. The magazine declared that Duke Power's management had "demonstrated unusual foresight in the planning of its system, based almost entirely on domestic fuels—coal and nuclear power." The company had "designed, engineered and constructed—using its own people—the most efficient generating system of any American electric utility."[30]

Just when the skies had brightened so much for Duke Power and the Endowment, however, an unforeseen, frightening event happened: in late March

1979, at a nuclear plant in Pennsylvania known as Three Mile Island, a major nuclear accident occurred. It was a first in the United States, for despite the vociferous protests against nuclear power that had increased throughout the 1970s, there had been no major accident — until Three Mile Island. The president of Duke Power, William S. Lee II, grandson of the brilliant William S. Lee who had worked alongside J. B. Duke to build the power system, was himself an outstanding engineer and one of the nation's recognized authorities on nuclear power. He and twenty-nine other hand-picked employees of Duke Power rushed to Three Mile Island to join a team of some 2,600 technicians, scientists, and others who worked successfully to bring the overheated unit under control. There were no deaths, no meltdowns, no escaping radiation — but it was a hair-raising close call.

About a month after the accident at Three Mile Island, Richard Henney reported to the trustees of the Endowment on a meeting that Bill Lee and other Duke Power experts in nuclear power had held with some twenty utility analysts. The purpose of the meeting was for Lee and his colleagues to report on the incident at Three Mile Island and to explain and answer questions about Duke Power's involvement in nuclear power facilities. One of the Duke Power experts stated that the problems at Three Mile Island were "basically some equipment malfunctions compounding human errors." Duke Power, it turned out, had units similar to those at the Pennsylvania facility and had encountered most of the operational problems that had occurred at Three Mile Island, but never in sequence.

In light of the incident, Duke Power had modified its operational procedures and equipment. Also, Duke Power's basic operational methods were different, but the company was reassessing all its reactors and operational methods, and operating personnel were undergoing resimulation training. National authorities had reviewed Duke Power's plant and operations but had found no problems. The licensing process for nuclear facilities would, nevertheless, be slowed down, and two of Duke Power's projected nuclear plants would be delayed. "Generally the analysts . . . seemed favorably impressed by Duke's presentation," the report concluded.[31]

There is no need here to outline the elaborate steps taken by the nuclear-power industry in the aftermath of Three Mile Island. Bill Lee and others from Duke Power played nationally prominent roles in designing and implementing the various measures and programs. The relevant point for this study is that Three Mile Island was what might be termed another wake-up call for the trustees of the Endowment about the possible danger of having two-thirds or so of its investments in one electric utility company. The Endowment requested three of the nation's top investment firms to comment on its investment objectives and its portfolios in the late 1970s, and despite the fact that Duke Power was "considered one of the best utilities in the country," the strongest emphasis in all three analyses was on the Endowment's need to reduce the concentration of its funds in Duke Power securities.[32]

As if that message were not clear enough, John Spuches in New York informed the trustees some months after Three Mile Island that, at the request of certain trustees, he had been reexamining certain well-recognized rules of trust administration. Accordingly, he had reaffirmed conclusions arrived at earlier that "the Trustees of The Duke Endowment will be deemed to be in 'control' of Duke Power Company for purposes of the Federal securities laws." That meant, for example, that the trustees would be liable to a purchaser of Duke Power securities in the event of a material misstatement or a material omission in a prospectus relating to such securities, with certain highly limited exceptions.

Spuches went on to explain that in order to provide themselves with an adequate defense with respect to such potential liability, the trustees ought to read the prospectuses issued by Duke Power and "otherwise keep themselves generally informed about its affairs." The trustees should personally review all material routinely sent to shareholders of Duke Power and keep informed generally about the electric-utility business, nuclear power, and other related matters. "In light of the fact that approximately two-thirds of the income of The Duke Endowment is derived from securities of the Duke Power Company," he wrote, "it appears to us imperative that each of the Trustees keep . . . fully informed about the Company and the myriad factors that affect or might affect it — now and in the future."

Spuches stressed the fact that each trustee had a personal duty in the matter, for under trust law the duty could not be delegated. While the corporate world might be different, in the administration of trusts "no such delegation is permissible." After citing several legal cases that illustrated the principles of nondelegability and personal responsibility of each trustee for investment decisions, he concluded, somewhat sternly, that any trustee "who remains inactive is guilty of a breach of trust."[33]

From both a personal as well as an institutional standpoint, therefore, the Endowment's trustees, with one important exception, had reason to want to reduce the holdings in Duke Power. Under the terms of the indenture, however, that would require the unanimous consent of all trustees — and Doris Duke absolutely opposed the sale of any Duke Power stock.

After Tom Perkins's death in June 1973, the task of trying to reason with Doris Duke fell to others. Marshall Pickens, who had been the vice-chairman of the Endowment, was elected as chairman to succeed Perkins. Because of Pickens's age, however (during a period when the Endowment was still observing certain age limitations), it was understood that his tenure as chairman would be limited. Accordingly, in January 1975 the trustees elected Archie Davis as chairman.

Davis vigorously led the Endowment in the last half of the 1970s to shake itself up a bit, reexamine its methods and objectives, and attempt to adapt as best as possible to fast-changing conditions. He did this first of all by reinvigorating the committee system under which the trustees had always operated. Then, aiming at careful self-study and self-criticism, each trustee committee met for an extended period with appropriate members of the staff as well as with representatives from the various beneficiaries to consider whether changes might be needed in the various programs of the Endowment. These self-study retreats or conferences helped accelerate certain changes that were already underway and even produce some new ones in the activities of the Endowment's different sections. These developments will be discussed in the following chapter.

The trustees of the Endowment, like any group that regularly gives away large sums of money, were accustomed to receiving many expressions of gratitude and plaudits in the editorial columns of Carolina newspapers. Inspired no doubt by the willingness of Archie Davis to open things up a bit, the trustees did something that the Endowment had never before risked: they invited an outside expert to evaluate its operation.

Merrimon Cuninggim, an alumnus of Duke University, among other institutions, and former Rhodes scholar, had climaxed an impressive academic career at several institutions by serving for a dozen years as president of the Danforth Foundation in Saint Louis, Missouri. The trustees of the Endowment initially invited him to study the relationship of the Endowment to its educational beneficiaries but then extended the scope of his study to cover the Endowment's method of making grants, its evaluation procedures, its board of trustees and staff, and other aspects. In accepting the task, Cuninggim advised Davis that the trustees "should be prepared to receive candid judgments, critical as well as appreciative." Cuninggim explained that he saw the consultant's work as "not merely descriptive but also normative, not merely a reporting of what is but also of what alternatives exist."[34]

True to his warning, Cuninggim stirred up the troops a bit—but not drastically. There were some references in his report, which he delivered to and discussed with the trustees in March 1980, to certain personnel problems that the Endowment faced at that moment, but with the passage of time those matters have receded in importance. As one might expect, he prefaced his report by hailing the visible and measurable "magnificent accomplishments" of the Endowment, "one of the great foundations." Then, because Davis had urged Cuninggim to make specific recommendations rather than simply pose queries, the report proceeded to deal with forty-four recommendations. Since some were obviously more important than others, only a selection of them will be mentioned here.

First, and concerning the indenture, Cuninggim noted that even the trustees themselves seemed not to have a uniform understanding concerning the scope of their powers under the indenture; some trustees, not all, believed that the board possessed more discretion than it had ever exercised. Consequently, Cuninggim urged the board to "undertake a full-dress discussion of its duties and powers, to the end that differences of understanding may be overcome." This related to the next recommendation that the board needed to consider "whether any [additional] changes in the Indenture" needed to be made. (The trustees had obtained the permission of the North Carolina Supreme Court to change the indenture's investment provisions in 1972.)

After noting that "few if any national foundations have ever had as able and dedicated" trustees as did the Endowment, Cuninggim made a series of recommendations concerning the board itself. One was that an ad hoc committee should carefully consider such matters as the processes of selection of the trustees, the breadth of representation, the adequacy of orientation, and certain other internal questions. Cuninggim was quite emphatic in one recommendation: "That a black be elected to the Board as soon as practicable, or perhaps a bit sooner." (It would not happen until 1993.)

Having delivered that well-deserved reproach, Cuninggim turned to what he admitted was the "most awkward matter" for him: the large size of the trustees' "commissions" or honoraria. "Respected foundation leaders uniformly believe," he reported, "that Duke's honoraria for Trustees are harmful to organized philanthropy in general." According to Cuninggim, only a minority of foundations provided compensation to their trustees and even then in modest amounts. (In the margin he noted trustee compensations ranging from $250 per meeting for the Carnegie Corporation to $5,000 per year for the Ford Foundation.) The Endowment's budget item at that time for the trustees' commissions ($1,015,827) was larger than the item for staff salaries

($1,008,795) and came to something over $70,000 per trustee for the year. (Although Doris Duke continued as a trustee, she had refused for some years to accept compensation.) Arguing that "nothing would build the Endowment's reputation quicker and higher nationally" — with other foundations, with universities and other beneficiaries, and with Congress — than "a forthright facing of this problem." Cuninggim proposed that "by one means or another" the board should cut back "in major amount" the commissions paid to trustees. (This recommendation was not followed.)

Cuninggim next turned to some detailed suggestions concerning the structure and functioning of the various committees, and, while important for the efficient functioning of the Endowment, these suggestions need not be addressed here. When he dealt with the committee on the educational institutions, Cuninggim admitted that as an educator himself he was more familiar with the problems and needs in that area. After a few general remarks about each of the four educational institutions, he concluded that they constituted a diverse group of which the Endowment could "indeed be proud." The four institutions shared one "overwhelming characteristic," he noted: they all needed more financial support. Accordingly he recommended that the Endowment make every effort to give "enlarged support to its four educational institutions, in light of the increasing pressure that all of them are going to feel in the days ahead."

Another place where Cuninggim stepped on toes was in suggesting that he considered the salary scale and benefits for the senior staff members of the Endowment to be on the high side, especially when compared with the pay patterns of universities. He also noted the "paucity of women on the professional staff" and the "lack of minority personnel throughout."

Concerning "the difficult question of evaluation," Cuninggim made an interesting observation. "Nearly every foundation I know performs this task poorly," he declared, "and for that matter so do most other non-profit organizations." The realization that such agencies had to be publicly accountable was slowly growing, he argued, "though the ultimate necessity is no longer in question." He urged that the trustees should develop a plan and a timetable for evaluations of the Endowment's work and that the "various evaluations from time to time be undertaken not only by in-house personnel but also by outside experts." For various reasons that he explained in his report, Cuninggim proposed to relieve the chairman of the Endowment of certain responsibilities by having the title of the executive director changed to president, with certain new tasks. (That title change would eventually be made.)

Summarizing what he thought would be the result if all or even a considerable part of the changes that he had proposed were adopted, Cuninggim noted that "they would change something of the temper of the Endowment — from relatively passive to relatively active, from somewhat hierarchical to largely collegial, from more to less indulgent, from less to more demanding, from occasionally isolated to habitually involved."[35]

A few months after Cuninggim delivered his report, two senior members of the staff, Marshall Pickens and Jim Felts Jr., responded in a memorandum to the trustees. At the outset they asserted their belief that Cuninggim's report showed "little understanding of the difference between a *private trust* and a foundation and the role of the founding Indenture in the day-to-day operation of The Duke Endowment." Pickens and Felt asserted that Cuninggim's comments about the routine operations of the various sections of the Endowment were "superficial," lacking supporting factual material, and more reflective of what he thought the Endowment should be than what it actually was.

As for Cuninggim's suggestion that the Endowment should give more support to the four educational institutions than it already did, Pickens and Felt presented certain historical data. Their main purpose was to show that, from an early date, the trustees had given a substantial monetary priority to the educational institutions and had done so by taking funds largely out of the hospital account. To illustrate this, they noted that between 1924 and 1979 a total of over $287 million had been paid to the four educational institutions and over $88 million of that had been withheld from other beneficiary accounts, principally the hospital. In addition, more than $18.5 million had been withheld from other beneficiary accounts (principally hospital) and added to corpus as mini-endowments for the four institutions. Pickens and Felt agreed that the educational institutions all needed more money but noted that the same was true for the other beneficiaries.

The two veteran officers of the Endowment reiterated that it was not a national foundation but a regional private trust fund with beneficiaries clearly specified by the indenture. While many changes had occurred in the nearly six decades that the Endowment had operated, "the needs of the beneficiary institutions are still largely the same, with the exception that the financial requirements are greater."

Insisting that the Endowment with only thirty-three employees was not comparable to the large national foundations, Pickens and Felts maintained that to try to fit the limited operations of the Endowment into an organizational chart better suited to those large foundations was unnecessary and futile. As for the compensation of the trustees, that had been set by J. B. Duke and was "not excessive when the legal liability and responsibility of each Trustee is considered and when compared with the compensation of Trustees of other similar trusts." Each trustee, they noted paid a pro-rata share of liability coverage of $10 million.

As for Cuninggim's suggestion that the salaries paid to the Endowment's senior staff were on the high side when compared with university salaries, Pickens and Felt made a telling point. Would it not be fairer, they asked, to compare the senior staff salaries with those of hospital professionals at comparable levels, those people with whom most of the staff worked? For example, the average salary paid to the eleven top Endowment staff members at that time was close to $54,000, whereas the average salaries of top administrators in twenty-four hospitals of over four hundred beds was $60,000; in a dozen hospitals of over five hundred beds it was nearly $70,000. (The average salary for a full professor at Duke University in 1979–80 was almost $32,000.)

Cuninggim's report had stated that the public image of the Endowment was positive and that it deserved to be because "the good that has flowed from its benefactions is immense." Pickens and Felt, responding to that judgment, concluded: "This public image did not 'just happen,' but represents the dedicated service of past and present trustees and staff over a fifty-year period."[36]

While the Cuninggim report clearly aroused the troops, another action that Archie Davis inspired led to even more internal controversy and debate in the Endowment. Primarily for the sake of greater operating efficiency and to save money, Davis and his allies proposed, after a committee had carefully studied the matter and a management consulting firm had recommended the move, that the Endowment close its impressive offices in Rockefeller Center in New York and consolidate into one headquarters office in Charlotte. (The office of the Rural Church section would remain in Durham.) Since all the financial records had been kept in the New York office since the beginning of the Endowment and all disbursements made from there, this proposal not only meant the overthrow of a well established way of doing things but also a drastic disruption in the personal lives of some of the staff officers and employees. Nevertheless, the economic advantages of consolidating in Charlotte were beyond dispute, and on one of the few occasions, if not the only one, where dissenting votes were recorded in the minutes of the trustees, they voted overwhelmingly in March 1979 to consolidate in Charlotte.

While two trustees abstained in the obviously tense voting (and one abstainer later changed his vote to negative), the trustee who apparently most deeply regretted and opposed the move to Charlotte was Richard Henney. Serving the Endowment in an almost Alexander Sands-style since 1953, Henney had been named as the first executive director in 1971. Already ill when the move to Charlotte was being considered, Henney died in May 1979 and was succeeded as executive director the following year by John Day.

The election of two unconventional or nonstereotypical trustees in the later 1970s also suggested that Davis, even before Cuninggim made his report, was helping the trustees to loosen up a bit and try for a broader representation on the board. In June 1978 the election of W. Kenneth Goodson, a bishop in the United Methodist Church, marked the first time that a clergyman had been named to the board. A native of Salisbury, North Carolina, and graduate of Catawba College and then the divinity school of Duke University, Goodson was retiring as the presiding bishop of the Virginia Conference of the United Methodist Church when he became a trustee. For a variety of reasons, he would prove to be a valuable addition to the board.

Then in November 1979 the trustees elected Juanita M. Kreps to the board. The fourth woman to serve as a trustee and the first outside the Duke family, she had had a distinguished career at Duke University, where she received her Ph.D. in economics, first as a professor and then in several top-level administrative posts. Having also served as Secretary of Commerce in the administration of President Jimmy Carter, she, like Goodson, brought special talents and perspectives to the board.

Just as the trustees, under the leadership of Archie Davis, demonstrated a willingness to accept changes and to adapt to new conditions, so too did the staff of the Endowment. In all four areas of the Endowment's work, the years after 1960 brought significant modifications. There were no abrupt or startling innovations, but gradually the staff, backed up by the trustees, found a variety of ways to make sure that the Endowment could continue to be relevant and helpful in serving the purposes that J. B. Duke had designated.

7 ·

THE

ENDOWMENT

AND ITS

EDUCATIONAL

BENEFICIARIES,

1960–1994

JUST AS UNFORESEEN economic and political circumstances forced the trustees of the Endowment to rethink its long-standing, legally mandated investment policy, so too did changing conditions inspire a gradual modification of policies concerning appropriations made to the Endowment's beneficiaries. Taking advantage of certain phrases in the indenture and sensibly responding to social needs that were different from those of the 1920s and 1930s, the staff, backed up by the trustees, found new ways to assist hospitals and promote health care; to underwrite diverse agencies and programs dealing with those children who were "societal" orphans even if they were not biological ones; and to help the rural Methodist church in North Carolina function more effectively in the late twentieth century.

There was also a significant change after 1960 in the Endowment's relationship with its educational beneficiaries. As mentioned earlier, from the very first the Endowment was as thoroughly entangled with Duke University as with the Duke Power Company. With Davidson, Furman, and Johnson C. Smith, however, the Endowment had a strange relationship: it annually provided financial support that was absolutely crucial for all three institutions, yet beyond that, the Endowment had virtually no contacts with them. That situation changed.

The trustees had decided early on, as has already been discussed, that they would make the educational institutions, and particularly Duke University, the primary beneficiaries of the Endowment, in a monetary sense, despite a provision in James B. Duke's will that could have made hospitals the top winner. The trustees chose to continue this policy of favoring the educational institutions after 1960 but changed the mechanism for implementing it.

The trustees passed the last of the resolutions making "additions to corpus" for the benefit of the four educational institutions in 1959. Although the minutes of the trustees' meetings contain no explanation for the cessation of that practice, which had begun in 1934, there were probably two reasons. First, the Treasury Department had been lax about enforcing certain legislation, enacted in 1950, designed to curb the practice of some foundations in "accumulating" income, that is adding the income from the asset base to the corpus or principal rather than distributing the income to beneficiaries; by the late 1950s, however, there were growing signs of the Treasury Department's concern about the matter. Second, because of the indenture's investment restrictions, the trustees could only buy Duke Power securities or certain types of government bonds; since there was a growing conviction on the part of many of the trustees, not all of them, that the Endowment owned more than enough Duke Power stock and since government bonds were not especially attractive at that time, the trustees opted to begin giving surplus money in the Endowment's reserve fund (money taken largely from the hospital account) directly to the four educational institutions.

These special appropriations, however, would not go to the four institutions in the form of unrestricted income to be used however the schools pleased, as was the case with the money distributed under the 32-5-5-4 formula. Rather, the annual special appropriations — so long as the trustees chose to make them — would be the subject of negotiations between representatives of the Endowment and each of the four institutions. In short, the Endowment would no longer remain passive in its relationship with Davidson, Furman, and Johnson C. Smith. Moreover, the point should be made at the outset that in general the Endowment attempted to steer most of the special appropriations toward the academic strengthening of the schools. That is, while some of the special appropriations went for buildings, the Endowment tried to direct most of them toward faculty salaries, library enhancement, scholarships, and other such mainline academic essentials.

The trustees had created a committee for Duke University affairs in 1929, but that committee had gradually become inactive. After all, George Allen, William R. Perkins, and Alexander Sands, plus one or two other Endowment trustees, had long played central roles in the governance of Duke University; Tom Perkins and, a bit later, Richard Henney and Marshall Pickens did the same thing from around 1960 onward. In late March 1960, however, soon after the explosive Gross-Edens affairs at Duke University, the trustees established a new committee on educational institutions and charged it with the responsibility of dealing with and making recommendations to the full board concerning all matters relating to the four educational institutions. With Ben Few, nephew of William P. Few, as chairman, the other members were Perkins, Pickens, Sands, and Mary Semans. Since Sands died less than a month after the creation of the committee, Doris Duke became a member also when she replaced him.

Early in 1961 the trustees employed Paul H. Clyde, a professor of history at Duke University, to serve as secretary of the committee on educational institutions. A meticulous scholar in the field of the United States' relations with China and Japan, Clyde had also served as director of Duke's thriving summer school and, most significantly for his position with the Endowment, had served under Paul Gross as the executive secretary for the long-range planning committee at Duke University. While Clyde, therefore, was an experienced scholar and administrator in his own right, he also had benefited from the rewarding experience of working with Gross on what became Duke University's single most important blueprint for institutional advancement — despite the fact that Gross himself lost his top administrative post in 1960.

Clyde's work for the Endowment involved him, in varying degrees, with all four of the educational institutions, but he probably proved to be more helpful to Johnson C. Smith than to any of the others. For so long a missionary enterprise of the northern Presbyterian church, Smith in the 1960s was ready to sink deeper roots in its local community and region and to strengthen itself as a liberal arts college. While Smith's own administrative, trustee, and faculty leaders played the central roles in the transformation that accelerated in the 1960s, Clyde and the Endowment also contributed significantly to the process.

Making an initial visit to the Johnson C. Smith campus in May 1961, Clyde was favorably impressed by the president of the institution, Rufus P. Perry. He was, Clyde reported, a dignified, friendly, and able person who was "frank in showing us some of the best and some of the worst features of the physical plant." On academic matters, "including the very difficult problem of upgrading what is essentially a teachers' college," Perry was reported to have spoken "with moderation and common sense, indicating far more than a superficial understanding of the obstacles to be overcome." Clyde noted that fewer than a third of the forty-seven full-time faculty members had the Ph.D. degree, and most of them carried a heavy teaching load of fifteen class-room hours per week. There were about 850 students, approximately evenly divided between men and women, in the college — the great majority of them said to be preparing to teach — and 30 students in the theological seminary. Perry and others with whom Clyde spoke suggested that one of the major problems that the college faced was the inadequate preparation of many of the first-year students, especially in English and mathematics.

Since Perry, however, was much concerned about projected buildings and improvements costing $2.25 million, Clyde suggested that Johnson C. Smith might find it advantageous to make even a modest beginning in the direction of professional help in the development or money-raising area. That might enable Smith to "use all proper means to match from other sources" whatever special grants it might receive from the Endowment in the future.[1]

Later in 1961 Clyde helped arrange for Perry to utilize the services of the same public relations agency in Charlotte that the Endowment used, with the Endowment picking up the tab. Clyde's most important move concerning Smith, however, came in 1962 when he tactfully steered Perry toward the idea of spending some of its money from the Endowment on long-range planning. It could deal to some extent with physical facilities but, Clyde believed, should be primarily concerned with academic matters such as faculty competence, teaching, problems of admission and retention of students, and related matters. Admitting that there were no easy answers to such difficult problems, Clyde nevertheless believed that those were the questions Johnson C. Smith "ought to be wrestling with," and a competent outside consultant might help get the whole process started.[2]

Clyde quietly proceeded to sell first Perry and then subsequently Smith's board of trustees on the idea of long-range planning and the need for an outside consultant. Having pushed inside the Endowment for a larger allocation of special-grant money for Smith, Clyde, on the basis of advice from an expert in the field of African American colleges, arranged for Donald C. Agnew, a Ph.D. alumnus of Duke University and then the president of Oglethorpe University in Atlanta, to serve as the consultant and advisor for Johnson C. Smith's initial effort at a comprehensive self-study and long-range planning. The self-study was a prerequisite for accreditation by the Southern Association of Schools and Colleges, and Clyde claimed that Johnson C. Smith was the first African American college in the Southern Association to undertake such a venture.

Even before Johnson C. Smith embarked on its pioneering self-study and planning, the trustees of the Endowment late in 1961 met for the first time on Smith's campus. Doris Duke felt strongly about the nation's need to deal more equitably with African Americans, and, although she missed the trustees' meeting on the Smith campus, Tom Perkins seized the opportunity to report to her about it. Admitting that it was the first time that he and many other trustees had even been on the campus, Perkins declared that the trustees had been impressed by President Perry and the people who worked with him. "What they were able to accomplish with the meager facilities they have," he noted, "is little short of miraculous and I can assure you they get more out of every dollar than any of the other educational institutions which we support." Perkins thought that the trustees had gone "a long way toward assuring them that The Duke Endowment is truly interested in their problems and aims and [is] prepared to assist them personally as well as with checks."[3]

What the Endowment's "checks" meant to Smith in the early 1960s is suggested by the fact that the school's total operating income for the year ending June 30, 1963, came to a bit over $1,315,000. Of that amount, approximately $400,000 came from tuition and fees, and over $524,000 came from the Endowment. In addition to the money, however, Clyde had helped to begin a valuable process of critical self-examination at Smith. When Agnew invited him to attend a meeting of Smith's trustees in Pittsburgh, Pennsylvania, Clyde responded that he would be glad to do so but only if Perry and one or two leading trustees of Smith asked him to attend the meeting. For the best interest of the Endowment, Clyde explained, he had to be "careful not to insinuate" himself into the picture in any way "except when the educational institution concerned clearly indicated that it wants me to do so."[4]

The proper invitations having been extended, Clyde went with Agnew to the meeting in Pittsburgh. One matter that worried Clyde but about which he felt inhibited in speaking was that Johnson C. Smith's theological seminary, which was not fully accredited, had very few students (there were seven graduates of the seminary in 1964), but it consumed about a third of Smith's income. Officers of the Endowment in New York had learned of the Interdenominational Theological Center (ITC) in Atlanta, which had been formed by the cooperative action of four predominantly African American seminaries representing four denominations in the late 1950s. Different foundations contributed almost $3.6 million to the ITC by 1964, but $2.3 million of that came from the Sealantic Fund, a Rockefeller philanthropy. The ITC did not replace the denominational training of theological students but, according to the president of the ITC, made it possible for each denomination to do this training better. The center also enjoyed close cooperation with the Methodists' Candler School of Theology at Emory University and the Presbyterians' Columbia Seminary, which was also in Atlanta.

In light of Johnson C. Smith's history and traditions, Clyde understood the sensitivity concerning its seminary, but he urged Agnew to broach the subject with Perry if and when the time seemed right. The matter did indeed take time and caused considerable debate and soul-searching, but by the end of the decade Smith's seminary had become a part of the Interdenominational Theological Center, thus allowing the Charlotte-based campus to focus its attention and resources on the arts and sciences for undergraduates.

Agnew, who had left Oglethorpe to become executive director of the Education Improvement Project of the Southern Association of Schools and Colleges, continued to serve as a consultant at Smith. Prior to a talk he was to give to the Endowment trustees in mid-1964, Clyde advised him concerning certain points that might be made. First, Agnew might explain about the Education Improvement Project's larger purpose of strengthening African American colleges in order to produce a healthier American society. Then, turning to Johnson C. Smith and its planning and self-study venture, Clyde thought "a mild compliment" to the trustees for underwriting the project might be in order. He hoped too that Agnew might urge the trustees to move toward the goal of helping to make it possible for Smith "to become first-class and the best predominantly Negro private liberal arts college in the South." Clyde explained that the point should be emphasized, however, that the pursuit of that goal would require patience and restraint and that Smith had to do its own planning and set its own goals. "These things cannot be thrust upon the college from the outside," Clyde cautioned. Yet, as the Endowment had demonstrated for the previous three years, outside forces could "exert a subtle constructive influence." And Agnew should certainly mention Perry's report that the planning process was helping the morale of both faculty and trustees.[5]

Although Clyde resigned as secretary of the Endowment's committee on educational institutions in early 1966, he continued to serve the Endowment as a consultant and to be involved and interested in developments at Johnson C. Smith. When Smith completed its self-study and a visiting committee of the Southern Association made its report on Smith in 1966, Clyde undertook to summarize the latter document for Tom Perkins. An important point that the visiting committee made at the beginning of its report, and something that Clyde and Agnew had long been concerned about, was that Smith's president, with too many persons reporting directly to him, was overburdened with administrative detail. The recent appointment of an executive dean was a hopeful development, the committee believed, if the dean should be given real powers.

Concerning the faculty, the Southern Association's committee noted that Smith failed to meet the requirement for four-year colleges to have at least 30 percent of the faculty with the Ph.D. and at least 60 percent with professional preparation equivalent to three years of study beyond the bachelor's degree; Smith had 13 percent and 11.5 percent respectively, and a marked increase in the salary scale would be required to recruit new Ph.Ds.

In the area of admissions, the visiting committee found that the mean verbal and mathematical score of applicants in 1964–65 was quite low. That meant that almost all of the first-year students would have difficulty in handling standard college courses, and the committee made many suggestions concerning the curriculum and the problem of underuse of the library.

Smith's physical plant, the committee found, was in better shape than the educational program. With three new buildings erected since 1961 and more slated to come, Perry had earned the designation by some in the Smith community as "the master builder."

In the business area, the visiting committee found the division of responsibility between the Pittsburgh and Charlotte offices, as mentioned earlier, to be perplexing. In Charlotte the president, in addition to preparing the budget in conjunction with the trustees, had to approve all requisitions and to sign all checks in payment of bills.

There were other matters that the visiting committee addressed, but Clyde urged Tom Perkins not to be discouraged by the report. The bright spot, Clyde avowed, was the self-study and the report of the visiting committee, "the first really critical examination of this institution ever made."[6] Clyde proved to be correct, for the self-study followed by the outside assessment prompted Perry and the Smith trustees to take a number of important, far-reaching steps.

In 1967 the trustees voted to close the business office in Pittsburgh and consolidate that aspect of the operation on Smith's campus. A revision of the bylaws enlarged the board from twenty-one to twenty-seven members, with the six new members coming from the Charlotte area. Increasingly, therefore, Smith would be rooted, and supported, in its own area. Moreover, both Clyde and Tom Perkins exerted themselves to interest other foundations in supporting Johnson C. Smith.

When Clyde persuaded William Archie, the executive director of the Mary

Reynolds Babcock Foundation in Winston-Salem, to visit President Perry, it turned out to be a most fortunate development for Johnson C. Smith. At a time when racial tensions in the United States were already increasing — and would do so even more dramatically in the years just ahead — Archie joined Clyde and others in seeing hope for the future in an institution like Johnson C. Smith. Following a series of conferences with Perry, certain trustees of Smith (including John P. Lucas Jr., a vice president of the Duke Power Company), and Duke Endowment leaders, Archie became interested in proposing to the Babcock Foundation that it join forces with the Endowment in making a major, multiyear commitment to support Johnson C. Smith. He proceeded most cautiously, however, and managed to have Smith's trustees request an examination of certain aspects of the institution's operations by outside experts, namely Hugh McEniry, the vice-chancellor of the University of North Carolina at Charlotte, and Lucius Wyatt, the business manager at Hampton Institute in Virginia. While Donald Agnew was not a member of the committee, he conferred and consulted with McEniry and Wyatt.

Following visits to the campus in October 1967 and then a long conference call concerning their views and findings, McEniry reported to Archie that, while he and Wyatt could claim no intimate understanding of the institution from such brief visits, they did believe they bought a certain objectivity to their task. They gave Smith high marks for its physical plant, strong community support in Charlotte, and good morale among students, faculty, and alumni. They had high praise for Perry and his eleven-year administration but pointed out that he had saved Johnson C. Smith from administrative expense at the cost of his own time and energy. There continued to be a great need, McEniry noted, for a real dean, a business manager, a development officer, and one or two other key personnel. In conclusion, however, McEniry and his colleagues considered Smith to be worthy of consideration for a major grant.[7] Although encouraged by this report, Archie was still not ready to recommend a major, multiyear commitment to the trustees of the Babcock Foundation. Rather he favored an interim step in the form of a grant to assist Johnson C. Smith in employing a new dean, a business manager, and perhaps someone to run a freshman-year program.

Meantime in New York, Tom Perkins and others on the Endowment's educational committee came up with the idea of special grants to Smith and Davidson, similar to a grant already made to Furman, which would enable them to supplement the salaries of two faculty members who could be named, as at Duke University, James B. Duke professors. Although Smith's trustees had already voted to name their new library the James B. Duke Memorial Library (since the Endowment had largely paid for it), they liked the idea of the named professorships. In 1968 Rufus Perry decided to retire as president of Smith at the end of the year, and the trustees named him as one of the new James B. Duke professors. To succeed him, the trustees elected Lonnie H. Newsom, who earlier in the 1960s had been for two years president of Barber-Scotia College in Concord, North Carolina, before becoming an officer of the Southern Regional Education Board in Atlanta.

This new leadership, combined with the appointment of a new academic dean and a business manager, augered well for Smith. Unfortunately, however, President Perry's zeal for new buildings and lack of adequate help in the financial area had an unforeseen consequence: just as the new administrative team took over, a leading auditing firm discovered current obligations at Johnson C. Smith in excess of $2 million, including a deficit of $575,000 projected for 1968–69. Caught by this painful surprise, Newsom had no choice but to turn to the Endowment and request that its forthcoming special grants to Smith be used for general operating expenses and that Smith be released from any restrictions on previous, unexpended grants totaling almost $103,000. The Endowment not only acceded to this request but made a special appropriation to Smith in June 1969 of $450,000 for general operating purposes to help it out of its predicament. One of the larger banks in Charlotte also extended credit in the emergency.

The officers of Johnson C. Smith may or may not have exaggerated, but they subsequently stated in a memorandum to the Endowment that 1968–69 was "the most critical period in the long history of this 102 year old institution" and its "very existence hung by only threads of faith and hope." Both faith and hope had been rewarded, the statement continued, when the Endowment came forth with its unprecedented help. "Needless to say that without the strong arm of financial support of the Endowment, Smith would have probably joined the scrap-heap or funeral pyre of more than two hundred other traditionally Negro colleges within the last hundred years."[8]

Cheered by the resolution of Smith's financial crisis and greatly impressed by Newsom's leadership, the Babcock Foundation, on Archie's recommendation, late in 1969 committed itself to support Johnson C. Smith in the amount of $2 million over a five-year period, that constituting almost a third of the Babcock Foundation's distributable income. As Archie informed a friend in the Ford Foundation, which would also eventually help Smith, there were two conditions to the Babcock grant: (1) that the Duke Endowment would match

Babcock money with special grants (that is, grants above and beyond the 4 percent of the income from the original corpus that Smith received annually), and (2) that the Babcock Foundation and the Endowment would have a study made in about a year and a half "to be sure that the kind of progress that should be made is being made and that our funds are being expended for the specific purposes covered by the grant."

Because the officer of the Ford Foundation also knew and liked Lonnie Newsom, Archie expressed the conviction that Newsom, with a little more help (perhaps from the Ford Foundation?) and with a firm resolve on the part of his faculty and some portion of the students, could do the job—which was "to make out of Johnson C. Smith in time, a collegiate institution worthy of the name and capable of turning out baccalaureate graduates who can compete fairly and equitably in the market place."[9]

The Endowment liked nothing better than to use its grants as leverage to gain additional support for a beneficiary. In responding to Archie's news of the Babcock grant to Smith, Richard Henney and Amos Kearns, the chairman of the Endowment's committee on educational institutions, expressed the delight of the trustees and their determination to do everything possible to match the Babcock funds during the five-year period. "The Duke Endowment most certainly shares the enthusiasm and hope of the Babcock Foundation," Henney and Kearns declared, "to make it possible for Johnson C. Smith to become a first-class liberal arts college."[10]

Linking two North Carolina-based foundations together in a joint undertaking was a relatively natural and easily accomplished matter, but the Endowment's leaders knew how to "network" on a much larger scale. Through the Foundation Executive Group in New York, Tom Perkins met regularly with top officers of many of the major foundations in the nation. "I know of the deep concern that the Ford Foundation has for the traditionally black colleges," Perkins wrote to McGeorge Bundy, the head of the Ford Foundation, "and think that this [Johnson C. Smith] might be a place where money could be well spent in conjunction with others." Accordingly, Perkins invited Bundy to a meeting with Archie, Newsom, and various Endowment officials in April 1970.[11] Further "networking" led to grants for Johnson C. Smith from the Seeley G. Mudd Fund, the Kresge Foundation, and others.

Foundations were not, certainly, the only source of new support for Smith. A fund-raising campaign for Smith in Charlotte, the first in the school's history, began in 1970. With a number of prominent local people, such as the president of the North Carolina National Bank, having been added to the board of trustees, Smith now had a growing and enthusiastic local constituency, not only among African Americans but also among the white business and professional community. An Endowment staff member who played a key professional role in the Charlotte campaign was Robert J. Sailstad. Following Paul Clyde's resignation as secretary of the committee on educational institutions, Richard Henney had served in that capacity until August 1968. At that time, the trustees named Sailstad as the Endowment's first director of educational affairs and public information. This was a significant new post, for the Endowment had long utilized both a public relations agency in New York and one in Charlotte for press releases and various other matters in the area of public relations. Sailstad, with wide experience in his field, had served as director of development and public relations at Davidson College for a number of years prior to joining the Endowment. In addition to his public-relations chores, he became a staunch ally of Bill Archie in the campaign to assist Johnson C. Smith.

Archie and Sailstad, after considerable negotiations by the former, succeeded in taking their case for Smith to the group that had first started and long stood behind the institution, the United Presbyterian Church. When the church's board of national missions finally agreed to allow the two foundation officers to address its administrative committee in New York in early 1971, Sailstad pointed out that Endowment had given over $9 million to Smith since 1924; that its special grants to Smith had increased from $293,000 in 1967 to $714,000 in 1969; and that it had joined with the Babcock Foundation in a tentative allocation to Smith of $4 million. Sailstad particularly emphasized the groundswell of support that Smith was enjoying in Charlotte and claimed that "more hard cash has already been contributed to Johnson C. Smith by those who live in Charlotte than has ever been raised in a general city campaign for any black institution in North or South, East or West."

Pointing out that the United Presbyterian Church could be proud of its past support of Smith, Sailstad added that it "now presents a particularly unique, once-in-a-lifetime opportunity for this church and its leadership." To serve as a model for other such private, predominantly African American colleges, Smith, Sailstad argued, needed a minimum of $12 million. With the people of Charlotte investing $1.5 million and the Babcock Foundation and the Duke Endowment allocating $4 million, a $1 million grant from the United Presbyterian Church would carry the campaign over the halfway mark.[12] Although the Presbyterians did lend Smith up to $500,000, they apparently were not financially situated so that they could comply with the request of Sailstad and Archie.

When Lonnie Newsom resigned as president of Johnson C. Smith in 1972 to accept the presidency of Central State University in Ohio, Sailstad, Archie, and others who were what might be termed "outside boosters" of Johnson C. Smith were keenly disappointed. The appointment of Wilbert Greenfield as Smith's tenth president later that year, however, promised a continuation of the efforts to strengthen the institution. A native of North Carolina who had done his undergraduate work at North Carolina Agricultural and Technical College in Greensboro, Greenfield had received his Ph.D. in physiology at the University of Iowa and had both taught and served as academic dean at Jackson State College in Mississippi before taking the presidency at Smith.

Both Archie and Sailstad, as well as the foundations they represented, continued to support Smith and its new president. In fact, in mid-1974 Archie informed Richard Henney that he felt better about Johnson C. Smith than he had at any time since the Babcock Foundation and the Endowment joined hands to try to assist it.

Although Sailstad continued to be more involved with Smith than with Davidson, Furman, or Duke, the Endowment was possibly not again as much directly involved in developments at Smith as it was through the 1960s and into the early 1970s. Smith had embarked on a new course in the 1960s, only partly as a result of Paul Clyde's urging. The process of strengthening itself as a liberal arts college was necessarily slow and sometimes difficult, but it continued in the 1970s, 1980s, and on into the 1990s.

The Endowment's annual financial support of Smith continued to be crucial, and there were some special grants that especially stood out. In 1981, for example, when much-feared cuts in federal student aid programs, which were critically important at Smith, failed to materialize, President Greenfield persuaded the Endowment's trustees that Smith's most pressing need was an additional dormitory. Fewer than half of the students were able to find on-campus housing, and Greenfield believed that the high rate of attrition at Smith was affected by the housing situation. (Nationally 50 percent of all entering students eventually graduated, but at Smith only 40 percent did so.)

Accordingly, the trustees of the Endowment voted to make a special, one-time grant for a new 220-bed dormitory. The preliminary feasibility study showed a cost of $2.9 million, and the Endowment agreed to provide $2 million over a three-year period. Although a one-time invasion of the reserve fund for approximately $500,000 would be necessary in the first year, the trustees believed that they could thus give the special help to Smith while continuing or exceeding the existing levels of special grants to Duke, Davidson, and Furman.

As another example of Smith's continuing push to strengthen itself and how the Endowment tried to facilitate that, the Lilly Endowment made a grant of $500,000 to enable Smith to establish an honors college. In both 1987 and 1988 the Endowment made special grants to help Smith meet the dollar-for-dollar match required by the Lilly Foundation.

By 1994 Smith was in the midst of a $50 million capital campaign to increase its endowment, strengthen its faculty, and provide support for its 1,400 students. It was also celebrating the inauguration of its first women president, Dr. Dorothy Cowser Yancy. She led an institution that had undergone dramatic changes since J. B. Duke decided in 1924 to make it a beneficiary of the Endowment.

After the Endowment decided in 1960 to become more involved than it ever had been with Davidson, Furman, and Johnson C. Smith, it became Paul Clyde's task, in conjunction with the committee on educational institutions, to implement the new policy. With Furman University, Clyde, as well as the Endowment, had the satisfaction of watching it grow progressively more ambitious even as it steadily grew stronger in its academic program. Moreover, Clyde's role concerning Furman was quite different from and less time consuming than his relationship with Johnson C. Smith.

Over a period of years from 1955 to 1961, Furman gradually moved to a quite beautiful and spacious new campus on the outskirts of Greenville, South Carolina. Using red brick and modified colonial style in the buildings to symbolize Furman's history and traditions, the architects also included numerous functional features to point toward the future. All in all the result provided Furman with an unusually handsome group of buildings on a splendidly landscaped campus.

Although officials made every effort to move various statues and other portable landmarks from the old campus, it took time for the students to settle into their new surroundings. There was anxiety about traditions and continuity, just as there had been at Duke University in the fall of 1930 when male students moved into the Tudor Gothic structures on Duke's new West Campus. All of that anxiety and unsettledness passed relatively quickly, however.

The Endowment's dealings with Furman in those first years on the new campus may be illustrated through a letter that Clyde wrote concerning how Furman would use the $125,000 special grant that the Endowment made to Furman late in 1961. John L. Plyler, president of Furman since 1939, had submitted a list of "immediately pressing needs" costing almost $200,000. Following a policy that the Endowment's committee on educational institutions had agreed on, Clyde suggested that rather than just appropriate the $125,000 and let Plyler decide how to use it, the committee should specify its own priorities among the items that Plyler had listed.

Furman had an excellent new library building, Clyde noted, but its "book collections are weak even for an undergraduate college." The faculty needed to be strengthened in terms of number, quality, and morale. Therefore Clyde argued that it would be highly desirable to encourage the raising of faculty salaries and the making of strong new appointments.

Clyde recognized that Plyler felt some urgency about completing the building program on the new campus. Thus in the president's list of immediate needs, the cost of buildings and outdoor athletic facilities totaled $82,000. Clyde thought, justifiably or not, that Plyler could "get this money from the Baptists much more easily than he can get them to provide funds for books or salaries." He recommended, therefore, that the Endowment would best serve Furman's interest in the long run if the committee on educational institutions specified that $75,000 of the $125,000 be devoted to academic purposes and only $49,300 to plant and grounds.[13]

This preference of the Endowment for strengthening the academic side did not, as the above letter shows, preclude money for buildings and grounds, but top priority went to the academic side. Fortunately for Furman, it had an unusually strong, able dean, Francis W. Bonner, who shared Clyde's view of educational priorities, so it was not as if the Endowment were forcing an unwanted dose of medicine down a resisting throat. It was more a matter of the four educational institutions having to learn to draw up their list of "immediate pressing needs" with some thought and care about the Endowment's preferences. After all, the special grants were what might be termed freewill offerings by the trustees to higher education. The trustees not only did not have to make them each year, but they were certainly free legally to terminate or redirect them whenever they might choose to do so.

In late 1963 the trustees allocated $375,000 to Furman, a significant increase over earlier special grants. With the Endowment's trustees scheduled to meet on Furman's campus in April 1964, Clyde pointed out that it would be Plyler's twenty-fifth anniversary as president. That was close to a record for mid-twentieth-century college and university presidents, Clyde suggested, and Plyler's tenure had brought "an extraordinary development not only in the facilities, but also in the quality of education offered by Furman University." Clyde urged that the trustees should recognize Plyler's unusual service, which they subsequently did, for "such action would have the additional advantage of serving the Endowment's public relations in a very dignified and proper way."[14]

One problem at Furman which bothered Clyde but even more so its own leaders, who had to live and cope with it almost daily, concerned relations with South Carolina's Baptists. William P. Few, while still the dean of Trinity College in 1908, had made some acute observations about the relationship of colleges and outside bodies, whether state legislatures or church groups. Fortunately for Trinity, it had already achieved what Few, as well as many other leading American educators, considered essential for a stable and secure college or university: a permanent and self-perpetuating board of trustees. From his knowledge of history as well as certain experiences at Trinity, Few balanced a genuine belief in democracy with a realistic awareness that periodic "gusts of unwisdom" were a characteristic and dangerous feature of democratic societies. In the long run, Few argued, "there can be no security for a college which in its actual control is too close to the untrained mass of people, whether this mass is represented by a state government subject to popular will or represented by a church organization that reflects too immediately the changing moods of the multitude."[15]

Southern Baptists would have benefited from pondering Few's words, for both Furman in South Carolina and Wake Forest in North Carolina long suffered from the nearly choking embrace of their respective Baptist state conventions. Concerning a wide range of topics from dancing and fraternities to the acceptance of federal grants, there were all too frequent battles about the policies of the Baptist-sponsored universities, battles that consumed too much time and energy of educators and that distracted attention from genuinely important academic concerns.

In the fall of 1964, just as a strong, new president, Gordon W. Blackwell, was about to assume office, the matter of integration — the admission of African American students — became the subject of controversy between Furman and the state's Baptist convention. As early as 1961 a majority of the faculty and students at Furman had indicated in a straw poll that they favored integration for the institution. In the spring of 1964 Furman's trustees voted in favor of admitting students without regard to race, and Blackwell accepted the offer of the presidency with the clear understanding that the board had determined this policy.

Although the executive committee of the convention recommended in the fall of 1964 that the action of the Furman board be approved, the full convention itself voted 943-915 to oppose the proposed change at Furman, and by a much larger majority to reject the whole idea of integration. Faced with this rebuff, Furman's board called a special meeting at which it seemed for a while that those who favored delaying the implementation of the integration policy might carry the day. One of the strongest proponents of Furman's sticking by its guns, however, was Dean Bonner, who had long led the fight for integration at Furman.

Among other, even stronger arguments that Bonner made, as he reported to Paul Clyde, was the fact that if Furman should refuse to admit African Americans, it would be the only one of the Endowment's educational beneficiaries with such a policy. "While this would not necessarily mean being dropped from the [Endowment's] program," Bonner maintained, "it could well mean that Furman could not expect any more of the 'bonuses' or supplementary grants which have frequently come our way in recent years." He asserted to Furman's board that the trustees of the Endowment felt "strongly about the matter of equal opportunity for education."[16]

Furman's board ended up standing firm and reaffirmed the decision to integrate. The first four African American students were enrolled in February 1965. When Blackwell asked Clyde if Bonner's remarks about the Endowment's position should be publicized, however, Clyde conferred with Paul Gross. They decided that Bonner's references to the Endowment should not be made public, obviously because the Endowment did not wish to be perceived as throwing its weight around, even if the cause were a morally sound one. Furman's trustees well understood, at any rate, that 14.4 percent of its income for 1963–64 came from the Endowment whereas only 8.2 percent came from the South Carolina Baptist convention.

Furman, like Wake Forest, ultimately freed itself from the constricting embrace of the Baptists, and that was one factor in the brightening image of Furman as an increasingly strong liberal arts college. Another was Bonner's encouragement of more international studies at Furman. As a result of conferences with Paul Clyde, Bonner used a portion of Furman's special grants from the Endowment to enable appropriate faculty members, mostly in the humanities and fine arts, to travel and study during the summer in Europe and India. New courses and enriched, broadened older ones resulted from this policy. Bonner later reported to the Endowment that no other program of encouragement had provided such a stimulus to Furman's faculty, both to those who received the travel grants and to their colleagues. "No other program has so dramatically demonstrated to the faculty that they are considered to be as important as buildings, trees, and athletic teams."[17]

On the occasion of Furman's completion of one of its periodic self-studies and the related report on Furman of a visiting committee of the Southern Association in 1966, Clyde summarized some of his thoughts about the institution. He believed that there was clear evidence that Furman under Gordon Blackwell's leadership was pursuing with increasing intensity the academic goals that had been emerging during the closing years of John Plyler's long tenure. As Clyde saw the matter, Plyler had put greater emphasis during most of his presidency on the demands of the new physical plant, to the relative neglect of insuring a strong faculty and library. During Plyler's last four or so years, however, Clyde thought the long-time president had given increasing attention to the quality of the education offered by Furman. Then Blackwell and Bonner accelerated the movement toward concern about educational quality, higher standards, and a more internationally minded and cosmopolitan faculty and student body. Furman, Clyde declared, had long been "tied to a narrow geographical region and to a strict, fundamentalist denominationalism." Well into the twentieth century it had not been a truly strong liberal arts college. Yet after World War II things changed. Furman built what Clyde, as well as many others, considered one of the most attractive campuses in the country; more importantly, it "has elevated in major degree the quality of practically all of its instructional programs." Its major problem, Clyde predicted, would be in "finding the funds to pay for its present high morale and for the quality that must yet be developed."[18]

Confirmation for Clyde's assertions about Furman's marked academic improvement came in 1973. The Council of the United Chapters of Phi Beta Kappa then voted to charter a chapter at Furman, making it one of 214 such chapters in the nation and the third in South Carolina. (The University of South Carolina had been awarded a chapter in 1926 and Wofford College one in 1941.) This was a mark of recognition that Furman had long sought and one which was by no means granted on a perfunctory or haphazard basis. Gordon Blackwell thought it "the most significant event ever in the academic life of Furman."[19]

While money from the Duke Endowment obviously played a role in the ascending curve that marked Furman's course after 1924, it took leaders like Plyler, Bonner, Blackwell, and numerous others not mentioned here to know how to use the money wisely.

Just as the Endowment enjoyed a happy, uncomplicated relationship with Furman after 1960, when the relationship began to become something besides a more or less automatic and purely monetary one, so too was that the case with Davidson. It went through a series of changes beginning in the 1960s that, while building on the inherited and basic strengths of the college, significantly and permanently altered it. Paradoxically, one of Davidson's greatest resources — the unusually loyal support of a high percentage of its alumni — also posed a problem. The alumni, including the many who were trustees and faculty members, loved and passionately stood by the Davidson that they had known. Believing that Davidson had been and was about as good an institution as it ought to be, they resisted change. Such complacency, which obviously hampers the full realization of any educational institution's potential, gave way in the 1960s, as will be illustrated, to a willingness to embrace many different types of far-reaching changes. The result was a much stronger, more nationally visible Davidson, no longer just a regionally strong liberal arts college but one that ranked among the best in the nation. The Endowment helped in that development.

When Davidson's trustees voted in May 1962 to drop racial barriers in admissions, they were simply doing what many other southern colleges and universities were also doing in the early 1960s. Fortunately for Davidson, the Presbyterian church bodies with which the college was linked accepted integration more graciously than did the South Carolina Baptists. Perhaps an even bigger jolt, especially for many alumni, would come a decade later when the trustees, following the faculty's recommendation, voted to make Davidson fully coeducational by admitting women students.

Meantime, Clyde negotiated easily with D. Grier Martin, Davidson's president since 1958, about how the Endowment's special grants should be spent. Reporting to Tom Perkins about "a good talk in a relaxed atmosphere" with Martin, Clyde noted that the president would probably include in his list of immediate needs (toward which the Endowment's special grant of $125,000 could be used) greater support for the library. "This would be good," Clyde added, "because their library is not nearly as strong as it should be."[20]

Sure enough, when Martin's list of immediate needs reached Clyde, library support was there along with a half-dozen other items. The estimated total cost of the immediate needs was, however, $150,000, meaning that Clyde faced the task of pruning it down to the $125,000 available before making his recommendation to the Endowment's committee on educational institutions. He reached the goal by halving the amounts requested in certain cases but suggesting the full amount requested in others. In the case of support for the library, Clyde not only recommended the full amount requested but added $2,600.

Grier Martin was adept at doing something that the Endowment's trustees and staff always appreciated, and that was making a full report on how the special grant had been utilized as well as thanking the Endowment. (Being quite human, the trustees naturally resented it when the Endowment's aid was taken for granted.) In the case of the $125,000 special grant for 1962, Martin noted that, while he had earlier sent a progress report on the use of the appropriation, it was "impossible for a statistical report . . . to express in any adequate sense the benefits which have accrued and which will accrue in the years ahead from the projects which were made possible by this generous appropriation to Davidson."

Getting down to specifics, Martin claimed that the new interdepartmental humanities course, the development of which and the essential facilities for which had been made possible by the Endowment's grant, was "the most significant and . . . promising development in Davidson's educational program during the past two decades." He went on to talk about other improvements that had been wholly or partly paid for by the Endowment's grant.

Important as all of those projects were, however, Martin believed, undoubtedly correctly, that they were not as significant as the basic improvement in faculty and staff salaries that had been made possible by the agreement of the Endowment's trustees in the previous year that $125,000 could be used annually for that purpose. "This 'giant stride' forward in Davidson's program of faculty development," Martin declared, "has been largely responsible for the success that Davidson has had in the improvement of its faculty during the past two years." He suggested that the significant increase in faculty and staff compensation would be increasingly effective in future years "as more and more people come to realize that Davidson has faculty compensation equal to the better colleges and universities, not only in the South but throughout the nation." Martin took pride in the fact that only one other educational institution in North Carolina at that time had higher average salaries than Davidson, and that was Duke University.

"I wish that there were some way in which all of us at Davidson could express adequately our gratitude for all that the Duke Endowment has meant to this college through the years," Martin concluded. "You may be sure that our efforts will be in the direction of showing this gratitude by the service which the college will render in the future."[21] Two developments in the mid-1960s brought Davidson closer to its goal of achieving national recognition for its quality. Out of more than 800 colleges and universities in the nation, the Ford Foundation in 1965 picked Davidson as one of the fifty-seven such institutions to receive a challenge grant. In Davidson's case, the Ford Foundation offered $2.3 million if Davidson could raise an additional $5.5 million. It was the largest fund-raising program of that type that Davidson had ever tackled, according to Grier Martin, and he believed that successful completion of the campaign would be another important step in "moving Davidson College from regional leadership to equality with the finest liberal arts colleges in the country."[22] Although the Endowment's annual support of Davidson had been a factor in the Ford Foundation's selection of Davidson for a challenge grant, Davidson could not use money from the Endowment to meet the challenge. Nevertheless, in October, 1967, some nine months ahead of schedule, Davidson reached and even exceeded (by over $30,000) its goal of raising $5.5 million.

To put the matter of Davidson's (as well as Duke University's) quest for national ranking in some perspective, one might note what a leading analyst of American higher education had to say about southern colleges and universities in 1965. Allan M. Cartter, a former professor of economics and dean of the graduate school at Duke University, left there in the aftermath of the Gross-Edens affair and eventually became vice president of the American Council on Education. The South, Cartter declared, "cannot as yet boast of a single outstanding institution on the national scene." The region had a fair share of good universities, he noted, "but perhaps more than its share of poor ones." In its colleges and universities, Cartter concluded somewhat unfairly, "the South has steadily chosen to expand quantity rather than improve quality."[23]

Notwithstanding Cartter's analysis, the Endowment was entangled with at least two educational institutions — Davidson and Duke — that certainly intended to do all that they possibly could do to prove him wrong concerning recognition on the national scene. In addition to the successful meeting of the Ford Foundation's challenge grant, the second important step that Davidson took in the 1960s to revitalize itself came in the way of curricular reform. Prior to the arrival of the visiting committee of the Southern Association of Colleges and Schools, the Davidson faculty completed its own self-study of the institution but made no suggestion for significant change in the curriculum, that is the course of study required of the students. According to an historian of Davidson, its curriculum in 1965 "was still strongly reminiscent of 1900" — and the mid-1960s was "no time for reminiscing." The visiting committee was reported to be "dismayed to find at Davidson such apparent contentment with the status quo" and urged that the faculty should "look at some new horizons" and "do some blue skying."[24]

Davidson, like Furman, was blessed with a strong, quite popular dean, Frontis W. Johnston, who was also a respected historian. The visiting committee's urging gave Johnston exactly the opportunity that he had been seeking, and the result was that Davidson's faculty totally scrapped its venerable course of study and launched its "blue sky" curriculum, which, while retaining a certain structure, gave the students much more choice and placed a new emphasis on independent study, the non-Western program, and the honors college. "I suspect that is the most important decision Davidson has ever made," Clyde reported to Tom Perkins.[25]

Clyde's chronic concern about Davidson's library proved quite appropriate, too, for the self-study report in 1965 pointed out that among twenty-eight comparable colleges, Davidson was in last place in the number of books and periodical subscriptions, in twenty-sixth place in library expenditures per student, and twenty-second in the percent of the college budget used for the library. In 1967 Davidson's trustees authorized the construction of a new library, one that would meet the college's long-term needs, and the Endowment, along with many other loyal supporters of Davidson, would play a significant role in the rectifying of that particular problem at Davidson.

The various changes that Davidson underwent in the 1960s were climaxed in 1972 when the trustees, accepting a recommendation of the faculty, voted to admit women. "It was, beyond doubt, the most dramatic change ever made in the nature of Davidson College," one historian argues, "and yet it seems impossible to treat it as dramatic, so natural and successful was the change and so calmly accepted."[26] With approximately 1,000 male students, Davidson proposed to expand sufficiently to include around 500 women.

Just to illustrate how the Endowment often assisted beneficiaries in other than a monetary fashion, one should note that two staff members from the Endowment's Hospital Section, Jere W. Witherspoon and Charles Hite, visited the Davidson infirmary and helped college officials begin to think about some of the new problems involved in coeducation. Networking "within the family" also gained ground, such as the arrangement that Sailstad facilitated and the Endowment subsidized whereby Davidson's faculty members and students engaged in research and in honors programs were given full use of the resources in the main library of Duke University. The fact that the Duke Power Company gave Davidson 106 acres on nearby Lake Norman, to be used for recreational purposes, merely added another dimension to the institutional intermingling and cooperation.

When Grier Martin resigned as president of Davidson in 1968 because of health reasons, Samuel R. Spencer Jr. succeeded him. Suggesting how well Davidson had succeeded in shaking off an earlier, alleged complacency, Spencer in his installation address called for a "chronic dissatisfaction with the status quo." He wanted "loving critics" of Davidson to look at every facet of college life and then ask, "Can it be better? How can we make it better?"[27]

Such a posture was beginning to pay off for Davidson, both in terms of a stronger, more cosmopolitan pool of applicants and in national recognition. In the early 1970s a large foundation, which wished to remain anonymous, made an objective comparison of 206 independent liberal arts colleges in the United States that enrolled 1,000 or more students. Davidson ranked thirteenth among the 206 and was the only college in the Southeast to rank among the top fifteen. According to Davidson's officers, if Davidson's full support from the Duke Endowment had been included in the study, Davidson's endowment-per-student rating would have improved, thus causing its overall national ranking to rise to tenth or eleventh place. In average faculty compensation, for example, where a good bit of Endowment money had gone since 1924, and especially since 1961 when the special grants began, Davidson ranked fifth. In the long run, that particular mark of academic strength augured especially well for the college.

As mentioned earlier, the Endowment's networking with other foundations redounded to Davidson's benefit. For example, when the trustees of the Seeley Mudd Fund visited Davidson and eventually made a significant building grant, Sam Spencer expressed his deep appreciation for the fact that "the Endowment is acting as a catalyst in the matter."[28] The fact that Davidson was hustling to do what it could to help itself was indicated by the fact that in 1973 it won an award from the U.S. Steel Company for having the highest percentage improvement among private colleges during the previous year in contributions to the annual fund.

Following Sam Spencer's resignation in 1983, John W. Kuykendall became the president of Davidson, and the push toward excellence and high national standing continued unabated. To illustrate the Endowment's ongoing role in the process, one might note that the Endowment in 1988 helped to finance a five-year, multimillion-dollar project at Davidson called Focus on Technology. It had the goal of infusing technology into and across the entire curriculum and was but one example from the many that could be cited of how the Endowment cooperated with Davidson's leaders to strengthen the college.

In 1989 Davidson launched the most ambitious financial campaign in its history and, at the time, the largest ever attempted by a liberal arts college. Six years later Davidson proudly announced that it had raised $160.3 million, funding a new sports complex, a visual arts center, three new dormitories, thirteen endowed professorships, 202 new scholarships, seven academic departmental endowments, and 50 new endowed library book funds. Among the Endowment's contributions to the campaign were gifts of $1 million for the establishment of the James B. Duke Scholars Program supporting eight students annually, two from each class; $1 million in support of the visual arts center; and another $1 million to fund a James B. Duke professorship. In the indenture, J. B. Duke had referred to his hope that Duke University should eventually attain and maintain "a place of real leadership in the educational world." The trustees of the Endowment, however, especially after 1960, were quite happy to do what they could to help another of the educational beneficiaries, Davidson College, pursue the same goal.

Thanks to the Endowment, Duke University in the early 1960s actually did take a giant, concrete step toward the national leadership that J. B. Duke had coveted for the institution. It was probably the single most significant step, in fact, in a whole series of developments that would push Duke into the top echelon of research universities by the 1990s. Acting on the belief that the quality of the faculty, while certainly not the only significant factor, was nevertheless the single most important determinant of an educational institution's academic strength, the university's trustees, backed by the Endowment, set out to make faculty compensation at Duke competitive with that of the best universities in the nation. The immediate beneficiaries of this dramatic new policy were, of course, Duke's faculty members; but in the long run, higher education throughout the South could only be strengthened by the then startling development, one signaling that historic regional disparities in faculty salaries were not to continue at Duke.

The temporarily demoralizing Gross-Edens affair at Duke happened just when the Endowment was about to embark on its new policy of making annual special grants to the four educational institutions. That juxtaposition, however, was simply an accident of history. The dismissal of Paul Gross as the vice president for education by the majority of the university's trustees by no means signaled the death of the long-range plan for Duke that Gross, Paul Clyde, and their associates had produced. Moreover, since the Endowment retained Gross as a special consultant for educational affairs, he continued to have close contact with Tom Perkins and other trustees and officers of the Endowment.

At a meeting of the committee on educational institutions in April 1961 both Gross and Deryl Hart, the veteran head of surgery at Duke who had been named acting president and then president of the institution, were present, and two memoranda from Gross constituted the principal items on the agenda. His thesis was that the best interests of Duke University required a quite substantial increase in faculty salaries across the board in order to bring Duke into a competitive position with the best institutions, to attract top scholars, and to retain able faculty members.

The committee and ultimately the full board of the Endowment agreed with the recommendation of Gross. The trustees recognized that such an improvement in faculty salaries was one of the necessary prerequisites if J. B. Duke's request in the indenture was to be honored, namely that Duke University secure for its officers, trustees, and faculty persons of such "outstanding character, ability, and vision as will insure its attaining and maintaining a place of real leadership in the educational world." Accordingly, the Endowment appropriated $1 million, to be matched by $1 million from the university, to be used for the salary hikes in 1961–62 and 1962–63.[29]

When Tom Perkins and Deryl Hart issued in June 1961 a joint statement to the public about the salary hike, they explained that the Endowment and the university were acting on "the firm conviction that, if southern higher education is to make its full contribution to the nation as a whole, the regional faculty pay differential must be eliminated, thus enabling southern colleges and universities to compete successfully with institutions elsewhere in holding and attracting the best men and women in their faculty ranks." The Endowment, according to the statement, hoped that its action would draw attention to the problem and "encourage similar steps by all individuals and organizations interested in financial support of southern institutions of higher education." Hart seized the occasion to note that the salary hike was merely the latest in a series of measures designed to give Duke a "truly national status." He pointed also to fourteen new endowed chairs at the University, the fact that ground had been broken for a new building for the School of Law, and that scholastic qualifications for admission to Duke were steadily improving.[30]

Press reaction to the joint action by the Endowment and the university was quite favorable. The *Durham Morning Herald* (June 4, 1961) predicted, correctly as it turned out, that the new Duke salary scale would "awaken southern legislatures, that of North Carolina among them, to the seriousness of the faculty pay situation." "It would also," the *Herald* added, "stimulate the private colleges to search the more industriously for sources of additional income to boost their pay scales." The *Winston-Salem Sentinel* (June 5, 1961) noted that, "Great teachers make great schools. Brick and mortar do not." Whatever greatness had been built into North Carolina colleges and universities thus far, the *Sentinel* astutely declared, had been "compounded largely of great human personalities."

When the American Association of University Professors, in its annual report on faculty compensation in the nation, announced in 1962 that only four institutions had achieved the top A rating—Harvard, Yale, Princeton, and Duke—it was a most gratifying development for both the Endowment and Duke University. The fact that the university's trustees, after lagging behind both faculty and student opinion throughout the late 1950s, finally voted in 1962 to admit students without regard to race added to the optimism and hopefulness that characterized Duke University in the early 1960s. Unfortunately, in the euphoria of the faculty members about their improved situation, they did not stop to note that the nonacademic employees of the university had received no dramatic pay increases. In fact, too many of the service personnel of the university, a high percentage of whom were African Americans, were being paid the lowest possible minimum wage. A few years later, as the nation reeled from the assassination of Martin Luther King Jr., this fact would return to haunt and torment the Duke University community.

In the fall of 1962, however, all the turmoil of the late 1960s lay hidden in the future, and the selection in late 1962 of Douglas M. Knight as Duke's fifth president seemed to promise well for the institution. An urbane, highly articulate professor of English, Knight had received his undergraduate degree and his Ph.D. from Yale in 1946 and then taught there until he became president of Lawrence College in Wisconsin in 1954. The fact that two earlier presidents of Lawrence had gone from there to become distinguished university presidents—Henry M. Wriston to Brown and Nathan Pusey to Harvard—made Duke's selection of Knight all the more auspicious.

Tom Perkins and others associated with the Endowment seemed enthusiastic about Knight as he assumed his new post at Duke in the fall of 1963. Apparently unfazed by the rebuff that the majority of the university's trustees had given to the Endowment in the Gross-Edens affair, Perkins continued to play a major role in the university through his position on the executive committee. In addition, Mary Semans, named a trustee of the Endowment in 1957, was elected as a trustee of the university in 1961, the first member of the Duke family to serve on the board since the death of her grandfather, Ben Duke, in 1929.

Douglas Knight did not know about the complicated relationship between the Endowment and the university when he first arrived on the scene. The search committee had assured him that the Gross-Edens storm had subsided. Originally, Perkins had been slated to give the principal address at the university's annual Founders' Day convocation in December 1962, and for many months various members of the Endowment's staff had been scurrying around trying to gather historical and other types of data that could be used in the speech. After Knight accepted the presidency, however, the plans were changed, and Perkins, to his relief, merely had the task of introducing Knight, who gave the principal address.

In his remarks, Perkins declared that the trustees of the Endowment regarded Duke University "as the embodiment of Mr. Duke's greatest dream and the primary beneficiary of his generosity." The Endowment, Perkins avowed, did not control the university and neither should nor could do so. Duke University did differ from other universities, he explained, in one major respect: "Instead of one group of Trustees standing guard over its independence, its growth, its integrity — shielding it from improper interference of any kind — this university has two. The two groups — Trustees of the University and Trustees of the Endowment — constitute a unique partnership in higher education, one which insures the University's academic freedom and independence, its freedom of inquiry, and freedom to teach as its sees fit."

Perkins, in making the above argument, may or may not have realized the fact, but he was making exactly the same explanation about the two sets of trustees that President Few had articulated in the late 1920s. In Few's case, as discussed earlier, the Rockefeller-backed General Education Board had questioned the long-term viability of the university when one group of trustees nominally controlled it and another group of trustees controlled most of the money then needed to operate the university. Using arguments echoed by Perkins, Few had succeeded in persuading the General Education Board that what it perceived as a liability for Duke University was in actuality an asset.

In December 1962, Perkins went on to point out that the Endowment contributed financial support to the university not only as specifically provided in the indenture but also through the special allocation of discretionary funds. That policy had resulted in making the university the recipient of approximately half (rather than 32 percent) of the Endowment's annual income. The Endowment, Perkins concluded, was "specifically charged with seeing to it that Duke University is operated in a manner calculated to achieve the leadership Mr. Duke intended." Perkins, in yielding the podium, pledged Knight "the whole-hearted support of best wishes of the Duke Endowment."[31]

In reality, of course, the relationship of the two boards had not been as magically harmonious as either Perkins or Few had suggested. Looking back some years later, Douglas Knight explained that he found the university, at least in its upper levels, under considerable stress in the early 1960s, primarily because of the tension between the Endowment trustees and their allies among certain senior administrators and faculty members on the one hand and the university's trustees and their allies on the other. "The question of final responsibility for the university's welfare," Knight noted, "was left unresolved after the resignation of Hollis Edens and Paul Gross and would remain so for another decade."[32]

On the particular matter of Paul Gross, Knight later stated that by appointing him (Gross) as a consultant on higher education, the Endowment was in effect saying, "You may take away his title but not his influence in the university." Knight believed that this arrangement helped perpetuate animosities that had been created by the great blowup of 1960. "There was always a shadow government in the wings," Knight wrote, "and I felt its presence whenever there was a crucial issue either with the faculty or with the Endowment." The result, Knight believed, was that those in charge of the university "had to live with one more level of disunity at a time when a united front was absolutely essential for the orderly and effective treatment of crises as they came along." If Gross did not agree with some policy or new development, "then it became measurably more difficult to accomplish these ends."[33]

Although Knight probably did not realize the situation at the time, at least some persons in the Endowment were aware of and sensitive about Knight's position. Paul Clyde, the secretary of the Endowment's committee on educational institutions, not only was a close friend and ally of Gross but also maintained his office in Durham. While it was not on the Duke campus, Clyde quite naturally had many close friends among both administrators and faculty members. Clyde at one point expressed his hope to Perkins that his office could move toward a position where, in addition to the functions involving the four educational institutions that it already performed, "it could give authoritative counsel to The Endowment and to the four institutions on major national trends in the picture of higher education." As a step toward that goal, Clyde suggested that a research and editorial assistant be added to the staff of his office and that it would enjoy greater status if it were called the Educational Section (and therefore be on an equal footing with the Hospital and Orphan Section).[34]

Clyde's hope for an enlarged and more visible role for the secretary of the committee on educational institutions was not to be realized. After Knight was named as president but before he actually assumed office, Perkins and his assistant in New York discussed various matters related primarily to Duke University, and the assistant summarized their conclusions in this fashion: (1) it was important to continue current efforts to build up the strength and independence of the university's board of trustees and its executive committee; (2) when vacancies occurred on the Endowment's board, new trustees should be persons experienced in and interested in educational affairs; (3) official policy-level relationships with the university should be carried on through the executive committee of the university as far as possible and minimum reliance placed on personal contacts with university administrators unless the university president was informed; (4) the Durham office of the committee on educational institutions, as it then existed, should be discontinued, and if a replacement was to be made when Clyde's contract ended, the new person should perform only such functions as "may be felt mutually valuable to the Endowment and the four educational institutions"; any future educational office should be located in Durham only after discussion with and approval by President Knight; and (5) despite the value of Paul Gross's contributions, the practice of inviting him to attend meetings of the committee on educational institutions should be discontinued as soon as possible — "If University representation at our meetings is desirable let it be Doug Knight."[35]

Just how much the above proposals reflected the actual thinking of Tom Perkins, rather than that of his assistant, is not known. The memorandum does clearly suggest, however, that the Endowment's top leadership was aware of the need to try to clear the way for Duke's new president. When Clyde's contracted term as secretary ended early in 1966 (and he became a consultant), the Durham office was turned over to the Rural Church Division of the Endowment, and the subsequent directors of educational affairs and public communications would be officed in Charlotte. None of them would, in fact, be quite as actively involved in the affairs of the educational beneficiaries — especially Johnson C. Smith, Furman, and Davidson — as Paul Clyde had been. Concerning Duke University, Clyde never played the same role as with the three other educational institutions, primarily because Tom Perkins and other Endowment trustees were so intimately and regularly involved in the affairs of Duke University.

In many ways Duke University flourished in the 1960s. The trend toward better prepared and harder working students, especially in Trinity College (which had lagged a bit behind the Woman's College in this respect), had begun in the 1950s, and it accelerated in the 1960s. An ambitious fund-raising campaign had been discussed during the last year or so of the Edens admin-istration but was then delayed by the turmoil that beset Duke in 1960. In 1965 the university launched the Fifth Decade campaign with the goal of raising $187.4 million over a ten year period, with the hope that $103 million of the total could be raised in three years — $75.5 million for physical plant, $15 million for endowment, and $12.3 million for current budget support. Once again, unforeseen events would impede and partly frustrate the ambitious campaign, but Douglas Knight took pride in the fact that between 1963 and 1969 gifts and grants to Duke (including significant sums from the Duke Endowment) totaled $195 million as compared with a total of $68 million during the previous six years. Knight also and quite understandably took great encouragement from the $8 million challenge grant to Duke that he obtained from the Ford Foundation, though it had to be matched on a four-to-one basis.

This is not the place to mention all of the important new programs and buildings at Duke in the 1960s, though the Endowment played a significant role in the realization of most of them. An addition to the main library that more than doubled its size was probably the most important and urgently needed new facility. In the area of art and music, Duke finally began to develop long-coveted but also long-delayed strength. Mary Semans played a major role in securing the new music building named for her mother, Mary Duke Biddle, and located on the East Campus. Since Mrs. Biddle's interest in helping Duke acquire such a facility in the late 1930s had been deflected by President Few (in favor of an earlier addition to the library), the belated and posthumous real-ization of her wish seemed most appropriate. The gift to Duke of a rich, unique collection of medieval art, which had been assembled by Joseph and Ernest Brummer, was conditioned on the university's providing suitable mu-seum space to display the collection. Since President Few's efforts to acquire an art museum (plus an endowment to go with it) had been thwarted back in 1941 by Tom Perkins's father, William R. Perkins, Knight and an enthusiastic group of trustees and faculty members who worked with him hit on the idea of renovating the science building on East Campus so that it could become the university's art museum. The fact that the final cost of the renovation exceeded the target, however, inspired some trustees as well as faculty members to criticize Knight for his alleged extravagance. Even earlier, that is by 1964, Clyde was complaining to Perkins about "the ineffective top organization of the University's administration."[36] He intended this as a criticism not only of Knight but also of the provost, R. Taylor Cole, a nationally distinguished

political scientist who, unlike many senior faculty members, had quite carefully avoided entanglement in the Gross-Edens affair. In early 1967 Clyde
seized on the occasion of a dispute between Knight and the faculty's representative body, the Academic Council, to supply Perkins with a memorandum, as
requested. "Unfortunately, evidence has been accumulating over the past two
years," Clyde reported, "which raises grave doubts concerning the University's
future." The Academic Council had unanimously approved a committee report charging that, as a result of administrative policies, "in many quarters
Faculty morale has been impaired seriously because of the lack of responsible
Faculty participation in matters of great Faculty concern." Clyde added his
own view that the report, sent in confidence to Perkins, was "symptomatic of a
general and very unfortunate condition and frame of mind which appears to
prevail now on the campus."[37]

Since verbal pushing and shoving matches between university presidents
and faculties are by no means rare events, the matters that Clyde commented
about to the powerful chairman of the Endowment were actually fairly routine. In the late 1960s, however, some decidedly nonroutine events were to
produce unprecedented consequences on the Duke Campus. Moreover, while
events at Duke paled in comparison to what happened on the campuses at
Berkeley, Columbia, Cornell, and numerous other institutions, Duke was not
only located in the most pervasively conservative section of the country, but it
was also the only university that the great majority of its trustees and alumni
either knew or cared about. When student activism dramatically arrived on
the Duke campus in the late 1960s, Douglas Knight would become the scape-
goat of first bewildered and then angry trustees and alumni, not to mention a
sizable faction of the senior faculty. Tom Perkins and other Endowment figures certainly played key roles in the resignation of Knight, which came in
April 1969. This resignation, however, was quite different from that of Hollis
Edens nine years earlier in the sense that it was not a case of the Endowment's
making an end run around the university's trustees. Rather, the Endowment
group, especially Perkins, joined with various leaders of the university's trustees to obtain Knight's resignation.

There is no need here to present the complicated story of the dramatic events
at Duke following the assassination of Martin Luther King Jr. in early April
1968. The denouement of the famous "Silent Vigil," in which a large group of
students and a relative handful of mostly junior faculty members camped out
for over four days and nights on the main quadrangle in front of the Duke University Chapel, came on April 10 when the chairman of the board of trustees,

Wright Tisdale (vice president and general counsel of the Ford Motor Company) announced to the assembled throng that Duke would make significant —
and costly — adjustments in its pay scales for nonacademic employees. The
existing federal minimum wage for most business and commercial organizations was $1.60 per hour; for the employees of universities and colleges it was
$1.50 per hour and was not scheduled to reach $1.60 until 1971. "We [at
Duke] will be at the $1.60 minimum wage by July 1, 1969," Tisdale declared,
"and we shall make a significant step toward this by July 1, 1968." He added
that the step would cost a lot of money and would require increased income as
well as a reexamination of the university's entire operation.[38]

Many, probably most, of the Duke faculty had to admit that the protesting
students had strong moral ground. Overjoyed by the much publicized boost to
their own salaries in the early 1960s, most of the faculty had simply not
stopped to worry about the plight of the nonacademic employees until the
Silent Vigil put the issue in the spotlight. The moral stance of the activists,
however, would have been even more impressive if they had offered to find
some way whereby they personally might have shared some of the financial
burden of the pay hike for the nonacademic employees, such as a call for a tuition increase to help defray new costs. Their assumption, however, like that of
many others, before and since, was that the university had "deep pockets" —
abundant resources — that could be easily tapped.

In actuality, Duke faced a serious budgetary deficit because of the unforeseen cost of the emergency pay hike. Moreover, large segments of the university's constituency not only refused to recognize the moral dimension of the
Silent Vigil but were also deeply alienated by such activism on the campus,
especially after there had been student calls to "shut down the university."
"My reaction to the so-called vigil," Marshall Pickens declared to two divinity
students who had written him, "is that it is a form of blackmail which should
not be used in a civilized community." Pickens, an influential trustee of both
the university and the Endowment, believed that the faculty had "a great
responsibility" for what had happened "in disrupting the normal university
activities through the student sit-in . . . and great harm has been done to
the University and its image and it will take many years to recover what has
been lost."[39]

Another trustee of the Endowment and a Duke alumnus, Kenneth C. Towe,
unburdened himself to a leading trustee of the university: "Concern for the
apparent lack of forceful and constructive leadership (which, in my humble
opinion, is a condition precedent to proper campus administration and ad-

herence to sound fiscal policies) continues uppermost among my apprehensions for the future of Duke University as a private institution of 'real leadership in the educational world.' " Towe, taking the position that Perkins and others in the Endowment would increasingly support, called for "numerical cutbacks to the bone in the faculty and reduction of enrollment for undergraduates (if not throughout)" as necessary steps to restore the university's moral and financial health.[40]

Faced with a threatened budget deficit of over $1.7 million, leaders in the administration came up with the idea of increasing income from tuition by admitting 150 or so additional undergraduates and allowing a limited number of upperclass students who preferred to live off campus to do so, thereby avoiding the need for additional dormitory beds. Tom Perkins and his Endowment allies opposed this plan, pushing instead for cutbacks in both the size of the student body and that of the faculty. While the budget crisis was ultimately resolved through other means and without a victory for either side in the debate, it does illustrate the role that the Endowment played in the internal policy-making of the university. In 1965, Duke's trustees had repealed the bylaw, sponsored and insisted upon by President Few in the early 1930's, that required that at least three trustees of the Endowment also serve as trustees of the university and sit on the powerful executive committee of the board. Having repealed the mandatory requirement, the university trustees turned right around and voluntarily reelected Tom Perkins and Amos Kearns from the Endowment to the executive committee.

Perkins, explaining his views to Kearns a few weeks after the Silent Vigil, noted that he had also conveyed them on the telephone to the chairman of the university's trustees, Wright Tisdale. First of all, Perkins declared that the university trustees needed to understand that the Endowment group believed that the proposed expansion of the student body was "very unsound fiscally" and that the Endowment had other beneficiaries to keep in mind besides Duke. Perkins argued that a large part of Duke's financial problems had came from over expansion, not only of facilities but also of faculty and student body. "We also feel," Perkins continued, "that a well-housed and uncrowded student body would be less restless and less apt to put on demonstrations." Along with certain other rather drastic ideas, Perkins advocated a reduction in the size of the faculty, possibly through attrition. He also suggested that if tuition and the charges for room and board could be increased for September 1968, that also might help reduce enrollment. (Administrators at Duke subsequently pointed out to Perkins that since students had already been admitted and reregistered for the fall semester of 1968 under published tuition rates and charges, the university could hardly break what was in effect a contract.)

Debate within the executive committee continued throughout 1968. In a meeting in early May, for example, John Day, the Endowment's treasurer, sat in for Perkins who could not be present. Following the eight-hour meeting, Day reported that the major obstacle to certain measures that the Endowment favored had proven to be the university's provost, Taylor Cole. For example, when the matter of immediately reducing the number of students and faculty came up, Cole, according to Day, said that was "impossible because the acceptances had already gone out for the next academic year, and he felt that a reduction in the faculty would be impossible because the ratio of students to faculty had been increasing over the past few years." When pressed further, Cole was said to have conceded that there might be a possibility of reducing the size of the faculty but refused to make any firm commitment about specific cuts.[41]

Perhaps a small, routine matter in and of itself, the above discussions suggest that, while Perkins and other Endowment figures had every right to be concerned about the university's financial bottom line, they were ill equipped to make judgments concerning the academic core of the university's life. Fortunately for Duke, richly experienced teacher-scholar-administrators like Taylor Cole and his successor, Marcus Hobbs, helped prevent unwise overreactions to what turned out to be a temporary crisis.

While the university's leaders still struggled with the financial repercussions of the negotiations that ended the Silent Vigil, another, more temporarily frightening episode of student activism at Duke sealed the fate of Douglas Knight. Early on the morning of February 13, 1969, a large group of about forty-five of Duke's African American students, some carrying large cans that they said were filled with gasoline, marched into Allen Building on West Campus. (The main administrative offices of the university were housed in the front portion of the large building.) Settling into the bursar's suite of offices after forcing out the staff and employees, the students presented a list of demands that was headed by the call for a separate department of Afro-American studies, the establishment of a "Black" dormitory, and other related changes in university policies. Although the fact that the metal containers carried into the building did not actually contain gasoline was later established, no one but the students themselves knew that at the time, and for a large part of the tension-filled day there was great anxiety, first about the possible danger to human lives and second about the security of vital academic records covering many years that were kept in the adjacent Central Records office. Security officers ordered all occupants in other portions of Allen to evacuate the building.

President Knight happened to be in New York at the time, but, upon being informed about the situation at Duke, he immediately flew back and arrived on campus before noon. After conferring with the provost, Taylor Cole, and others who had been attempting in vain to talk the students into ending their occupation of the building, Knight decided to call on the state government for help from specially trained police forces and to convene the faculty for a special meeting at 4:00 P.M. to announce his decision. Claiming to be outraged by Knight's decision, some of the radical faculty members rushed from the faculty meeting to alert the occupiers of Allen. Thereupon they marched out of a side door of the building, but when the crowd of people assembled in the quadrangles outside of Allen surged forward, the state police used tear gas. No lives were lost and no serious injuries suffered, but it was a turbulent, troubled ending to a deeply divisive episode.

Looking back much later, Knight declared, with considerable accuracy, that when Duke integrated earlier in the 1960s it had said to its African American students, who were by no means numerous anyhow, "Come in, be white."[42] That alleged insensitivity on the part of the predominantly white institution was neither recognized nor conceded at the time of the Allen Building affair, however, by a large portion of the faculty and student body, not to mention the trustees and alumni. The two last-named groups were angrily appalled and perhaps much less divided and less ambivalent in their reaction to the manifestation of "Black Power" at Duke than were the faculty and students. That fact spelled trouble for Douglas Knight.

Without naming Tom Perkins, Knight merely states in his later book that the Endowment group among the university's trustees figured largely in the movement that led to his resignation in April 1969. Charles B. Wade Jr., a prominent Duke alumnus and an executive of R. J. Reynolds Tobacco company, had succeeded Tisdale as chairman of the university's trustees late in 1968, and while Tisdale also pushed for Knight's resignation, Wade had formed a close personal friendship with the beleaguered president. When a number of trustees pressed for a specially called meeting where Knight's resignation could be formally demanded, Wade successfully took on the painful task of persuading Knight to resign before he could be formally asked to do so. Wade subsequently explained the resignation to Marshall Pickens in this way: "Basically, Doug Knight has been a most generous man in allowing us to work this thing out so that it does not reflect [badly] on him or the University, and to him is due most of the credit for the way I was able to handle it."[43]

To illustrate the Endowment's and Tom Perkins's influence in Duke's affairs during the troubles of the late 1960s, one need only note a letter to Charles Wade written by another prominent trustee and member of the executive committee, Fred Von Canon. "It is my opinion that we cannot ignore the wishes of the Duke Endowment," Von Canon declared, "if so doing could mean that they might divert many large special gifts now coming to Duke." The Endowment had bailed the university out of many critical situations over the years, Von Canon continued, and "I do not feel that the Trustees can afford to treat Tom's demands lightly." Wade replied that he thought Von Canon was "exactly right" about the attitude the trustees should take toward the Endowment. "Whenever we have conflicts," Wade noted, "we must find a way to resolve them."[44]

University trustees like Von Canon and Wade had ample reason to view the Endowment with what might be termed wary respect — or nervous gratitude. Richard Henney in early 1971 made a study of Duke University's finances from the 1953–54 academic year through that of 1968–69. Since a steadily increasing amount of money had come to Duke, as to other research universities, from the federal government in the form of research grants, in making his calculations Henney excluded the federal "turn-around" income, also sometimes referred to as "soft" money (which has threatened to become even more disturbingly "soft" at a much later time). Rather, he calculated Duke's expenses that were covered by endowment income, tuition, fees, gifts, and nongovernmental grants. On that basis, the university's expenses in 1953–54 came to almost $6 million, and income from the Endowment covered 29.8 percent of those expenses. By 1968–69 the university's expenses had increased almost five times the earlier figure, being almost $30 million, and income from the Endowment covered 20.6 percent of those expenses. In other words, while Duke was somewhat less dependent on the Endowment by 1968 than it had been in 1954, the money from the Endowment was still absolutely crucial to the university.[45] Despite that dependence, there came times when the university's trustees, believing that they acted in the institution's best interests, stood up to the Endowment. The most memorable example of that was, of course, in March 1960 at the climax of the Gross-Edens affair. There would be nothing like that in the troubled period between 1968 and 1971, but there were clear signs that certain trustees of the university, if pressed far enough, would challenge Tom Perkins. Henry Rauch, for example, as an influential member of the executive committee, asserted that he thought Perkins, in fighting to get his way about the budget and the university's admissions policy, had "hit below the belt" when he cited that portion of J. B. Duke's indenture that allowed the trustees of the Endowment to withhold funds from Duke University under certain conditions.[46]

In the bitter aftermath of the occupation of Allen Building and as Perkins and other trustees pushed to have Knight ousted, Wade himself worried about the relationship of the university and the Endowment. At one point he declared that, "without setting any devious rumours afoot or politicking the matter in any way," he felt he "ought to face right up to Mr. Perkins and tell him what the Endowment influence is doing to the university." Believing that it would be unfair to have a "crisis" without giving prior notice, Wade avowed that he would confer with Perkins within the next two or three weeks.[47]

Exactly what Wade said to the powerful chairman of the Endowment or when he said it is not known. Wade probably did have a careful, candid discussion with Perkins, however, for there is convincing evidence pointing in that direction. When Terry Sanford, the former Democratic governor of North Carolina, learned that the committee searching for a new president of Duke might end up recommending him, he sought a confidential interview with his longtime friend, Charles Wade. The two men met in Greensboro in early December 1969, and Sanford had two principal matters that concerned him, Duke's budgetary situation and its relationship with the Endowment.

Concerning the budget, Wade assured Sanford that the problems growing out of the unforeseen expenses incurred after the Silent Vigil in 1968 had been taken care of and that Duke's financial situation was quite sound. As for the Endowment, Wade promised Sanford (1) that Tom Perkins had pledged the fullest possible support of Sanford if he became Duke's new president; and (2) that "the Endowment would not get in his [Sanford's] way."[48] The acid test of Perkin's pledge of support for and noninterference with Terry Sanford's administration would come in less than a year, and, fortunately for Duke University, Wade proved to have been quite correct in his assurances to Sanford.

By the time Sanford was named as Duke's sixth president in December 1969, a movement to restructure Duke's board of trustees was already well underway. A group of angry partisans of Paul Gross among the Duke faculty had called for reform of the board of trustees back in 1960, but their statement had been intemperate, insulting to the majority of the trustees at that time, and therefore counterproductive. In 1969 the push for restructuring the board came partly, and significantly, from some of the trustees themselves.

In searching for the roots of the tension and turmoil that characterized so many campuses in the 1960s, a special committee of the American Council on Education had suggested that one clear problem that at least contributed to the trouble was that too many boards of trustees consisted of remote, aging people who were not in close touch with either students or faculty but who nevertheless made important decisions that directly affected the lives of everyone connected with the institution. That such ideas were percolating among at least some of Duke's trustees is shown by Charles Wade's assertion to another trustee in May 1969 that he believed Duke would have to change the structure of its board of trustees. "I am concerned about representation and tenure," Wade declared. "We complain about the latter in academia, and think nothing of the weight and meaning of a 'lifetime' appointment to the Board." Wade went so far as to suggest that Duke would not be able to find a president to succeed Knight "unless we are willing to change our structure and our attitude."[49]

With authorization from the executive committee, Wade appointed a special trustee committee to study the functions and organization of the university's governing board. When the group presented its report in December 1969, it argued that since the average age of board members was then sixty (with only three members under fifty) and two-thirds of the trustees were in business or business-related occupations, the special committee believed that the board would be strengthened if there were a greater diversity of membership, particularly with respect to age and occupation. "There is an inherent danger in any self-perpetuating body," the report declared, "that it will preserve its own stereotypes even when circumstances require changes in membership circumstance."[50]

In addition to the special committee of the trustees, the chancellor of the university, Barnes Woodhall, a distinguished neurosurgeon, had appointed a commission on university governance some months before Sanford was named as the new president. Instead of calling for the inclusion of faculty members and students on the board of trustees, as many colleges and universities were doing, this commission, which was chaired by William Van Alstyne, a professor of law at Duke, came up with the idea of having trustees nominated, not by the executive committee as was then the practice, but by a committee consisting of trustees, faculty members, and students. The fact that this report was released to the public before the board had considered it angered Tom Perkins, but the *Charlotte Observer* editorialized that Duke had been handed a proposal for correcting one of the "genuine problems exposed by campus disruptions — the make-up of university trustees." The *Observer* asserted that especially at private universities and most especially at Duke there was a glaring case for trustee reform. "Over the years these distant and self-perpetuating bodies have made themselves into boards of look-alike brothers with limited insights into the complex campus communities they are responsible for." The difference in outlook between Duke's trustees and elements of the university community were accentuated, the *Observer* argued, "by the extra measure of power held by the Duke board and exercised by its executive committee members." On occasion Duke's trustees had "literally run the place" and "created the impression of a campus dominated by a remote, unfeeling 'establishment.'" By changing the method of nominating trustees, Duke could, over time, "presumably expect a very different composite trustee — or better yet, a diverse board that suggested no composite."[51]

Although Duke's trustees, who freely gave many hours — and sometimes even days — in attempting to serve the university, were hardly the remote, unfeeling plutocrats that the *Charlotte Observer* editorial suggested, there clearly was, as Charles Wade himself had recognized, a need for some changes. Among several proposed reforms in addition to the trustee-nominating process, two other important ones were that faculty members and students should serve on the standing committees of the trustees (except the investment committee) and that continuous board membership should be limited to no more than two full, six-year terms. Trustees emeriti, however, would be welcome as nonvoting members of standing committees other than the executive committee.

Prominent among the group of trustees who were not happy about the proposed bylaw changes was Tom Perkins. When Charles S. Murphy, another Duke trustee and prominent lawyer in Washington, D.C., circulated his argument against any proposal for the board of trustees "to enter into compromising relationships with the students and faculty," Perkins promptly announced that he agreed with Murphy's position and hoped that other Endowment-related trustees of Duke such as Marshall Pickens and Amos Kearns, as well as some others Perkins named, would feel the same way. Noting that he had been on the executive committee far too long, Perkins nevertheless declared that he had "learned that it takes time (lots of it) to make the University work." For example, he figured that he had been to Durham on university business more than 180 days during the previous eleven years, including a lot of Saturdays and holidays. (An ardent golfer, Perkins particularly disliked meetings on Saturdays.) "I'll be happy to get out," he stated, "but only when I *know* we have a system that will work — and that means professional management by the President, the Chancellor, the Provost, and the Financial Vice President, and not by a bunch of amateur committeemen."[52]

Even such a generally mild-tempered person as Marshall Pickens seemed to be digging in his heels to resist any basic reforms concerning the university's trustees. "Apparently the 'in thing' is to change just to be able to say that we are part of a changing world," Pickens informed Murphy. "The University has operated successfully under its present charter for more than a hundred years [including the life of Trinity College] and to say that a system does not work because a small minority disagrees is in my opinion absolutely wrong."[53]

Since changes in the bylaws required a two-thirds majority vote of the trustees, the possibility of meaningful reforms seemed rather dim by the late spring of 1970. Murphy received reactions from eighteen trustees, and twelve trustees appeared to oppose changing the nominating procedure. Then Tom Perkins signaled an important shift. Whether Charles Wade had again communicated with Perkins is not known, but he may well have done so. At any rate, in mid-July 1970 Perkins wrote the chairman of the trustees' special committee that since Duke had a new president as well as a new chancellor (Kenneth Pye) and a new provost (John Blackburn), he favored hearing from them before making any changes in the bylaws. Perkins added that he assumed Sanford and his colleagues would have their recommendations by the time of the board's meeting in early September, and if they did not, then he thought that the meeting should be canceled.[54] Perkins had decided that he would defer to Terry Sanford's judgment about reforming the board.

At the trustees' request, Sanford did let his views be known, and he came down clearly on the side of reform. In addition to the five trustees, two faculty members, two students, and president of the alumni association on the nominating committee, the president of the university would also serve on it and obviously would have great influence in the process. Instead of saying that no person who had reached the age of sixty-five should be elected a trustee, Sanford favored seventy as the cutoff, on the grounds that retirement at age sixty-five often freed up persons who would be valuable on the board. There were other minor modifications, but the important point is that Terry Sanford threw his support and prestige behind changes in the bylaws.

When the board met in September 1970, Tom Perkins retreated altogether from his earlier position and wholeheartedly supported Sanford and the changes in the bylaws that Sanford wanted. Soon after the meeting, Wade wrote thanking Perkins and declared that if Perkins had not spoken out in support of Sanford's position and his more open, trusting attitude toward all segments of the university community, then Wade did not believe that the bylaws could have been changed. Wade added that he was even more grateful to Perkins because he (Wade) knew that Perkins did not fully agree with the proposed changes. Without the changes, however, Wade declared Duke would have been "in for a rough time," and it would have been difficult for Sanford to establish his leadership. "This action goes a long way toward establishing it," Wade concluded. "With the kind of support you gave, I am convinced he [Sanford] will make us a great President."[55]

Perkins, in acknowledging Wade's letter, stated that he was glad that the trustees had finally settled the bylaw changes in what appeared to be a workable manner. "The time has come to fish or cut bait," Perkins continued, "and I meant what I said that in Terry we have gotten great leadership and we should give him all the support he needs."[56]

True to his word, Perkins did give his own and the Endowment's wholehearted support to the Sanford administration. In fact, Perkins and Sanford enjoyed a personal friendship that extended beyond university matters.[57] The days of the Endowment's helping to bring about the resignation of Duke University's presidents, as in the cases of Hollis Edens and Douglas Knight, were over.

Tom Perkins died on June 21, 1973. Having succeeded George G. Allen as chairman of the Endowment in 1960, Perkins lacked the authority that Allen had derived from his close, personal association with J. B. Duke. Yet Perkins, like Allen, was both a strong-willed leader and something of an autocrat as far as the Endowment was concerned. Mary Semans, who served as a trustee of the Endowment under both Allen and Perkins, later recalled that meetings of the trustees in the 1950s and 1960s tended to be cut-and-dried affairs, with the powerful chairmen getting pretty much whatever they wanted and with the trustees, operating on a consensual basis, routinely going along with the recommendations of the staff. The staff officers, of course, first cleared any recommendation that was not routine with Allen and Alexander Sands and, after 1960, with Tom Perkins.[58] The trustees elected Marshall Pickens to succeed Perkins as chairman of the Endowment's trustees. This was largely a courteous gesture to honor the widely admired Pickens, however, for the understanding was that, because he would soon be seventy years old (and the trustees were then still observing age restrictions, which were later dropped), he would serve as chairman for only a short period. Accordingly, in January 1975 the trustees elected Archie K. Davis as the chairman to succeed Pickens.

Davis's leadership of the Endowment for the following six years was significant in several ways, as has been mentioned earlier. With reference to the educational institutions, and especially Duke University, Davis hammered away at the idea that, because of a possible conflict of interest, trustees of the

Endowment should not also serve as trustees of the Endowment's beneficiary institutions.[59] The trustees adopted no new bylaw or rigid rule but, again proceeding by consensus, they gradually adhered to the policy that Davis championed.

When Duke University's trustees were considering changes in their bylaws in 1969–70, one member of the trustees' special committee, whose identity is not known, prepared a statement, never publicized, on Duke's relationship to the Methodist church and to the Endowment. While the relationship to the church is not relevant here, and nothing ever came of the discussion anyhow, what the trustee had to say about the university and the Endowment is indeed germane. At the outset of the analysis, the trustee emphasized, quite correctly, that Duke University had been "greatly enriched by its intimacy" with both the Methodist church and the Endowment and that the university "would be immensely the poorer in all sorts of ways if it had not received the sustaining interest of these two partnerships through the years."

On the other hand, the statement continued, "each relationship is potentially compromising," and "to the extent to which any university, in order to be well structured and well administered, should be the full master of its own destiny, to that extent Duke fails by a small measure to possess its complete sovereignty." The Endowment played such a major role in determining the fortunes and thus the nature of the university, that many outsiders, according to the trustee, believed that Duke University had two boards of trustees, with authority and power divided between them. Then forgetting various episodes in Duke's history since the late 1920s or, what is more likely, not even knowing about them, the trustee cheerily declared that the fact "that this situation has not caused major difficulty is a tribute to the degree of harmony that has been achieved."

While the danger in fact seemed to be less than the danger in theory, the trustee nevertheless concluded that for the university's situation "to be theoretically sound (as well as pragmatically beneficial, as is now the case), an arm's-length relationship between the Boards of the Endowment and the University might be desirable." Just as a governor of a state is often an ex-officio member of the state university's board, the chairman of the Endowment's trustees might well be a member of Duke's board. But "a larger number of interlocking memberships might be thought by experts in university governance to be inadvisable." Perhaps no structural changes were called for (since Few's bylaw mandating the membership of three Endowment trustees on the university's executive committee had already been repealed), but "custom might be altered, and common understanding, especially for the benefit of the general public, might be improved."[60]

That the trustee who prepared the above analysis was gingerly walking on hitherto forbidden territory is clear enough. Tom Perkins undoubtedly read this statement, and it, along with his friend Charles Wade's persuasiveness, may have helped Perkins to soften his opposition to changes in the university's bylaws and to line up solidly behind Sanford. At any rate, the end result of the combined awareness on the part of the university's trustees and the Endowment's trustees that disentanglement — a friendly but arm's-length relationship — might be advantageous all around meant that three successive presidents of Duke University — Terry Sanford, H. Keith H. Brodie, and Nannerl O. Keohane — have simply not faced some of the difficult problems related to the Endowment that confronted Presidents Few, Edens, and Knight. Since about 1970, the way has indeed been easier and clearer for Duke University — and the ever increasing amounts of monetary support from the Endowment, especially as its income rose dramatically in the boom of the 1980s, continued to be crucial in the strengthening of the institution.

In August 1980 M. Laney Funderburk Jr. succeeded Robert Sailstad as the Endowment's director of educational affairs and public information. Continuing a vigorous program of producing and arranging for the showing of slideshows and other types of material about the Endowment's multifaceted activities that Sailstad had begun, Funderburk also served as the key intermediary between the four educational institutions and the Endowment. He prepared a five-year review of the Endowment's special grants to the educational beneficiaries in 1981, and it showed that 75 to 86 percent of the special grants to Davidson, Furman, and Johnson C. Smith had gone for purely academic purposes, such as faculty salaries, scholarships, and libraries. The much larger special grants that had gone to Duke University, however, were more broadly directed, with 36 percent of the total going for capital purposes.

Another type of activity that Sailstad had begun and that Funderburk continued was Endowment sponsorship (and cosponsorship) of seminars and symposia designed to help nonprofit agencies in the Carolinas improve their fund-raising skills and programs. Since the Endowment itself was limited by the indenture as far as its own grants were concerned, it exerted itself to assist a broad range of charitable and nonprofit organizations and agencies to operate more effectively in the increasingly complex world of fund-raising.

This was a part of the Endowment's public service that Funderburk's successor, Elizabeth Locke, refined and expanded even further. A Duke undergraduate as well as Ph.D. in English, Locke became the first woman to hold a major staff position in the Endowment when she was named as director of both the educational division and communications in 1982. Having served as director of university publications at Duke in the late 1970s and also as the corporate contributions officer for the Bethlehem Steel Company from 1979 until 1982, Locke brought valuable work experience as well as unusual ability to her position with the Endowment. She was destined to become its first woman director in 1996.

The Endowment has made so many significant grants to Duke University during the past three decades or so that singling out one or even a few becomes virtually impossible. Clearly one of the most creative and also one of the largest grants, however, and one that the Endowment itself initiated, after full consultation with university officers, was to the Benjamin N. Duke Leadership Fund at Duke University. Its purpose was to make sure that Duke, as it grew more nationally and even internationally prominent, kept at least a certain minimum number of outstanding undergraduate students from the two Carolinas in its student body.

From the late 1920s onward, Duke, quite understandably, gradually acquired a more cosmopolitan student body than Trinity College had known. In the 1930s President Few noted with satisfaction that three components of the university—the Woman's College, the Medical School, and the summer session—were increasingly attractive to students outside of the Carolinas and the South. Admission to the Woman's College and the Medical School became intensely competitive, so much so in the case of the former that informal geographic quotas were introduced to make sure that able Carolina and southern women were properly represented. Otherwise the Woman's College could easily have been filled with students solely from the mid-Atlantic states. By 1946–47, women from North Carolina made up 34 percent of the student body in the Woman's College and men from the state constituted 36 percent of the enrollment in Trinity College (the undergraduate men's college between 1930 and 1972, when the separate Woman's College was abolished). Since the trend for this in-state enrollment was steadily downward, however, many trustees and older alumni worried a great deal about the matter, especially as Duke's tuition began gradually to move upward after World War II. "There is a growing feeling that we [at Duke] are much more interested in becoming a national university than we are in serving the state," one trustee asserted in 1947. He thought that there seemed to be "a very general disposition among high school graduates in this state to feel that they are not wanted at Duke."[61]

The trustee was quite wrong in suggesting that Duke did not want North Carolina students. Wisely avoiding rigid geographical quotas that might have compromised academic standards, however, Duke with the help of Alexander Sands and others, came up with a significant and creative new type of scholarship in 1947, one that both signified the university's commitment to North Carolina and at the same time promised to enhance the academic quality of the undergraduate student body. The Angier Buchanan Duke regional scholarship program was the university's first organized, publicized effort to bring some of North Carolina's ablest students to the university.

Benjamin N. Duke had established the Angier B. Duke Memorial Fund in 1925 as a special kind of living monument to his deceased son, and he requested the trustees of the Duke Endowment to administer the fund. It became for many years the principal source of financial aid offered at the university, mostly in the form of low-interest loans to needy students. Paul Gross and others on the faculty saw the need, however, for a scholarship program specifically targeted toward recruiting outstanding students. Alexander Sands became an enthusiastic supporter of the idea, and he and certain administrators came up with a plan to divide North Carolina into six regions and offer six Angier B. Duke scholarships, four for men and two for women. The candidates were to be chosen primarily on the basis of their secondary-school records, college aptitude as shown by special tests, and demonstrated leadership abilities. As one early memorandum stated, the Angier B. Duke scholarships were intended neither "to produce grade-getting machines nor the leisurely scholar." Rather, they were to bring to Duke young men and women from North Carolina who gave "promise of becoming leaders in their chosen fields." The planners hoped that the scholarships would be awarded to students who possessed academic ability of a creative, imaginative sort as well as integrity and vitality — students who would become mature citizens with "a genuine interest in society and the ability to influence and direct the course of affairs."[62] In the indenture, J. B. Duke urged Duke University to admit as students "only those whose previous record shows a character, determination and application evincing a wholesome and real ambition for life."

The Angier B. Duke scholarship program from its beginning had a significant impact on the university. The program grew larger in subsequent years but also took a different direction. Expanded first into the states closest to North Carolina, it then became regional and, by the end of the 1950s, national in its scope. In other words, while it brought excellent students to Duke, they increasingly were not from North Carolina.

The fact of the matter was that many faculty members as well as some top-level administrators came to Duke from other parts of the country and typically knew nothing of the institution's history, traditions, or obligations. The more conscientious and institutionally minded newcomers set about remedying that situation, but those whose focus remained on their disciplines and their own careers maintained a studied ignorance about Duke's past. To this latter group, concern about where students came from seemed quite beside the point and even parochial. The only thing that mattered, in their eyes, was that the students be the most academically promising that could be brought to Duke. As for any possible moral obligation to J. B. Duke, whose initial gift and then ongoing benefactions made the university possible, their question was this: Where in the indenture was it stated that Duke should enroll a certain number of students from the Carolinas?

The answer to such a question is, of course, that J. B. Duke made no reference to the geographical origins of the university's students. He simply declared that he hoped Duke would attain and maintain "a place of real leadership in the educational world." In the paragraph of the indenture above the one containing that statement, however, J. B. Duke explained (1) that he had been engaged for many years in developing water powers in certain sections of the two Carolinas; (2) that he had observed how such development "gives impetus to industrial life and provides a safe and enduring investment for capital"; and (3) that his ambition was that the revenues from such developments should "administer to the social welfare" of the "communities which they serve." In other words, J. B. Duke declared that he was giving the controlling interest in the Duke Power Company to the Duke Endowment so that the Endowment could "administer" to the social well-being of people in the Carolinas.

There was — is — tension, not necessarily conflict, between J. B. Duke's dual goals of Duke University's "leadership in the educational world" and its service to the people of the Carolinas. This has been a matter of ongoing debate among those interested in Duke since the late 1920s, and, as in the Gross-Edens affair of 1960, it has been all too easy for various individuals and groups to distort the alleged regional-versus-national dichotomy. That it actually is not a matter of either-or was best explained, as has been mentioned earlier, by an eloquent professor of history at Duke, William B. Hamilton. He proposed a resolution, enthusiastically endorsed by the faculty in 1960, that "the aim of creating a university which will rank with the best is in no way in conflict with the special opportunities and obligations we acknowledge to the area in which we live." Duke, the resolution concluded, "could perform no better service to this region than to erect a university second to none in those fields in which its resources permit it to operate."[63]

As persuasive and excellent as Hamilton's statement was, however, it remained on a rather elevated, theoretical plane and did not speak to such practical matters as admissions policy and whether Duke should be concerned about its ever dwindling number of students from the Carolinas. Certain university administrators remained more aware of and sensitive to the views of the trustees of both the university and the Endowment than were some faculty members, and these administrators almost continuously grappled with the problem. In 1980, for example, Chancellor Pye reported to the executive committee on a number of steps that Duke was taking in an attempt to reverse the decline in the enrollment of students from the Carolinas. Despite these efforts, and they were not new or isolated, some people in North Carolina took a dim view of developments at Duke. When the Duke trustees announced a 14 percent tuition increase in 1980, a small-town newspaper editor in eastern North Carolina angrily declared that J. B. Duke's dream of an educational institution for North Carolina "boys and girls" had been "completely forgotten," and the "dream has turned into a nightmare." The "fellows in charge there [at Duke] care nothing about the North Carolina story." Since there would be "enough rich Yankees from New York to fill up the institution," why worry about North Carolina? The editor charged that Davidson and Wake Forest were traveling the same road, but Duke was "a little more blatant about it all and a little quicker to act."[64]

Such bitter attacks on Duke were old hat. Trinity College, financially backed by rich Republican industrialists, had come in for more than its share of brickbats from irate Tar Heel Democrats back around 1900. While politics no longer inspired such attacks on Duke, the institution clearly had public relations problems with some of the local folk. It was not really those problems, however, that lay behind the creation of the Benjamin N. Duke Leadership Fund but rather the larger matter of the university's purposes and how they related to its history — and the Endowment's history and purposes in so far as Duke University was concerned.

In the fall of 1984 Elizabeth Locke, director of the Endowment's education and communications division, reported to the committee on educational affairs that she and Mary Semans had met with certain officers of Duke University to discuss the Endowment's concern about the low rate of application and matriculation of students from the Carolinas. The university officials shared the concern, Locke reported, and had (1) commissioned an independent agency to survey selected Carolina high-school students and their parents to determine why and how students selected their colleges; (2) begun a reorganization of the Duke admissions office; and (3) instituted a "Duke Day" program at high schools throughout North Carolina.

Subsequently, Elizabeth Locke and certain trustees of the Endowment, who were members of the educational affairs committee, had a routine conference at Duke about how the university wished to use the forthcoming special grants from the Endowment. Locke recalls that after the main business had been dealt with, one of the Endowment trustees asked the new president, Keith Brodie, to speak frankly and say what he saw as worrisome in Duke's situation. After mentioning that the low number of Carolina students continued to disturb him and other Duke leaders, Brodie had to leave the room. When he did, William McGuire, one of the Endowment trustees present and former president of the Duke Power Company, spoke out. A normally quiet person, McGuire, according to Locke, pounded on the table and declared, "By God, we are going to do something about that, and I don't care if it takes $10 million."[65]

The "something" became the Benjamin N. Duke Leadership fund — and it would end up costing even more than $10 million. Preceded by elaborate studies done both by the university and the Endowment, the Benjamin N. Duke program, in one sense, harked back to the original Angier B. Duke scholarship, though the new plan was both more ambitious and more expensive. The naming of the new program for J. B. Duke's older brother was an interesting, if somewhat belated, recognition of two facts: (1) for many years Benjamin N. Duke was the principal link between Trinity College and the Duke family; and (2) the Endowment, at least in its nonhospital portions, was the systematization (on a princely, perpetual basis) of a pattern of family giving that went back to the 1890s, and Ben Duke had served as the family's chief agent in implementing that pattern of giving.

The Benjamin N. Duke program was jointly planned by the university and the Endowment and launched in 1985. It had as its goal to increase the number of undergraduates from the two Carolinas at least to about 15 percent of the student body. To achieve that, the Endowment made a pledge of $10 million, payable over a ten-year period, and the university agreed to raise $3 million to create a permanent endowment fund. It would establish ten merit scholarships per year for students from the Carolinas with high leadership potential, and would address the financial needs of all undergraduates from the Carolinas who were admitted to and then came to Duke by replacing the loan portion of the standard financial aid package with a grant. In other words, students at Duke from the Carolinas might have to earn part of their tuition and costs through part-time employment or work-study programs, but, thanks to the Benjamin N. Duke program they could graduate debt free. In addition, the university undertook to create public awareness of the program by intensifying recruitment efforts, creating brochures, and working with Duke alumni.

By 1989, as the first Benjamin N. Duke students graduated, the number of undergraduates from the Carolinas had risen to 16.8 percent. The approximately forty Benjamin N. Duke merit scholars on campus were enough to form a significant group for planned programs and community service. Some 293 students from the Carolinas received grants instead of loans in their aid packages, and North Carolina headed the list of states from whence Duke students came. Despite the Endowment's pledge and the university's contribution, which had already exceeded its $3 million pledge by almost $2 million, the Benjamin N. Duke program proved to be underfunded because of necessary increases in Duke's tuition; the Endowment and the university together, however, scrambled to provide the funds needed. It was a splendid example of cooperation between the university and the Endowment to "achieve the results intended hereby," as J. B. Duke stated in the indenture concerning Duke University.

To those few faculty members and administrators who might protest that Duke's prestige in the academic world would be greater if the admissible but not necessarily top-scoring Carolina students were replaced by stellar academic performers from other sections of the country, one answer might be this: just as humans do not live by bread alone, universities have some purposes in addition to, and perhaps loftier than, the single-minded pursuit of prestige.

THE ENDOWMENT

AND HOSPITALS,

CHILD CARE,

AND THE RURAL

METHODIST

CHURCH,

1960–1994

WHILE CHANGES IN THE Endowment's relationship with its educational beneficiaries were the most striking ones in the years after 1960, modifications in policies concerning hospitals and health care, orphanages and child care, and the rural Methodist church in North Carolina were also significant. Responding to new needs and new circumstances, both the staff and the trustees took advantage of certain latitudinarian phrases in the indenture — particularly one concerning the power of the trustees to use any withheld, accumulated funds "for the benefit of any such like charitable, religious or educational purpose" — to break loose gradually from past, more restrictive policies and to expand the scope and therefore the usefulness of the Endowment's grants. By thus adapting to the times, the Endowment managed to be just as socially useful, although in partly different ways, in 1994 as it had been when it was launched in 1924.

Hospitals and Health Care

The greatest influence on hospitals in the Carolinas, as in the rest of the nation, came in the 1960s from the federal government. The Medicare program providing substantial hospital and medical benefits to all Americans sixty-five and over became effective in 1966; the joint federal-state Medicaid program for the poor was a smaller but also significant extension of the federal government's role in the health-care area. Both programs together had an enormous, expansionary impact on the nation's hospitals, and in the Carolinas, the Endowment helped in coping with many of the consequences. Just as the Hill-Burton program to help build community hospitals had led to an increase in the calls on the Endowment for assistance, so too did the ambitious new medical programs of the 1960s.

Even before they arrived on the scene, however, the Endowment began to try to help in addressing a medical problem that would grow even more crucial in later decades: the shortage of general practitioners or, as they were increasingly termed, family doctors. Alerted by numerous assisted community hospitals about their difficulty in securing interns, Marshall Pickens turned to Dean Wilburt C. Davison at Duke. Pickens knew, as did anyone at all knowledgeable about the medical profession, that more and more doctors had long been turning away from family practice in favor of the medical specialties. Not only did the specialists generally make more money and have better control over their hours of work, but they also, especially in university-related hospitals, had opportunities for research. What neither Pickens nor anyone else at the time knew was what, if anything, might be done to counter the trend, which had been accelerating for many years. That was where Pickens hoped that the popular and prestigious dean, who had played such a large role in making the Duke Medical Center one of the nation's best, might have some ideas.

Davison did, indeed, have a number of ideas, and he set about trying them out with his characteristic energy and ebullience. As Davison prepared to retire from his thirty-three-year deanship at Duke, he proved to be quite receptive to Pickens's suggestion that he (Davison) become a consultant on medical education to the Hospital Section. Tell Dr. Rankin, Davison wrote Pickens, that "there is nothing I would rather do than be his Junior Medical Consultant. . . . He has been more than a father to me and to be his junior would be the greatest compliment I have ever received."[1] Not only, then, did Davison become a part-time, active consultant, but he also was elected early in 1961 as a trustee of the Endowment.

The shortage of family doctors had one of its sources in the type of internships chosen by the graduates of medical schools. For example, Duke, according to Davison, had offered a rotating internship since the medical center opened in 1930; the new graduate was supposed to spend a year in medicine and then six months each in obstetrics and pediatrics. Davison explained that while four persons usually started in the rotating internship each year, out of over a hundred who had begun in the program he knew of only four who had completed it. If they started in obstetrics, they usually stayed there, or the same thing in pediatrics, due to the persuasiveness of the residents or full-time teachers in those fields.

As for obtaining interns for hospitals not connected with medical schools, Davison saw the greatest problem as one of "persuading research-minded faculties [in the medical schools] that an intern would profit greatly from a year in a community-type hospital." The intern would see types of patients not usually encountered in what Davison termed the "ivory towers" and, he added, would render an invaluable service to the hospital itself. Davison toyed with the idea of a state law or a requirement of the state board of medical examiners that would require at least one year of a rotating internship in a hospital not connected with a medical school before the granting of a medical license. The dean of Wake Forest's medical school informed Davison, however, that he believed that "to require that a graduate of a medical school serve a rotating internship in a 'non-medical school hospital' would be almost in the same category as the segregated lunch counter situation." In a free country, the dean argued, he did not see how one could require interns to take their training in a particular class of hospital if other types were available to them and if they wished to choose the other types. The dean did concede, on the other hand, that the idea of requiring a rotating internship without specifying what type of hospital it had to be in, as in Pennsylvania and Michigan, might be a different matter.[2]

Fully aware that he was swimming against the tide as far as most members of medical-school faculties were concerned, Davison believed, no doubt correctly, that the opportunity to engage in research was a major inducement to interns to remain in university hospitals. The medical faculty at Duke and other such centers, he noted, "can have an almost unlimited amount of money from the National Institutes of Health and the foundations if they will submit a plausible research or training program." Such projects needed personnel, so the number of residents increased dramatically at the federal government's expense. Duke's house staff, he claimed, had risen from 90 to 331 in a three-year period, and many titles had been changed from residents to fellows, with the latter receiving good salaries, with $4,200 of the total being tax free.

With quite a few medical students enrolled on part or full-time fellowships, Duke even had a course entitled "How to Do Research" for which the medical school gave credit toward the M.D. degree and that could also be used toward the Ph.D. degree. Davison conceded that it was an interesting course with attractive fellowships, so that all who were eligible tended to take it. "I know from personal experience," he added, that once one was "infected by the 'research virus,' it is very difficult to recover sufficiently to practice medicine." He cited the case of one medical professor who was trying to bring in retired medical faculty from other schools to teach Duke students so that his own "young men can proceed uninterruptedly with their research programs and careers."[3]

One result of what was happening in the medical schools, aside from the burgeoning research empires, could be seen in Durham itself according to Davison. When he first arrived there in 1927, he stated that he found 60 physicians, of whom 6 were specialists and 54 general practitioners. By 1960, however, of the 75 medical doctors in Durham (exclusive of the Duke staff), only 6 were listed as family doctors. Another manifestation of the problem showed up in the difficulty that most nonuniversity hospitals had in recruiting interns. In 1961, for example, Duke sought 52 interns and got 51. On the other hand, Watts Hospital in Durham sought 22 and got 4; Charlotte Memorial Hospital wanted 10 but got only 2; and several hospitals that were approved for internships got none. Although Davison thought it wrong for the three university hospitals then in North Carolina — Duke, Wake Forest, and the University of North Carolina at Chapel Hill — to absorb more interns than the rest of the hospitals in the state needed, he made no headway in attempting to persuade them to reduce their number of interns by appointing more assistant residents and residents after they had served rotating internships in community hospitals.

Despite all the daunting problems, Davison persisted in his new task of trying to increase the number of family doctors by, among other strategies, persuading more medical graduates to serve rotating internships in community hospitals. In September 1960 he arranged for a meeting in the Endowment's offices in Charlotte of the three medical school deans, the president of the state medical society, the secretary of the state board of medical registration, Pickens, Watson Rankin, himself, and several others. Although the group explored the many facets of the complicated problem, Davison believed that medical deans, agreeing with the great majority of their faculties, paid mere "lip service" to the idea of rotating internships, especially in community hospitals. Accordingly, Davison, with the support of the Endowment, went directly to the medical students themselves.

Starting in the fall of 1960 and repeating the event in subsequent years, Duke medical students (at Davison's request) invited senior medical students at the state's three medical schools to attend a meeting and free barbecue dinner at Turnage's, a down-home type restaurant on the outskirts of Durham that was a favorite spot of Davison's. A group of interns then serving in community hospitals was also invited, and the idea was to have them speak frankly about their experiences and have the students question them freely. With over a hundred medical students and thirteen interns present, the Duke students in charge of the affair reported that the meeting had been "extremely valuable," maybe not so much for any immediate results but as a first step for the prospective intern and the community hospitals to "grow closer in their understanding of what each offers and desires" — and "little such understanding presently exists." There were thirteen community hospitals in the Carolinas approved by the American Medical Association for rotating internships, and an intern representative from eight of them spoke briefly to open the meeting. According to the minutes, all eight "appeared enthusiastic in their support for their particular hospital and program." Almost all "commended the Staff for the high ethical level of their practice and their diligent efforts to insure the intern a program of merit." None felt that the year was "merely a 'clerkship,' and all felt they enjoyed supervised responsibility consistent with their expectations."

Then after one of Turnage's famous barbecue dinners, complete with live piano music (and one wonders what beverage), there was an hour-long moderated discussion that was "brisk, quite frank, and of immense value in helping all to understand the various fac[e]ts of the many problems which surround the type of internship one chooses, the nature of the hospital selected for training, and the criteria the student employs in their selectivity."[4]

Reporting on the meeting to Pickens, Davison declared that the students "represent my best hope, and they are very enthusiastic about the possibilities, provided the hospital administrators, staff and trustees recognize their responsibilities like those at the Cone Hospital [in Greensboro, North Carolina] and Spartanburg, Greenville, and Columbia [all in South Carolina]."[5] Part of Davison's new job was to alert the community hospitals about their need to make their rotating internships as educationally meaningful as well as generally attractive as possible. He pointed to the hospital in Spartanburg, South Carolina, which had the distinction of being the only community hospital in the Carolinas in 1960 to fill its quota of interns. Not only did the trustees and staff of the Spartanburg hospital work carefully to provide a good training program for interns, Davison noted, but they recruited interns "as keenly and as successfully as a football coach" went after top players. The Spartanburg hospital hosted cocktail parties in Charleston and Augusta for the senior medical students at several schools and arranged expense-paid visits by the students to inspect the hospital.[6]

Davison arranged for medical leaders in general practice in the Carolinas to help outline a proper training program in family medicine that the community hospital could offer to interns. Then Davison got the Endowment to appropriate funds so that five community hospitals in North Carolina could offer, as an experimental pilot project, a $600 summer fellowship to one rising senior from each of the state's three medical schools so that the student could spend two months in a family-practice internship, or, as it was then termed, an externship. This pilot program proved to be so successful that it was expanded and continued for a number of years. When the Duke Medical Center established a Department of Community Health Sciences in 1966, its head, Dr. Harvey Estes, became the faculty advisor for the Endowment's clinical scholarship program.

In a twelve-year review of the program in 1972, Estes sent a questionnaire to the former medical students who had participated in it. Of 246 respondents, he reported that 210 believed that the summer externship had had a clear impact on their professional careers, with all but a handful viewing the impact as positive. Estes noted that 80 of the respondents had volunteered the comment that their choice of private rather than academic practice had been materially influenced by the externship experience. Only 9 respondents (3.7 percent) indicated that they had been negatively influenced about private practice. Estes thought that the most pervasive theme that emerged from the responses was "the scope of Dr. Davison's impact on participants and, in a larger sense, his stature as a man and physician." A great many of the past participants in the program had made specific references to the inspiration and guidance that they had received from Davison. To a lesser but still significant degree, other doctors who had served as preceptors had had a similar impact. While the matter was not quantifiable, Estes believed that a significant aspect of the externship program was the function of the preceptors as role models, both as physicians and persons.

In view of the growing awareness of the pressing problems in the delivery of health care and the concomitant change in the physician's public image, Estes suggested that experiences such as those offered in the summer externship program had become all the more important as an early component of medical education. Moreover, social awareness was causing a growing number of medical students to seek out community-based experiences.[7]

Estes's point about preceptors, other than Davison himself, who became inspirational role models for medical students is nicely illustrated by a letter that a student wrote concerning his experience at a hospital in Lincolnton, North Carolina. The time spent with Dr. John P. Gamble Jr., the student reported, was "probably the most valuable and meaningful experience of my entire medical training to date." He described Gamble as being at ease with the poorest farmers as well as high government officials and "an absolute genius" in explaining difficult medical terms in understandable phrases. The student stated that he had been surprised, even overwhelmed, by the teaching aspect, for in a country hospital he had expected to see nothing more than sore throats and diabetes; on the contrary, he had been "shocked to see the very wide range of interesting pathology and that it all just is not referred on to the big city hospitals or to the medical centers." Gamble had been one of the best one-on-one teachers he had ever encountered, and as a result of the experience, the student declared that his career plans had taken a 180-degree turn toward just such a medical practice.[8]

Such a letter obviously vindicated Davison's belief that some medical students, even if not enough of them, could be inspired to go into both family practice and community hospitals. Davison was undoubtedly correct in his belief that the vast medical centers, such as Duke's, had gone too far, under the lure of lavish federal and foundation support for research, in turning away from family practice and service to the community hospitals. On the other hand, Davison himself probably went too far in denigrating research as one important function and purpose of a university-related medical center. Just as Duke strove constantly in its work in the arts and sciences to maintain a balance between teaching and research on the part of the faculty, so too, one suspects, did the medical centers need greater balance between admittedly important research, on the one hand, and various additional, important medical purposes that needed to be served, on the other hand. Davison, for all of his undoubted success in helping to launch the Duke Medical Center, may not have fully understood, especially as he grew older, the complex mission of a research university. An undergraduate alumnus of Princeton, Davison declared late in his life (and he died in 1972) that, "Princeton was a better place before the graduate school invaded the college." He admitted that he might be prejudiced in saying that, but apparently he did not realize or fully appreciate that without its graduate school, Princeton, which has no professional schools such as medicine and law, would not even be a university, much less one of the leading research universities in the nation.[9]

Watson Rankin, still mentally vigorous at age eighty, came at the problem of getting interns and residents into the larger community hospitals so that they might thus be channeled into general practice from a different perspective, albeit one that Davison fully endorsed. The key to the problem, Rankin argued, lay in outpatient clinics and services. To establish that essential service in the larger community hospitals, they had to have interns and residents, for without them outpatient services simply could not be developed. Outpatient clinics, according to Rankin, provided arguments addressed to the medical profession but also even more important and effective arguments addressed to the public: (1) they provided an essential element in hospital service, giving the hospital full maturity; (2) they economized in hospital expenses, both in construction and maintenance; (3) they provided a valuable auxiliary facility to the welfare services of the country, which had grown to be one of its largest and most expensive services; and (4) they helped take care of one of the larger problems of the local health department, namely screening and immunization.

Rankin emphasized that the force of the argument about the role of interns and residents in the outpatient clinics would appeal more to the public than to the medical profession. Accordingly, he suggested that Davison should, after consulting first with the hospital chiefs of staff, consider another conference with a larger group that included the chairmen of hospital boards, welfare officials, and public health officers.[10]

Davison, responding enthusiastically to Rankin's idea, did arrange such an expanded conference in the fall of 1961. Davison noted that he and the chief pediatric nurse at Duke had observed in the early 1950s that the outpatient service and teaching in the Duke hospital were more important than what was done in the wards; in fact, Davison and the nurse had published an article about the matter. Moreover, the powerful head of Duke's large and important Department of Medicine had been converted to the importance of the outpatient clinic. The greatest difficulty Davison had noted about outpatient clinics in community hospitals was that many staff members failed to give them adequate supervision and some staff members felt that the outpatient clinics competed with private practice. As a result, many interns and residents regarded outpatient duty as a thankless chore rather than as a prime opportunity for learning about general practice. Since, however, Davison personally knew two highly influential chairmen of hospital boards who were more enthusiastic about outpatient clinics than were their staffs, he particularly welcomed Rankin's notion about appealing to the public on the subject rather than just to the profession.

As a result of all this brainstorming and negotiating, one of the areas where the Endowment appropriated large sums of money in the years after 1960 was helping those larger community hospitals in the Carolinas that wished either to add or expand outpatient clinics to do so. Nobody knew at the time, of course, that in pursuing such a program both the hospitals involved and the Endowment were considerably ahead of the curve as far as the medical trends of the 1990s would be concerned.

In the late 1970s the Endowment joined forces with two other North Carolina foundations, the Kate B. Reynolds Health Care Trust and the Z. Smith Reynolds Foundation, in an ambitious, multiyear program to provide better access to health-care services for North Carolinians. After studying the problems that blocked access to health care, especially in rural and underdeveloped areas, the consortium launched a comprehensive effort to assist community hospitals in having physicians to provide full-time coverage of emergency rooms. As of early 1977, thirty-one hospitals had received Endowment grants totaling $1.45 million for that purpose, and the hospitals had recruited thirty-three physicians, twenty-one of them from outside the state.

The consortium also gave $400,600 to help establish three hospital-sponsored satellite clinics, with emergency transportation available. Another component of the program was support for four hospital-based centers for primary-care group practice, these centers being particularly designed to aid in recruiting and training physicians to serve in areas that had acute shortages of doctors.

The initial study for the Access to Health Care program had revealed that there was great need for better dental care by large segments of North Carolina's population. The national ratio of dentists to patients was one to 2,000, but in North Carolina the ratio was one to 3,000; and eight North Carolina counties were found to have no practicing dentists. Accordingly, the consortium made grants to support three demonstration projects — one in Elizabeth City in the eastern part of the state and others in Boone and Murphy, both in the western portion. Mobile trailers equipped with dental chairs and laboratories visited elementary schools, where screening and treatment procedures were given to children. The project was closely coordinated with local health departments, school and county government officials, and practicing dentists. Another project in the area of dental care was support for a comprehensive dental-care program in the Duplin General Hospital in Kenansville, which was believed to be the first example in North Carolina of a community hospital's sponsoring a comprehensive program in dental health.

Another group targeted for help from the consortium was senior citizens with special problems of access to health care. The aim in this area was to make it easier for elderly persons to take advantage of existing health resources. Finally, the three foundations supported the Neighborhood Medical Clinic in Charlotte, the training program for family-practice doctors at Wake Forest's Bowman Gray School of Medicine, and a new residency program in emergency medicine at Charlotte Memorial Hospital.

While the Endowment had a long history of friendly cooperation with certain other foundations, particularly the Kellogg Foundation in Michigan, the Endowment's participation in the consortium supporting the Access to Health Care program was the first time that it had, on a formal basis, jointly funded a health-care program with other foundations. The Endowment's staff, including, among others, Marshall Pickens and Jim Felts, had long worked closely with the two Reynolds foundations, both of which had much smaller staffs. The Access to Health Care program had grown out of discussions that the Endowment's staff had with the staffs of the two Reynolds foundations and then subsequently with state officials and representatives from the hospitals and medical schools.

As the case of the Access to Health Care program illustrates, the staff members of the Hospital Section often played a creative part in shaping important programs that the Endowment supported. While there was remarkable continuity and stability in the key staff positions, able new people entered the scene all along. In 1961, Ashley H. Gale Jr. became a field representative in the section. A native New Yorker, Gale served as an administrator in a hospital in Greenwood, South Carolina, for six years before taking the position with the Endowment. In 1980 he became director of the section. Other newcomers to the section in 1969 were Jere W. Witherspoon and Charles L. Hite; when Billy McCall retired as executive director of the Endowment in 1992, Witherspoon succeeded him in that post. Likewise, when Gale retired as director of the Hospital Section in 1991, Eugene Cochrane succeeded him. Since Watson Rankin had died in 1970, the "late comers" to the Hospital Section were denied the direct tutelage and inspiration that had so much influenced Graham Davis, Marshall Pickens, George Harris, Jim Felts, and one or two others. Yet Rankin cast a long shadow, and a vast number of his key ideas lived on in the work of the Hospital Section.

Helping Carolina communities to build new hospitals or transform proprietary hospitals into publicly supported ones was, after around 1960, not the major activity that it had been during Rankin's long directorship of the section. Nevertheless, hospitals continued to have urgent capital needs that the Endowment helped them to meet. Outpatient clinics and emergency rooms have already been mentioned; in the area of expensive new equipment that quickly became regarded as indispensable, one might only mention, for example, the computerized axial tomography (CAT) scanners that appeared on the scene in the 1970s. In a memorandum to the trustee committee on hospitals in 1976, Ashley Gale explained that the new technology had had a rapid, dramatic impact in the early diagnosis of diseases in areas of the body that theretofore had been virtually impossible to detect in time to offer a fair hope of recovery for the patient. There was every reason to believe, Gale continued, that a significant number of hospitals in the Carolinas would request the Endowment's assistance in purchasing the equipment. To prevent unnecessary duplication of such equipment, the various Health System agencies scattered across the state had first to approve the purchase, and the agency for the Charlotte area already had requests for the purchase of four full-body scanners. (Charlotte Memorial Hospital already had a head scanner.) The costs ranged from $300,000 to $800,000, but Gale noted that he and his colleagues believed that the equipment was used efficiently and paid for itself without too much difficulty. The staff wished to participate in the provision of this equipment to a minimal extent in the range of appropriations from $25,000 to $50,000 and to make commitments well in advance so that the hospitals would have assurance of the Endowment's assistance and know its extent. The committee and then the full board approved such procedure.[11]

The CAT scanner was, of course, only one of dozens of important new technologies that appeared in recent decades, but there is no need even to attempt to list them. The point is that the Endowment continued to help hospitals in the areas of both construction and equipment, but the trend was toward greater programmatic assistance.

At an Endowment-sponsored Hospital Conference in 1976, which grew out of the Endowment's comprehensive self-study, Billy McCall pointed out that already, and from an early date, the Endowment had done much more than assist hospitals with indigent care and capital needs. It had helped to start Blue Cross Associations in both Carolinas and to establish vigorous Hospital Associations with full-time staffs. It had assisted in establishing graduate medical education programs for interns and residents in community hospitals as well as educational and training programs for hospital managers. It had created programs to expose young medical students to the realities and rewards of family and community medical practice and encouraged hospitals to share services in many areas such as data processing, industrial and biomedical engineering, purchasing, and contract management. The Endowment joined with other foundations to improve access to health care, and it was encouraging the development of hospital systems and multiple-hospital arrangements to improve efficiency.

McCall emphasized two principles that continued to guide the Endowment in its hospital work: (1) a reasonable degree of concentration that directed "enough resources to any given problem or opportunity to have a positive impact, to make a difference, rather than scatter bread on so many waters at once as to dissipate resources and fail to achieve any positive results"; and (2) the Endowment's interest was always secondary to the hospital's or to that of the community that supported the hospital. The Endowment seldom funded a program in its entirety, McCall noted, and "the wisdom of this approach has been demonstrated over and over again." The Endowment and its Hospital Section saw themselves, McCall explained, as partners with the hospitals, and while the trust indenture clearly imposed certain limitations, it was sufficiently flexible to permit the Hospital Section to respond to most demonstrated and perceived needs. He invited the conferees to help the Endowment identify new directions and to speak out candidly if certain existing activities had outlived their usefulness.[12]

McCall was saying, in effect, that the Endowment was more ready than ever to respond to changing needs in the health-care area. In 1978 the trustees approved the hospital committee's recommendation that $2 million of the estimated income available for hospital purposes (over $13 million) be earmarked for "special programs" not necessarily directly related to indigent care or the building and equipment of hospitals. By 1993, following a special retreat where the staff of the section and the trustees on the hospital committee had carefully considered the matter, the Endowment took an explicitly proactive stand and requested the hospitals to consider making proposals in three areas—access-to-care programs, programs for children, and hospital networking and community affiliation programs. In response to this initiative, the Endowment funded twenty-four new programs, and the ratio of programmatic spending to the more traditional appropriations for indigent care and capital needs was about fifty-fifty in 1993.

The examples that could be cited to illustrate this steadily growing trend toward support for programs are myriad, but a scattered sampling at least suggests where the Hospital Section was headed. In 1974 the trustees had pledged $100,000 over a four-year period to help the Spartanburg General Hospital establish a training program for hospital chaplains. (The hospital itself provided $120,000.) Each of four intern chaplains put in a seventy-two-hour week so that a chaplain could be on call in the hospital twenty-four hours a day. The chaplains answered over 1,000 calls after normal working hours during the first year of the program, not casual visitations but calls in response to specific requests from patients, families, and staff. Sunday worship services, bedside weddings, communion services — all were part of the chaplains' work.

While helping to make chaplains available in hospitals addressed a simple, basic human need, the Endowment's ten-year pledge of $2.5 million in 1981 to help the Duke University Medical Center establish a Center for Health Policy Research and Education pointed toward a quite different type of concern. The basic idea behind the center was to frame problems in health policy so that quantitative tools and methods could be applied. For example, the Duke center worked with the Endowment, the North Carolina Hospital Association, and four other foundations over a period of several years to analyze a variety of approaches for taking care of the medical needs of the uninsured poor (shades of Graham Davis and the 1930s). One of the center's staff members developed a computer model that provided estimates of the cost and the impact of various policy options. Since the study dealt with North Carolina, the state legislature responded by creating an Indigent Health Care Study Commission to recommend steps for legislative action. The model was then extended to South Carolina. The Duke center also did much work for the World Health Organization and the National Cancer Institute.

Much easier for a lay person to understand was the first in a series of annual health-care conferences that began in 1984. Jointly sponsored by the Endowment and the two hospital associations of the Carolinas, the first conference dealt with the then emerging issue of medical-ethical decisions, and it lead to some forty community programs held over the following two or three years. The next year the conference focused on the mounting problems of small rural hospitals. Then in 1986 the conference turned to a long-standing problem in the Carolinas, infant mortality, and the intertwined matters of maternal and child health.

Just as the health-care conferences were a far cry from the Endowment's bricks-and-mortar spending during its early years, so too was the joint project with the two state hospital associations to send thirty hospital leaders from the Carolinas to Washington, D.C., for a two-and-a-half-day seminar on how to deal effectively with government agencies and the public policy process. In line with the partnership tradition, the Endowment paid the group's tuition at the highly specialized center that presented the seminar, and the hospital associations covered the costs of travel and lodging. The response to the first group's experience in 1993 was so favorable that a second group went for the training in 1994.

An appropriation that nicely illustrated the Endowment's growing interest in programs that linked hospitals with other agencies and groups in the community was one that the Endowment, again acting in conjunction with the Kate B. Reynolds Charitable Trust, made to the Pitt County Memorial Hospital in Greenville, North Carolina. A regional referral center for AIDS patients in twenty-nine counties in the eastern part of the state, Pitt Memorial joined with a diverse group of community leaders to form an AIDS Interagency Council, the purpose of which was to improve the care and quality of life of AIDS patients while at the same time reducing the social and economic impact on the region. Representatives from the Burroughs-Wellcome pharmaceutical company; the Pitt County department of social services, mental health, and public health; the East Carolina University medical and nursing schools; Pitt Memorial Hospital; and physicians in private practice formed the core of the Interagency Council. It developed a plan for an AIDS case-management system, which had as its main goals to try to meet AIDS patients' needs more effectively while also lowering costs and preventing long hospital stays. Sticking with the project until positive, encouraging results were obtained, the Endowment appropriated $475,000 for it from 1992 through 1994.

Appropriating almost $18.7 million for health-care purposes in the Carolinas during 1994, the Endowment gave 15 percent of that sum (or nearly $3 million) toward charity care; 27 percent (or a bit over $5 million) for capital needs; 15 percent (or almost $3 million) for access-to-care projects and programs; 11 percent (or over $2 million) for children's programs; 12 percent (or over $2 million) for hospital-community affiliations or networking; and 20 percent (or over $3.6 million) for all other programs.

"In attempting to see clearly the new and multiple roles of hospitals," the annual report for 1994 declared (p. 19), "in trying to bridge the gap between 'what used to be' and 'what is to come,' the Endowment aims to be just a little ahead of the curve." Neither did it wish to get "too far ahead in visionary anticipation," nor did it wish to lag behind "in supporting outworn systems." A difficult position to maintain, it was also one that required constant education and study, field work, meetings, and conferences with a host of interested groups. But that, of course, is exactly what the staff and trustees of the Endowment had been doing since James B. Duke and Watson Rankin launched the endeavor in 1924. Altogether between then and the end of 1994, the Endowment appropriated almost $411 million for hospitals and health care in the Carolinas. The resulting impact on the lives of Carolinians — of all races and classes, living and dead, in the last three-quarters of the twentieth century — can hardly be imagined and can never be tabulated.

Orphans and Child Care

One telling bit of evidence about the direction in which the Endowment's program of assistance in the child-care area moved came in 1965: the name of the Hospital and Orphan Section was officially changed to Hospital and Child Care Section. (In 1989, the Child Care Division became fully separate.) This was more than a mere change of names, for it signified that the trustees, though legally and morally bound by the terms of J. B. Duke's indenture, were gradually finding new ways whereby the Endowment could respond to significant changes in the area of child care.

As discussed in an earlier chapter, the trustees during the first two decades of the Endowment's existence interpreted the relevant (and tortuous) section of the indenture to mean that they could give assistance only for orphans (children without a living parent) and half orphans (children who had only one parent living) who were institutionalized. That is, until 1944 the Endowment made annual appropriations to the orphanages in the two Carolinas based on the days of care given to their biological orphans and half orphans. Although Watson Rankin and at least one other trustee, Doris Duke, chafed under this restriction, which kept the Endowment several steps behind more progressive and modern policies concerning child care, William R. Perkins had probably played a major role in influencing the trustees to stick to a rigid, increasingly outdated formula.

When Perkins became unwell in the early 1940s and less active in the Endowment's affairs, Rankin finally managed to get the trustees in 1944 to agree to give assistance also for orphans and half orphans who were placed in foster homes under the supervision of the orphanage. The merits of extramural or foster-home care, as compared with institutionalized care, were hotly debated by the superintendents, trustees, and others involved in the Carolinas. While a majority of the institutions then stood by the status quo, there were a few forward-looking leaders who pushed for change. One of them was A. J. Jamison, superintendent of the Baptist-sponsored Connie Maxwell Orphanage in Greenwood, South Carolina. Under Jamison's leadership, it had pioneered in the Carolinas in 1924 by implementing a carefully supervised mother's-aid program that assisted mothers, whose husbands had died (or disappeared?), to keep their children in their homes. This program, which was a decade or more ahead of a similar program of the New Deal, required the service of a social worker (later termed a family service worker), and Connie Maxwell was one of the first orphanages in the Carolinas to employ such trained personnel. In fact, Jamison used the annual appropriations from the Endowment to help pay for them. As other orphanages began also to do, Connie Maxwell moved away from merely custodial congregate care (i.e., one or two large dormitories) to family-type care in cottage units with cottage parents.

In response to Rankin's request in 1944, Jamison wrote to elaborate on certain ideas they had discussed. He began by noting that the biggest changes in the child-care field had come about as a result of federal, state, and county programs that had made it possible to care for large numbers of children, who formerly would have been applicants for admission into orphanages, in their own homes or the homes of close relatives. The New Deal's Social Security Act offered assistance whenever there was an adequate surviving parent or a bona fide relative of close kin. That program had changed the type of children applying for care in private (voluntary) orphanages, and, Jamison explained, they were "faced in a tremendously serious way with the need to care for children from disrupted or unhappy home situations." Frequently one or even both parents were living but proved to be "utterly inadequate and unable to carry on in a decent way in the matter of supervision and care of the child." This meant that many of the children applying for admission to the orphanage were more difficult to care for. "They have so frequently been damaged in their basic security," he noted, "that they are inclined to strike out at the world which has hurt them."

Jamison explained that, at that time, public or governmental agencies had little or no facility for placing children in foster homes, and few institutions in the Carolinas had foster-home programs. The result was that most of the care offered was one-sided. If orphanages could, however, develop closely supervised boarding-home programs, that would allow them to remove from the group those children who needed individual care and leave the provision for group care to those who grew and thrived on it.

Jamison declared that he was strongly convinced that in those states with large, sparsely settled rural areas, such as the Carolinas, the institution would continue to play a large part in children's programs. "Well-planned institutional life" he conceded, "is giving a fine type of training to many boys and girls who come especially from rural communities." He was also convinced, however, that when a child had special needs, placement in boarding homes, especially in rural areas, should be used. He therefore hoped the Endowment's trustees could work out a satisfactory adaptation to changed conditions that had developed during the previous decade.[13] Jamison's letter helped Rankin to persuade the trustees to liberalize the Endowment's policy in 1944, and it was merely the first in a long series of moves that provided greater flexibility in the child-care program.

The appointment in 1961 of Robert A. Mayer II as the first staff member to devote full time to the Endowment's child-care work was an important development. A native of Charlotte and graduate of Duke University, Mayer received some graduate training in accounting at the University of South Carolina and worked for several years for Duke Power before joining the Endowment. Acquiring considerable expertise and stature in the field of child care, Mayer was destined to remain with the Endowment for many years and to be an important player in the effort to improve the standard of child care in the Carolinas.

By the time Mayer began his work for the Endowment, the long-building trend toward a decline in the number of true, biological orphans or half orphans applying for admission had become even more noticeable. In 1963, for example, of 5,468 children cared for in forty-four assisted institutions, 55.6 percent had both parents living. Twenty years earlier the percentage had been 26.7 percent. Moreover, a growing percentage of the institutionalized children were attending public schools and were being given the opportunity, which the Endowment contributed toward, to seek education beyond the high-school level.

Some years before Mayer's appointment, in the mid-1950s in fact, the Endowment began to help support an important Group Child Care Project sponsored by the School of Social Work at the University of North Carolina at Chapel Hill. The Endowment had begun to support workshops or summer institutes for superintendents and others who worked in child-care institutions in the 1930s, but the Chapel Hill program was both more structured and permanent. In the workshops, groups prepared reports on such topics as a code of ethics for the houseparent; the responsibilities and privileges of parents of institutionalized children; the hostile adolescent in the institution; and punishment—why, when, how, and by whom. The summer workshops of the

Group Child Care Project had an impact not only in the Carolinas but across a much wider area, for in 1957, for example, seventy-two houseparents and others caring for children came from fourteen states and one foreign country for the first week of the program.

In addition to support for programs such as those sponsored by the Group Child Care project, programs which indirectly benefited all children in child-care institutions and not just orphans and half orphans, the Endowment began in the 1960s to assist in the addition of day-care centers by some institutions. An early one was established, with the help from the Endowment, at the Elon Children's Home in North Carolina, and at the Barium Springs (North Carolina) Home for Children, where the Endowment contributed $45,000 over a three-year period toward a total cost of $154,000.

Doris Duke continued to be interested in trying to liberalize the Endowment's child-care policies. Partly in response to that fact, the trustees formally embraced a more flexible policy for child-care appropriations in 1965. Mayer and Wilburt C. Davison conferred with Doris Duke and one or two members of her staff at Duke's Farm near Somerville, New Jersey, in July 1965. In response to the suggestion of Davison and Mayer, Doris Duke agreed to chair a special advisory committee consisting of Davison, Anthony D. Duke (grandson of Benjamin N. Duke and Doris Duke's first cousin once removed), and Pete E. Cooley (Doris Duke's business manager at Duke Farms). The trustees requested the special committee to advise and make recommendations to the regular Hospital and Child Care committee. Thanking Doris Duke for the gracious reception, Mayer added, "Not only should this give you a certain amount of satisfaction, but also [it] should bring closer to fulfillment the vision that your father had for children without parents."[14]

Privately, Mayer cautioned Davison that there were strong reasons in favor of a go-slow approach to special projects or programs in child care. For one thing, he thought it important that there be no drastic reduction in the Endowment's traditional per-capita assistance to the institutions. Moreover, he believed that, in the long run, the Endowment could do more good by being quite selective at the outset about special projects as opposed to a "sudden, shotgun-type approach." Consequently, the four projects that he considered worthy of special assistance were these: (1) additional facilities (two classrooms and a library) at Boys' Home; (2) a program for emotionally disturbed children that the Baptist Children's Homes of North Carolina wished to establish in cooperation with the psychiatric out-patient clinic at the North Carolina Memorial Hospital in Chapel Hill; (3) a day-care center at the Elon Children's Home as part of its total services to the community and as the first such center to be established by a child-care institution; and (4) support for the workshops in Chapel Hill for staff development and group-care projects through the North Carolina Child Care Association. Finally, Mayer reminded Davison that the Endowment preferred, as in the past, that the first impetus for projects should come from the child-care institutions rather than from the Endowment.[15]

Davison responded enthusiastically to Mayer's suggestions and thought that Doris Duke would also like them. She had, Davison noted, given the Duke Medical Center $25,000 around 1955 to build a day-care facility at Duke, which subsequently was operated by the Durham Nursery School Association. Davis urged Mayer to discuss the letters they had exchanged with Pickens and Rankin; he would do the same thing with Tom Perkins, and then they would be ready to send the list to Doris Duke.

As so carefully planned, her advisory committee approved the four projects, as did the Hospital and Child Care committee, and the trustees made the appropriations for them in December 1965. "All of us who are interested in child care," Davison wrote Doris Duke, "are sure that these projects will greatly improve the quality of child care [in the Carolinas]."[16]

To reconcile this more expansive use of child-care funds with the indenture's restrictive language about using the funds for orphans and half orphans, the trustees agreed that the requirements of the indenture would be met if the ratio of an appropriation to the total estimated cost of a program or project did not exceed the percentage of days of care of orphan and half-orphan children cared for in the previous year. In the appropriation to the Child Welfare League for the Group Care Project, for example, something in which all the child-care institutions participated, the Endowment's contribution was well below 44 percent of the total cost, a figure derived from the fact that in 1964, 44 percent of the days of care in the assisted institutions had been for orphans and half orphans. In other words, the trustees, following the lead of Mayer as well as of Doris Duke and her fellow members on the advisory committee, recognized that the funds available for distribution to child-caring institutions were increasing each year. At the same time, there was a corresponding decrease in the ratio of orphan and half-orphan days of care to the total days of care. Thus, an increasing number of special-purpose appropriations could be made from child-care funds without decreasing the per diem appropriation for orphan and half-orphan days of care.

In addition to the growing focus on assistance for special programs or projects, Mayer began pushing in 1967 for a change in the method of distributing funds from the child-care account. It took him several years to secure the modification, but he succeeded in 1970. What he wished to do, and what the Endowment actually began doing in the 1970s, was to differentiate for the first time between those child-caring institutions that incurred higher costs because they provided a more comprehensive service (through the use of social workers, for example) and the lower-cost institutions that provided minimum services. Mayer prefaced his argument by noting the already-mentioned, steady decline in the number of institutionalized orphans and half orphans. Yet the Endowment had seen the money available for distribution to the child-care institutions double every six to nine years, and the expectation was that such a pattern would continue. By 1975 Mayer estimated that there would be about $1 million available in the child-care account.

This combination of fewer eligible children and more available money might, he feared, create an additional imbalance in the funds received by assisted institutions. In 1967 some institutions received as little as 3 percent of their annual income from the Endowment, but four or five institutions received 15 percent or more of their annual operating expenses from the Endowment. Even though the number of such institutions in the latter group was small, Mayer believed that the high percentage of support from the Endowment was "one of the contributing causes to their lack of initiative and incentive to develop new sources of income."

Despite the addition of the grants for special projects, Mayer argued that the existing method of distribution took "the course of least resistance" and did "little in the way of recognizing the institution that [was] honestly trying to meet a community need." He wondered if the Endowment's support might be doing more harm than good in those cases where the Endowment was the largest or second largest contributor to the institution's annual budget, and he asked if the Endowment should not be concerned with whether its annual investments in the various institutions were doing the maximum good for child welfare in the Carolinas.

One of the Child Care Section's operating principles — or hopes — had been that continued help to the disadvantaged or below-standard institutions would encourage them to improve their programs. But, Mayer asked, had that actually happened? In 1934 when Marshall Pickens visited one particular institution, it received a score of 416 out of a possible 1,000. In 1967 Mayer said he doubted that the institution would score that well. With the Endowment's "no-strings-attached" policy, it was "difficult to encourage the institutions toward better programming if they don't see the value of it."

Mayer recognized the resistance that would meet any effort to change a method that had been employed for over four decades, but he nevertheless believed that "the responsibility for seeing that better child welfare services are provided in the Carolinas outweighs all other responsibilities." And in the absence of any other agency pushing for such improvement, someone — that is, the Endowment — ought to assume the responsibility.

Mayer suggested two possible options. One, which the trustees ultimately embraced, was that appropriations, hitherto made solely on the basis of orphan and half-orphan days of care, should be based on a combination of cost and days of care. That, he argued, would recognize and reward those institutions that were providing a higher quality of service and thus a costlier one. Alternatively, the appropriation might be based on the total days of care with the amount paid to each institution not exceeding the cost of caring for the orphan and half-orphan children in the institution. In either case, the trustees should consider establishing a top limit to the amount available for assistance on the basis of days of care. Then the balance of the annual allocation could go toward special projects, with the Endowment making a careful effort to involve the superintendents as a group in determining areas in which the Endowment could best promote and help provide better child-care services.[17]

As stated, Mayer succeeded in selling his ideas, first to the committee on hospitals and child care and, through it, to the full board. The child-care institutions were given two years' advance notice of this change so that they could plan accordingly. For those institutions with the more comprehensive programs, including full social service, the change meant more money; for the weaker institutions it meant less money, though they always had the option of upgrading, with partial assistance from the Endowment, if they chose to do so.

When the trustees made this policy change in 1970, they asked Mayer to identify those child-care institutions that were operating at a level below the minimum standards established by the two states' departments of social service and public welfare. Mayer admitted that the development of such a list was hazardous, since the list-maker's subjective, value judgments came into play; the standards of each state's welfare agency had few benchmarks to assist in evaluation; the whole climate of an institution could change with the naming of a new superintendent; and location and the availability of funds affected quality. Nevertheless, he suggested that one could divide the institutions into three categories: (1) those that had programs that allowed children able to grow and develop to do so in a way that made the experience of group care the least damaging; (2) those that either were moving toward the first category or had the potential to do so; and (3) those whose conditions were such that the majority of the children in care might be seriously scarred as a result—though the "scars" might be no worse than if the children were receiving no care at all. Another characteristic of the third category, according to Mayer, was the virtual impossibility of any of them moving into the second much less the first category. Accordingly, he estimated that the Carolinas had twelve in the first group, twenty-four in the second, and four in the third.[18]

Mayer joined other leaders in the child-care field in pushing for the Carolinas to have a program of licensing child-care institutions. Some superintendents, trustees of the children's homes, and other fought this idea because they feared entanglement with state bureaucracies. Mayer admitted to one superintendent, who worried about state licensing of the children's homes, that he shared the expressed concerns about governmental controls and the possibility of standards that would prove too expensive for some hard-pressed institutions. Mayer added, however, that he believed there were enough checks and balances within the framework of the proposed statute for mandatory licensing to prevent the feared problems. Licensing, Mayer argued, was a better alternative than the conditions children were forced to live in some other states. He cited one institution where five adults, two of whom were in the kitchen, looked after thirty-eight children. Another home, he reported, fed its children on 68 cents per child per day.

Mayer admitted that society had never developed a system of monitoring organizations—child care, industrial, or whatever—that absolutely guaranteed adequate management. He nevertheless believed that there were approaches that could be taken to avoid serious shortcomings in the delivery of child-care services, and licensing was one of those. Some people misunderstood, he continued, and thought it was only a tool to close weak institutions. Consultative aspects of licensing could be provided, however, and they would assist institutions to remain open and also to offer at least a minimum level of services. "Licensing in North Carolina is a long range goal of mine and some executive directors of children's homes," he declared. Giving the state such authority would not only provide needed information to policy makers, but it would also eliminate some of the inequities prevalent in state programs of grants-in-aid.[19]

The proponents of state licensing won their battle, and by 1981 the Endowment adopted a policy of accepting applications of assistance only from those children's homes that were licensed by the state or that could present a letter from the state licensing agency certifying that the minimum standards for licensure had been met. Mayer reported that, as of 1981, thirty-four of the forty-one assisted child-care institutions in the two Carolinas were licensed.

By the closing decades of the twentieth century, therefore, the children's homes in the Carolinas were, in the main, significantly different from what they had been in the late 1920s: minimum standards had been both raised and clearly established, family-service workers had become an important part of most of the homes, and there were a variety of efforts to meet the special needs of emotionally disturbed children, a group that steadily increased each decade. While the Endowment had been directly involved in all those changes, it had moved far beyond the early, rigid policy of assistance based only on the days of care given to institutionalized orphans and half orphans.

Nothing illustrates the broader and more imaginative approach of the Endowment in the child-care area than the support it gave over many years to Children Unlimited. A nonsectarian, not-for-profit adoption agency based in Columbia, South Carolina, Children Unlimited dealt with children, between the ages of six and seventeen, who were once considered "unadoptable." That is, they were children who were older, biracial, or handicapped in one way or the other; some were in sibling groups that needed placement together. With fifty or so children normally waiting for adoption, the agency advertised widely. Some people criticized that as exploitation of the children, but the director of the agency replied, "I think fifteen years of foster care or institutionalization is far more exploitative."

Once prospective parents expressed interest, they went through a preparation-for-adoption program. A visitation by the child followed, and if all went well, the child moved in and the adoption process began. Children Unlimited continued to work with the family for about a year, to offer counsel, to help secure needed services, and to try to help the child and the parents become a united family. Over a decade the agency placed over 250 children and had a 76 percent success rate; in light of the severe problems of so many of the children, that rate was considered good. Government agencies supplied a bit over half of the necessary funding, but the rest had to come from private donations. Long-term funding by the Endowment, beginning in 1979, helped provide a level of confidence that attracted other funds, and by 1993 the Endowment had given over $1.4 million to Children Unlimited.

Programs in therapeutic wilderness camping, especially for emotionally disturbed children, garnered support from the Endowment, and the Endowment made one interesting grant in 1991 that did double duty. The Thornwell Home for Children in Clinton, South Carolina, owned a camp about eighty miles away, which the Home used for retreats and summer outings. The camp had gotten run-down, but a group of police officers in Pickens County, South Carolina, where the camp was located, used it for day outings for preteenagers as part of a drug education program. It was a strictly volunteer activity for the police who had come to realize that there were "so many borderline children, kids of alcoholic parents, kids who had had a minor brush with the law, kids who came from a home where there was drug abuse." The police volunteers believed these children needed more than a school program that tried to teach them to say no to drugs, and the day camp outing offered that opportunity.

The Endowment gave the funds to restore the camp, and police officers took forty to forty-five children there every Tuesday and Thursday. One officer reported: "We have games, and picnics, football players and other athletes who talk to the kids, people who are role models of all kinds. We do a lot of work on self-esteem and role-playing on how to 'say no.'" The experience also gave youngsters a different perspective on police, the officer noted, for at the camp "we can be friends" and on the same team.[20]

By 1994 the Endowment was giving as much or more in support of special programs in the child-care areas as for general operating support of the children's homes. The actual figures were $1,318,000 for general operating support and $1,332,097 for special programs. Altogether in the seventy years since J. B. Duke established the Endowment in 1924, it had given over $50 million to help those whom he called "wards of society" in the Carolinas; and the definition of those "wards" had come to be much broader than biological orphans and half orphans.

The Rural Methodist Church in North Carolina

Just as the Hospital and Child Care Sections gradually modified many of their policies after 1960, so too did the Rural Church Section. Of the three categories of aid that the Endowment extended to the rural Methodist churches in North Carolina — to retired pastors or their widows, for building programs, and for operating support — the biggest change came under the last category. Under the rubric of "operating support" the trustees and staff increasingly met requests for program grants whereby the churches broadened their social ministry. Establishing soup kitchens, day care and elder care programs, a wide variety of recreational activities for young people, and numerous other endeavors, the rural churches of the late twentieth century became active and involved in their communities in a manner that had not been dreamed of in the 1920s and 1930s. In order to establish various programs of social ministry, many small, rural churches found it necessary to join with other Methodist churches in the area to form a parish that could facilitate cooperative action. Not only, then, did the Endowment make grants for social programs but also to assist in the establishment of the parishes.

Studies in the early 1970s revealed that more than 40 percent of the Methodist churches in the United States had fewer than 100 members; in North Carolina 45 percent of the Methodists (or approximately 222,000 persons) were members of rural churches in sparsely settled communities or towns of less than 1,500 people (which was the indenture's cutoff point). Since more than 1,350 of the 1,975 United Methodist churches in the state were in these small communities, the Rural Church Section still had plenty to do and continued to help meet genuine needs.

From the beginning and as J. B. Duke intended, the Rural Church Section worked closely with Duke University's School of Religion or, after 1941, the Divinity School. The summer internships for Duke's theology students, as explained in an earlier chapter, continued to be an important component of the school's program that was funded by the Endowment. Moreover, Jesse Ormond and then, after Ormond's retirement, A. J. Walton held appointments in the Divinity School while they also worked for the Endowment.

When Walton retired in 1959, M. Wilson Nesbitt Jr. succeeded him. A native North Carolinian, Nesbitt graduated from Lenoir-Rhyne College and then received his divinity degree at Duke in 1941. After holding several pastorates, he worked for the Western North Carolina Conference for several years before becoming a member of the faculty at the Duke University Divinity School in 1958 and beginning his work in the Rural Church Section of the Endowment.

In 1968 the Endowment significantly altered the Rural Church program by naming Nesbitt as its first full-time director and secretary of the trustee committee on the Rural Church. Moving off of the Duke campus, Nesbitt and his small secretarial staff occupied the Endowment offices in Durham formerly used by Paul Clyde as secretary of the educational affairs committee. At the same time, a new Bishops Advisory Committee to pass on all requests was established as a replacement for the old Durham Committee. With representatives from the two Methodists conferences in North Carolina and from Duke University, the Bishops' Advisory Committee served to link the Endowment even more closely with the two Methodist conferences.

That the Divinity School continued to play a crucial role in the Rural

Church program was clearly illustrated when the Endowment helped the school establish the Jesse M. Ormond Center for Research, Planning, and Development in 1969. Directed by Robert L. Wilson, a member of the Divinity School's faculty, the Ormond Center received significant support from the Endowment in employing the methods of the social sciences to assist in church planning and in giving divinity students training in the field. In addition to consultative services for local churches, the Ormond Center undertook general studies to broaden the understanding of the church at large. For example, it analyzed the trends in the number of Methodist preachers available during the 1960s and early 1970s.

Another illustration of how the Endowment and local Methodist churches utilized the resources of the Ormond Center may be seen in the establishment of one of the early parish programs in eastern North Carolina. The district superintendent of the Goldsboro District, Albert F. Fisher, became concerned about the Kenansville charge in Duplin County. "There were four churches on the charge," Fisher later noted, and they were "at odds with one another, having difficulty paying out [i.e., meeting their financial obligations], unwilling to assume responsibilities, and discouraged." For many reasons, Fisher added, the churches were unable to get and keep strong leadership.

Prior to the annual conference of 1972, Fisher, in consultation with the bishop of the North Carolina Conference, decided that the Kenansville charge needed a pastoral change. He met with key lay leaders from the four churches, discussed the problems, and secured their agreement to talk with the members of the churches about organizing into a parish. In the following months the churches organized a parish council and elected a parish treasurer. At the 1972 annual conference the bishop named an energetic new pastor for the charge, Jack M. Benfield, and by 1975 Fisher, who had moved on in 1974 to become the associate director of the Endowment's Rural Church Section, could report that "tremendous things have been happening" in Duplin County. Benfield had helped build a new spirit of cooperation in the parish, and the results had been "extraordinary." Fisher noted that before he resigned from his post as district superintendent, he had observed that the members of the churches had begun "to develop a new sense of their own worth and their own ability, and a spirit of unity began to evolve." By 1975 Fisher believed that "the Kenansville Parish is the best model that we have of how small rural churches can join together for a significant ministry."[21]

While Benfield and the members of the four Methodist churches on the charge were clearly the principal actors in creating "the best model" of a rural parish, the Endowment and the Ormond Center also played supporting roles. Wilson Nesbitt met with Benfield and representatives of the four churches in September 1973. At this meeting in Duplin County, the conferees agreed that a comprehensive church-and-community study, based on a guide prepared by the Ormond Center, should be made before the cooperative ministry was launched. This study resulted in an extensive typed document that included numerous maps, a wide variety of data about the county, and detailed analysis of each of the four churches with reference to membership, budgets, facilities, and other matters.

As for changes that were occurring in the community and how they might affect the church, the study noted that Duplin County ranked seventh in the state in land area, yet in 1970 had a population of only 38,015–27,000 on farms and the remainder in nine small towns. Whites constituted 66 percent of the population and nonwhites 34 percent. About 10 percent of the population was elderly, with a higher percentage in and around Kenansville. Other data about the schools, medical facilities, civic clubs, and various other matters followed.

"Kenansville and the surrounding areas are proud of their heritage," the study pointed out, and that "pride has hampered growth in the past, especially in Kenansville." In 1963, however, a Duplin Development Commission began to try to encourage economic change, and the county expected to experience greater growth in the next decade.

What were some of the needs of the people and the community? Highlights here were day care for small children and especially for children of migrant workers during the harvest season. In all of the churches, a major concern was about the needs of the youth, for the churches were so small that only through a group effort could a meaningful program for the young people be sustained. There was a glaring need for a youth center, for at that time "the local hamburger drive-in serves that role." The adults needed leadership training about church-school teaching and work on administrative boards.

From April to October each year, migrant workers arrived in Duplin, over 500 or so. A Roman Catholic nun-nurse helped monitor the migrants' physical needs and had expressed a willingness to assist in ecumenical religious services for the migrants.

The permanent residents of the county also faced many problems. For example, approximately 30 percent of all the houses in the county lacked some or all indoor plumbing, and a recent survey had revealed that 55 percent of the houses were substandard.

The particular problems of the four small Methodist churches, all served by one pastor, were suggested by the fact that one church had regular Sunday morning services at 9:45 on the second and fourth Sundays in the month, with an average attendance of twenty-two; another had its services on the same second and fourth Sundays at 11:00, with an average attendance of seventy; the third church had services at 9:45 on the first and third Sundays, with an average attendance of fifty; and the church in Kenansville held services on the first and third Sundays at 11:00. (Talk about a mobile circuit-rider!) In addition, the churches provided Sunday-school classes for adults and children, Youth Fellowships (the old Epworth League), and one or two held Wednesday-evening prayer services.

The goals that the new parish set for itself as a result of the study were these: (1) to employ a part-time assistant minister so that worship services could be held weekly at each church; (2) to employ a part-time secretary for the parish; (3) to establish an active youth program in each of the two high-school districts in the parish; (4) to provide ecumenical services to meet the spiritual needs of the migrant workers in cooperation with the Roman Catholic nun-nurse; (5) to hold special worship services on a parish-wide basis (on the fifth Sundays and other times such as Easter, Thanksgiving, and Christmas); (6) to sponsor a Parish Day at a camp located in the county; (7) to organize the Parish United Methodist Men and the Parish United Methodist Women, with circles at each church; (8) to sponsor a leadership training school, inviting other Methodist churches and other denominations to participate; (9) to hold parish confirmation classes for children and youth; and (10) to promote an "advance special" (a mission project, usually in a foreign country) toward which all the churches would work for the entire year. In addition to the above plans or hopes, the parish proposed to name a church-and-community worker to help with services to migrant workers, youth programs, and assistance to the elderly.[22]

Thanks largely to the efforts and generosity of the local members, with only limited assistance from the Endowment and certain United Methodist church boards, the Kenansville Parish had achieved many of its goals and was a thriving organization by the mid-1970s — "One Church in 4 Locations" according to a brochure prepared by the parish. It had a parish office in a building in Kenansville across from the Duplin General Hospital, and Benfield and others believed that, since there was no space in any of the four churches for the office, having it located "on the street" helped give the parish an identity in the community; it also provided the pastor with an opportunity to give more counseling and service to the entire community. In less than two years, both stewardship (giving) and participation had increased in the parish, as evidenced by a 47 percent increase in the budgeted amounts for salary and travel, a 24 percent increase in the churches' contribution to the various causes of the annual conference, and a 10 percent increase in church-school attendance.

Urban folk accustomed to relatively large churches, or possibly to no church at all, might well wonder why rural and small-town Methodists clung so strongly to their little churches. Jack Benfield provided at least one clue when he prepared a brief history of the Kenansville Parish in 1976. One of the four churches, Wesley Chapel, went back to 1815, when it was but one Methodist church on a circuit so large that it took a preacher six weeks to make a round on horseback. (Since the Methodist Episcopal church in America had not been formally organized until 1784, Wesley Chapel was obviously one of the pioneer Methodist churches, although two other Methodist churches in Duplin had a founding date of 1790.) The building used by the Wesley Chapel congregation in 1975 had been erected in 1844, making it one of the oldest Methodist buildings in North Carolina still in continuous use. The pews and other furnishings in the church were all homemade and handcrafted, with the pulpit believed to be original. "An ascent to the attic is an inspiring trip to the past," Benfield declared, for the rafters, beams, and joists were hand-hewn logs, many with bark still intact, and most were joined with pegs.

The Methodists in Kenansville organized their church in 1850 and erected a modest wooden building in 1858. It was remodeled several times in subsequent years, and with help from the Endowment, the members added a brick veneer in 1935. The other two churches on the charge were organized in the twentieth century, one in 1903 and one in 1955, but at least two of the churches were venerable (by American standards), well-loved links with the past. Marriages, deaths, and other important events in the lives of the members were intimately associated with the churches, so much so that there was probably no other institution in the community that rivaled them in their hold on the loyalty and love of their communicants.[23]

Following Methodist custom, the bishop moved Benfield to another charge in 1976, but the Kenansville Parish continued to carry out its multisided ministry. Wilson Nesbitt or Albert Fisher met periodically with the leaders there, and the Endowment continued to contribute support. Wishing to avoid a permanent dependent relationship, however, the Endowment in the late 1970s informed the Kenansville Parish that aid from the Endowment would be on a declining basis each year until it ended altogether in 1981. Any new programs or projects that the parish might wish to undertake would certainly be eligible for assistance from the Endowment, but its grants were intended always as incentives rather than as permanent funding.

In the western part of the state, five small Methodist churches in the Pisgah National Forest formed the Mitchell-Yancey Parish in the early 1970s, and the Endowment helped. At a meeting of the parish leaders and Endowment representatives in 1979, the former reported that one of the greatest benefits of the parish program had been the ability of the churches to hold services every Sunday. The parish representatives also noted that the congregations enjoyed the fellowship of the parish-wide meetings on the fourth Sunday evenings, the rotating preachers, and the stronger youth programs. Between 1974 and 1979 the Endowment contributed $46,000 to the parish but gradually phased out its assistance, except for any new programs that might be developed.

Despite the apparent success of the parish plan in certain cases, it did not really take hold in North Carolina. An especially capable and energetic preacher might manage to get a parish organized, but under the Methodist system the preacher got moved to a new church on a regular basis. On the whole, therefore, the parish plan did not permanently alter the way in which rural Methodist churches operated.

A rarely used alternative to the parish plan for some small, rural Methodist churches was merger, and in the late 1960s three churches in Lincoln county, Gastonia District, followed that route. They received help from the Endowment to build a new church for the 321 members in the combined congregation. "Our merger continues to thrill us in many ways," the minister reported to Nesbitt. The members were not only pleased with their new building but also relished other signs of growth. The church planned to participate in an interdenominational child-development center, which would be housed in one of the buildings formerly used by one of the merged churches. The new, merged church sponsored two Girl Scout troops (one a new one) and a new Boy Scout troop. The minister noted also that more of the members were participating in district and conference camps and assemblies and that the church-school teachers were doing an excellent job.[24] The Endowment made its final grant toward the merger program in 1978.

Under the terms of J. B. Duke's indenture, the Endowment could not make direct grants to interdenominational or ecumenical agencies. It could and did, however, assist rural and small-town Methodist churches that wished to participate in such programs. One good example of this developed in Cleveland County in the Piedmont region. The small Methodist churches in the upper or northern part of the county, churches which began a cooperative program in the mid-1950s, ended up in an interracial and interdenominational coalition—one which included Methodist, Baptist, Missionary Methodist, Holiness, and Seventh-Day Adventists churches. The coalition sponsored a wide-ranging program of community service and social ministry, and the Endowment helped through the Methodist churches involved.

In 1970 the health department of Cleveland County suggested to a group of church and civic leaders that the upper part of the county needed a health clinic. Having already become aware of the need, the community leaders soon organized the Upper Cleveland Health Committee and began to find a host of new ways to serve the community. When a doctor's large residence, which had also housed a medical clinic, became available in 1971, the health clinic moved there, and the various churches, civic clubs, and interested individuals organized the nonprofit Upper Cleveland Area Needs, Inc.—U-CAN—with its headquarters in the former residence. Its purpose was "to co-ordinate the efforts of all people, to minister to the physical, spiritual, social, economic and psychological needs of one another under God."

U-CAN's ministries covered a broad spectrum: (1) a Sunday-school class for special children with leadership, transportation, and refreshments provided by local churches; (2) a burn-out shelter with appliances, furniture, and small household items to give to families who lost their homes by fire; (3) an emergency clothes closet; (4) an answering service staffed by volunteers to help meet needs by referring people to other agencies if necessary; (5) tutoring, by prior arrangement; (6) transportation provided by volunteers to doctors' offices, hospitals, and grocery stores and a hot lunch program for the shut-in elderly (meals on wheels); (7) weekly ministries to the four rest homes in the area; (8) annual Christmas parties in several locations and Santa Claus for foster-care children in the area; (9) library; (10) emergency and disaster aid through funds for fuel oil, electricity, medicine, groceries, and other necessities; (11) space in the U-CAN center for club meetings, Alcoholics Anonymous, adult education, the office of the Upper Cleveland Group Ministry, a day-care center, counseling, and a little theater; (12) a health clinic staffed by the county health department each Tuesday morning and periodic special clinics for glaucoma, high blood pressure, and other chronic conditions; and (13) a hot lunch program provided through the county's social service department.[25]

Earlier, and in addition to the above programs centered in U-CAN's headquarters, the Endowment had assisted the Methodist group ministry in upper Cleveland to equip an office with filmstrips and other visual-aid materials; to establish a coffeehouse ministry for youth in one of the towns; to conduct workshops in music and choirs, missions, teacher, and other leadership training; to provide a week of day camping for children and also a week of "rough camping"; to conduct on an ecumenical basis, a week of activities for young people in junior high and one for those in senior high; to publish a group-ministry newsletter; and, among other things, to sponsor a Duke summer student program.

When the bishop of the Western North Carolina Conference visited upper Cleveland in 1972, he reported that the people there singled out two characteristics as fundamental in the U-CAN program: (1) the cooperation had grown out of the needs of the people, and the program was designed to serve those needs rather than to get people to "join the church"; and (2) it was primarily a lay movement and would proceed regardless of the tenure or leadership of the pastors. "I still think," the bishop added, "they have been and are motivated by wise and dedicated pastors." Moreover, the bishop confided his additional impression that "the major leadership and motivation" behind the interracial, interdenominational program of U-CAN had come from the cooperative United Methodist Ministry.[26]

Meeting with a "strong contingency" of U-CAN's lay leaders in 1979, the Endowment representative, Jack Williams, advised them of the Endowment's new policy of grants on a declining basis for a limited period, with incentive money still available to get new programs started. "I encouraged them to dream and be bold in looking at their ministry," Williams noted.[27] If the past record was a reliable indicator, one must suspect that the imaginative folk of upper Cleveland met Williams's challenge.

In 1969 Wilson Nesbitt provided a brief, revealing insight not only into the thinking of himself and the Rural Church Section but also into an important trend in the United Methodist church. According to Nesbitt, there were two major characteristics in United Methodism's program in Town and Country if it was to be significant and to minister to the needs of people in future decades. First, long-range planning was essential, which meant that local congregations, with help from the conference and other agencies (such as the Ormond Center), would need to become thoroughly informed about what was happening in the community and what its potential might be. On the basis of cultural, economic, educational, and religious data, the local congregation had to prepare in writing a long-range approach that set forth goals and principles of operation.

Second, cooperation had become crucial. "No longer are churches islands unto themselves," Nesbitt insisted, "for they must join together in a common responsibility for a much larger area than the small neighborhoods which once characterized the area served by individual congregations." The destinies of all the churches in a county in the mountains of North Carolina, for example, were tied together according to Nesbitt, and "it is very important that they begin working together as a unit."[28] Nesbitt had a generous, idealistic vision but, unfortunately, it proved to be one that did not fit the facts.

Under its charge to help support and maintain North Carolina's rural Methodist churches, the Endowment and its Rural Church Section assisted a striking variety of programs from the 1960s onward, programs that were designed to help the small churches "work together as a unit" as they steadily expanded their understanding of social ministry. In many respects, the late-twentieth-century churches were vastly different from the ones that the Endowment had begun to assist in the mid-1920s. Yet the trustees and the staff of the Endowment had proven themselves capable and eager to adapt and change under new conditions. Altogether between 1924 and 1994, the Endowment allocated over $18.3 million for maintaining and operating rural Methodist churches.

The Endowment's program for assistance in the building of rural Methodist churches also underwent some changes not in so far as the Endowment's policies were concerned but in response to the requests that came in from the churches. For one thing, help in the building from scratch of new church structures took a secondary position to help with renovations, the addition of Sunday-school wings, and assembly halls — "luxuries" about which the poverty-stricken rural churches of the late 1920s and 1930s could hardly have dreamed.

There were new churches to be built, of course, and the Endowment continued to play its traditional role of offering limited assistance. Old battles about the use of architects also continued. Church buildings, while by no means as complicated and technologically demanding as hospitals, did pose certain quite important problems. For example, the importance of adequate parking areas, with access to all parts of the church building from the parking areas, had grown steadily more crucial over the decades. From the standpoint of worship and liturgy, there were numerous matters that needed to be considered carefully, such as access to both ends of the sanctuary from the rest of the building. The organist or pianist needed to be so situated that he or she could direct the choir, and the communion rail and kneeling strip (as used by Methodists) had to be placed so that it was accessible to the aged and handicapped.

These were only three of the twenty-five considerations in one memorandum concerning the worship aspects of church architecture.

From the educational point of view, adequate space for all age groups was an obvious point. Also, however, there should be an exterior window in each classroom, and the recommended minimum width for corridors was six feet. More than a dozen other matters needed to be carefully planned concerning the church schools.

From the standpoint of fellowship, the question of what dining capacity would be needed in an assembly room and how often it would be used needed to be carefully weighed. There was a need for ample storage space provided for chairs, tables, and recreational equipment. There were more than a dozen other matters concerning the fellowship hall, and similar considerations about office space and safety features. In short, church building had become a vastly more complicated matter than Washington and "Uncle Billy" Duke had experienced back in the nineteenth century.

Persuading some rural Methodists that such was the case, however, proved tricky. Aside from the money involved in using an architect, another obstacle arose from the fact that rural builders or contractors often tried to persuade congregations not to use an architect. Some builders even argued that working drawings and specifications were unnecessary. When the builder or the congregation maintained that a new building should be exactly like the one they originally had, there was also a problem. When the Bishops' Committee on Church Architecture discussed this matter in 1962, those assembled agreed that maintaining the enthusiasm of the congregation was essential. At the same time, however, congregations urgently needed to take the time to plan adequately. The final consensus of the group was that when a congregation expected to apply for assistance toward a new building from the district board of missions, the department of church extension, and the Endowment, all three groups should issue joint recommendations, "one of which would be to hire an architect to plan and supervise the program."[29] Finally, in 1978 the Endowment announced that it would not accept applications for assistance in building projects where no architect was used.

In certain cases, congregations managed to have the best of both worlds, that is, to keep their beloved old church building while also gaining a new structure. In 1972 the Endowment assisted the Carver's Creek United Methodist Church in Bladen County in the eastern part of the state in an unusual building program. The Carver's Creek church, the oldest Methodist church in Bladen county, dated back to 1790, and the wooden structure still in use in the

1970s was built in 1859. An architectural firm in Wilmington, North Carolina, incorporated the 114-year-old wooden structure in the design for a new church plant and received for the project the Endowment-sponsored Randolph E. Du Mont certificate of recognition for excellence in church design.[30]

A less colorful undertaking than the above project but one that proved helpful to many rural Methodist congregations was the Endowment support for a program to weatherize the churches. With North Carolina's Alternative Energy Corporation providing the expertise, the congregations supplied the labor. The endowment participated by making grants in 1987 that totaled $123,000 and went to 67 churches. Altogether between 1985 and 1994, the Endowment allocated more than $1.1 million in helping 487 rural Methodist churches save energy (and money) through the weatherization program.

A nice example of a new church that the Endowment helped to build was provided by that of Hinton's Memorial United Methodist Church in Lincolnton, North Carolina, in the western part of the state. When the Reverend Habakkuk Taylor, an African American minister newly appointed to the church, arrived in mid-1986, he found a small, concrete-block structure that was filled with dust and cobwebs. After he and his wife cleaned the place, he preached to a congregation of eleven people. Subsequently, Taylor met with some of the church leaders and learned that they had acquired land for a new church. While the preacher agreed about the need for a new building, he argued that, "Before we can build *a* church, we have to build *our* church — that is, we need our people, our congregation; then the building can come."

Taylor began visiting and inviting people to join the congregation at Hinton's Memorial. He also issued a challenge: "If we get $5,000, we'll break ground." Through rummage sales, fish fries, and "a lot of sacrificial giving by families," he later reported, the congregation of fifty-two members surpassed the $5,000 goal in less than six months. Then with help from the Endowment and the Western North Carolina Conference, the congregation began early in 1987 to see its dream of a handsome, new brick church begin to become a reality. The next goal was to burn the mortgage note as quickly as possible, and, Taylor declared, "With God's help, we'll do it." He, incidentally, had come late to the ministry after serving for twenty-two years in the armed forces and being wounded three times in Vietnam. "Then I got the call [to preach] and began training," he explained. "I go every summer to Duke University and have two years left before I finish the Ministerial Course of study program."[31]

For building rural Methodist churches in North Carolina during 1994, the last year covered by this study, the Endowment appropriated $1,173,000.

Altogether since the beginning of the Endowment late in 1924, it had by the end of 1994 appropriated nearly $27.7 million for that purpose.

The help that Washington, Ben, and J. B. Duke began to give to "worn-out Methodist preachers" in the late nineteenth century became an integral part of the Endowment. Meant only as an extra bonus or a supplement to the regular pension received by the retired preachers of the two Methodist conferences or their surviving spouses and dependents, the Endowment's gifts took the form of checks mailed out by the president of Duke University just before Christmas each year. As mentioned earlier, it was a task that gave particular pleasure to William P. Few as well as to his successors down through Terry Sanford in the 1970s.

Then the Internal Revenue Service, clearly the Grinch that meant to steal Christmas, began to raise questions. As a result, the Endowment late in 1974 decided that it needed a better understanding of the actual financial conditions of the recipients in its Superannuated Gift Program. Accordingly, the Endowment employed a management consulting firm that specialized in the field of attitude and opinion research to develop a plan for the study. In consultation with Endowment officials and the Ormond Center, the consulting firm, which employed an opinion research company to undertake the basic data gathering, sent out a questionnaire to a small test group in the Durham area. Each recipient of the questionnaire also got a letter from the bishop explaining the purpose of the study and assuring anonymity and confidentiality. The test proved successful, so the professional pollsters mailed a scientifically drawn sample of 181 individuals the questionnaire along with a letter from the appropriate bishop. The goal was about 100 completed questionnaires, roughly divided equally between retired ministers and their widows, and samples from both groups had been randomly drawn from lists of recipients.

A total of 113 completed questionnaires, a 62 percent response, proved to be adequate to represent the condition of the whole group. The survey revealed that the typical gift recipient had been receiving the check from the Endowment for upward of ten years and found that the money contributed importantly to his or her welfare. This gained significance when added to the fact that a clear majority reported having "greater difficulty making financial ends meet" than was the case a year earlier. Some of the volunteered comments were: from a retired minister, "Can make no major purchases to replace vehicles or appliances," and "I am a widow living in an apartment, and with only my small pension and Social Security as income [it] has made it *very* difficult financially. I am also helping my brother who has only Social Security when he quit work. He has no retirement."

The survey revealed that the median net worth of the entire group as of 1974 was $20,894. For the widows in the sample, it was $14,246 and for the ministers $30,539. In both instances a significant portion of net worth involved assets of a nonliquid nature such as homes, automobiles, and household possessions.

The median income from all sources for the group in 1974 was $6,940, and the figure for the retired ministers was higher than for the widows. About half the group reported that they paid no federal income taxes because their incomes fell below the minimum taxable level. Over a third of the sample group reported that they had to work to supplement their income.

Despite their relative poverty, the long-ingrained commitment to charitable giving of the retirees and widows persisted: over 88 percent reported contributions at a median figure of $350, and over half indicated that they were contributing some support to persons other than themselves.

Despite their modest incomes and outside obligations, people in the sample clearly demonstrated that they struggled to live within their means and most managed to set aside at least some of their 1974 income for future needs. Of the comments volunteered, the consultants believed that this one from a widow captured both the determination to save and an underlying motivation: "Everything, phone, gas, electricity, food, clothes, etc., are up. My income is less, but by doing without, making do, and economizing in every way, I have saved that little to take care of myself when I get completely helpless. I would rather die than go on welfare."

The consultants concluded their report by declaring that the overall picture that emerged from the survey was one of a group of men and women of basically quite modest means who were having progressively greater difficulty making ends meet (because of inflation). Yet they managed "to do so with determination, and, to judge from the comment material, with considerable grace as well."[32]

If the staff and trustees of the Endowment had ever harbored any doubts about the usefulness of the Superannuated Gift Program, which they probably had not until the Internal Revenue Service began making inquiries, this carefully conducted survey of the financial condition of the target group clearly laid those doubts to rest. The Internal Revenue Service, however, persisted in its niggling about the Endowment's Christmas checks, and beginning in 1974 the Endowment arranged for the checks to be sent through the office of the two Methodist bishops in North Carolina rather than through the office of the president of Duke University.

In 1994 the Endowment distributed a little more than $800,000 to the retirees and surviving spouses, and altogether since 1924 the total amount so appropriated came to a bit over $13,777,000. For many years, too, the trustees had allocated for this purpose more than the 2 percent of the total income from the original corpus that the indenture suggested. It was a warmhearted and most welcome gesture of thanks in remembrance of the circuit riders.

As mentioned earlier, Albert F. Fisher became the associate director of the Rural Church Division in 1974. When Wilson Nesbitt retired in 1977, Fisher became the director. Early in 1979 J. J. (Jack) Williams became the assistant director of the division and served in the post for ten years. He was succeeded as assistant director in 1989 by W. Joseph Mann who, upon Fisher's retirement in 1996, the trustees named as director of the division.

9 ·

J. B. DUKE

WINS

AND

LOSES

The Partial Collapse

of the Grand Design

WHEN JAMES B. DUKE established the Duke Endowment late in 1924, he
made an audacious bet that he could, with the help of his lawyers, establish a
perpetual charitable trust, one that would last forever and continue to be
useful. By 1994, when the Endowment turned seventy, what finally became
clear was that J. B. Duke had both won and lost his bet. In so far as the
charitable purposes in the Carolinas that he selected for the Endowment to
serve — higher education, hospitals and health care, orphanages and child
care, and the rural Methodist church in North Carolina — he had won. Those
four areas continued to be just as crucially important in human welfare
in 1994 as they were in 1924. Moreover, as circumstances and conditions
changed through the seven decades, the trustees and the staff of the Endowment managed to find ways to follow the exacting stipulations of the indenture
of trust while at the same time modifying policies and broadening the scope of
the Endowment's usefulness.

An intrinsic part of J. B. Duke's Grand Design for perpetual philanthropy
was, however, a tight interlocking relationship between the Endowment and
the Duke Power Company. For reasons explained earlier, he intended for the
Endowment to own a controlling interest in the power company and to derive
the larger part of its annual income from its stock in Duke Power. Further-

more, he explicitly requested in the indenture that the trustees of the Endowment "see to it that at all times these companies be managed and operated by the men best qualified for such a service."

In the 1920s few people questioned this linking together of a charitable trust and an investor-owned, for-profit business. Numerous other foundations had similar structures; and while there certainly were always politicians and others who preferred for the government, rather than private foundations, to address social needs, there were no legal barriers to such an arrangement as J. B. Duke's Grand Design provided for the Endowment and Duke Power.

After World War II, however, and especially in the 1960s, views about this matter underwent a significant change. As described in an earlier chapter, the dominant view in the United States Congress came to be that the federal government should take action to prevent too close a linkage between a tax-exempt foundation and a for-profit business. Finally, the Tax Reform Act of 1969 required, among other things, that within a certain number of years no foundation could own more than 25 percent of the outstanding common stock of a for-profit business. For the Endowment, this meant, in effect, that it could no longer invest in the common stock of Duke Power. Since the indenture restricted the Endowment's investments to Duke Power stocks and bonds or certain types of government bonds, the trustees felt they had no alternative but to seek relief from the indenture's investment restrictions in the North Carolina courts.

When the courts granted this relief in 1972 and allowed the Endowment to diversify its investments, this marked a significant modification of the Grand Design, a modification made necessary by the great change in public policy that was embodied in the Tax Reform Act of 1969. Despite the newly won permission to diversify its future investments, the fact remained that the overwhelming majority of the Endowment's assets consisted of Duke Power common stock. As late as 1993, for example, almost 79 percent of the Endowment's income was from dividends on Duke Power stock. A series of events in the 1960s and 1970s, as discussed earlier, convinced the majority of the trustees that the wisest and most prudent course for the Endowment to follow was to lessen its financial dependence on Duke Power by selling some, not all, of the Endowment's stock in the company.

To the extent that the Endowment sold Duke Power stock it would, obviously, be moving farther away from J. B. Duke's Grand Design. That he hoped that would never happen was made clear in the indenture where he included these words: "I advise the trustees that they do not change any such

investment [in Duke Power] except in response to the most urgent and extraordinary necessity." While J. B. Duke chose simply to "advise" the trustees
in this matter, he further stipulated elsewhere in the indenture, in language
that was not merely advisory, that the trustees should sell no Duke Power
stock "except upon and by the affirmative vote of the total authorized number
of trustees at a meeting called for that purpose." In other words, even if the
trustees should decide that "the most urgent and extraordinary necessity"
compelled the sale of some Duke Power stock, that would require unanimous
agreement of all the trustees. This was the part of the indenture that gave one
trustee, Doris Duke, the power to prevent the remainder of the trustees from
doing what they had collectively decided most emphatically needed doing:
lessening the Endowment's financial dependence on Duke Power by a sale of a
portion of the Endowment's stock in the company. Doris Duke, in short,
managed to keep a significant portion of her father's Grand Design intact as
long as she lived.

Doris Duke's relationship with the Endowment was, from the time she
became a trustee at age twenty-one in 1933, as her father mandated, strange in
a number of ways. As a young, socialite newlywed in the 1930s, her apparent
lack of any sustained interest in the work of the Endowment was understandable enough. As she matured, however, she continued to have a sort of on-and-
off involvement with the Endowment. Traveling a great deal and, after World
War II, spending the winter months in her mansion in Honolulu, Hawaii, she
only occasionally attended one or two of the ten meetings each year of
the trustees.

Even in the child-care area, where she clearly had a genuine interest, her
involvement in the Endowment's activities was spasmodic rather than continuous. She would somewhat suddenly display a keen interest in the Endowment's child-care program, as for example around 1944 and later around
1965, but would then disappear from the picture — and the archival record.
(What Doris Duke did through her own highly secretive foundations — first
Independent Aid, Inc., and then later the Doris Duke Foundation — is another
matter. There she possibly did maintain a more consistent, sustained interest
in philanthropy, but unfortunately, if any records of these agencies survive,
they have not been made available to scholars.)

Small signs of Doris Duke's impatience about the Endowment's policies and
methods began to crop up early. As mentioned earlier, both George G. Allen,
the chairman of the trustees from 1925 until his death in 1960, and Tom
Perkins, Allen's successor and chairman until his death in 1973, were strong-

willed individuals who tended to run the Endowment in an autocratic fashion. With staff members doing most of the real work and first clearing their recommendations with Allen, William R. Perkins, and Alexander Sands Jr. in the early period and with Tom Perkins after 1960, the meetings of the trustees tended to be rather dull, perfunctory affairs, and Doris Duke lost patience with them.

As Doris Duke grew older, the Endowment's way of operating clearly annoyed her more and more. Accustomed to having her own way about so many things because of her immense wealth, she did not enjoy being constrained by the Endowment's unvarying methods and stodgy style. For example, she attended a meeting of the trustees in May 1968 and raised some questions about a certain policy at Duke University concerning bids for a construction project there. When she received the typed minutes of the meeting for her signature — the indenture required that all trustees present at any given meeting sign the minutes — she refused to sign and wrote in her own hand at the bottom of the page, "These minutes are incomplete — Doris Duke."

After missing the meeting in June 1968, she attended the one in July and "raised an objection to the minutes of the meeting held May 28, 1968, stating that in her opinion the minutes were incomplete since they did not include her comments and questions regarding Duke University's policy." Further, she felt that the policy was wrong and wanted a full explanation from Duke University.

One can only imagine the consternation of the trustees in this situation, for trustees' meetings were traditionally harmonious, sedate affairs. Indeed, if there had ever before been such a hint of passion or emotion at a meeting of the trustees, it had not been recorded in the minutes. In this case, Chairman Perkins, according to the minutes, "informed Miss Duke that it is customary to record in the minutes only actions taken by the Board; however, the minutes of this meeting would record her objections and questions and a full explanation would be requested from Duke University."[1]

A trivial matter, certainly, but it shows that Doris Duke was tiring of her role as Endowment trustee and felt frustrated by what she perceived as rule by the patriarchy. At exactly what point around 1970 she decided that she had had enough and would no longer even occasionally attend meetings of the trustees is not known. Adding to her disenchantment with the Endowment was her serious falling-out with Tom Perkins. The details about this are not known, but one story from reliable sources has it that Doris Duke requested Perkins to dismiss one of her employees at Duke Farms, her estate near Somerville, New

Jersey. When Perkins refused to take action, believing that it was not his but Doris Duke's own responsibility, she became exceedingly angry and vowed never again to have anything to do with Perkins.[2]

Tom Perkins died in 1973, and by the time Archie Davis began to reinvigorate and shake up the Endowment as chairman of the trustees from 1974 through 1980, the withdrawal of Doris Duke from its affairs had become complete — except for her refusal to allow the sale of any Duke Power stock. The timing of Doris Duke's alienation from the Endowment was ironic in a way because the trustees and their committees did begin to play a larger, more significant role in the 1970s, and the Endowment began to support a wide variety of new and imaginative programs in health care, child care, and the rural Methodist church in North Carolina.

The loosening up and reinvigoration that Archie Davis had helped to begin got carried even further in the 1980s after Mary Semans became the chairwoman of the Endowment. The two trustees with whom Doris Duke maintained the friendliest relations were Mary Semans, her first cousin once removed, and Wilburt C. Davison. When Duke University proposed in 1972 to honor Davison on his eightieth birthday by establishing two professorships in pediatrics to be named for him, the Doris Duke Foundation gave $500,000 for the purpose and the Endowment gave a similar amount. While Davison died later in 1972, thus ending that link with the Endowment for Doris Duke, she continued to communicate, usually by telephone, with Mary Semans.

The trustees elected Robert McCormack to succeed Davis as chairman late in 1981. A trustee since 1965, McCormack was a lawyer who had long been associated with the Endowment through his partnership in the New York law firm of Perkins, Daniels, and McCormack. When McCormack died less than a year after assuming the chairmanship, the trustees in December 1982 elected Mary Semans to lead the Endowment. The first woman to hold the post, she was the second graduate of Duke University in the position, Marshall Pickens having been the first. Pickens, however, served as chairman only about a year and, as of 1996, Semans's tenure in the chair was already second in duration only to George Allen's. Deeply informed about her family's history and strongly committed to its tradition of philanthropy, Semans also possessed a knowledge about and love for the Endowment's prime beneficiary, Duke University, that was unsurpassed in the Endowment's history.

The election of atypical trustees such as Kenneth Goodson and Juanita Kreps began even before Semans assumed leadership. She encouraged even more such elections, however, and by 1994 the board of trustees was more diversified that it had ever been. In light of the relatively enlightened racial views of Washington, Ben, and J. B. Duke and of the carefully biracial character of the beneficiaries of the Endowment, the trustees were surprisingly slow in inviting an African American to join their number. When they finally did that in 1993, however, they chose superbly. Widely recognized as the dean of African American historians in the nation, John Hope Franklin capped a distinguished academic career by becoming a James B. Duke professor of history at Duke University in 1982. A former president of the American Historical Association, the Organization of American Historians, and the Southern Historical Association, Franklin also served as the president of the United Chapters of Phi Beta Kappa, received the Presidential Medal of Freedom, and had had bestowed upon him a record-breaking number (108 as of mid-1996) of honorary degrees. A strong and effective champion of justice for African Americans because of his judiciousness as well as knowledge and wide-ranging experience, Franklin brought an unparalleled distinction to the Endowment's governing board.

If Franklin's becoming a trustee represented a significant breakthrough for the Endowment, so too did the election of Richard W. Riley as a trustee in 1989. Over the years the Endowment had scrupulously steered clear of any involvement in politics and overt association with politicians. Riley, however, had been the Democratic governor of South Carolina from 1978 until 1986. A native of Greenville County, South Carolina, and a graduate of Furman University, he received his law degree from the University of South Carolina's law school before entering practice and politics. Following four years in South Carolina's lower house and ten in the state senate, he was elected governor in 1978. The reason the trustees broke their taboo about politics and politicians in Riley's case was that he had particularly distinguished himself during his governship by his leadership, in both South Carolina and the nation, in the fields of education, health, and child care — the exact areas of prime concern to the Endowment. His remarkable ability was suggested by the fact that a poll of the nation's governors in 1986 ranked Riley as the third most effective governor in the nation. It was a distinct loss to the Endowment, therefore, when he resigned as trustee in early 1993 to become secretary of education in the administration of President Bill Clinton.

The election of two trustees, even before Riley, brought new and interesting perspectives to the board. Russell M. Robinson II, elected a trustee in 1987, was a native of Charlotte who received both his undergraduate and law degrees at Duke University. While he was prominent in a wide variety of civic activities as well as in legal circles, Robinson brought something special to the board of trustees: through his earlier legal work for the Endowment he, together with John Spuches in New York, had come to know more about the history of the Endowment's structure and the intricacies of the indenture than any one else. His presence on the board, therefore, brought a valuable legal and historical perspective.

When the trustees elected Mary Duke Trent Jones to the board in 1988, she brought something long missing from it — relative youth. Born in Durham in 1940, she was the oldest child of Mary Semans and her first husband, the late Dr. Josiah C. Trent. After graduating from Duke in 1963, Mary Trent taught school briefly before marrying James P. Jones of Durham in 1964. Along with helping to raise three sons (who were grown by the time she became a trustee), Mary Trent Jones involved herself in a wide variety of civic and educational affairs in Bristol, Virginia, where she lived, and in the state of Virginia as a whole. She was, in short, a younger version of her civic-minded and energetic mother and thus became an additional link between the Endowment and the Duke family.

When William G. Anlyan became a trustee in 1990, he brought to the board a rich background in medicine and medical education that had been lacking since the death of Wilburt C. Davison a decade earlier. After receiving his undergraduate and medical degrees from Yale University, Anlyan went to Duke in 1949 for his internship and then residency in general and thoracic surgery. Remaining at Duke for the remainder of his career, he eventually served as dean of Duke's School of Medicine and then, among other things, as the executive vice president and chancellor for health affairs. Leading the Duke Medical Center in one of its most expansive and impressive eras, Anlyan held so many important positions in national and even international medical and scientific organizations that it would be impossible to list them here. Suffice it to say that his vast experience in the fields of medicine and medical education made him an invaluable resource for the Endowment board.

Bishop Goodson died in 1991, and in the areas of Methodism and higher education in general, Thomas A. Langford brought to the board in 1992 experience and knowledge comparable to Anlyan's in medicine. A native North Carolinian, Langford graduated from Davidson College in 1951 and received his divinity degree as well as his Ph.D. (in religion) from Duke University. Remaining at Duke as a highly successful teacher and scholar, he later served as dean of the Divinity School for a decade before becoming vice-provost for academic affairs in the 1980s and finally provost (the top academic post under the president of the university) from 1990 until the fall of 1994. Just as active and prominent in national and even international spheres of Methodism as Anlyan was in the medical arena, Langford also possessed a profound knowledge about and understanding of Duke University — and higher education in general — that made him a valuable trustee of the Endowment.

These six trustees named between 1987 and 1993 — Russell Robinson, Mary Trent Jones, Richard Riley, William Anlyan, Thomas Langford, and John Hope Franklin — brought unusual talents and experience to the board even though they did not have the corporate or business background that the great majority of the Endowment's trustees had traditionally possessed.

As 1994 ended, in addition to five of the above-named persons (Riley resigned in 1993), the board consisted of ten others. Mary Semans, the most senior trustee in point of service (since 1957), has already been discussed, as has Juanita Kreps (since 1979). Archie Davis, who chaired the board during a period of significant change in its operations in the 1970s, has also been discussed earlier.

The seven other trustees serving as 1994 ended all possessed impressive credentials in the business world as well as records revealing a wide variety of civic and church-related activities that were too numerous to be mentioned here. The most senior of the seven in terms of service as a trustee was James C. Self (since 1974), a native of South Carolina and graduate of The Citadel; he was long associated with the Greenwood Mills (textiles) and rose from assistant treasurer of the company to become president (from 1955 to 1981) and then chairman of the board and of the executive committee. Next in point of service was Charles F. Myers (since 1976), a native of West Virginia who attended the Harvard business school after graduating from Davidson. Like Self, Myers made his career in textiles and rose to become chairman of Burlington Industries from 1968 to 1974.

Louis C. Stephens Jr. became a trustee in 1980. A native North Carolinian, he graduated from the University of North Carolina at Chapel Hill before serving three years in the United States Navy during World War II. Subsequently he graduated from Harvard's business school and then took a position with the Pilot Life Insurance Company in Greensboro in 1949. Elected president of the company in 1971, Stephens served as chief executive officer from 1973 until his retirement in 1987.

While Stephens represented the insurance industry on the board, Hugh M. Chapman came from the banking world. A native South Carolinian who graduated from the University of North Carolina at Chapel Hill and later did some graduate work in banking at Rutgers University, Chapman became a trustee in 1981 and was elected vice-chairman of the board in 1989. He held various executive positions in the Citizens and Southern National Bank of South Carolina in Columbia before becoming its president in 1971 and then its chairman and chief executive officer from 1974 until 1986. In the latter year he became president of the Citizens and Southern Corporation in Atlanta and then in 1992 the chairman of NationsBank South.

Thomas S. Kenan III became a trustee in 1992 and had a background in both business and philanthropy. The son of a longtime trustee, Frank H. Kenan, who resigned in 1990, Thomas Kenan was born in Durham and graduated from the University of North Carolina at Chapel Hill in 1959. Involved as an officer and director of various business interests of his family — such as the Kenan Transport Company, the Westfield Company, and Flagler System, Inc. — Kenan also served as an officer and trustee of various family-connected charitable organizations such as, among others, the William R. Kenan Jr. Charitable Trust, the Randleigh Foundation, and the Kenan Family Foundation. He also served from the early 1980s onward as a trustee of the Mary Duke Biddle Foundation and other, smaller foundations with which Mary Semans was involved.

The board elected two new trustees of the Endowment in 1994. The first was Richard Jenrette, a native of Raleigh. After graduating from the University of North Carolina at Chapel Hill, Jenrette obtained a degree from the Harvard business school. In 1959 he became one of the founding members of Donaldson, Lufkin, and Jenrette, an investment banking firm in New York. When the Equitable Insurance Company purchased the firm in 1984, Jenrette continued to oversee the operations of his old firm but also became Equitable's chief investment officer and then in 1990 its chief executive officer until his retirement in 1994. Keenly interested in historic preservation, he was involved in the restoration of several important historic homes in the two Carolinas.

The most recently elected trustee as of the end of 1994 was Edwin Craig Wall Jr., a native and resident of Conway, South Carolina. A Davidson graduate (1959) who also went on to business school at Harvard, Wall began his business career with Canal Industries, a wood products company, in 1962 and served as its president from 1969 onward.

The fifteen trustees in December 1994 were, therefore, a more diversified group than the Endowment had ever before known. One thing that did not change, however, was the strong desire on the part of a majority of the trustees to lessen the Endowment's financial dependence on the Duke Power Company. This desire gathered momentum throughout the 1970s, and no trustee seemed to hold it more strongly than Archie Davis.

Late in 1979 Davis wrote to request a conference with the elusive Doris Duke. "I am surprised by your letter requesting a meeting at this time," she replied. She claimed that she had "agreed wholeheartedly" to a meeting some six months earlier, but it had never materialized because the Endowment's lawyers had changed their minds. "It is, in fact, common knowledge," Doris Duke continued, "that I spend the winter months in Hawaii" and that was why she found it "very curious" that Davis "would be asking for a meeting again" on the eve of her departure. If he wished to meet her in California (where she also owned a home in Beverly Hills) the following week or the following April when she returned, he should let her know.[3] Davis apparently failed to catch her.

The trustees arranged to hold a special meeting in the Mayfair Regent hotel in New York in September 1981. Believing that there was a chance that Doris Duke might be prevailed upon to attend the meeting and listen to the various arguments in favor of greater diversification of the Endowment's portfolio, all of the other trustees gathered for what they hoped would be a most important meeting. Doris Duke, however, did not show up.

Mary Semans, no less than Archie Davis, grappled with the problem. In 1983 she requested the Endowment's longtime counsel in New York, John Spuches, to report to the trustees about developments concerning Duke Power. Spuches reported on the general improvements in the prices of electric utility stocks and noted that Duke Power had figured prominently in that movement. The market value of Duke Power common stock had not been as high as it was in 1983 since the early 1970s. Moreover, for the first time in many years the shares were selling at levels approximating book value, and both major bond-rating agencies had recently granted Duke Power's first mortgage bonds an AA rating, a stature they had not enjoyed for many years.

Spuches went on to point out that the operating efficiencies of Duke Power remained impressively high. The most recent report of the Federal Energy Regulatory Commission had placed six coal-fired generating facilities of Duke Power among the top ten in the nation. Spuches also noted that observers of the electric utility industry were predicting that in the years ahead, the industry would feel significantly less pressure from financing needs imposed by construction programs and that, in general, utilities would be in a position where they would have to exert efforts to utilize their cash profitably rather than stretch themselves to raise it.

Duke Power, according to Spuches, had announced that it would be doing less debt and equity financing during the next several years, and it was buying shares of its common stock on the open market to satisfy the needs of certain employee and shareholder dividend-reinvestment plans. Spuches thought this new development might present a most attractive opportunity for the Endowment, since any sales of its Duke Power common stock directly to Duke Power would obviate the necessity of a registration statement, result in significantly reduced transaction costs, and provide fewer risks for the trustees.[4]

Here, then, was an additional reason why the time was especially right for the Endowment to sell some of its Duke Power stock to the power company itself. Efforts of Mary Semans and the chairman of the Endowment's investment committee to confer with Doris Duke about the matter proved fruitless, however, and the trustees were left in their quandary.

That the matter continued to loom large in the trustees' minds is indicated by another request that they made of John Spuches late in 1985: what legal obligations, if any, were imposed on the Endowment's trustees by the provision in the indenture that they should oversee the operations of the Duke Power company? Spuches began his careful analysis by arguing that J. B. Duke in his indenture *recommended* securities of the Duke Power company as the prime investment for Endowment funds, *advised* against changing the investment except in the most urgent necessity, and *requested* the trustees to see to it that Duke Power was managed and operated by the men best qualified for the job.

"As we have previously advised you," Spuches continued, "we believe this entire provision is precatory only, that is, having the nature of or expressing an entreaty, and not mandatory." If that were so, then the "provision would not be legally binding upon the trustees and would impose no enforceable obligation on them." Spuches went on to say that it was generally conceded that William R. Perkins was a "superb practitioner" and that, since the indenture had been under consideration for a considerable time before it was signed, the language used in it was "chosen carefully to express exactly what Mr. Duke had in mind." There were numerous examples in the indenture, Spuches suggested, that demonstrated that J. B. Duke (and W. R. Perkins) knew the difference between words of entreaty and words of command. For example, Duke stated that it was his "*wish* . . . and he so *directs*" (italics added) that his daughter be elected a trustee when she reached the age of twenty-one. In the paragraph immediately preceding, however, he "suggests, but does not require" that a majority of the trustees be natives or residents of one of the

Carolinas. In short, J. B. Duke used certain words in the indenture to indicate a preference without imposing any binding obligation.

Even if one assumed that J. B. Duke had meant to impose a legally binding obligation on the trustees to oversee the management and operation of Duke Power, Spuches continued, "it is now impossible for the Trustees to fulfill such obligation," because the circumstances were so different from what they were when J. B. Duke established the Endowment. Immediately prior to his death in 1925, Spuches noted, he, his family, and entities controlled by him and his associates owned almost 93 percent of the outstanding common stock of Duke Power, and J. B. Duke was its president. He planned for the same persons to serve as trustees of the Endowment and the Doris Duke Trust (except for Doris Duke, who was to become a trustee of the Endowment only) and for those persons to control the management and operation of Duke Power. He named as the original trustees twelve persons, six of whom were directors of Duke Power (and in four cases also officers of the company) and one of whom, George G. Allen, succeeded J. B. Duke as president of the company. As W. R. Perkins declared in a public speech in 1929, "What Mr. Duke really contributed [to the Endowment] in major part was control and operation of a business."

J. B. Duke's expectations concerning Duke Power, Spuches explained, were fully realized for many years after his death. Until April 1971 each president of Duke Power came from the ranks of the Endowment's trustees, and as late as June 1973 a trustee, Thomas L. Perkins, served as chairman of the board of Duke Power. Trustees constituted a majority of the board of directors of the company at least until the late 1960s. As the percentage of the combined common-stock ownership of the Endowment and the Doris Duke Trust declined from approximately 56 percent in 1956 to approximately 15 percent in 1985, the number of trustees on the Duke Power's board of directors also declined; by 1985 only one trustee served as a director, and none of the Duke Power officers was a trustee.

Spuches explained that the decline in the percentage of common-stock ownership by the Endowment and the Doris Duke Trust was due to two developments, neither of which was reversible: (1) The Tax Reform Act of 1969 had required the Endowment to reduce its percentage of ownership in the common stock of Duke Power to not more than 25 percent by 1979 and prevented it from purchasing any more of the stock; and (2) the fact that the Doris Duke Trust and (during the period to 1970) the Endowment had not possessed sufficient funds to enable them to subscribe for all the shares of common stock to which they had been entitled in the various subscription offerings of Duke Power.

Spuches conceded that one might argue that, in a modern publicly held corporation, the ownership by a group of approximately 15 percent of the outstanding common stock would in many circumstances confer effective working control of such a company on the group. "However, the provisions in the Internal Revenue Code, referred to previously, regarding the disposition of excess business holdings effected by the Tax Reform Act of 1969 were expressly occasioned by the strong desire of Congress to preclude control of public corporations by private foundations. Accordingly, any attempt by the Trustees of The Endowment to effectuate Mr. Duke's intention with respect to the management of Duke Power Company would run squarely afoul of current public policy."[5]

Just as Spuches had provided legal arguments that supported the Endowment's post-1973 policy of distancing itself from the day-to-day operation of Duke University, so too did he elaborate on the legal basis of the Endowment's ridding itself of the task of overseeing the management and operation of Duke Power. He did not, obviously, address the matter of the indenture's requirement, which was not just "precatory," that the Endowment could not sell any of its Duke Power stock except by the unanimous agreement of all the trustees. And Doris Duke stubbornly and defiantly planted her feet firmly on that stipulation. Furthermore, she demonstrated a keen appetite for litigation if she and her expert lawyers believed she had good reason for it.

On one occasion Doris Duke elaborated on her reasons for objecting to the sale of any Duke Power stock by the Endowment. During a civil proceeding concerning the Doris Duke Trust in 1979 she went to a law office in Newark, New Jersey, to make a deposition. When asked at the outset of the proceeding if she were in any way concerned about the heavy concentration in the Endowment's portfolio of Duke Power stock, she replied that she was not concerned about it because, "I have read the Indenture and I know what my father wanted." When next asked if she believed in the principle of diversification, her counsel advised her not to answer the question.

When one of the lawyers present asked Doris Duke why she had stopped going to the meetings of the Endowment trustees, she answered: "I just thought there was very little I as a single vote could contribute. . . . I felt continually frustrated by just being the only one that ever spoke up. Otherwise it was always a rubber stamp [process] and I was always the one asking the questions and bringing up different points. It seemed like nobody really wanted to hear me. So I said, what's the use of my going? So I stopped."

When asked if she had ever considered resigning as a trustee, Doris Duke replied, "I don't think I can." Then when a lawyer asked if he told her that she could resign would that make any difference, her counsel advised her not to answer. "I wouldn't [resign] anyway," she interjected and added that she had informed Mary Semans that she (Doris Duke) did not think her father's plans as spelled out in the indenture should be changed.

Although a bit vague in some of her testimony and generally uninformed about her own business affairs, Doris Duke deposed that she had never sold any of her own Duke Power stock but might have given away some of it for charitable purposes. She stated that she had never read the indenture of trust that established the Doris Duke Trust and had never had anyone explain it to her in detail. "All I know is that it provides me with some money," she declared. She added that her father never discussed it with her, either, but that he had discussed the Endowment with her, telling her that its primary purpose was "to benefit the South."

As for the Endowment's heavy reliance on Duke Power stock, Doris Duke asserted that her father "wanted something that would be a very stable source of income for the foundation — something that was non-speculative." Also he "had great belief in water power as one of the necessities of our particular society." She stated that her father had not discussed the Duke Power company with her but that he "took me around to see it . . . all through [and] around the generators, the turbines and all the mechanics." (Doris Duke was almost thirteen years old when her father died in 1925.) The deposition ended with Doris Duke reiterating her opposition to the sale of any Duke Power stock because it would be "contrary to what my father wanted." He had considered it "the most stable stock that he could give" for his foundation, that "you couldn't have your money in anything safer."[6]

Like a tree planted by the water, Doris Duke would not be moved — as far as the Endowment's holdings in Duke Power were concerned. No doubt, some of the remaining trustees of the Endowment worried more about the matter than others did, but the majority consensus among the trustees throughout the 1980s and into the 1990s seemed to be that it was long past time for the Endowment to seek greater diversification in its portfolio. Just to give the trustees something to think about, John Spuches, from time to time, sent each of them copies of news stories and judicial decisions concerning trustees of foundations or family trusts who were sued for failure to diversify holdings in a timely manner.

The fact seemed to be that nothing short of the death of Doris Duke could alter the situation. Falling and breaking her hip two days after facelift surgery in California in April 1992, she entered what would be a prolonged period of declining health. In January 1993 she underwent surgery to have one arthritic knee replaced. Despite various complications that followed that surgery and against the advice of one of her doctors and some friends, she insisted on having surgery on her other knee in July 1993. Two days after leaving the hospital and going to her home in Beverly Hills, California, she suffered a stroke and nearly died. She returned to the hospital for two months, however, before returning to her home on September 20. There her bedroom had been equipped for her to receive intensive care, with two nurses on duty around the clock, but death came on October 28, 1993, less than a month before what would have been her eighty-first birthday on November 22.[7]

The trustees of the Duke Endowment, and particularly Mary Semans, had long deeply regretted the alienation of Doris Duke from the Endowment. It had gone on, however, for over twenty years and had proven to be something that the trustees could not change and therefore something that they simply had to accept as a given. After passing an appropriate and traditional resolution concerning the death of a fellow trustee, however, the trustees also decided in December 1993 that the officers of the Endowment should begin proceedings looking toward a sale of a large portion of the Duke Power stock. As of the last day of 1993, the Endowment held over 26 million shares of the stock, valued at more than $1.1 billion. Then at their meeting in March 1994 the trustees voted to sell 16 million of those shares.

The sale of such a large block of utility stock was obviously not a routine transaction. John G. Mebane Jr., the Endowment's senior investment officer, along with other representatives from the Endowment and from Duke Power, began conferring with leading investment banking firms in New York in December 1993. The trustees then selected Goldman, Sachs & Company to serve as the lead underwriter of the massive sale, and Merrill Lynch & Company and Morgan Stanley & Company to serve as comanagers. After elaborate preparation of documentary material as well as slides and other material for on-screen presentation, several teams composed of representatives from the investment houses, the Endowment, and Duke Power embarked on a whirlwind tour of many of the major cities in the United States and in western Europe. Mebane and his colleagues referred to the tour as "the road show," the purpose of which was, of course, to create interest in acquiring large blocks of Duke Power stocks on the part of banks, investment groups, and others. By March 29, 1994, the task was done, and the final sale took place.[8]

From holding over 57 percent of Duke Power's common stock in 1962, the Endowment had seen its share shrink to 12.7 percent in 1993. Yet that percentage consisted of over 26 million shares. After the big sell-off of March, 1994, the Endowment continued to hold approximately 10 million shares of Duke Power stock, but that was only about 5 percent of the company's outstanding stock. From the Endowment's investment perspective, the sale of the Duke Power stock permitted the creation of a more diversified portfolio, with the concentration in one company being reduced from 77.5 percent as of the end of 1993 to only 30.8 percent at the end of 1994.

As of the end of 1994, of the Endowment's total income received on investments since December 1924, over $955,445,000 or 71 percent represented dividends on Duke Power stock. That relationship between J. B. Duke's perpetual charitable trust and the power company he had established and so much esteemed had, however, finally been terminated. A substantial part of his Grand Design for perpetual philanthropy in the Carolinas no longer existed.

From the Endowment's inception late in 1924 until the end of 1994, its total income amounted to almost $1,167,945,000. Duke University, the prime beneficiary, had received almost $481 million of that; Davidson and Furman had each received over $46 million; and Johnson C. Smith almost $40 million. In the hospital and health-care area, the Endowment had contributed almost $411 million and in the child-care field over $50 million. Superannuated Methodist preachers or their surviving spouses had received almost $14 million; almost $28 million had been given to help build rural Methodist churches and over $18 million to help maintain and operate them.[9]

Unlike the trustees of some foundations that have been known to stray fairly far from the original intent of the donor, the trustees of the Endowment had both faithfully and imaginatively continued for seventy years to do precisely those things that J. B. Duke had wanted done. After 1994, however, they would do them with drastically less of the total income being derived from stock in his cherished Duke Power Company. The Endowment's annual assistance to its beneficiaries went on, in ever increasing amounts and in more imaginative ways than ever, but an important part of James B. Duke's Grand Design was gone.

APPENDICES

| Name | Duke University | | Duke Power Company | | |
	Trustee	Exec. Com.	Director	Officer	Officer-dates
Allen	1923–1958	1923–1958	3-04-25/10-10-60	Vice President President Chairman Hon. Chairman	3-23-25/10-27-25 10-27-25/3-29-49 3-29-49/3-26-57 3-26-57/3-13-59
Burkholder			3-04-25/3-13-48	Vice President	12-07-27/3-13-48
Cocke	1947–1960 Chairman: 1954–1960	1951–1960	3-04-25/7-25-66	Vice President President	3-07-28/9-29-53 9-29-53/1-01-59
Lee			3-04-25/3-24-34	Vice President	3-23-25/3-24-34
Marshall			10-27-25/9-21-53	Vice President President	3-27-34/3-29-49 3-29-49/9-21-53
Parker			3-04-25/11-13-55	Sec. & Treas.	3-23-25/11-13-55
Perkins	1924–1945	1937–1945	3-04-25/6-15-45	Vice President	10-27-25/6-15-45
Sands	1946–1960	1946–1960	4-04-35/4-22-60	Assistant Sec. Vice President Chair., Fin. Com.	4-04-35/4-26-55 4-26-55/4-22-60 11-26-57/4-22-60
Duke	1924–1925		3-4-25/10-10-25	President	3-23-25/10-10-25
Flowers	1927–1951 President: 1941–1948	1927–1951			

Name	The Duke Endowment			
	Birth	Elected	Resigned	Died
Jonathan E. Cox	11-1-1856	10-26-26		3-29-32
William N. Reynolds	3-22-1863	2-24-31		9-10-51
William S. O'B. Robinson Jr.	6-25-1885	4-26-32		1-11-67
Doris Duke	11-22-1912	11-28-33		10-28-93
Thomas L. Perkins V. Chairman 4-26-60/10-25-60 Chairman 10-25-60/6-21-73	11-9-1905	3-30-48		6-21-73
Walker P. Inman	8-21-1894	10-30-48		9-19-54
Philip B. Heartt Asst. Sec. 9-27-38/10-27-53 Secretary 10-27-53/2-28-61	2-16-1896	1-30-51	12-31-75	1-9-83
Benjamin F. Few V. Chairman 11-29-60/1-27-70	11-10-1894	9-25-51	12-31-73	3-05-78
Marshall I. Pickens Asst. Sec. 1-29-46/2-28-61 Secretary 2-28-61/1-25-66 V. Chairman 1-25-66/6-27-73 Chairman 6-27-73/12-31-74	1-23-1904	9-25-51		11-26-91
R. Grady Rankin V. Chairman 11-29-60/1-25-66	2-25-1891	10-27-53		7-13-76
Kenneth C. Towe	1-19-1893	10-26-54		1-6-78
Thomas F. Hill	12-3-1889	11-29-55		12-31-70
Mary D. B. T. Semans V. Chairman 1-27-70/12-1-82 Chairman 12-1-82	2-21-1920	4-30-57		
Randolph E. DuMont Asst. Treas. 1-30-45/11-29-55 Treasurer 11-29-55/7-9-61	6-8-1902	5-31-60		7-09-61

Duke University		Duke Power Company			
Name	Trustee	Exec. Com.	Director	Officer	Officer-dates
Reynolds	1927–1951	1933–1951			
Robinson			2-24-27/4-27-66	Vice President	3-25-41/3-26-57
				Vice-Chairman	10-27-53/3-26-57
				Chairman	3-26-57/3-31-59
				Mem., Fin. Com.	11-26-57/4-27-66
Perkins	1958–1973	1958–1973	11-29-55/6-21-73	Chairman	4-24-61/6-21-73
				Mem., Fin. Com.	11-26-57/6-21-73
Inman	1949–1954		2-25-47/9-19-54		
Heartt			6-27-60/2-26-48	Assistant Sec.	4-26-55/11-29-55
				Secretary	11-29-55/2-27-61
				Mem., Retire Com.	4-27-48/2-26-68
				Mem., Fin. Com.	6-27-60/1-29-68
				Chair., Fin. Com.	7-25-60/1-29-68
Few	1941–1967	1960–1965	10-29-57/9-27-69	Mem., Fin. Com.	11-26-57/9-27-69
Pickens	1963–1974		4-22-64/4-30-82	Mem., Fin. Com.	9-26-66/4-30-82
Rankin			2-26-35/7-25-66	Mem., Fin. Com.	11-26-57/7-25-66
Towe	1954–1963	1960–1963	10-29-57/2-26-68	Mem., Fin. Com.	11-26-57/2-26-68
Hill			9-25-45/3-31-59	V. President	3-28-50/3-31-59
Semans	1961–1981	1971–1981			
DuMont				Asst. Treasurer	11-29-55/7-9-61

Name	The Duke Endowment			
	Birth	Elected	Resigned	Died
Wilburt C. Davison	4-28-1892	2-28-61		6-26-72
Amos R. Kearns	7-22-1905	1-30-62		7-28-79
Robert McCormack Chairman 1-1-82/11-8-82	7-31-1913	3-30-65		11-8-82
William B. McGuire V. Chairman 12-1-82/12-31-88	7-26-1910	3-30-65	12-31-88	
Richard B. Henney Asst. Treas. 11-29-55/10-31-61 Treasurer 10-31-61/1-25-66 Secretary 1-25-66/6-27-73 Exec. Dir. 1-26-71/5-30-79	6-21-1918	3-28-67		5-30-79
James R. Felts Jr. Asst. Sec. 2-28-61/1-30-74	8-5-1912	4-26-71		8-20-87
J. Kelly Sisk	3-3-1913	4-26-71		11-6-80
Archie K. Davis V. Chairman 6-27-73/12-31-74 Chairman 1-1-75/12-31-81	1-22-1911	10-31-72	12-31-95	
John D. deButts V. Chairman 1-29-75/1-27-82	4-10-1915	12-5-73		12-17-86
James C. Self	10-19-1919	6-26-74	9-14-95	
Charles F. Myers Jr.	7-17-1911	5-26-76		
Frank H. Kenan	8-3-1912	1-26-77	1-4-90	6-4-96
W. Kenneth Goodson	9-25-1912	6-28-78		9-19-91
Juanita M. Kreps	1-11-1921	11-28-79		
Louis C. Stephens Jr. V. Chairman 1-27-82	12-19-1921	1-30-80		
Hugh M. Chapman V. Chairman 6-6-89	9-11-1932	5-27-81		

Name	Duke University		Duke Power Company		
	Trustee	Exec. Com.	Director	Officer	Officer-dates
Kearns	1945–1975	1948–1962 1963–1975			
McGuire			12-28-54/4-29-75	Asst. to President President Mem., Fin. Com. Consultant	10-30-56/1-1-59 1-1-59/4-28-71 1959–71; 1973–75 1971–75
Henney			1-29-68/4-29-75	Asst. Treasurer Mem., Fin. Com. Chair., Fin. Com.	7-24-61/3-1-68 2-26-68/4-29-75 2-26-68/1-1-75
Self			4-30-82/4-23-92	Mem., Fin. Com.	4-30-82/4-23-92
Goodson	1966–1969 1972–1978				

Name	The Duke Endowment			
	Birth	Elected	Resigned	Died
Charles B. Wade Jr.	7-8-1915	5-4-83		7-16-94
Russell M. Robinson II	3-13-1932	5-5-87		
Mary D. T. Jones	7-15-1940	2-2-88		
Richard W. Riley	1-2-1933	5-2-89	1-21-93	
William G. Anlyan	10-14-1925	6-5-90		
Thomas S. Kenan III	4-19-1937	4-7-92		
Thomas A. Langford	2-22-1929	4-7-92		
John Hope Franklin	1-2-1915	4-6-93		
Richard H. Jenrette	4-5-1929	3-1-94		
E. Craig Wall Jr.	8-22-1937	10-4-94		3-5-97
John G. Medlin Jr.	11-23-1933	3-5-96		
Constance F. Gray	8-27-1947	6-4-96		

Duke University		Duke Power Company			
Name	Trustee	Exec. Com.	Director	Officer	Officer-dates
Wade	1964–1977 1979–1983	Chairman: 1968–1971	7-71/4-76	Mem., Audit Com.	1974
Robinson			1-13-95	Mem., Audit Com.	1995

James B. Duke

TO

Nanaline H. Duke and Others, Trustees

Indenture and Deed of Trust of Personalty
Establishing
The Duke Endowment
December 11, 1924

THIS INDENTURE made in quadruplicate this 11th day of December, 1924, by and between JAMES B. DUKE, residing at Duke Farms, near Somerville, in the County of Somerset, and State of New Jersey, United States of America, party of the first part, and NANALINE H. DUKE, of Somerville, N.J., GEORGE G. ALLEN, of Hartsdale, N.Y., WILLIAM R. PERKINS, of Montclair, N.J., WILLIAM B. BELL, of New York City, N.Y., ANTHONY J. DREXEL BIDDLE, JR., of New York City, N.Y., WALTER C. PARKER, of New Rochelle, N.Y., ALEX H. SANDS, of Montclair, N.J., WILLIAM S. LEE, of Charlotte, N.C., CHARLES I. BURKHOLDER, of Charlotte, N.C., NORMAN A. COCKE, of Charlotte, N.C., EDWARD C. MARSHALL, of Charlotte, N.C. and BENNETTE E. GEER, of Greenville, S.C., as trustees and their successors as trustees under and in accordance with the terms of this Indenture, to be known as the Board of Trustees of the Endowment, parties of the second part,

WITNESSETH:

That in order to effectuate the trusts hereby created, the first party has given, assigned, transferred and delivered, and by these presents does give, assign, transfer and deliver, the following property, to wit:

122,647 Shares of Stock of Duke Power Company, a corporation organized and existing under the laws of the State of New Jersey.

100,000 Ordinary Shares of the Stock of British-American Tobacco Company, Limited, a corporation organized and existing under the laws of Great Britain.

75,000 Shares of the Common "B" Stock of R. J. Reynolds Tobacco Company, a corporation organized and existing under the laws of said State of New Jersey.

5,000 Shares of the Common Stock of George W. Helme Company, a corporation organized and existing under the laws of said State of New Jersey.

12,325 Shares of the Stock of Republic Cotton Mills, a corporation organized and existing under the laws of the State of South Carolina.

7,935-3/10 Shares of the Common Stock of Judson Mills, a corporation organized and existing under the laws of said State of South Carolina.

unto said trustees and their successors as trustees hereunder, in trust, to be held, used, managed, administered and disposed of, as well as all additions and accretions thereto and all incomes, revenues and profits thereof and there-from, forever for the charitable purposes, in the manner and upon the terms herein expressly provided, and not otherwise, namely:

FIRST.

The trust established by this Indenture is hereby denominated The Duke Endowment, and shall have perpetual existence.

SECOND.

Each trustee herein named, as well as each trustee selected hereunder, shall be and remain a trustee so long as such trustee shall live and continue mentally and physically capable of performing the duties of a trustee hereunder, subject to resignation and to removal as hereinafter stated. The number of trustees within two years from the date of this Indenture shall be increased to, and thereafter remain at, fifteen, such increase being made by vote of the trustees at any meeting. He suggests, but does not require, that, so far as practicable, no one may be selected trustee if thereby at such time a majority of the trustees be not natives and/or residents of the States of North Carolina and/or South Carolina. It is the wish of the party of the first part, and he so directs, that his daughter, Doris Duke, upon attaining the age of twenty-one years, shall be made a trustee hereunder, for that purpose being elected to fill any vacancy then existing, or, if there be no such vacancy, added to the trustees thereby making the number of trustees sixteen until the next occurring of a vacancy, whereupon the number of trust again become and remain fifteen.

Subject to the terms of this Indenture, the trustees may adopt and change at any time rules and regulations which shall govern in the management and administration of the trust and trust property.

Meetings of the trustees shall be held at least ten times in each calendar year at such time and place and upon such notice as the rules and regulations may provide. Other meetings of the trustees may be held upon the call in writing of the chairman or a vice-chairman or any three trustees given in accordance with the rules and regulations, at such place and time and for such purpose as may be specified in the call. A majority of the then trustees shall constitute a quorum at any such meeting, but less than a majority may adjourn any such meeting from time to time and from place to place until a quorum shall be present. The affirmative vote of the majority of a quorum shall be necessary and sufficient at any such meeting to authorize any action by the trustees hereunder, except as herein otherwise expressly provided. Written records, setting forth all action taken at said meetings and the voting, thereon, shall be kept in a permanent minute book of the trustees, and shall be signed by each trustee present at the meeting.

The trustees shall select annually from their number a chairman and two vice-chairmen, and a secretary and a treasurer, who need not be trustees. Such officers shall hold office for one year and thereafter until their respective successors shall be selected. The compensation of the secretary and treasurer shall be that fixed by the trustees.

The trustees shall establish an office, which may be changed from time, which shall be known as the principal office of this trust, and at it shall be kept the books and papers other than securities relating to this trust.

By the affirmative vote of a majority of the then trustees any officer, and by the affirmative vote of three-fourths of the then trustees any trustee, may be removed for any cause whatever at any meeting of the trustees called for the purpose in accordance with the rules and regulations.

Vacancies occurring among the trustees from any cause whatever (for which purpose an increase in the number of trustees shall be deemed to cause vacancies to the extent of such increase in number of trustees) may be filled by the remaining trustees at any meeting of the trustees, and must be so filled within six months after the vacancy occurs; provided that no person (except said Doris Duke) shall remain or become a trustee hereunder who shall not be or at once become a trustee under the trust this day being created by the party of the first part by Indenture which will bear even date herewith for his said daughter and his kin and their descendants, so long as said latter trust shall be in existence.

Each trustee shall be paid at the end of each calendar year one equal fifteenth part of three percent of the incomes, revenues and profits received by the trustees upon the trust properties and estate during such year, provided that if any trustee by reason of death, resignation, or any other cause, shall have served during only a part of such year, there shall be paid to such trustee, if alive, or if such trustee be dead than to the personal representatives of such trustee, such a part of said one-fifteenth as the time during which said trustee served during such year shall bear to the whole of such year, such payment to be in full for all services as trustee hereunder and for all expenses of the trustees. In the event that any trustee shall serve in any additional capacity (other than as chairman or vice-president) the trustees may add to the foregoing compensation such additional compensation as the trustees may think such trustee should receive by reason of serving in such additional capacity.

No act done by any one or more of the trustees shall be valid or binding unless it shall have been authorized or until it shall be ratified as required by this Indenture.

The trustees are urged to make a special effort to secure persons of character and ability, not only as trustees, but as officials and employees.

THIRD.

For the purpose of managing and administering the trust, and the properties and funds in the trust, hereby created, said trustees shall have and may exercise the following powers, namely:

To manage and administer in all respects the trust hereby created and the properties and funds held and arising hereunder, in accordance with the terms hereof, obtaining and securing for such purpose such assistants, office space, force, equipment and supplies, and any other aid and facilities, upon such terms, as the trustees may deem necessary from time to time.

To hold, use, manage, administer and dispose of each and every of the properties which at any time, and from time to time, may be held in this trust, and to collect and receive the incomes, revenues and profits arising therefrom and accruing thereto, provided that said trustees shall not have power to dispose of the whole or any part of the share capital (or rights of subscription thereto) of Duke Power Company, a New Jersey corporation, or of any subsidiary thereof, except upon and by the affirmative vote of the total authorized number of trustees at a meeting called for the purpose, the minutes of which shall state the reasons for and terms of such sale.

To invest any funds from time to time arising or accruing through the receipt and collection of incomes, revenues and profits, sale of properties, or otherwise, provided the said trustees may not lend the whole or any part of such funds except to said Duke Power Company, nor may said trustees invest the whole or any part of such funds in any property of any kind except in securities of said Duke Power Company, or of a subsidiary thereof, or in bonds validly issued by the United States of America, or by a State thereof, or by a district, county, town or city which has a population in excess of fifty thousand people according to the then last Federal census, which is located in the United States of America, which has not since 1900 defaulted in the payment of any principal or interest upon or with respect to any of its obligations, and the bonded indebtedness of which does not exceed ten per cent of its assessed values. Provided further that whenever the said trustees shall desire to invest any such funds the same shall be either lent to said Duke Power or invested in the securities of said Duke Power Company or of a subsidiary thereof, if and to the extent that such a loan or such securities are available upon terms and conditions satisfactory to said trustees.

To utilize each year in accordance with the terms of this Indenture the incomes, revenues and profits arising and accruing from the trust estate for such year in defraying the cost, expenses and charges incurred in the management and administration of this trust and its funds and properties, and in applying and distributing the net amount of such incomes, revenues and profits thereafter remaining to and for the objects and purposes of this trust.

As respects any year or years and any purpose or purposes for which this trust is created (except the payments hereinafter directed to be made to Duke University) the trustees in their uncontrolled discretion may withhold the whole or any part of said incomes, revenues and profits which would otherwise be distributed under the "FIFTH" division hereof, and either (1) accumulate the whole or any part of the amounts so withheld for expenditures (which the trustees are hereby authorized to make thereof) for the same purpose in any future year or years, or (2) add the whole or any part of the amounts so withheld to the corpus of the trust, or (3) pay, apply and distribute the whole or any part of said amounts to and for the benefit of any one or more of the other purposes of this trust, or (4) pay, apply and distribute the whole or any part of said amounts to or for the benefit of any such like charitable, religious or educational purpose within the State of North Carolina and/or the State of South Carolina and/or any such like charitable hospital purpose which shall be selected therefor by the affirmative vote of three-fourths of the then trustees at any meeting of the trustees called for the purpose, complete authority and discretion in and for such selection and utilization being hereby given the trustees in the premises.

By the consent of three-fourths of the then trustees expressed in a writing signed by them, which shall state the reasons therefor and be recorded in the minutes of the trustees, and not otherwise, the trustees may (1) cause to be formed under the laws of such state or states as may be selected by the trustees for that purpose a corporation or corporations so incorporated and empowered as that the said corporation or corporations can and will assume and carry out in whole or in part the trust hereby created, with the then officers and trustees hereof officers and directors, thereof, with like powers and duties, and (2) convey, transfer and deliver to said corporation or corporations the whole or any part of the properties then held in this trust, to be held, used, managed, administered and disposed of by said corporation or corporations for any one or more of the charitable purposes expressed in this Indenture and upon all the terms and with all the terms, powers and duties expressed in this Indenture with respect to the same, provided that such conveyances, transfers and deliveries shall be upon such terms and conditions as that in case any such corporation or corporations shall cease to exist for any cause the property so transferred shall forthwith revert and belong to the trustees of this trust and become a part of the corpus of this trust for all the purposes thereof.

Said trustees shall have and may exercise, subject to the provisions of this Indenture, any and all other powers which are necessary or desirable in order to manage and administer the trust and the properties and funds thereof and carry out and perform in all respects the terms of this Indenture according to the true intent thereof.

Any assignment, transfer, bill of sale, deed, conveyance, receipt, check, draft, note, or any other document or paper whatever, executed by or on behalf of the trustees, shall be sufficiently executed when signed by the person or persons authorized so to do by a resolution of the trustees duly adopted at any meeting and in accordance with the terms of such resolution.

FOURTH.

The trustees hereunder are hereby authorized and directed to expend as soon as reasonably may be not exceeding Six Million Dollars of the corpus of this trust in establishing at a location to be selected by them within the State of North Carolina an institution of learning to be known as Duke University, for such purpose to acquire such lands and erect and equip thereon such buildings according to such plans as the trustees may in their judgment deem necessary and adopt and approve for the purpose, to cause to be formed under the laws of such state as the trustees may select for the purpose a corporation adequately empowered to own and operate such properties under the name Duke University as an institution of learning according to the true intent hereof, and to convey to such corporation when formed the said lands, buildings and equipment upon such terms and conditions as that such corporation may use the same only for such purposes of such university and upon the same ceasing to be so used then the same shall forthwith revert and belong to the trustees of this trust as and become a part of the corpus of this trust for all of the purposes thereof.

However, should the name of Trinity College, located at Durham, North

Carolina, a body politic and incorporate, within three months from the date hereof (or such further time as the trustees hereof may allow) be changed to Duke University, then, in lieu of the foregoing provisions of division "FOURTH" of this Indenture, as a memorial to his father, Washington Duke, who spent his life in Durham and whose gifts, together with those of Benjamin N. Duke, the brother of the party of the first part, and of other members of the Duke family, have so largely contributed toward making possible Trinity College at that place, he directs that the trustees shall expend of the corpus of this trust as soon as reasonably may be a sum not exceeding Six Million Dollars in expanding and extending said University, and improving such lands, and erecting, removing, remodeling and equipping such buildings, according to such plans, as the trustees may adopt and approve for such purpose to the end that said Duke University may eventually include Trinity College as its undergraduate department for men, a School of Religious Training, a School for Training Teachers, a School of Chemistry, a Law School, a Co-ordinate College for Women, a School of Business Administration, a Graduate School of Arts and Sciences, a Medical School and an Engineering School, as and when funds are available.

FIFTH.

The trustees hereof shall pay, apply, divide and distribute the net amount of said incomes, revenues and profits each calendar year as follows, to wit:

Twenty per cent of said net amount shall be retained by said trustees and added to the corpus of this trust as a part thereof for the purpose of increasing the principal of the trust estate until the total aggregate of such additions to the corpus of the trust shall be as much as Forty Million Dollars.

Thirty-two per cent of said net amount not retained as aforesaid for addition to the corpus of this trust shall be paid to that Duke University for which expenditures of the corpus of the trust shall have been made by the trustees under the "FOURTH" division of this Indenture so long as its name shall be Duke University and it shall not be operated for private gain, to be utilized by its Board of Trustees in defraying its administration and operating expenses, increasing and improving its facilities and equipment, the erection and enlargement of buildings and the acquisition of additional acreage for it, adding to its endowment, or in such other manner for it as the Board of Trustees of said institution may from time to time deem to be to its best interests, provided that in case such institution shall incur any expense or liability beyond provision already in sight to meet same, or in the judgment of the trustees under this Indenture be not operated in a manner calculated to achieve the results intended hereby, the trustees under this Indenture may withhold the whole or any part of such percentage from said institution so long as such character of expense or liabilities or operations shall continue, such amounts so withheld to be in whole or in part either accumulated and applied to the purposes of such University in any future year or years, or utilized for the other objects of this Indenture, or added to the corpus of this trust for the purpose of increasing the principal of the trust estate, as the trustees may determine.

Thirty-two percent of said net amount not retained as aforesaid for addition to the corpus of this trust shall be utilized for maintaining and securing such hospitals, not operated for private gain, as the said trustees, in their uncontrolled discretion, may from time to time select for the purpose and are located within the States of North Carolina and/or South Carolina, such utilization to be exercised in the following manner, namely: (a) By paying to each and every such hospital, whether for white or colored, and not operated for private gain, such sum (not exceeding One Dollar) per free bed per day for each and every day that said free bed may have been occupied during the period covered by such payment free of charge by patients unable to pay as the amount available for this purpose hereunder will pay on a pro rata basis; and (b) in the event that said amount in any year shall be more than sufficient for the foregoing purpose, the whole or any part of the residue thereof may be expended by said trustees in assisting in the erection and/or equipment within either or both of said States of any such hospital not operated for private gain, payment for this purpose in each case to be in such amount and on such terms and conditions as the trustees hereof may determine. In the event that said amount in any year be more than sufficient for both of the aforesaid purposes, the trustees in their uncontrolled discretion may pay and expend the whole or any part of the residue thereof in like manner for maintaining and securing hospitals not operated for private gain in any other State or States, giving preference, however, to those States contiguous to the States of North Carolina and South Carolina. And said trustees as respects any year may exclude from participation hereunder any hospital or hospitals which the trustees in their uncontrolled discretion may think so financed as not to need, or so maintained and operated as not to deserve, inclusion hereunder.

Five per cent of said net amount not retained as aforesaid for addition to the corpus of the trust shall be paid to Davidson College (by whatever name it may be known) now located at Davidson, in the State of North Carolina, so long as it shall not be operated for private gain, to be utilized by said institution for any and all of the purposes thereof.

Five per cent of said net amount not retained as aforesaid for addition to the corpus of the trust shall be paid to Furman University (by whatever name it may be known) now located at Greenville, in the State of South Carolina, so long as it shall not be operated for private gain, to be utilized by said institution for any and all of the purposes thereof.

Four per cent of said net amount not retained as aforesaid for addition to the corpus of the trust shall be paid to the Johnson C. Smith University (by whatever name it may be known), an institution of learning for colored people, now located at Charlotte, in said State of North Carolina, so long as it shall not be operated for private gain, to be utilized by said institution for any and all of the purposes thereof.

Ten per cent of said net amount not retained as aforesaid for addition to the corpus of this trust shall be paid and distributed to and among such of those organizations, institutions, agencies and/or societies, whether public or private, by whatsoever name they may be known, not operated for private gain, which during such year in the judgment of said trustees have been properly operated as organizations, institutions, agencies and/or societies for the benefit of white or colored whole or half orphans within the States of North Carolina and/or South Carolina, and in such amounts as between and among such organizations, institutions, agencies and/or societies as may be selected and determined as respects each year by said trustees in their uncontrolled discretion, all such payments and distributions to be used by such organizations, institutions, agencies and/or societies exclusively for the benefit of such orphans.

Two per cent of said net amount not retained as aforesaid for addition to the corpus of the trust shall be paid and expended by the trustees for the care and maintenance of needy and deserving superannuated preachers and needy and deserving widows and orphans of deceased preachers who shall have served in a Conference of the Methodist Episcopal Church, South (by whatever name it may be known) located in the State of North Carolina.

Six per cent of said net amount not retained as aforesaid for addition to the corpus of the trust shall be paid and expended by the trustees in assisting (that is, in giving or lending in no case more than fifty per cent of what may be required for the purpose) to build Methodist churches under and connected with a Conference of the Methodist Episcopal Church, South (by whatever name it may be known) located in the State of North Carolina, but only those churches located in the sparsely settled rural districts of the State of North Carolina and not in any city, town or hamlet, incorporated or unincorporated, having a population in excess of fifteen hundred people according to the then last Federal census.

Four percent of said net amount not retained as aforesaid for addition to the corpus of the trust shall be paid and expended by the trustees in assisting (that is, in giving or lending in no case more than fifty per cent of what may be required for the purpose) to maintain and operate the Methodist churches of such a Conference which are located within the sparsely settled rural districts of the State of North Carolina, and not in any city, town or hamlet, incorporated or unincorporated, having a population in excess of fifteen hundred people according to the then last Federal census.

Expenditures and payments made hereunder for maintaining such superannuated preachers, and such widows and orphans, as well as for assisting to build, maintain and operate such Methodist churches, shall be in the uncontrolled discretion of the trustees as respects the time, terms, place, amounts and beneficiaries thereof and therefor; and he suggests that such expenditures and payments be made through the use of said Duke University as an agency for that purpose so long as such method is satisfactory to the trustees hereof.

SIXTH.

Subject to the other provisions of this Indenture, said trustees may pay, apply, divide and distribute such incomes, revenues and profits at such time or times as may in their discretion be found best suited to the due administration and management of this trust, but only for the purposes allowed by this Indenture.

In the event that any stock dividend or rights shall be declared upon any of the stock held under this instrument, the said stock and rights distributed pursuant thereto shall for all purposes be treated and deemed to be principal though the said stock dividend and/or rights shall represent earnings.

No trustee hereby appointed and no trustee selected in pursuance of any powers herein contained shall be required to give any bond or other security for the performance of his, her or its duties as such trustee, nor shall any trustee be required to reserve any part of the income of any investment or security for the purpose of creating a sinking fund to retire or absorb the premium in the case of bonds or any other securities whatever taken over, purchased or acquired by the trustees at a premium.

The term "subsidiary" as herein used shall mean any company at least fifty-one per cent of the voting share capital of which is owned by said Duke Power Company.

The party of the first part hereby expressly reserves the right to add to the corpus of the trust hereby established by way of last will and testament and/or otherwise, and in making such additions to stipulate and declare that such additions and the incomes, revenues and profits accruing from such additions shall be used and disposed of by the trustees for any of the foregoing and/or any other charitable purposes, with like effect as if said additions, as well as the terms concerning same and the incomes, revenues and profits thereof, had been originally incorporated herein. In the absence of any such stipulation or declaration each and every such addition shall constitute a part of the corpus of this trust for all of the purposes of this Indenture.

SEVENTH.

The party of the first part hereby declares for the guidance of the trustees hereunder:

For many years I have been engaged in the development of water powers in certain sections of the States of North Carolina and South Carolina. In my study of this subject I have observed how such utilization of a natural resource, which otherwise would run in waste to the sea and not remain and increase as a forest, both gives impetus to industrial life and provides a safe and enduring investment for capital. My ambition is that the revenues of such development shall administer to the social welfare, as the operation of such developments is administering to the economic welfare, of the communities which they serve. With these views in mind I recommend the securities of the Southern Power System (the Duke Power Company and its subsidiary companies) as the prime investment for the funds of this trust; and I advise the trustees that they do not change any such investment except in response to the most urgent and extraordinary necessity; and I request the trustees to see to it that at all times these companies be managed and operated by the men best qualified for such a service.

I have selected Duke University as one of the principal objects of this trust because I recognize that education, when conducted along sane and practical, as opposed to dogmatic and theoretical, lines, is, next to religion, the greatest civilizing influence. I request that this institution secure for its officers, trustees and faculty men of such outstanding character, ability and vision as will insure its attaining and maintaining a place of real leadership in the educational world, and that great care and discrimination be exercised in admitting as students only those whose previous record shows a character, determination and application evincing a wholesome and real ambition for life. And I advise that the courses at this institution be arranged, first, with special reference to the training of preachers, teachers, lawyers and physicians, because these are most in the public eye, and by precept and example can do most to uplift mankind, and, second, to instruction in chemistry, economics and history, especially the lives of the great of earth, because I believe that such subjects will most help to develop our resources, increase our wisdom and promote human happiness.

I have selected hospitals as another of the principal objects of this trust because I recognize that they have become indispensable institutions, not only by way of ministering to the comfort of the sick but in increasing the efficiency of mankind and prolonging human life. The advance in the science of medicine growing out of discoveries, such as in the field of bacteriology, chemistry and physics, and growing out of inventions such as the X-ray apparatus, make hospital facilities essential for obtaining the best results in the practice of medicine and surgery. So worthy do I deem the cause and so great do I deem the need that I very much hope that the people will see to it that adequate and convenient hospitals are assured in their respective communities, with especial reference to those who are unable to defray such expenses of their own.

I have included orphans in an effort to help those who are most unable to help themselves, a worthy cause, productive of truly beneficial results in which all good citizens should have an abiding interest. While in my opinion nothing can take the place of a home and its influences, every effort should be made to safeguard and develop these wards of society.

And, lastly, I have made provision for what I consider a very fertile and much neglected field for useful help in religious life, namely assisting by way of support and maintenance in those cases where the head of the family through devoting his life to the religious service of his fellow men has been unable to accumulate for his declining years and for his widow and children, and assisting in the building and maintenance of churches in rural districts where the people are not able to do this properly for themselves, believing that such a pension system is a just call which will secure a better grade of service and that the men and women of these rural districts will amply respond to such assistance to them, not to mention our own Christian duty regardless of such results. Indeed my observation and the broad expanse of our territory make me believe it is to these rural districts that we are to look in large measure for the bone and sinew of our country.

From the foregoing it will be seen that I have endeavored to make provision in some measure for the needs of mankind along physical, mental and spiritual lines, largely confining the benefactions to those sections served by these water power developments. I might have extended this aid to other charitable objects and to other sections, but my opinion is that so doing probably would be productive of less good by reason of attempting too much. I therefore urge the trustees to seek to administer well the trust hereby committed to them within the limits set, and to this end that at least at one meeting each year this Indenture be read to the assembled trustees.

EIGHTH.

This Indenture is executed by a resident of the State of New Jersey in said State, is intended to be made, administered and given effect under and in accordance with the present existing laws and statutes of said State, notwithstanding it may be administered and the beneficiaries hereof may be located in whole or in part in other states, and the validity and construction thereof shall be determined and governed in all respects by such laws and statutes.

It being the purpose and intention of this Indenture that no part of the corpus or income of the trust estate hereby created shall ever for any cause revert to the party of the first part, or to his heirs, personal representatives or assigns, it is hereby declared that: (a) Each object and purpose of this trust shall be deemed and treated as separate and distinct from each and every other object and purpose thereof to the end that no provision of this trust shall be deemed or declared illegal, invalid or unenforceable by reason of any other provision or provisions of this trust being adjudged or declared illegal, invalid or unenforceable; and that in the event of any one or more of the provisions of this trust being declared or adjudged illegal, invalid or unenforceable that each and every other provision of this trust shall take effect as if the provision or provisions so declared or adjudged to be illegal, invalid or unenforceable had never been contained in this Indenture; and any and all properties and funds which would have been utilized under and pursuant to any provision so declared or adjudged illegal, invalid or unenforceable shall be utilized under and in accordance with the other provisions of this Indenture which shall not be declared or adjudged illegal, invalid or unenforceable; and (b) in the event any beneficiary for which provision is made shall cease to exist for any cause whatever, then so much of the funds and properties of this trust as otherwise would be utilized for the same shall be thereafter utilized for the remaining objects and purposes of this trust.

IN WITNESS WHEREOF, the said JAMES B. DUKE, at his residence at Duke Farms in the State of New Jersey, has subscribed his name and affixed his seal to this Indenture, consisting with this page and the preceding and following pages of twenty-one pages, each page of which, except the following page, he has identified by signing his name on the margin thereof, all on the day and year first above written.

JAMES B. DUKE (L.S.)

A NOTE ON

SOURCES

SINCE THERE ARE rather few secondary accounts that were important for this study — and they are cited in the footnotes — this brief essay will focus on the principal source, the backbone, of the volume, the Duke Endowment Archives.

Housed in Special Collections of the W. R. Perkins Library, Duke University, the Endowment's archives constitute a mammoth treasure trove of data, only a portion of which was used in the research for *Lasting Legacy*. Materials covering the period from 1924 (and some are of an earlier date) through 1992 occupy over 282 linear feet of shelf space, and more material has come in regularly since 1992.

Access to portions of the archives is restricted, although scholars and others may apply for the Endowment's permission to use specified parts of them. The staff of Special Collections has prepared a careful Inventory File of the Endowment's archives, and it presents detailed information about the various series in the collection. Some of those series — such as the voluminous financial records in the Controller's Office (CO) Series and the Investment Office (IO) Series — were not useful for this study. The same thing was true of various other series.

The Board of Trustees (BOT) Series consists of bound volumes of minutes of the meetings (ten per year) of the trustees, and Box BOT1 contains an index to the minutes. As mentioned earlier in this book, however, the trustees' minutes are designed for the purposes of lawyers and accountants and are of highly limited use to the historian. The minutes record action taken, predominantly those appropriating money to beneficiaries, but give no clues as to how the trustees reached their decisions, what differing viewpoints there may have been, or about countless other matters that are of primary interest to the historian.

The most valuable material concerning the Endowment's history (as distinct from the history of its many beneficiaries) is found in the Central Files (CF) Series. There are twenty-four boxes (about the width and height of a shoe box but longer) in this series, and they contain many thousands of microfiches, that is sheets of microfilm that contain rows of microimages of pages of writing, be it printed, typed, or handwritten. The first eleven boxes in this CF Series (Box CF1–CF11) were the crucial ones for this study, for they contain the general correspondence, reports, and various other types of documents that the historian must have to flesh out a narrative about the Endowment.

The microfiche files are difficult to use, not so much because they require a special machine to read them but because of how they are arranged and because of certain flaws in the manner in which they were made (or in the original files from which they were made?). The fiches are arranged chronologically by grouping of years and then by alphabetized subject codes. For example, the Endowment's files concerning, say, Duke University from 1950 to 1955, may be located easily enough. The researcher must be careful, however, for the material from 1950 is at the end of the section, and one must therefore proceed from the back to the front of the block of material in order to keep any semblance of chronological order. Moreover, some pages are out of order and, more seriously, some are simply missing. Whether this happened through the carelessness of those who made the microfiches or because the pages were missing from the original files cannot now be determined.

Regardless of these problems, these eleven boxes of microfiches are the indispensable sources for a study of the inner working of the Endowment. The remaining thirteen boxes in the series contain the Hospital Files and Child Care Files, arranged chronologically and then alphabetically by institutional names, but they were not used for this study.

Portions of the Hospital and Child Care Divisions (HCCD) Series were used. HCCD Box 1 contains an important feasibility study or report made by Alexander H. Sands Jr. in 1924. It also contains the original copies of some of the marvelously rich correspondence and writings of Graham Davis. The fact that they are the original copies makes them a special pleasure for the researcher. The annual application for assistance from the community hospitals and childcare institutions in the Carolinas are on microfilm in this series but were not used for this study.

The Rural Church Division (RCD) Series contains correspondence from 1918 through 1943 in Boxes RCD1 and 2 and this material proved most revealing and helpful. Limited, random sampling of material on various rural Methodist churches provided illustrations of Endowment activity in this area.

From the beginning the Endowment has published an *Annual Report,* and this proved to be a valuable source. Aside from the financial data in each volume, the report covers the Endowment's activity during the year in its four fields of concern. There are two main problems about the annual report, however. The first is that it is just annual and provides no long-term view. The second problem, which is related to the first, is that some activity in, say, the Rural Church program looks most promising in 1965 and is so described in the annual report for that year. By 1968 or 1970, however, it turns out that what looked promising in 1965 has pretty much fizzled—but later annual reports do not reveal that. This is not meant to suggest that there is or ever has been any conscious or deliberate misleading, but there are simply built-in limitations to reports that cover only one year, no matter how conscientious their compilers might be.

NOTES

PREFACE

1 Waldemar A. Nielsen, *The Big Foundations* (New York: Columbia University Press, 1972), p. 50.

2 J. B. Duke's indenture of trust creating the Duke Endowment is included in this volume as appendix 2.

I THE ORIGINS OF THE DUKE ENDOWMENT

1 Greater detail about these various business interests of Washington Duke and his sons may be found in Robert F. Durden, *The Dukes of Durham, 1865–1929* (Durham, N.C.: Duke University Press, 1975). Hereinafter cited as Durden, *The Dukes*.

2 W. R. Perkins, "An Address on the Duke Endowment: Its Origins, Nature, and Purposes," delivered before the Sphex Club at Lynchburg, Virginia, October 11, 1929. Printed pamphlet in Duke University's Perkins Library.

3 Earl W. Porter, *Trinity and Duke, 1892–1924: Foundations of Duke University* (Durham, N.C.: Duke University Press, 1964), is authoritative and comprehensive.

4 B. N. Duke to J. B. Duke, December 29, 1893, in B. N. Duke Letterbook, Special Collections, Duke University's Perkins Library. This letter was written by hand and the letterpress copy pasted in the back of the letterbook.

5 W. P. Few to J. B. Duke, March 31, 1914, William P. Few Papers, Duke University Archives. Hereinafter cited as Few Papers.

6 J. C. Kilgo to W. P. Few, July 13, 1915, Few Papers.

7 J. B. Duke to Board of Church Extension and Board of Trustees, Trinity College,

April 22, 1920, J. B. Duke Letterbook, J. B. Duke Papers, Special Collections, Duke University's Perkins Library.

8   W. P. Few to J. B. Duke, February 1, 1919, Few Papers.

9   W. P. Few to J. B. Duke, February 27, 1919, Few Papers.

10 This latter development, a portion of which J. B. Duke ultimately sold to the Aluminum Company of America for one-ninth of that company's stock (approximately $17 million), is discussed in Durden, *The Dukes,* pp. 191–192, 242–243, and in John W. Jenkins, *James B. Duke: Master Builder* (New York: George H. Doran Company, 1927), pp. 185–193. Hereinafter cited as Jenkins, *J. B. Duke.*

11 For a fuller discussion of "The Origins of the University Idea at Trinity," see chapter 1 of Robert F. Durden, *The Launching of Duke University, 1924–1949* (Durham, N.C.: Duke University Press, 1993). Hereinafter cited as Durden, *Launching.*

12 In Few's unpublished and unfinished history, "The Beginnings of an American University," Few Papers, and also in *Duke University Alumni Register* 18 (December 1932): 341–342.

13 W. P. Few to J. H. Separk, May 28, 1921, and W. P. Few to C. W. Toms, July 23, 1921, Few Papers.

14 James F. Gifford Jr., *The Evolution of a Medical Center: A History of Medicine at Duke University to 1941* (Durham, N.C.: Duke University Press, 1972), pp. 11–34, has the most detailed study of this episode.

15 Raleigh *News and Observer,* December 28, 1922.

16 This attempt to suggest J. B. Duke's personal responsibility for the health-care area of the Endowment represents a modification of the thesis presented in the author's *The Dukes of Durham,* where only the family's long-standing pattern of giving is emphasized.

17 A. Sands to W. P. Few, October 27, 1923, and W. Rankin to W. P. Few, December 29, 1923, Few Papers.

18 W. Rankin to W. P. Few, January 4, 1924, Few Papers.

19 There is more detail on these matters in both Durden, *The Dukes,* and Durden, *Launching.*

20 G. G. Allen to W. P. Few, September 18, 1924, Few Papers.

21 R. L. Flowers to W. P. Few, October 29 (two letters) and 30, 1924, Few Papers.

22 Flowers to Few, November 1, 1924, Few Papers.

23 A copy of the indenture is reproduced in this volume as appendix 2.

24 Frank Rounds's interview with Norman A. Cocke, Charlotte, N.C., 1963, pp. 106–107, the Duke Endowment Archives, Special Collections, Duke University's Perkins Library. Hereinafter cited as Duke Endowment Archives.

25 W. P. Few to J. H. Reynolds, December 29, 1924, Few Papers.

26 The indenture establishing the Doris Duke Trust also stipulated that if Doris Duke should die without lineal descendants, the two-thirds share of the trust's holdings held for her benefit should go to the Duke Endowment. In 1988 when Doris Duke was seventy-five, she adopted as her daughter an adult woman, Charlene Heffner (who was thirty-five). Following the death of Doris Duke in October 1993, Heffner,

claiming to be a lineal descendant of Doris Duke, sought to obtain the two-thirds share (approximately $127 million) of the Doris Duke Trust. The trustees of the Endowment, pointing out that adult adoptions were not legal in New Jersey when J. B. Duke established the Doris Duke Trust in 1924, argued, among other things, that Heffner could not be considered a lineal descendant. The New Jersey superior court agreed with the trustees in July 1995 and awarded the $127 million to the Endowment. Attorneys for Heffner appealed the ruling, but as of mid-1996 the final decision had not been made.

27 In 1924 Ben Duke attempted to draw up lists of all the living descendants of his aunts and uncles, that is, his cousins. Since the families had been large on both the paternal and maternal sides, Ben Duke ran into puzzling complications as he tried to distribute over $500,000. J. B. Duke, in his will, left the sum of $2 million to be divided among the descendants of his aunts and uncles, whom he did not attempt to specify by name. This meant that the executors of the will encountered a diffi- cult drawn-out task, which is described in Robert F. Durden, "Troubled Legacy: James B. Duke's Bequest to His Cousins," *North Carolina Historical Review* (Octo- ber 1973): 394–415.

28 These matters are dealt with in greater detail in both Durden, *The Dukes*, and Durden, *Launching*.

29 Frank Rounds's interview with Roy A. Hunt in Pittsburgh, October and December, 1963. Duke Endowment Archives.

30 Jenkins, *J. B. Duke*, p. 259.

31 "Last Will and Testament of James B. Duke," J. B. Duke Papers; John W. Jenkins, *James B. Duke: Master Builder* (New York: George H. Doran Company, 1927), pp. 263–264, 299–302.

2   LAUNCHING THE ENDOWMENT: THE HOSPITAL AND ORPHAN SECTION (PART I)

1 Rosemary Stevens, *In Sickness and in Health: American Hospitals in the Twentieth Century* (New York: Basic Books, 1989), pp. 119–120, 124. On a smaller and more scattered basis, the Commonwealth Fund, a philanthropic foundation of the Harkness family in New York, also began to assist in the building of rural hospitals in the late 1920s. The first one was in Tennessee in 1927, and it was soon followed by three others in Virginia, Maine, and Kentucky, with others to come later.

2 W. S. Rankin to H. Folks, October 11, 1930, Box CF3, Duke Endowment Archives. James E. Gifford Jr. is preparing a study of Rankin's career prior to his assumption of the position with the Duke Endowment.

3 Minutes of the Trustees, December 17, 1924, and February 22, 1927, vol. 1, Box BOT2, Duke Endowment Archives.

4 W. R. Rankin to Alexander Sands, October 20, 1925, under Charlotte office, Box CF1 (Central Files General Correspondence), Duke Endowment Archives. These "Central Files" are on microfiche, are voluminous, and are difficult to use since they are topically rather than chronologically arranged.

5 W. S. Rankin, "A Million Dollars a Year for Hospitals," February 23, 1926, under Committee on Public Information, Box CF1, Duke Endowment Archives.

6 [W. S. Rankin], "Preliminary Considerations with Reference to the Development of the Hospital Problem of the Duke Endowment," [November 1925 is penciled in margin], under Insurance, Hospital Policies, Box CF3, Duke Endowment Archives.

7 G. Davis to E. F. Majer, February [3?], 1927, under Charlotte office, Box CF2, Duke Endowment Archives.

8 G. Davis to T. R. Ponton, November 12, 1927, G. L. Davis Correspondence, 1927–34, three folders in Box HCCD 17, Duke Endowment Archives. Hereinafter cited as Davis Correspondence. Fortunately, when the Endowments files were put on microfiche in the 1960s, someone recognized the unique value of Davis's correspondence, and the original copies were retained along with a few incoming letters.

9 G. Davis to M. T. MacEachern, May 6, 1932, Davis Correspondence.

10 G. Davis, "Operative Nomenclature Problems," April 6, 1933, under North and South Carolina Hospital Association, Box CF2, Duke Endowment Archives.

11 W. S. Rankin to W. B. Bell, November 4, 1931, Davis Correspondence.

12 Statement concerning the Duke Endowment Hospital and Orphan Section's Bulletin Number 3, under Hospital Construction, Box CF1, Duke Endowment Archives.

13 Report of the committee on hospitals and orphanages, May 26, 1931, Minutes of the Trustees, vol. 4, pp. 19C1–3, Box BOT2, Duke Endowment Archives.

14 G. Davis, "The Small Hospital Problem," *Hospitals,* November 1940, a paper presented at the meeting of the American Hospital Association in 1940. G. Davis Folders, Box HCCD 18, Duke Endowment Archives.

15 Charles E. Rosenberg, *The Care of Strangers: The Rise of America's Hospital System* (New York: Basic Books, 1987), pp. 4–5.

16 Ibid., p. 149.

17 G. Davis to J. L. Melvin, August 9, 1934, under Hospital Care Association, Box CF2, Duke Endowment Archives.

18 G. Davis to Newton Fisher, May 31, 1934, G. Davis Folders, Box HCCD 17, Duke Endowment Archives; James W. Davis to G. Davis, July 29, 1934, under North and South Carolina Hospital Association, Box CF2, Duke Endowment Archives.

19 G. Davis, "The Cost of Nursing in Small General Hospitals," under Nursing, Box CF3, Duke Endowment Archives.

20 M. Burgess, "Costs in Small Schools," *American Journal of Nursing,* August, 1931, under Nursing, Box CF3.

21 The background and early phase of this battle is well treated in Rosenberg, *The Care of Strangers,* pp. 212–236.

22 W. L. Jackson and J. W. Davis to "Dear Doctor," May 29, 1937, under North and South Carolina Hospital Association, Box CF2, Duke Endowment Archives.

23 G. Davis to Newton Fisher, October 6, 1933, Davis Correspondence.

24 Davis to Fisher, April 30, May 5, 1934, Davis Correspondence.

25 Davis to Fisher, June 11, 1934, Davis Correspondence.

26 Davis to Fisher, June 14, 1934, Davis Correspondence. Neither Davis's picture nor even his name appeared in the publication.

27 G. Davis to W. C. Davison, June 22, 1934, Davis Correspondence.

28 G. Davis to J. L. Horne Jr., June 7, 1934, Davis Correspondence.

29 G. Davis to W. T. Sanger, November 24, 1934, Davis Correspondence.

30 G. Davis to J. M. Beeler, January 17, 1935, Box HCCD18, Duke Endowment Archives.

31 G. Davis to R. L. Brandt, December 26, 1935, Box HCCD18.

32 F. M. Walker to G. Davis, June 12, 1939, and Davis to Walker, June 13, 1939, Box HCCD18.

33 Rosenberg, *The Care of Strangers*, p. 343.

34 G. Davis to A. E. Hardgrove, March 24, 1936, Box HCCD18. See also, James F. Gifford Jr., *The Evolution of a Medical Center: A History of Medicine at Duke University to 1941* (Durham, N.C.: Duke University Press, 1972), p. 58.

35 W. C. Davison to W. P. Few, March 22, 1927, Few Papers.

36 Gifford, *Evolution of a Medical Center*, pp. 58–59, has more details.

37 Stevens, *In Sickness and in Health*, p. 6.

38 Ibid., p. 154.

39 W. S. Rankin to H. H. Moore, May 25, 1932, under Insurance, Cost of Medical Care, Box CF2, Duke Endowment Archives.

40 G. Davis to F. A. Grisette, April 25, 1934, Davis Correspondence.

41 *New York Times*, January 3, 1934; *Durham Morning Herald*, November 29, 1934.

42 Jay Franklin in "We the People," column in *Charlotte Observer*, January 16, 1937.

43 *Charlotte Observer*, July 11 and October 5, 1934.

44 G. Davis to C. R. Rorem, October 6, 1934, Davis Correspondence. Lamb, in his report to the Association of Hospital Officers in Britain, declared that the "greatest impression" of his month-long visit in America was the "deep-seated affection and warm-heartedness to England, its ideals and traditions." He had found the Americans to be "quite cheerful during the present severe wave of industrial depression . . . and [they] are now cultivating fortitude, courage, sacrifice, comradeship, and other eternal qualities, that cannot be bought with dollars." He thought America possessed "driving forces and creative genius to an unusual degree," but he made this interesting qualification: "America is not one nation but still a collection of many nations with varying climates, differing languages and stupendous distances, which make it infinitely more difficult to determine and enforce a National policy than in a country of the size and traditions of dear old England." Sydney Lamb, "30 Happy Days in America," January 16, 1935, under Hospital Care Association, Box CF3, Duke Endowment Archives.

45 G. Davis to the Joint Committee on Group Hospitalization, July 23, 1934, Davis Correspondence.

46 G. Davis to I. Manning, October 30, 1934, under Hospital Care Association, Box CF3, Duke Endowment Archives.

47 G. Davis to A. Sands, June 12, 1934, Box HCCD18, Duke Endowment Archives. This letter was misfiled in a folder for late 1935.
48 W. Rankin to W. S. O. B. Robinson Jr., March 8, 1935, under Hospital Care Association, Box CF3, Duke Endowment Archives.
49 G. Davis to I. Manning, May 3, 1935, Box HCCD18, Duke Endowment Archives.
50 Davis to Manning, April 15, 1935, Box HCCD18.
51 Manning to Davis, April 17, 1935, Box HCCD18.
52 Manning to Davis, May 25, 1935, Box HCCD18.
53 Manning to Davis, July 11, 1935, Box HCCD18.
54 Davis to Manning, July 31, 1934, Davis Correspondence.
55 G. Davis to H. F. Sanger, August 18, 1934, Davis Correspondence.
56 G. Davis to F. Grisette, August 21, 1935, Box HCCD18, Duke Endowment Archives.
57 G. Davis to Frank Van Dyk, March 17, 1936, Box HCCD18.
58 G. Davis to M. L. Sutley, January 31, 1939, Box HCCD18.
59 G. Davis to A. Oseroff, January 31, 1939, Box HCCD18. Davis's Greenville plan attracted considerable national attention. He also, in 1937, drafted a remarkable and long—fourteen, closely spaced typed pages—memorandum outlining a proposed hospitalization plan for Mississippi, a state whose economic and social problems were then even more severe than those of the Carolinas. See G. Davis to A. M. McCarthy, July 15, 1937, Box HCCD18.
60 G. Davis to D. H. Dabbs, October 11, 1939, Box HCCD18.
61 G. Harris to G. Davis, January 23, 1940, and Davis to Harris, January 29, 1940, Box HCCD18. When Davis soon wrote that the head dietitian at the Kellogg clinic had helped him gain fifteen pounds in three weeks, Harris replied, "If the dietitian there can guarantee to cut down on one's weight in the same proportion that she can increase it, I might arrange to get out that way sometime soon." Harris to Davis, February 24, 1940, Box HCCD18.
62 Copy of R. C. Nye to G. Davis, February 9, 1940, Box HCCD18.
63 M. Pickens to J. B. Norman, July 8, 1958, under Charlotte Office, Box CF2, Duke Endowment Archives.

3 LAUNCHING THE ENDOWMENT: THE HOSPITAL AND ORPHAN SECTION (PART 2)

1 Only those members of the staff who had their full careers, or a substantial part of them, with the Endowment will be mentioned in the text.
2 G. Harris, "Field Work of the Duke Endowment," April 16, 1937, and July 17, 1937, under Charlotte Office, Box CF2, Duke Endowment Archives.
3 "Comments by Registrants Attending Institute . . . ," Banner Elk, N.C., June 22–26, 1953, under Medical Record Librarians, Box CF3, Duke Endowment Archives. In later years, the Endowment held such workshops in a variety of locations.
4 G. Harris to medical record librarians at Tri-State Hospital Conference, April, 1939, under North and South Carolina Hospital Associations, Box CF2, Duke Endowment Archives.

5 M. Pickens to C. C. Clark, July 5, 1949, under Hospitals, Miscellaneous, Box CF2, Duke Endowment Archives.

6 M. Pickens to G. W. Hill Sr., February 22, 1956, under Hospital Organization and Management, Box CF2, Duke Endowment Archives.

7 M. Pickens, "General Hospital Development in the Carolinas—A Review," *Charlotte Observer,* February 13, 1951.

8 M. Pickens, "Hospital Statistics for a Ten-Year Period," under Hospital Reports and Statistics, Box CF3, Duke Endowment Archives.

9 Undated [c. 1951] memorandum concerning hospital costs, under Hospital Reports and Statistics, Box CF3.

10 *Toledo* (Ohio) *Blade,* April 28, 1962.

11 C. Rowland to A. E. Rappaport, October 3, 1960, under Consultants, Miscellaneous, Box CF1, Duke Endowment Archives.

12 C. H. Clark to M. Pickens, February 1, 1951, General Correspondence, Box CF1, Duke Endowment Archives.

13 G. L. Davis, president of the American Hospital Association, "Memorandum of Conference . . . ," December 16, 1947, under American Hospital Association, Box CF2, Duke Endowment Archives.

14 J. R. McGiboney to W. Rankin, October 26, 1949, under Hospitals, Miscellaneous, Box CF2, Duke Endowment Archives. A more detailed analysis of the Hill-Burton Act may be found in Rosemary Stevens, *In Sickness and in Health: American Hospitals in the Twentieth Century* (New York: Basic Books, 1989), pp. 216–219.

15 "The Duke Endowment and Negroes in North Carolina," n.d. [ca. 1936], under Insurance, Hospital Policies, Box CF3, Duke Endowment Archives. The Carolina hospitals that admitted both races, like others in the South at that time, followed legally mandated segregation policies. That most hospitals outside the South followed a *de facto* system of racial segregation that was not much different is suggested by Charles E. Rosenberg, *The Care of Strangers: The Rise of America's Hospital System* (New York: Basic Books, 1987), pp. 301–302, and Stevens, *In Sickness and in Health,* pp. 137–138.

16 W. Rankin to ?, n.d. [1927], under Hospital Reports and Statistics, Box CF3, Duke Endowment Archives.

17 [W. Rankin], "Memoranda for M. Edwin R. Embree" [of the Rosenwald Fund], March 30, 1929, under Insurance, Hospital Policies, Box CF3, Duke Endowment Archives. For an account of Rankin's and Davison's successful efforts to help Lincoln Hospital regain accreditation by the American College of Surgeons in the early 1930s, see James F. Gifford Jr., *The Evolution of a Medical Center: A History of Medicine at Duke University to 1941* (Durham, N.C.: Duke University Press, 1972), pp. 163–167. Lincoln temporarily lost its accreditation when the fatality rate in major operations, as revealed in the reports required by the Endowment, rose to twice that of the region's other African American hospitals. Lincoln Hospital also gained assistance from the Rosenwald Fund.

18 G. Davis to T. C. Taylor, November 2, 1931, Davis Correspondence, Box HCCD17, Duke Endowment Archives.

19 G. Davis to A. M. McCarthy, July 15, 1937, Box HCCD18, Duke Endowment Archives. One of Davis's friends in the North wrote that he had found the fourteen-page, single-spaced letter to McCarthy "so interesting that it did not occur to me you had written a volume to rival 'Gone With the Wind.'"

20 Peter C. English, "Pediatrics and the Unwanted Child in History: Foundling Homes, Disease, and the Origins of Foster Care in New York City, 1860 to 1920," *Pediatrics* 73 (May 1984): 700.

21 Alexander H. Sands to J. B. Duke, January 16, 1924, under Child Care Statistics, N.C. and S.C., Box CF3, Duke Endowment Archives.

22 C. W. Areson to M. Pickens, July 31, 1962, under Child Care, Statistics, N.C. and S.C., Box CF3.

23 English, "Pediatrics and the Unwanted Child," pp. 699–700.

24 M. Pickens, "The Duke Endowment as Related to the Child Caring Institutions in the Carolinas," with G. Davis to A. B. Stevenson, February 3, 1937, under Public Utilities, Box CF3, Duke Endowment Archives.

25 Undated announcement of fellowship, under Social Service, Box CF3, Duke Endowment Archives.

26 C. C. Carstens to A. F. Jamison, May 18, 1934, under Social Case Work Project, Box CF3, Duke Endowment Archives.

27 C. C. Carstens to Mrs. W. T. Bost, December 19, 1935, under Social Case Work Project, Box CF3.

28 A. T. Jamison to C. C. Carstens, August 28, 1937, under Social Case Work Project, Box CF3.

29 C. C. Carstens, "A Project for the Development of Social Service in the Children's Institutions of North and South Carolina," n.d. [1937], under Social Case Work Project, Box CF3.

30 W. S. Rankin's Report for the Committee on Hospitals and Orphanages, with Minutes of the Trustees, May 31, 1944, vol. 17, pp. 25ff., Box BOT2, Duke Endowment Archives.

31 Minutes of the Trustees and accompanying documents, June 26, July 13, 1934, vol. 7, Box BOT2, Duke Endowment Archives.

32 Harold L. Ickes, *Back to Work: The Story of PWA* (New York: Macmillan, 1935), pp. 140–146.

33 *New York Times,* December 8, 1937, pp. 21, 23, and January 4, 1938, p. 1.

34 "Trail of the Circuit Rider," portions of the script, Box CF2, Duke Endowment Archives. Since the file is not clear as to whether this is the complete script, a missing portion may have dealt with the Endowment's work with the rural Methodist church in North Carolina. Since the film was made to be shown primarily in both Carolinas, however, and since the church work was limited to North Carolina, the trustees may have decided to make only the indirect reference to "many thousands of dollars annually for religion."

35 Colored Ministers Union to the Duke Endowment, February 22, 1937, with "The Trail of the Circuit Rider," Box CF2, Duke Endowment Archives.

36 Jonathan Daniels, "The Forgotten Man," clipping from the Raleigh *News and Observer,* with "The Trail of the Circuit Rider," Box CF2.

37 Sheldon Dick to W. Rankin, February 3, 1942, with "The Trail of the Circuit Rider," Box CF2.

38 W. Rankin to A. Sands, May 1, 1950, with Minutes of the Trustees, June 27, 1950, vol. 23, Box BOT2, Duke Endowment Archives.

4 THE ENDOWMENT AND THE FOUR EDUCATIONAL INSTITUTIONS, 1924–1960

1 W. Rankin to A. H. Ditteau, July 9, 1927, under Miscellaneous, Box CF3, Duke Endowment Archives.

2 Trustees' meeting of December 31, 1929, vol. 3, p. 21, Box BOT1, Duke Endowment Archives.

3 Allen and Perkins later paid for the carillon as their personal gift.

4 D. Grier Martin, "Highlights of Davidson since 1924," presented to trustees of the Duke Endowment, February 24, 1959, with Minutes of the Trustees, vol. 30, Box BOT3, Duke Endowment Archives.

5 Mary D. Beaty, *A History of Davidson College* (Davidson, N.C.: Briarpatch Press, 1988) is a useful survey.

6 Alfred S. Reid, *Furman University: Toward a New Identity, 1925–1975* (Durham, N.C.: Duke University Press, 1976), p. 6.

7 Ibid., p. 17.

8 Ibid., pp. 33, 41.

9 Ibid., pp. 63, 98.

10 Inez Moore Parker (and Helen V. Callison, ed.), *The Biddle-Johnson C. Smith Story* (Charlotte, N.C.: Charlotte Publishing, 1975), pp. 3–12. There was already one African American on the faculty before 1891.

11 Arthur A. George, *The History of Johnson C. Smith University, 1867 to the Present,* Ph.D. dissertation in education, New York University, 1954 (facsimile print of University Microfilms International, 1986), p. 76.

12 Statement by H. L. McCrorey, *The Duke Endowment Yearbook* 1 (December 1924–December 1928 [1929]): 49–52.

13 Since this matter and certain others relating to the Endowment's relationship with Duke University down to 1949 are fully developed in Robert F. Durden, *The Launching of Duke University, 1924–1949* (Durham, N.C.: Duke University Press, 1993), they will only be sketchily treated here.

14 Raymond B. Fosdick, *Adventure in Giving: The Story of the General Education Board* (New York: Harper and Row, 1962), p. 150.

15 W. P. Few to A. Flexner, June 28, 1926, Few Papers.

16 W. P. Few, "The Duke Endowment and Duke University," 8 pp., privately printed, n.d., n.p., Duke University Archives.

17 W. R. Perkins to W. P. Few, March 24, 1927, Few Papers.

18 W. Few to Trevor Arnett, October 10, 1929, Few Papers.

19 Although the record reveals no mention of the matter, a factor that may or may not have entered into this negotiation had to do with the salaries of faculty members in medical schools. It was a highly controversial matter in academic medical circles, but Abraham Flexner and the GEB strongly favored full-time, salaried faculty members for medical schools, as at John Hopkins, Chicago, and certain other top institutions. When Davison first spoke to the Medical Society of North Carolina in 1927, he stated that Duke would follow the Johns Hopkins model in this respect as in so many others. In the spring of 1929, however, Davison changed his mind and opted to follow the Harvard model whereby the medical faculty remained "geographically full-time" in the hospital but saw private patients who supplied a significant part of the doctors' incomes. Duke's private diagnostic clinics became the mechanism for this system. For a fuller discussion of this matter, see Fosdick, *Adventure in Giving,* pp. 150–173. Between 1923 and 1960, the GEB gave over $17,560,000 to Vanderbilt University's medical school and $300,000 to Duke's. See ibid., p. 328.

20 W. P. Few to W. R. Perkins, January 12, 1930, Few Papers.

21 W. P. Few to G. Allen, August 5, 1933, and Allen to Few, August 8, 1933, Few Papers.

22 W. P. Few to W. R. Perkins, December 19, 1930, Few Papers.

23 Perkins to Few, January 15, 1931, Few Papers.

24 Few to Perkins, January 1, 1934, Few Papers.

25 J. F. Bruton to W. P. Few, December 17, 1934, Few Papers.

26 [Mary Garland Allen Gregg and Lucy Burwell Allen Fowlkes], *George Garland Allen: A Life to Be Honored* [privately published, 1983], p. 21. The daughters also state that their father, in dealing with Few and others at Duke, was "unfailingly courteous" but "made it clear he expected his wishes to be fulfilled." Ibid., p. 39.

27 W. R. Perkins to T. D. Bryson, September 19, 1941, and R. L. Flowers to W. R. Perkins, September 23, 1941, Robert L. Flowers Papers, Duke University Archives. Hereinafter cited as Flowers Papers.

28 W. R. Perkins to J. F. Bruton, February 4, 1942; G. Allen to R. Flowers, February 6, 1942; and J. F. Bruton to W. R. Perkins, February 9, 1942, Flowers Papers.

29 A. Brower to W. Davison, June 8, 1948, Willis Smith Papers, Special Collections, Duke University Library.

30 For a fuller account of matters treated in the remainder of this chapter, see Robert F. Durden, "Donnybrook at Duke: The Gross-Edens Affair of 1960," *North Carolina Historical Review* 71 (July and October 1994): 331–357 and 451–471. Here the focus will be on the Endowment's role.

31 P. Gross to A. H. Edens, January 17, 1955, A. H. Edens Papers, Duke University Archives. Hereinafter cited as Edens Papers.

32 Undated, unsigned memorandum written by P. Gross, ca. October 1957, Bunyan S. Womble Papers, Duke University Archives. Hereinafter cited as Womble Papers.

33 H. Edens to Bunyan S. Womble, June 30, 1960, Edens Papers.

34 Ibid.

35 Ibid.

36 *Report of the President . . . for 1958–1959* (Duke University: Duke University Press, 1959), pp. 7–10.

37 C. B. Houck to H. Edens, February 24, 1960, Womble Papers.

38 E. F. Spears to Huber Hanes, February 28, 1960, Womble Papers. Letters similar to this from other trustees and alumni leaders may be found in this collection.

39 Russell Clay and Bill Frue, "Resignation of Edens Goes to Trustees Today," *Durham Morning Herald,* March 23, 1960.

40 P. H. Hanes to A. Sands, March 17, 1960, Womble Papers.

41 Richard E. Thigpen, *90 Years into the Twentieth Century: The Autobiography of R. E. Thigpen* (Charlotte: n.p., 1991), pp. 154–155.

42 Roma Cheek to Bunyan Womble, n.d. [ca. April 1960], Womble Papers.

43 Minutes of board meeting, March 23, 1960, Records of the Board of Trustees, Duke University Archives.

44 Minutes of board meeting, March 23, 1960, Records of the Board of Trustees.

45 Minutes of board meeting, March 23, 1960, Records of the Board of Trustees. Eden's impromptu statement was probably never edited or corrected for punctuation and the like and is, therefore, stylistically flawed.

46 The Endowment trustee had conveniently forgotten that under the university's bylaws the president is not only a member of but the head of the faculty.

47 Minutes of board meeting, March 23, 1960, Records of the Board of Trustees. The five dissenters in the dismissal asked that their votes be recorded, and they were: Tom Perkins, Alexander Sands, C. A. Cannon, Amos Kearns, and B. F. Few.

48 University Council resolution, March 16, 1960, Womble Papers.

49 Minutes of specially called faculty meeting, March 25, 1960, Womble Papers.

50 "Petition to the Board of Trustees of Duke University, March 27, 1960," with a cover letter sent to all faculty members, April 13, 1960, from "A committee of thirty-two administrative faculty members," Womble Papers.

51 P. B. Heartt, secretary, for trustees of the Duke Endowment, to Special Committee of the Faculty, April 26, 1960, *Durham Morning Herald,* May 4, 1960.

52 Raleigh *News and Observer,* May [5?], 1960, clipping in newspaper clipping file, Duke University Archives.

53 Memorandum by Earl Porter, March 29, 1960, Edens Papers.

54 Memorandum by Earl Porter, April 11, 1960, Edens Papers. On the following day, Tom Perkins said virtually the same thing to Edens.

55 One of the sadder casualties of the Gross-Edens affair was the death of Alexander Sands. He flew back to New York after attending the trustee meeting at Duke on April 21, 1960, and died in his sleep during that night. One can only surmise that prolonged worry and stress about affairs at Duke hastened his death.

5 IN REMEMBRANCE OF THE CIRCUIT RIDERS: THE ENDOWMENT AND THE METHODIST CHURCH IN NORTH CAROLINA, 1924–1960

1 Jean B. Anderson, *Durham County* (Durham, N.C.: Duke University Press, 1990), p. 87.

2 John W. Jenkins, *James B. Duke: Master Builder* (New York: George H. Doran Company, 1927), p. 27.

3 J. B. Duke to Board of Church Extension and to Board of Trustees, Trinity College, April 22, 1920, J. B. Duke Letterbook, Special Collections, Duke University Library.

4 W. P. Few, "Statement on Superannuate Preachers Fund," *The Duke Endowment Yearbook* 1 (December 1924–December 1928 [1929]): 61–62.

5 W. P. Few to "My dear Friend," December 17, 1934, Few Papers.

6 Emily A. Siler to W. P. Few, January 3, 1935, Few Papers.

7 W. P. Few to Alexander Sands, January 8, 1925, Box RCD1, Duke Endowment Archives.

8 J. Ormond to H. M. King, July 7, 27, 1926, Box RCD1.

9 J. Ormond to Mrs. Kitty McKenzie, September 28, 1926, Box RCD1.

10 H. M. North to J. Ormond, April 16, 1929, Box RCD2, Duke Endowment Archives.

11 Ormond to North, April 23, 1929, Box RCD2.

12 R. G. L. Edwards to J. Ormond, November 12, 1929, Box RCD2.

13 J. Ormond to W. C. Martin, February 5, 1932, Box RCD2.

14 R. J. Lough to W. C. Martin, January 1, 1925, Box RCD2.

15 R. E. Pittman to J. Ormond, January 21, 1932, Box RCD2.

16 B. A. Sisk to J. Ormond, December 19, 1935, Box RCD2.

17 Speech by R. E. DuMont to the North Carolina chapter of the American Institute of Architects, March, 1957, under Trustees, Box CFI, Duke Endowment Archives.

18 S. E. Mercer to W. P. Few, September 22, 1926, Box RCD1, Duke Endowment Archives.

19 Few to Mercer, September 23, 1926, Box RCD1.

20 *The Duke Endowment: First Quarter Century, The Duke Endowment Yearbook* 18 (December 1950): pp. 19–20.

21 J. W. Johnson and G. S. Duffie to Paul Garber, July 13, 1931, School of Religion Papers, Duke University Archives.

22 M. B. Shives to J. Ormond, June 19, 1939, School of Religion Papers.

6 TRANSITIONS AND TROUBLES IN THE 1960S AND 1970S

1 Nanaline H. Duke to Trustees of the Endowment, n.d. [ca. April 1957], BOT, vol. 30, p. 38b1.

2 A list of the trustees, with their dates of service, is included in this volume as appendix 1.

3 Asheville, North Carolina, *Citizen Times,* July 25, 1971, and *Charlotte Observer,* January 2, 1970.

4 *Wall Street Journal,* July 23, 1962.

5 *Greensboro Daily News,* December 11, 1962, and *Charlotte Observer,* December 11, 1962.

6 Copies of portions of the 1963 opinion, under Duke Endowment, Box CF4, Duke Endowment Archives; *Cocke v. Duke University,* 260 NC1, 131 SE 2nd 909 (1963).

7 T. Perkins to Trustees of the Endowment, August 21, 1963, Box CF4, Duke Endowment Archives.

8 *Wall Street Journal,* February 9, 1965.

9 Statement of Principles and Practice, the Trustees of the Ford Foundation, September 24, 1964, under Revenue Department, Box CF5, Duke Endowment Archives.

10 T. Perkins to M. Pickens, October 8, 1965, enclosing a draft of statement for the Ways and Means Committee, under Revenue Department, Box CF5.

11 Alan Pifer to J. B. Connolly Jr., February 15, 1972, under Revenue Department, Box CF7, Duke Endowment Archives.

12 This quotation and subsequent quotations in this portion of the study are from two legal briefs prepared by the Endowment's lawyers and submitted to the courts. The copies were kindly made available to the author by Mr. John Spuches and will be added to the Duke Endowment Archives in Perkins Library.

13 Complicated litigation touching on these mini-endowments held by the Endowment for the four educational institutions went on until 1977 but does not need to be discussed here.

14 Alfred E. Kahn's letter, "Let's Play Fair with Utility Rates," *Wall Street Journal,* July 25, 1994.

15 Joe Maynor, *Duke Power: The First Seventy-Five Years* (Charlotte: Duke Power Company [ca. 1980]. This in-house publication consists mainly of articles first published in *Duke Power News* and then combined into a book.

16 Ibid., p. 155.

17 Carl Horn Jr. to the Trustees of the Duke Endowment, February 4, 1974, under Public Utilities, Box CF8, Duke Endowment Archives.

18 Ibid.

19 Arnold Miller to M. Pickens, January 22, 1974, under Public Utilities, Box CF8, Duke Endowment Archives.

20 Doris Duke to Arnold Miller, February 7, 1974, under Public Utilities, Box CF8.

21 Carl Horn Jr. to Doris Duke, April 3, 1974, under Public Utilities, Box CF8.

22 Arnold Miller to P. J. Collins, July 5, 1974, under Public Utilities, Box CF8.

23 R. Henney to C. Horn Jr., August 6, 1974, under Public Utilities, Box CF8.

24 Memorandum from Perkins, Daniels, and McCormack, [John Spuches] to Securities and Exchange Commission, April 18, 1974, under Public Utilities, Box CF8.

25 Ibid.

26 Philip W. Moore to R. Henney and also to R. Robinson, June 28, 1974, under Duke Endowment, Box CF6, Duke Endowment Archives.

27 R. Robinson to W. L. Felts, December 31, 1974, under Duke Endowment, Box CF8, Duke Endowment Archives.

28 Draft of petition to U.S. District Court, with certain shareholders in Duke Power Company as plaintiffs and directors and trustees of Duke Power and the Duke Endowment as defendants, with P. Moore to R. Henney, June 28, 1974, under Duke Endowment, Box CF8.

29 Analysis by Hornblower and Weeks-Hemphill, Noyes, Inc., n.d. [ca. 1976], under Public Utilities, Box CF9, Duke Endowment Archives.

30 Carl Horn Jr. to M. Pickens, November 14, 1977, under Public Utilities, Box CF9.

31 R. Henney, memorandum for files, April 26, 1969, with attached report, under Duke Endowment Trustees, Box CF10, Duke Endowment Archives.

32 Undated [ca. 1977?], incomplete memorandum, from Treasurer's Files, under Duke Endowment Trustees, Box CF10, Duke Endowment Archives.

33 Reid and Priest [John Spuches] to Trustees of the Endowment, July 25, 1979, under Duke Endowment Trustees, Box CF10.

34 M. Cuninggim to A. Davis, September 17, 1979, under Duke Endowment Trustees, Box CF10.

35 Merrimom Cuninggim, "Report to the Trustees of The Duke Endowment," March 26, 1980. Copy of report kindly supplied by Dr. Cuninggim.

36 M. Pickens and J. Felt Jr. to the Trustees, n.d. [ca. August ?, 1980], under Duke Endowment, Box CF11, Duke Endowment Archives.

7 THE ENDOWMENT AND ITS EDUCATIONAL BENEFICIARIES, 1960–1994

1 Report [by P. H. Clyde] on first visit to Johnson C. Smith University, May 2, 1961, under Committee on Educational Institutions, Box CF1, Duke Endowment Archives.

2 P. Clyde to M. Pickens, May 1, 1962, under Johnson C. Smith University, Box CF3, Duke Endowment Archives.

3 T. Perkins to Doris Duke, December 28, 1961, under Johnson C. Smith University, from Treasurer's Office, Box CF10, Duke Endowment Archives.

4 P. Clyde to D. Agnew, February 18, 1964, under Johnson C. Smith University, Box C35, Duke Endowment Archives.

5 Clyde to Agnew, May 15, 1964, under Johnson C. Smith University, Box C35.

6 P. Clyde to T. Perkins, with accompanying memorandum, June 29, 1966, under Johnson C. Smith University, Box C35.

7 [Hugh McEniry], Consultation Report on Johnson C. Smith, November 6, 1967, under Johnson C. Smith University, Box C35.

8 Undated [ca. December 1969?] memorandum from Johnson C. Smith University officers, under Johnson C. Smith University, Box CF6, Duke Endowment Archives.

9 W. Archie to J. W. Armsey, December 19, 1969, under Johnson C. Smith University, Box CF6.

10 R. Henney and A. Kearns to W. Archie, December 16, 1969, under Johnson C. Smith University, Box CF6.

11 T. Perkins to M. Bundy, March 24, 1970, under Johnson C. Smith University, from Treasurer's Office, Box CF10, Duke Endowment Archives.

12 Statement by R. Sailstad to the administrative council of the general council of the United Presbyterian Church, March 9, 1971, under Johnson C. Smith University, from Treasurer's Office, Box CF10.

13 P. Clyde to B. Few, under Furman University, Box CF3, Duke Endowment Archives.

14 P. Clyde to M. Pickens, September 5, 1963, under Furman University, Box CF3.

15 W. P. Few, "The Standardization of Southern Colleges," *South Atlantic Quarterly* 7 (October 1908), as reprinted in Robert H. Woody, ed., *The Papers and Addresses of William Preston Few* (Durham, N.C.: Duke University Press, 1951), p. 222–223.

16 F. Bonner to P. Clyde, December 14, 1964, under Furman University, Box CF5, Duke University Archives.

17 Alfred S. Reid, *Furman University: Toward a New Identity, 1925–1975* (Durham, N.C.: Duke University Press, 1976), p. 200.

18 P. Clyde to T. Perkins, May 16, 1966, under Furman University, Box CF5, Duke Endowment Archives.

19 Reid, *Furman University,* p. 255.

20 P. Clyde to T. Perkins, January 15, 1962, under Davidson College, Box CF3, Duke Endowment Archives.

21 G. Martin to P. Clyde, September 19, 1962, under Davidson College, Box CF3. The committee on educational institutions instructed Clyde to send a copy of Martin's letter to all the trustees.

22 G. Martin to M. Pickens, September 30, 1965, under Davidson College, Box CF4, Duke Endowment Archives.

23 As quoted in *Charlotte Observer,* May 20, 1966.

24 Mary D. Beaty, *A History of Davidson College* (Davidson, N.C.: Briarpatch Press, 1988), p. 377.

25 P. Clyde to T. Perkins, May 17, 1966, under Duke Endowment, Committee on Educational Institutions, Box CF6, Duke Endowment Archives.

26 Beaty, *History of Davidson College,* p. 390.

27 Ibid., p. 389.

28 S. Spencer to M. Pickens, July 14, 1972, under Davidson College, Box CF7, Duke Endowment Archives.

29 Minutes of the Committee on Educational Institutions, April 21, 1961, and memorandum from P. Clyde to Trustees, April 22, 1961, Box CF5, Duke Endowment Archives.

30 *Charlotte News,* June 1, 1961.

31 T. Perkins, Founder's Day remarks [December 1962], under Duke University, Box CF3, Duke Endowment Archives.

32 Douglas M. Knight, *Street of Dreams: The Nature and Legacy of the 1960s* (Durham, N.C.: Duke University Press, 1989), pp. 96–97.

33 Ibid., pp. 105–106. In a later memorandum, Knight stated that Gross and some of his allies on the faculty wished to see Taylor Cole ousted from the provost's job. An Endowment trustee on the executive committee, Amos Kearns, also gave Knight a list of those administrators, including Cole, whom the Endowment wished to see removed from office. When Knight failed to comply, Kearns, at a later date, criticized him in a meeting of the executive committee for the failure. Memorandum from Douglas M. Knight to the author, May 4, 1996.

34 P. Clyde to T. Perkins, September 10, 1962, under Committee on Educational Institutions, Box CF5, Duke Endowment Archives.

35 Joseph Allen to T. Perkins, July 12, 1963, under Committee on Educational Institutions, Box CF3, Duke Endowment Archives.

36 P. Clyde to T. Perkins, July 8, 1964, under Duke University, Box CF4, Duke Endowment Archives.

37 P. Clyde to T. Perkins, February 1, 1967, with enclosed memorandum, under Duke University, Box CF4.

38 Theodore David Segal, "'A New Genesis:' The 'Silent Vigil' at Duke University, April 5th–12th, 1968," senior honors thesis in History, 1977, p. 111. Knight, who had suffered a serious bout with hepatitis in the fall of 1967, had to be hospitalized again after several hundred students marched to his home on April 5, 1968, and wound up staging a sit-in. It ended the next morning when the students proceeded to the West Campus and began the Silent Vigil.

39 M. Pickens to T. J. Herin and C. D. White Jr., April 17, 1968, and M. Pickens to Howard Wilkinson, April 18, 1968, under Duke University, Box CF5, Duke Endowment Archives.

40 K. C. Towe to H. M. Rauch, May 10, 1968, under Duke University, Box GF5.

41 J. Day to T. Perkins, May 3, 1968, under Duke University, Box GF5.

42 Knight, *Street of Dreams,* p. 134.

43 C. Wade to M. Pickens, April 14, 1969, Charles B. Wade Jr. Papers, Duke University Archives. Hereinafter cited as Wade Papers. See also Knight, *Street of Dreams,* pp. 139–140.

44 F. Von Canon to C. Wade, January 29, 1969, and Wade to Von Canon, February 3, 1969, Wade Papers.

45 Memorandum from R. Henney to the Committee on Educational Institutions, January 27, 1971, under Duke University, Box CF6, Duke Endowment Archives.

46 H. Rauch to C. Wade, January 20, 1969, Wade Papers.

47 C. Wade to D. Knight, March 30, 1969, Wade Papers.

48 Interview with Terry Sanford, November 17, 1995, in the Sanford Building, Duke University.

49 C. Wade to J. W. Harris, May 28, 1969, Wade Papers.

50 Report of the Special Committee on Functions and Organizations of the Board of Trustees, December, 1969, under Duke University Trustees, Box C76, Duke Endowment Archives.

51 *Charlotte Observer,* January 30, 1970.

52 C. S. Murphy to C. Wade, March 11, 1970, and T. Perkins to C. S. Murphy, May 18, 1970, under Duke University Trustees, Box C76, Duke Endowment Archives.

53 M. Pickens to C. S. Murphy, March 17, 1970, under Duke University Trustees, Box C76.

54 T. Perkins to K. B. Watson, July 16, 1970, under Duke University Trustees, Box C76.

55 C. Wade to T. Perkins, September 10, 1970, under Duke University Trustees, Box C76.

56 Perkins to Wade, September 15, 1970, under Duke University Trustees, Box C76.

57 Interview with T. Sanford, November 17, 1995.

58 Interview with Mary Semans, October 27, 1995, Durham, North Carolina.

59 Ibid. An earlier conversation with John Day had also conveyed this information.

60 "Relationship of Duke University to the Methodist Church and to the Duke Endowment," [1970], under Duke University Trustees, Box C76, Duke Endowment Archives.

61 Don Elias to Willis Smith, June 7, 1947, Willis Smith Papers, Special Collections, Duke University Library.

62 Memorandum from the Duke University Committee to the trustees of the Angier B. Duke Memorial, July 20, 1946, Charles E. Jordan Papers, Duke Endowment Archives.

63 Minutes of specially called faculty meeting, March 25, 1960, Womble Papers.

64 Washington, North Carolina, *Daily News,* January 1, 1981.

65 Interview with Elizabeth Locke, March 15, 1995, Charlotte, North Carolina. An undergraduate alumnus of Davidson, McGuire received his law degree from Duke University.

8 THE ENDOWMENT AND HOSPITALS, CHILD CARE, AND THE RURAL METHODIST CHURCH, 1960–1994

1 W. Davison to M. Pickens, March 24, 1960, under Medical Education, Dr. Davison, Box CF3, Duke Endowment Archives.

2 C. C. Carpenter to W. Davison, March 17, 1960, under Medical Education, Dr. Davison, Box CF3.

3 W. C. Davison, "Community Hospital Internships and General Practice," with W. Davison to M. Pickens, January 6, 1961, under Medical Education, Dr. Davison, Box CF3.

4 J. A. Feagin to W. Davison, November 8, 1960, and accompanying minutes, under Medical Education, Dr. Davison, Box CF3.

5 W. Davison to M. Pickens, November 7, 1960, under Medical Education, Dr. Davison, Box CF3.

6 W. Davison to W. R. Berryhill, March 30, 1960, under Medical Education, Dr. Davison, Box CF3.

7 [Harvey Estes], "The Duke Endowment's Clinical Scholarship Program: A Twelve-Year Review," [November ?, 1972], under Duke University, Department of Community Health Services, Box CF7, Duke Endowment Archives.

8 Michael Price to Lynn Hartwig, May 14, 1975, under Duke University, Department of Community Health Sciences, Box CF8, Duke Endowment Archives.

9 W. Davison to P. Clyde, September 26, 1966, under Committee on Educational Institutions, Box CF5, Duke Endowment Archives.

10 W. Rankin to W. Davison, January 9, 1961, under Medical Education, Dr. Davison, Box CF3, Duke Endowment Archives.

11 Memorandum from A. Gale, September 9, 1976, under Duke Endowment, Trustee Meetings, Box CF9, Duke Endowment Archives.

12 Billy McCall's historical sketch at the Endowment's Hospital Conference, June 6–8, 1976, under Duke Endowment, Box CF9, Duke Endowment Archives.

13 A. J. Jamison to W. Rankin, May 13, 1944, under Connie Maxwell Children's Home, Box CF22, Duke Endowment Archives.

14 R. Mayer to D. Duke, July 9, 1965, under Apportionment of Child Care Funds, Box CF5, Duke Endowment Archives.

15 R. Mayer to W. Davison, August 9, 1965, under Apportionment of Child Care Funds, Box CF5.

16 W. C. Davison to D. Duke, December 13, 1965, under Apportionment of Child Care Funds, Box CF5.

17 R. Mayer to J. Felts Jr., October 25, 1967, under Apportionment of Child Care Funds, Box CF5.

18 [R. Mayer], "Memorandum to the Child Care Committee," February 9, 1971, under Duke Endowment Trustee Meetings, Box CF6, Duke Endowment Archives.

19 R. Mayer to B. D. Schwartz, April 20, 1973, under Legislation and Legislators, Box CF7, Duke Endowment Archives.

20 *The Duke Endowment Annual Report for 1991* (Duke Endowment), p. 30.

21 A. F. Fisher to Division of Missions of the United Methodist Church, March 7, 1975, under Kenansville Parish, 1973–1980, Box RCD5, Duke Endowment Archives.

22 "A Study of the Needs and the Program Plans, 1974"—Kenansville United Methodist Parish, under Kenansville Parish, 1973–1980, Box RCD5.

23 Jack M. Benfield, *The Kenansville Parish of the United Methodist Church: A Brief History . . .* (n.p., 1976), under Kenansville Parish, 1973–1980, Box RCD5.

24 Garland Young to W. Nesbitt, July 20, 1970, under Messiah Cooperative Ministry, 1969–1978, Box RCD5, Duke Endowment Archives.

25 Brochure, "Who Am I? The Story of U-CAN," May 1977, under Upper Cleveland Group Ministry, 1955–1981, Box RCD5, Duke Endowment Archives.

26 Bishop E. Garrison to B. Wilson and W. Nesbitt, October 5, 1972, under Upper Cleveland Group Ministry, 1955–1981, Box RCD5.

27 J. Williams, notes on meeting with Upper Cleveland Group Ministry, May 15, 1979, under Upper Cleveland Group Ministry, 1955–1981, Box RCD5.

28 W. Nesbitt to J. C. Christy Jr., September 4, 1969, under Watauga Charge Ministry, 1969–1981, Box RCD5, Duke Endowment Archives.

29 Notes of meeting of Bishops' Committee on Church Architecture, September 10, 1962, under Methodist Church, Box CF3, Duke Endowment Archives.

30 Whiteville, North Carolina, *News Reporter,* May 11, 1972, clipping under Methodist Church, Box CF7, Duke Endowment Archives.

31 *The Duke Endowment Annual Report for 1987* (Duke Endowment), p. 49.

32 W. G. Barlow to trustees of the Duke Endowment, August 4, 1975, under Duke Endowment, Box CF8, Duke Endowment Archives.

9   J. B. DUKE WINS AND LOSES: THE PARTIAL COLLAPSE
OF THE GRAND DESIGN

1   Minutes of Trustee's Meetings of May 28 and July 30, 1968, vols. 41A and 41B, BOT minutes, Duke Endowment Archives.

2 Interview with John Day, Lake Wylie, South Carolina, March 14, 1995, and John Spuches, New York City, October 12, 1995.
3 Doris Duke to A. Davis, November 29, 1979, under Duke Endowment Trustees, Box CF10, Duke Endowment Archives.
4 Minutes of Trustee's Meeting of November 2, 1983, vol. 56B, BOT minutes, Duke Endowment Archives.
5 Reid and Priest (John Spuches) to Trustees of the Endowment, November 26, 1985, in vol. 58B, BOT minutes, Duke Endowment Archives.
6 Deposition of Doris Duke, November 8, 1979, under Doris Duke Trust (depositions), from Treasurer's Office, Box CF10, Duke Endowment Archives.
7 The *New York Times,* May 21, 1995, p. 41.
8 Interview with J. G. Mebane Jr., Charlotte, North Carolina, March 15, 1995. Mr. Mebane also kindly supplied a copy of the prospectus for the sale and other data.
9 For the exact figures, see *The Duke Endowment Annual Report for 1994* (Duke Endowment), p. 59.

INDEX

Academic Council of Duke University, 252

Access to Health Care program, 279, 280

Ackland, William Hayes: decides to give art museum and endowment to Duke University, 136–137; dies and leaves estate in trust, 137–138

"additions to corpus resolutions," 134–135, 200, 224

African Americans: and the Endowment's relationship with, 85–89

Agnew, Donald C., 226–228

AIDS Interagency Council, 284

Alabama Hospital Association, 56

Alcoholics Anonymous, 301

Allen, George Garland: elected a trustee of Trinity College, 13; inherits much of J. B. Duke's power and influence, 27–28; opposes government-aided power plant in Greenwood, South Carolina, 103–107; and the erection of the Chapel at Duke University, 115; works to carry out J. B. Duke's plans for Duke University, 125–126; critical of free speech at Duke University, 131–133; moves to keep educational institutions as top priority of Endowment, 134–135; plays major role in selection of Flowers as president, 135–136; pushes Davison as Flowers's successor, 140–141; urges that Davison be named as acting president in 1960, 162; runs Endowment in autocratic style, 262; mentioned, 16, 23, 24, 26, 31, 137, 183, 201, 224

Allen Building at Duke University, 255

Allendale, South Carolina, 108

Alternative Energy Corporation in North Carolina, 305

Aluminum Company of America, 24, 198

American Association of University Professors, 131, 247

American Bankers Association, 186

American Bar Association, 140

Design for perpetual philanthropy,
189–201, 309–313, 317–324; mentioned, 138, 267

Duke, Nanaline H. (Mrs. James B.): resigns as trustee of Endowment and urges election of Mary Semans, 184–185; dies in 1962, 184; mentioned, 23, 27, 187

Duke, Washington: steers family toward charitable giving, 2; supports Oxford Orphan Asylum, 3; befriends African Americans and joins Republican party, 3–4; and Methodist circuit riders, 4; early experiences with Methodism, 165–166, 182; mentioned, 1, 20, 27, 107, 138, 304

Duke, William J. ("Uncle Billy"): exerts large influence on Washington Duke, 165; mentioned, 304

Duke Farms, Somerville, New Jersey, 288, 312

Duke Homestead, 107

Duke Medical Center, 272, 283

Duke Memorial Methodist Church, 27

Duke Power Company: linkage with the Duke Endowment and Doris Duke Trust, 21–22; is hit by floods in 1916, 24; builds first large-scale steam plant, 25; why J. B. Duke linked the Endowment to it, 25; and its tie with the Endowment under scrutiny of the federal government, 183–196; runs into problems in early 1970s, 202–205; labor troubles at its Kentucky coal mines, 205–214; the Endowment's move to lessen its involvment with, 309–313, 317–324; mentioned, 2, 12, 13, 17, 19

Duke's Chapel Methodist Church, 165

Duke University: name first suggested by Few in 1921, 9–10; named as principal beneficiary of Duke Endowment, 17–18; widespread misunderstanding about its naming, 18–19; special protection in the indenture, 113–116; early relationship with the Endowment, 123–164; serves as J. B. Duke's agent in aid to Methodist causes, 167–168; relations with the Endowment after 1960, 245–270; relationship with the Endowment examined by a university trustee, 263–264; and the tension between dual goals of national leadership and regional service, 267; and the continuing relationship between its Divinity School and the Endowment's Rural Church Section, 295–296; mentioned, 200, 201

DuMont, Randolph E.: is treasurer of Endowment with keen interest in Rural Church Program, 177–178; mentioned, 186, 305

Duplin County, 296–297

Duplin Development Commission, 297

Duplin General Hospital, 279, 298

Durham County, 165

Durham Morning Herald: carries important interview of Gross, 152, 154; hails salary hike at Duke, 246

Durham Nursery School Association, 289

East Carolina University, 284

Eastover Mining Company: labor troubles as a Duke Power subsidiary, 205–214

Edens, Arthur Hollis: names as third president of Duke University, 142; selects Gross as vice president for education, 143; leads university in a hopeful era but is criticized secretly by Gross, 143–144; is pushed by Endowment group and Gross to make important changes before being forced to resign in 1960, 145–162; dies in 1968 and is memorialized at Duke University, 163; mentioned, 249

Edison Award: won by Duke Power Company in 1973, 202

Eisenhower, Dwight, 190

Electric Light and Power: names Duke Power the nation's outstanding electric utility for 1977, 214

Elizabeth City, North Carolina, 279

Elon Children's Home, 288